T0291538

Social and Solidarity Economy in Cuba

LEXINGTON STUDIES ON CUBA

Series Editor: John M. Kirk, Dalhousie University and Mervyn Bain, University of Aberdeen

This series will publish texts on all aspects of Cuba, focusing on the post-1959 period. It seeks to be truly interdisciplinary, with studies of all aspects of contemporary Cuba—from foreign policy to culture, sociology, to economics. The series is particularly interested in broad, comprehensive topics (such as women in Cuba, economic challenges, human rights, the role of the media, etc.). All ideological positions are welcomed, with solid academic quality being the defining criterion. In exceptional circumstances edited collections will be considered, but the main focus is on high quality, original, and provocative monographs and innovative scholarship.

Recent Titles in This Series

Social and Solidarity Economy in Cuba: Foundations and Practices for Socialist Development Edited by Rafael J. Betancourt and Jusmary Gómez Arencibia

Cuba, Africa, and Apartheid's End: Africa's Children Return! By Isaac Saney

Disaster Preparedness and Climate Change in Cuba: Management and Adaptation Edited by Emily J. Kirk, Isabel Story, and Anna Clayfield

Cuban International Relations at 60; Reflections on Global Connections Edited by Mervyn J. Bain and Chris Walker

Soviet Influence on Cuban Culture, 1961–1987: When the Soviets Came to Stay By Isabel Story

Entangled Terrains: Empire, Identity, and Memory of Guantánamo By Asa McKercher and Catherine Krull

God and the Nation: A Social History of Cuba's Protestants By James A. Baer

The People's Professors: How Cuba Achieved Education for All By Kathryn Moody

Youth and the Cuban Revolution: Youth Culture and Politics in 1960s Cuba By Anne Luke

Cuba's Forgotten Decade: How the 1970s Shaped the Revolution Edited by Emily J. Kirk, Anna Clayfield, Isabel Story

Social and Solidarity Economy in Cuba

Foundations and Practices for Socialist Development

*Edited by Rafael J. Betancourt
and Jusmary Gómez Arencibia*

Translated by Catharine Vanderplaats
Vallejo and Rafael J. Betancourt

LEXINGTON BOOKS
Lanham • Boulder • New York • London

Published by Lexington Books
An imprint of The Rowman & Littlefield Publishing Group, Inc.
4501 Forbes Boulevard, Suite 200, Lanham, Maryland 20706
www.rowman.com

86-90 Paul Street, London EC2A 4NE

British Library Cataloguing in Publication Information Available

Library of Congress Cataloging-in-Publication Data

Names: Betancourt Abio, Rafael, 1952- editor. | Gómez Arencibia, Jusmary, editor. | Vallejo, Catharina V. de (Catharina Vanderplaats), translator.
Title: Social and solidarity economy in Cuba : foundations and practices for socialist development / edited by Rafael J. Betancourt and Jusmary Gómez Arencibia ; translated by Catharine Vanderplaats Vallejo.
Description: Lanham : Lexington Books, [2023] | Series: Lexington studies on Cuba | Includes bibliographical references and index.
Identifiers: LCCN 2023014520 (print) | LCCN 2023014521 (ebook) | ISBN 9781666929034 (cloth) | ISBN 9781666929041 (ebook)
Subjects: LCSH: Cuba--Economic conditions--1990- | Cuba--Economic policy. | Economic development--Cuba. | Solidarity--Cuba. | Socialism--Cuba. | Social responsibility of business–Cuba.
Classification: LCC HC152.5 .S6326 2023 (print) | LCC HC152.5 (ebook) | DDC 330.97291–dc23/eng/20230525
LC record available at https://lccn.loc.gov/2023014520
LC ebook record available at https://lccn.loc.gov/2023014521

Contents

List of Figures   ix

List of Tables   xi

Prologue   xiii
    Rafael J. Betancourt and Jusmary Gómez Arencibia

Chapter 1: Socialism Is the Solution, Not the Problem: A Solidary
    and Socially Responsible Formula for a Prosperous Economy   1
    Enrique Gómez Cabezas

Chapter 2: Now More than Ever, a Social and Solidary Economy Is
    Necessary to Build Socialism in Cuba   7
    Rafael J. Betancourt

Chapter 3: The Social and Solidarity Economy: Integrating
    Bases, Experiences, and Possible Projections for Socialist
    Development in Cuba   27
    Ovidio D'Angelo Hernández

Chapter 4: The Foundations of Popular and Solidarity Economics
    as Fulfillment of the Social Property of All People in the
    Socialist Transition   43
    Luis del Castillo Sánchez

Chapter 5: Participatory Budgeting: A Management Tool for Local
    Development in Cuba, Seen from the Experiences of the Office
    of the Historian of the City of Havana   53
    Orestes J. Díaz Legón and Maidolys Iglesias Pérez

Chapter 6: The Inclusion of Vulnerable Groups as Subjects of
      Development: Proposals from the Viewpoint of the Solidarity
      Economy   69
      Geydis Fundora Nevot and Reynaldo Miguel Jiménez Guethón

Chapter 7: Population, Value Chains and Social and Solidarity
      Economy: Epistemological Alignments   83
      Dianné Griñan Bergara

Chapter 8: Do Public-Private Partnerships Have Room in the
      Present Cuban Context?: Notes from a Practical Experience   99
      Mirlena Rojas Piedrahita

Chapter 9: Business Social Responsibility of the State Enterprise:
      The Experience of the Center of Molecular Immunology   119
      Jusmary Gómez Arencibia and Mirlena Rojas Piedrahita

Chapter 10: Cooperatives in the Restarted Reforms: Some
      Proposals for a Law of Cooperatives   139
      Camila Piñeiro Harnecker

Chapter 11: The Cooperative as an Energizing Agent of the Social
      and Solidarity Economy Model in Cuba   163
      Yamira Mirabal González and Iriadna Marín de León

Chapter 12: Participation in the Strategies and Social Management
      of Nonagricultural Cooperatives in Centro Habana Municipality   183
      Francisco Damián Morillas Valdés

Chapter 13: Committing to Cooperative Solidarity Labor: The Taxi
      Rutero 2 Experience   197
      Mirell Pérez González

Chapter 14: Cooperative Social Balance: A Useful Tool to Establish
      a Social and Solidarity Economy   215
      *Oscar Llanes Guerra, Mercedes Zenea Montejo, Annia Martínez
      Massip, and Lienny García Pedraza*

Chapter 15: Gender Perspective Viewed from the Model of Social
      Balance in Agricultural Cooperatives in Villa Clara   227
      *Annia Martínez Massip, Lienny García Pedraza, Oscar Llanes
      Guerra, Mercedes Zenea Montejo, Lázaro Julio Leiva Hoyo,
      Anelys Pérez Rodríguez, and Elianys de la Caridad Zorio González*

Chapter 16: Business Social Responsibility in Local Development:
A Look at the Training of Local Actors in the Province of
Mayabeque 237
*Orquídea Hailyn Abreu González, Yuneidys González Espinosa,
and Joanna Gasmury Roldán*

Chapter 17: "Go for it: You can do it!": The Solidarity Experience
of Female Entrepreneurs 253
Jusmary Gómez Arencibia

Chapter 18: Business Social Responsibility Does Not Go Unnoticed
in Cuban Private Enterprises 271
William Bello Sánchez

Chapter 19: Institutional Social Responsibility and Subjectivity 287
Consuelo Martín Fernández and Jany Bárcenas Alfonso

Index 303

About the Editors and Contributors 317

List of Figures

Figure 2.1 Independent Workers (TCPs) Employed in Cuba, 2003–2019   10

Figure 2.2 Cooperatives of Industrial Labor and Service Workers (CTIS)   13

Figure 6.1 Women in the Cooperative and Self-Employment Spheres (in %)   70

Figure 11.1 Integration of the Socioeconomic Agents   178

Figure 13.1 Structure of the Cooperative Taxi Rutero 2   206

Figure 13.2 The Importance of Labor According to the Workers   210

Figure 14.1 Modular Plan of the ICA-FLACSO-PC Cooperative Social Balance Model   216

Figure 18.1 Spaces of the Program [business social responsibility]   275

Figure 18.2 Premios [Prizes]   277

Figure 19.1 Symbolic Representation of Social and Environmental Responsibility   294

List of Tables

Table 6.1 Participation in Socioeconomic Spheres, by Skin
    Color (%)   70

Table 8.1 Types of Public-Private Alliances (PPA)   104–105

Table 11.1 Analysis of the Constitutional Principles and Those
    of the ESS Sector   167–168

Table 11.2 Proposals for the Improvement of Cooperative
    Management   173–177

Table 13.1 Indicators to Evaluate the Management of the
    Cooperative Taxi Rutero 2. (Scale of 1 [Negative] to
    5 [Positive])   208

Table 19.1 Representational Contents of Social Responsibility   293

Prologue

Rafael J. Betancourt and Jusmary Gómez Arencibia

The idea for this book arose during the last part of 2019, based on a project of the Red Cubana de Economía Social y Solidaria y Responsabilidad Social Empresarial—ESORSE [Cuban Network of Social and Solidarity Economy and Social Business Responsibility].[1] ESORSE is composed of a group of people who belong to university and scientific institutions and non-governmental organizations, cooperatives, businesses and others interested in contributing to the study and implementation of the social and solidarity economy (ESS in Spanish) and social responsibility (RS in Spanish) in our country, as a contribution to local sustainable development (DL in Spanish). It is also a network of networks that develop similar activities and incorporate ESS and RS among their objectives and practices. It constitutes a space of dialogue and exchange in keeping with socialist principles and supporting the economic and social development of the country. It is a way to integrate social and economic stakeholders into the building of socialism in Cuba through participation, association, solidary, and social commitment towards a way of economic organization that prioritizes human values above those of the market (Betancourt & Gómez Arencibia, 2019).

In 2017, the Red published *Construyendo socialismo desde abajo: la contribución de la economía popular y solidaria* [Building socialism from the bottom up: the contribution of the popular and solidarity economy]. (Betancourt, 2017) That edited collection includes articles by national and international authors from many institutions, with the stated objective of reflecting on the immediate reality and the theoretical principles behind ESS, its organizational instruments and tools for its application. That publication is the primary precedent for the book presented here.

During the following years, the members of the Red produced a torrent of knowledge, the result of research and fieldwork from different disciplinary perspectives and theoretical approaches, that called for systematization and dissemination. At the same time, there has been an evolution and deepening of the process of updating of the economic and social development model, that Cuba began in 2011 and accelerated in 2019–2020. Defining the space and role of ESS and RS in this changing national context has become imperative and its contribution to the implementation of the new model takes on a key importance.

The pages that follow are born of the need to show the work that has been accomplished during the past few years and to position the foundations of ESS and RS in such an important moment in this reality. They present practical experiences that suggest niches of ESS and favorable ecosystems for its development within the strategies of DL. The authors assembled in this collection are all Cuban and members of the Red, with the added value that they live in and write from different provinces, institutions and disciplines.

The book re-creates elements that make up the conceptual map of ESS: public-private relations, ESS stakeholders (state enterprises, cooperatives, the private sector), and production chains. Other topics of vital importance are portrayed: gender, vulnerable groups, social participation, social balance, the training of stakeholders. The subjective dimension of Social Institutional Responsibility is broached for the first time.

The volume begins with an article by Enrique Gómez Cabezas—Assistant Director of Cuba's Center for Psychological and Sociological Research (CIPS)—who considers the topic of efficiency and participation in Cuban socialism. In it he argues: "Socialism does constitute an opportunity to build new social relations: symmetrical, solidary, liberating. However, this does not appear to be an easy task, and requires the un-learning of the structures of the hegemonic mindset established by the dominance of capital."

His text is followed by that of Rafael Betancourt Abio—coordinator of the Red Cubana de Economía Social y Solidaria y Responsabilidad Social (ESORSE)—in a chapter that deals with some of the impacts of the new and necessary post-COVID-19 measures of recovery and the improvement of the economic activity in the country, on economic and social inequalities that exist. It shows that by consciously and assiduously implementing social and solidary economy (ESS) and business social responsibility (RSE), the country will have more tools to face social inequalities and motivate local inclusive economic development while building socialism.

Ovidio D'Angelo Hernández—researcher at CIPS and coordinator of the Group on Creativity for Social Transformation—explores the variety of theoretical positions, the nonlinear interpretations of some of the experiences in Cuba and their potential routes for building socialism.

Based in the Faculty of Economics at the University of Havana, Luis del Castillo Sánchez contributes a chapter that incorporates the socioeconomic system of the popular and solidarity economy (EPS) into the Cuban economic and social model of socialist development, as a community and associative dimension related to the social property of all people.

Orestes J. Díaz Legón—of the Faculty of Law of the University of Havana—and Maidolys Iglesias Pérez—sociologist of the Master Plan of the Office of the Historian of the City of Havana show the viability of the master plan for the participatory management of local development on the island, seen from a legal standpoint and based on the methodology and the lessons learned from the experiment carried out in Old Havana.

Based in FLACSO—Latin American Faculty of Social Sciences at the University of Havana—the researcher Geydis Fundora Nevot and Reynaldo Jiménez Guethón reflect on the relevance of developing the solidarity economy as an effective option to overcome inequalities and the importance of nurturing abilities in groups that are in vulnerable condition, and other stakeholders, based on proposals that foster this form of organization.

Researcher Dianné Griñan Bergara, formerly at the Center for Demographic Studies (CEDEM) of the University of Havana, analyzes the points of contact between the population-development approach, the theory of value chains and the theoretical-methodological positions of social and solidarity economics.

As part of the project "Strengthening the environmental transformations related to the adaptability to climate change by Cuban communities," which is coordinated and directed by the Cuban NGO Centro Félix Varela, the researchers Mirlena Rojas Piedrahita and Ania Mirabal Patterson ask themselves "Do public-private partnerships have room in the present Cuban context?" Their objective is to socialize the potential public-private relations in the Cuban context based on a practical experience in the community of Yarual, in the municipality of Bolivia in Ciego de Avila province.

Jusmary Gómez Arencibia, Mirlena Rojas Piedrahita—both from the Group for the Social Studies of Labor at CIPS—and Idania Caballero Torres of the Center of Molecular Immunology bring us "Business Social Responsibility of the State Enterprise," a chapter that situates BSR/RSE in the current Cuban context and in the socialist state enterprise. In addition, it includes a series of actions that can be extrapolated to other organizations beyond the biotechnology sector.

Camila Piñeiro Harnecker, former Professor of Cooperative Governance in the master's program in management and development of cooperatives of the Latin American Faculty of Social Sciences (FLACSO) at the University of Havana, proposes some ideas for achieving the objective of facilitating the expansion and consolidation of the Cuban cooperative sector so that it can play the very important role that the Conceptualization of the Cuban Economic and Social Model of Socialist Development has assigned to it.

Yamira Mirabel González and Iriadna Marín de León, of the Center for Studies on Management, Local Development and Tourism (CE-GESTA), of the University of Pinar del Río, show parallels between the principles of the Cuban socialist system and the social and solidarity Eeconomy, the foundations of the cooperative as an energizing element of ESS in Cuba, and proposals for the improvement of its performance.

Francisco Damián Morillas Valdés delves into the topic of cooperativism. He was a consultant to the president of the municipal government relating to the contribution of the nonagricultural cooperatives, the training of its members, and their role in the sustainability of the municipal development strategy. As a CIPS researcher, he subsequently carried out an investigation from 2014 to 2018, whose results are presented here.

For many years the Group on Latin America, Social Philosophy and Axiology (GALFISA) of the Institute of Philosophy has been studying the experience of the cooperative of urban transport, Taxi Rutero 2. With the aim of showing the need to rescue the centrality of work and to bring to light the potentials of cooperative and solidary work, the researcher Mirell Pérez González presents "Committing to Cooperative Solidarity Labor."

A team consisting of Oscar Llanes Guerra of the Agrarian University of Havana (UNAH), Mercedes Zenea Montejo of the Center of Studies of Management Techniques (CETED) of the University of Havana, and Annia Martínez Massip and Lienny García Pedraza of the Central University "Marta Abreu" of Las Villas (UCLV) contribute the chapter "Cooperative Social Balance." It is the outcome of research carried out in Cuba toward the analysis of cooperative social responsibility, used as a tool by the ICA-FLACSO-PC Model of Cooperative Social Balance and contextualized for the Cuban cooperative organizations. It encompasses the novelties of the intervention area of equity relations and the analysis of inequalities related to region, age, gender, class, and profession.

Annia Martínez Massip, Lienny García Pedraza, Lázaro Julio Leiva Hoyo, Anelys Pérez Rodríguez, and Elianys de la Caridad Zorio González (all from UCLV), joined by Oscar Llanes Guerra from UNAH and Mercedes Zenea Montejo from CETED-UH, reveal that the application of the Model of de Cooperative Social Balance in two cooperatives in Villa Clara during the project Via Lactia from 2016 to 2018, shows the dissatisfactions and contradictions with the organization of cooperative social responsibility.

Orquidia Hailyn Abreu González and Joanna Gasmury Roldán from the Center of Studies for Development Management (CEGED) of the UNAH join Yuneidys González Espinosa of the Department of Management of Sustainable Agro-Ecosystems of the National Institute of Agricultural Sciences (INCA) to identify the role of RSE in local development founded on the training of local stakeholders by universities and research centers which, based on knowledge networks, contribute to the building of enterprises and innovations that could transform the context grounded on the links between enterprise, government, and location.

Jusmary Gómez Arencibia, co-coordinator of the ESORSE Network, analyzes the experience of Cuban women entrepreneurs based on some of the ESS principles. The chapter identifies the potential of ESS for local development and for women's empowerment.

William Bello reminds us that finding a space to talk and work according to RSE in the community of private entrepreneurs has been an exhaustive undertaking of seven years, motivated by the Proyect CubaEmprende and managed from its Program OASIS, which the author directs.

And to conclude, there is the different perspective and innovative contribution of the psychologists Consuelo Martín Fernández and Jany Barcenas Alfonso, of the University of Havana and the InterCreAction Section of the Cuban Society of Psychology. In their chapter, they combine business, cooperative, corporative, and university social responsibility in a proposal that includes them all: institutional social responsibility (RSI). This involves an integrative and interdisciplinary perspective where the need arises to include the psychosocial approach for the study and implementation of RSI. They propose the integration of subjective indicators of RSI such as motivations and satisfaction of needs; performance and transformation of institutional roles; social participation; processes of social inclusion and exclusion; representational perceptions and arrangements.

Cuba is living through a period that the country's top authorities label a process of updating the Cuban economic and social model. This process "establishes greater inclusion of market elements in the allocation of resources in the economy, greater decentralization of the state enterprises, more prerogatives for the regions, as well as a greater participation in the economy of the private forms of ownership" (Cubadebate, 2020, p. 3). To this can be added the restructuration and modernization of the state apparatus and the eradication of prohibitions that limit the population's opportunities (Triana, 2020). Within the mosaic that will result from this modernization, what can social and solidarity economics and social responsibility contribute? The novelty and importance of this book lies in the response to this question. It is grounded in service to society by being committed to the distribution of services in an equitable and inclusive form. It recognizes the different forms of property management and their articulation by prioritizing the society of people over the society of capital.

The greatest achievement of this book lies in the proposal of definitions and terms adapted to Cuban reality. It reveals experiences that have come from and developed within the framework of the updating of the model and its contribution to Cuban development. And in tune with this, it presents good practices, challenges, and opportunities that allow for a dialogue with a multifaceted context that urgently needs to act with responsible social solidarity.

NOTE

1. In its Clause 95, the Scientific Committee of the Center for Psychological and Sociological Research (CIPS) approved the patronage of the Red de Economía Social y Solidaria y Responsabilidad Social Empresarial ESORSE as part of the activity of the Social Studies Group on Labor. It also operates under the auspices of multiple participants of other networks, institutions, and individuals including: the Center for Studies on Management, Local Development and Tourism (CE-GESTA) of the University of Pinar del Río; CTS+I Chair, Faculty of Psychology, Center of Research on the International Economy (CIEI), Center of Study on the Cuban Economy (CEEC). all of the University of Havana. In addition, the following have also joined: Center for Local and Community Development (CEDEL) and the Master Plan of the Office of the Historian of the City of Havana. ESORSE is led by a multidisciplinary coordinating team which is in charge of organizing and promoting the Red in a participative and inclusive manner, by articulating it with the plans and activities of its members.

BIBLIOGRAPHY

Betancourt, R. (Ed.) *Construyendo socialismo desde abajo: la contribución de la economía popular y solidaria* [Building Socialism From the Bottom Up: The Conctribution of Popular and Solidary Economy]. La Habana: Editorial Caminos. 2017

Betancourt, R., and J. Gómez Arencibia. *Sinopsis de la Red Cubana de Economía Social y Solidaria y Responsabilidad Social ESORSE* [Synopsis of the Cuban Network of Social and Solidarity Economics ESORSE]. La Habana: Centro de Investigaciones Psicológicas y Sociológicas CIPS. 2019.

Cubadebate. "Gobierno cubano informa sobre nuevas medidas económicas" [Cuban Government Announces New Economic Measures]. *Cubadebate*. From http://www.cubadebate.cu/noticias/2020/07/16/gobierno-cubano-informa-nuevas-medidas-economicas-video/-. 2020.

Triana, J. "Lo público, lo privado y el bienestar" [The Public, the Private and Wellbeing]. *OnCubaNews*. From https://oncubanews.com/opinion/columnas/contrapesos/lo-publico-lo-privado-y-el-bienestar/ 2020.

Chapter 1

Socialism Is the Solution, Not the Problem

A Solidary and Socially Responsible Formula for a Prosperous Economy

Enrique Gómez Cabezas

It would seem that economic inefficiency is an innate characteristic of Cuban socialism. Beyond the circumstantial achievements and emblematic experiences—which are the rule—there is a national consensus on this issue. The idea of the inefficiency of the state economy is deeply rooted in the popular creed—together with the pride in Cuba's audacious sovereignty. Such acknowledgment is also a central matter in the contemporary national political debates and public discourses. It is necessary to indicate that such judgments essentially refer to the production of goods and services. But it cannot be denied that the economy, as a system of relations for the production of the material and spiritual life of society, is a constructive space of societies, a producer of values, behaviors, symbols, and creeds—essential to ideologies.

From this side of the fence—that of independence and social justice—and not from the other side, we cannot understate the disastrous consequences of the blockade policies and aggressions of the greatest world power against Cuba; in particular, on its economy, which is very poor and peripheral. The survival of the country in blockade conditions is not an unimportant outcome—and also economic—and neither is maintaining a system of social services with results that stand out in the geographical region and even at a global level.

But the reserves of efficiency acquire major relevance in the face of the daily shortages and the mercantile turbulence of the social network. If the decision is to build an alternative society, one that is just and prosperous—in spite of the imperial efforts to impose its designs—an efficient management of the economy is called for, as is earning social recognition for it. Efficiency means obtaining the best possible results, not only according to the productive indicators but also in terms of social distribution, the satisfaction of needs, equity, and the fostering of solidary relations.

The association of socialism with inefficiency damages the trust in the viability of the Cuban emancipatory project. This perception is reinforced by the emergence of a private sector of the economy which presents prosperous experiences and attractive offers for professionals and qualified workers. Such a differentiation between the private and the state sectors of the economy gains a place as a social representation of the economic activity that is built from the communal wisdom. Although it is a matter of a questionable judgment that needs more complex analyses, the fact that it is reflected in this way in the social subjectivity must be seen as having the highest importance, because it is at the symbolic level where consensus is built and where values and ways of acting are legitimized.

The process of updating the model[1] that has been ongoing—for more than a decade now—defined the economy as a priority and center of attention. It proposed the diversification of the forms of property, the broadening of controlled foreign investment, the independence from the State for non-primary activities of production and services, the rationalization of the workforce in the budgeted sector, the expansion of self-employment, private hiring of the workforce, the discretionary creation of nonagricultural cooperatives, the surrender in usufruct of idle land and the leasing of state-owned buildings to other forms of management, the adjustment of social services, the reduction of subsidies and gratuities (PCC 2011), the redirection of care obligations and economic responsibilities toward families (Gómez Cabezas et al. 2017; Gómez Cabezas, et al. 2020)—among other measures of reform, with the aim of a prosperous and sustainable economy.

The measures taken in the economic sector have not had the timing nor the effect that the expectations of prosperity had established. Five years after the approval of the Guidelines during the VI Congress of the Party, 21 percent of the measures that had been approved were reported as having been achieved, and the rest were in process (PCC 2016). Another five years have passed without there being an appreciable turnaround of the economy, and hardly any transformations have been initiated in the socialist state enterprise. The VIII Congress of the Communist Party of Cuba that was recently held determined that:

> Negative effects associated with an excessive bureaucracy and a deficient control of resources persist, which are cause and condition *par excellence* of

the damaging phenomenon of corruption and other illegalities which limit the increase in productivity and efficiency. Structural problems of the economic model, which does not offer sufficient incentives for work and innovation, continue to be present. (Castro Ruz 17 April 2021, 5)

The updating strategy identified as the primary aim to unblock the development of the productive forces. This implies finding answers to some basic questions: What are these potential productive forces that the country has at its disposal? What obstacles slow down their development? In Cuba the main element of the productive forces are their workers, their intelligence, professional capacities and training, their tested ingenuity to face a thousand and one daily difficulties in their labor and family surroundings. In a country with limited natural resources, like Cuba, in a global economy that is based on knowledge, the value of human resources should not be underestimated. The significant social investment accomplished by the Cuban revolutionary project is there, in its people: trained, healthy, solidary, and in a condition to contribute much more. So what slows down the creative contribution that the labor collectives can make to the economic launch of the nation?

It is common in state enterprises to find a climate that is not very stimulating to the creative ingenuity of the collectives. At the subjective level, the reserves of efficiency have been linked to formal discipline, requirements and control. A culture of rigid standards, subordination to management directives, and participatory asymmetries are the rule. The dynamics of the relations with which higher management operates are reflected within the enterprises and their productive bases. The strong dependencies in decision making and the limited margins to think creatively from diverse realities generate strong inertia.

In this daily panorama of the workers, the forms of state property at the level of the labor entities can produce a dehumanizing working atmosphere: the environments of indifference and indolence—which is a reflection of a lack of belonging—the inefficiency, lack of control, and corruption are evident in this situation. This certainly is to a great extent conditioned by the insufficient income and the lack of satisfaction of basic human needs. But it is also a result of the limitations of the worker collectives to manage for themselves, to transform their organizations, to rethink themselves in the changing contexts, to define alternative paths and make decisions: It is difficult to undertake new roads without encountering tough hurdles. These daily living experiences build a symbolic representation of the work, disconnected from its conception as a source of human fulfillment.

Socialism does constitute an opportunity to build new social relations: symmetrical, solidary, liberating—although this does not seem to be an easy task and requires the unlearning of the hegemonic cultures that were instituted by the dominance of capital. The road forward will be to empower the labor collectives beyond all formality. At the day-to-day level they should operate as the true owners of the means of production. Responsibility, creativity and self-control spring from the structural prominence of the workers in their concrete labor contexts. Corruption has its strongest deterrent through internal oversight, exercised by the workers as an organized collective subject with the capacity to ask for a reckoning given their legitimate authority and their knowledge of what is happening.

A climate of appropriate autonomy—adjusted to previously accepted social commitments—constitutes a motivating factor in the collective thinking and cooperative actions—based on concrete realities and knowledge—aimed at their own developmental objectives and social responsibilities. This empowerment of the labor collectives as the principal subjects of the work process—and not as subordinates to disciplinary standards and external rules—is a basic condition in order to release their creative potential. The challenge to untie the knots that slow down the development of the productive forces requires embarking on this path: more socialist, producer of new meanings, and a liberation from the alienation of labor.

Another defining condition of the labor institutions is the relations they have with their closest surroundings: the neighborhood, the local area, the labor union, and even with other broader ones which include institutions at the national and even global level. The institutions necessarily interact with these contexts: they complement each other and are allies in synergetic dynamics, or in emerging conflicts of interests that generate discontent. These relations form an essential part of the social network and constitute a model of social and human development.

What values does an institutional design that is disconnected from its most immediate social context generate? It can be an expression of an opposing alienating indifference at the start of a socialist development. Systemic coherence is essential to the articulation of solidary ways of acting that will overcome the hegemonic culture established by the capitalist world. The intentional involvement of the institutions in community and local development strategies, and their contribution to the broadening of social justice and equity, strengthen a socialist workers' culture. The rapport and commitment with this context, in which institutions operate, should not exclude any form of property or management. Solidarity and social responsibility—if they are intended to be a distinctive characteristics of the system—should constitute nuclear values in the institutions.

Supporting greater local and entrepreneurial autonomy opens opportunities for building links between institutions and the communities in which they operate. The potential institutional contributions go beyond the provision of material and financial resources. They can include job offers, training options, support for enterprises or community projects that are socially and economically synergistic, environmental commitments, provision of services—among others, within an infinite repertory of contextualized actions.

The decision to establish the Regional Contribution for Local Development, a territorial tax of 1 percent of the gross profits paid by local organizations to the municipality (Romero López 2018) is a step in the right direction to connect the institutions to the surroundings in which they operate. But other formulas are also necessary, facilitating the possibilities to direct the contribution of resources generated by the institutions toward the development of concrete social projects and making the results of these contributions visible. In fact, a part of the work done by the labor collectives contributes to the state as support of agreed-upon guarantees—social rights, living conditions, equity and social justice, local and national development. To connect this contribution—or a part of it—to more nearby destinations would work as a mechanism of direct participation of the labor collectives in the redistribution of their work and the oversight of the process. This would strengthen the understanding of the solidarity meaning of their contribution and their inclusion as a category in the social project.

The challenges of the economic development of the nation generate a continuous debate, and its common denominator is the need for more efficiency. The contradictions of the current model demand changes: strengthening the social forms of property of the means of production becomes essential to sustain a participative socialism. The proposals for social and solidarity economy and institutional social responsibility, contextualized and developed in Cuba along the lines of this debate, respond to these requirements.

The Social and Solidarity Economy and Social Enterprise Responsibility Network (ESORSE in Spanish) is working on the conformation of proposals of a socialist nature, viable in the current conditions of the country. The network is located in the Center of Psychological and Sociological Research (CIPS in Spanish), and articulates the labors of several institutions, cooperatives, and solidarity enterprises. Its members, beyond the institutional representatives, constitute a thinking and acting community with the capacity to elaborate theoretical-methodological proposals, and at the same time gain experience in practices modeled on social institutional solidarity and responsibility.

The conviction that socialism is the solution, and not the problem, justifies the support of a social and solidarity economy. The obstructions of state management and other social forms of production are not attributable to socialism. They form part of the capitalism that needs to be overcome. Significant supplies of efficiency are present in socialism, ready to be captured.

NOTE

1. The economic and social reform in progress since the end of the first decade of the 21st century in Cuba. This reform was legalized after a public consultation and its approval in April of 2011 by the VI Congress of the Communist Party of Cuba, of the Guidelines of the Economic and Social Policies of the Party and the Revolution (PCC, 2011).

BIBLIOGRAPHY

Castro Ruz, Raul. "Informe Central al 8vo Congreso del Partido Comunista de Cuba" [Central Report to the 8th Congress of the Communist Party of Cuba] La Habana: Partido Comunista de Cuba, 17 April 2021.

Gómez Cabezas, E. J., et al. *Política social y equidad a escala local-comunitaria en el contexto de actualización del modelo económico y social cubano* [Social Policy and Equity at the Local-Community Scale in the Context of the Updating of the Cuban Economic and Social Model]. Research Report. La Habana: Centro de Investigaciones Psicológicas y Sociológicas CIPS, 2017.

———. "Las desigualdades sociales en el contexto cubano: Un recorrido por las investigaciones del Grupo Estructura Social y Desigualdades del CIPS" [Social Inequalities in the Cuban Context: A Review of the Research Conducted by the Group Social Structure and Inequalities at CIPS]. *Caudales*. La Habana: Centro de Investigaciones Psicológicas y Sociológicas CIPS, 2020.

PCC. *Resolución sobre resultados de la Implementación de los Lineamientos de la Política Económica y Social del Partido y la Revolución aprobados en el VI Congreso y su actualización para el periodo 2016–2021* [Resolution on the Implementation of the Guidelines of the Economic and Social Policies of the Party and the Revolution Approved in the VI Congress Updated for the Period 2016–2021]. La Habana: VII Congreso del Partido Comunista de Cuba, 2016.

———. *Informe Central* [Central Report]. La Habana: VIII Congreso del Partido Comunista de Cuba, 2021.

———. *Lineamientos de la Política Económica y Social del Partido y la Revolución* [Guidelines of the Economic and Social Policies of the Party and the Revoluion]. La Habana: VI Congreso del Partido Comunista de Cuba, 2016.

Romero López, R. "Procedimiento contable y financiero aplicable a la Contribución Territorial para el Desarrollo Local en La Habana." [Accounting and Financial Procedures Applicable to the Regional Contribution to Local Development in Havana] *Revista Cubana de Finanzas y Precios* 2 (2): 44–60. 2018. From http://www.mfp.gob.cu/revista_mfp/index.php/RCFP/article/view/06.

Chapter 2

Now More than Ever, a Social and Solidary Economy Is Necessary to Build Socialism in Cuba

Rafael J. Betancourt

2020 was the year of the double pandemic in Cuba: COVID-19—a disease caused by the new coronavirus SARS-CoV-2—and the sixty-year-old brutal economic, commercial, and financial blockade by the United States—worsened as never before by the Donald Trump administration.

Cuba intends to promote a model of development that aims to combine innovation and continuity, expressed in two documents produced by the VI Congress of the Communist Party of Cuba: the Conceptualization of the Economic and Social Cuban Model of Socialist Development and the National Plan of Economic and Social Development to 2030 (PCC, 2016a); and the Proposal of the Vision of a Nation, Axes and Strategic Sectors (PCC, 2016b).The first document states the following:

> The system of business enterprises is composed of all the types of property that are stipulated by law: socialist property of all the people [state-owned enterprises], cooperatives, joint ventures, private businesses. . . . All business organizations interact to the benefit of the social and economic development. . . . The system of planned management of the economic and social development takes into account the validity of market relations and regulates their actions in pursuit of socialist development, thus contributing, in the most efficient and effective way, to facilitate the access by the economic actors of the different forms of property and management to supplies and markets. (PCC 2016a, 11)

Faced with the new situation, the Cuban government once again had to adopt a strategy of survival, and simultaneously, try to relaunch the project

7

of updating the economic and social model in order to boost the country's development. On June 11, 2020, President Miguel Díaz-Canel Bermúdez announced a proposal that consists of two phases: the post-COVID-19 recovery—return to normalcy, avoid new outbreaks, develop the capacity to face and reduce risks and vulnerabilities—and the strengthening of the economic activity of the country. This last point includes the adjustment of the Economic Plan for 2020 and 2021: increase savings, generate more cash income, make more efficient use of the country's resources, and boost national production—especially that of food (Cubadebate, July 16, 2020).

The president insisted that Cuba will resume the process of updating the economic and social model, which for many academics and analysts has moved with sluggishness, discontinuities, and lack of decisiveness during an entire decade of a prolonged crisis of economic growth. Díaz-Canel stated that in order to confront the crisis provoked by the COVID-19 pandemic, "We have to come up with different ideas . . . ; we cannot continue doing things in the same way." He emphasized the need to orient the work of the Permanent Commission for Implementation and Development to evaluating "how we can implement more rapidly, more decisively, in a more organized way, a series of issues that are pending implementation in the Conceptualization of the Economic and Social Model." Among the elements that have not been put into practice, he mentioned: some forms of management and property; the reconfiguring of the public and the private sectors; the appropriate relation that should exist between both of them, on which he noted that "we have good experiences in this period of pandemic" (Martínez Hernández 2020, 3).

This chapter reveals some impacts of the new and necessary measures on the economic and social inequalities that exist and demonstrates that, by consciously and harmoniously assuming Social and Solidary Economics (SSE) and Business Social Responsibility (BSR), the country will have more tools to confront social imbalances and promote local inclusive economic development, within the frame of the construction of socialism.

BEYOND EGALITARIANISM: SOCIAL COMPLEXITY

The crisis of the 1990s, triggered by the downfall of the European socialist alliance, forced the country's administration at that moment to adopt a series of policies that shook the society, built in the first three decades of the Revolution and basically egalitarian. As a result of establishing multiple currencies, opening up to tourism and to remittances, the increase in permanent, temporary, and return emigration, the growth of communications, access to the internet, and the emergence of a private sector in which some struggle for survival while others enjoy comfortable and even luxurious living standards—have generated levels of inequality that did not exist decades ago. At the same time, these measures energized the economy, diversified employment, increased the insertion of Cuba in the world, broadened transnational family connections and overcame this crisis, while many people improved their material well-being as others were left behind (Martínez Heredia, 2005).

The public tools and policies used to tackle the inequalities arising in a more diversified and complex society, however, have basically been the same: universal and free public services—health, education, social security—subsidies for goods and services—culture, public transport, and the basic food basket—and access to employment in the state-owned sector—although after the 1990s this took place with salaries too low to overcome inflation and cover the basic necessities. With few exceptions, these are centralized, generic, and egalitarian policies, mainly financed through fiscal mechanisms of redistribution of income, in which the taxes paid by the private and cooperative sectors of the economy play a growing role.

The Evolution of the Private Sector in Cuba (2010–2020)

The tug-of-war of the government with the private and cooperative sectors since 2010—in spite of their validation as part of the socialist system—has become a source of polemic, delays in the implementation of approved policies, disenchantment by those who bet on forming cooperatives, and insecurity for those who wanted to start private businesses. As a result—in not reaching income potential or well-paid jobs—the country has had to pay high economic, social, and individual costs as well as disillusionment and frustration.

In 2010, there were a total of 589,000 workers in the private sector—12 percent of the workforce—of which 147,000 were self-employed workers (*trabajadores por cuenta propia*, TCP in Spanish), who labored in 178 authorized activities. In August of that year, the government broadened the possibilities for self-employment by increasing the allowed activities to 201 (Betancourt, 2018). Between 2010 and 2011, the number of TCPs increased 2.7 times. The average annual rate of increase between 2011 and 2019 was 6 percent (Betancourt, 2018).

The year 2019 ended with a total of 1,030,000 private workers—22.6 percent of all workers—of whom 617,000 were TCPs, and of those, 35 percent were women. The percentage of women among the TCPs increased from 16 percent in 2011 to 36 percent in 2019 (ONEI, 2020).

Sixty-five percent of the licenses were conferred in five provinces: Havana, Matanzas, Villa Clara, Holguín, and Santiago de Cuba. With respect to the range of the principal activities, 9 percent were licensed for the preparation and sale of food, 8 percent for the transportation of freight and passengers,

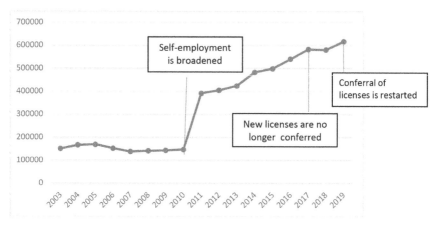

Figure 2.1.   Independent Workers (TCPs) Employed in Cuba, 2003–2019.

Source: ONEI. Anuario Estadístico de Cuba, 2019 [Statistical Annual of Cuba, 2019]. La Habana: Oficina Nacional de Estadística e Información de Cuba, 2020.

6 percent were housing rentals, while 26 percent were workers contracted by other TCPs (Tamayo & Labacena, 2019), which indicates the de facto existence of micro, small, and medium-sized businesses (MSMEs), whose number can be estimated at 32,000 if we assume an average of five workers per enterprise. In that year of 2019, it was reported that 10 percent of the total TCPs consisted of retirees and 15 percent simultaneously worked for the state.

The boundaries between the popular and the business economy are often diffuse and connected through formal and informal links. As the actual salaries are insufficient to cover people's basic needs—and their families'—many workers in the state-owned sector do part of their work in the popular sector in order to supplement their income, monetary and in kind. Having two jobs, or three, is common in today's Cuba. And if the informal workers who do unauthorized private work are added, the number of people who earn money in nongovernmental jobs could reach two million people—40 percent of the workforce—or even more (Feinberg, 2013).

The growth in the number of TCPs was not an easy road. From 2010 to the present, policies and regulations sometimes promoted and other times slowed and limited the sector—undoubtedly a reflection of the lack of consensus and political will among the appropriate authorities. In September 2010, the newspaper *Granma* stated:

> General Raúl Castro Ruz announced in the National Assembly the decision to broaden the sector of self-employed workers and use it as another alternative employment for workers who may become available after the reduction in the inflated rosters that the country must undertake. At the parliamentary meeting it

was also mentioned that several of the current prohibitions for conferring new licenses and the commercialization of some products would be eliminated, in addition to making the possibility to contract workers in specific activities more flexible. (Martínez Hernández 2010)

Without a doubt, the growth of the private sector, especially of small businesses like rentals and restaurants, increased tax evasion—partly in response to an excessively progressive tax system (between 25 and 35 percent) and a cash economy—and the purchase of supplies sidetracked from the public sector or imported by people ostensibly for their personal use—in response to the lack of a wholesale market and shortages in retail stores. The Government reacted in August of 2017 by freezing new licensing for a group of activities (Betancourt, 2018).

As part of a process of *enhancing* self-employment and of cooperatives, the Ministry of Labor and Social Security (MTSS in Spanish) stated that this suspension would be temporary. In order to justify the decision a wide range of reasons were asserted, among them: fiscal evasion, use of raw materials of illegal origin, lack of precision and insufficient controls, and deficiencies in the economic contract processes for the provision of services or goods between legal and natural persons. Unfortunately, as the economist Ricardo Torres observes, "to *enhance* has been equated with *braking, slowing, or increasing control*; and there are good reasons for this" (Torres, 2017).

On December 7, 2018—after sixteen months—the MTSS resumed granting licenses to restaurants, rental houses, and transporters. The new standards, decrees, and complementary resolutions included the regrouping of authorized activities from 96 to 28, and so the 201 that existed before were reduced to 123 (MINJUS, 2018).

Self-employed workers themselves considered that the modifications of December 2018 were akin to a rectification that canceled the most controversial aspects of the regulations enacted in 2017. The controversy started in academic circles and the private sector itself—and spilled over into the social networks—contending that these restrictions could bring harm. It was also encouraging for entrepreneurs that the new Constitution of the Republic of Cuba approved in April of 2019 recognized private property and included it in the matrix of economic actors of the country (Boza Ibarra, 2019).

In May 2019, there were more than 605,000 licensed TCPs in the country, distributed among the 128 activities then authorized. This figure represented an increase of 4.3 percent in five months, in spite of the fact that more than 77,000 closures had taken place (Romeo, 2019).

Beginning in mid-2019, a set of legislative improvements were passed that, compared with the two previous years, favored TCPs. Most important in the new package of standards was the possibility to establish contractual and commercial relations with both natural and legal persons (Cubans and foreigners), as well as the addition of seventeen new categories with which TCPs can establish contractual relations for services (Boza Ibarra, 2019).

In June 2020, as part of the strategy to strengthen the country's economic activity after the post-COVID-19 recovery, the government announced that it would move forward in the constitution of micro, small, and medium private businesses—MSMEs (mipymes, in Spanish)—of private, state, and mixed property, as well as the liberalization of self-employment, broadening the activities that can be exercised and modifying the applicable taxation system (MEP, Julio 2020).[1]

The Cooperatives of Industrial Employment and Service Workers: An Experiment at an Impasse

The 2011 Guidelines of the Economic and Social Policies of the Party and the Revolution establish that the cooperatives are considered to be "a socialist form of collective property . . . , which constitute an economic organization with legal personality and own patrimony, constituted by persons who join by contributing goods or labor, with the aim of producing and offering useful services to society, and who assume all their expenses with their incomes" (PCC 2011, 14). Therefore, they are different from both state and private property, and can be qualified as a social or associative property.

Since the triumph of the Revolution until 2012, the only authorized cooperatives were agricultural. That year, the Council of Ministers began to approve the experimental constitution of the first nonagricultural cooperatives (CNA in Spanish), which we prefer to qualify as cooperatives of industrial labor and service workers (CTIS in Spanish). From the start, the CNAs were considered experimental, supported by a legal framework that regulated their creation and operation. According to these laws, the new entities had legal personality and would be voluntarily constituted by its members, with economic and social aims carried out by collective management (Fonticoba Gener, 2012).

By March 2014, 498 CNAs had been approved, in the sectors of commerce and gastronomy, construction, technical and personal services, recycling, light industry, public transport, and energy. Of the total of the approved cooperatives, 77 percent were state enterprise units that were detached and turned over to its workers (induced cooperatives), and 23 percent were formed voluntarily at the request of TCPs interested in associating (grassroots cooperatives). The absence of university professions among the 128 authorized activities for self-employment limited the number of grassroots cooperatives, in spite of the many applications received by the authorities (Piñeiro Harnecker, Mayo 2014). The number of functioning cooperatives increased

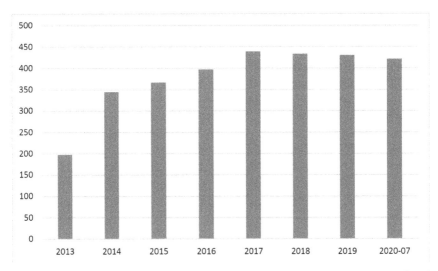

Figure 2.2.   Cooperatives of Industrial Labor and Service Workers (CTIS). Agricultural Cooperatives / Nonagricultural Cooperatives / Self-Employed Workers.

Source: ONEI. Anuario Estadístico de Cuba, 2019 [Statistical Annual of Cuba, 2019]. La Habana: Oficina Nacional de Estadística e Información de Cuba, 2020; ONEI. RE,ME,CNoA.zip. La Habana: Oficina Nacional de Estadíasticas e Información, 2016–2020.

annually until it reached 439 in 2017, and then it began to decline: 434 in 2018, 431 in 2019, and 422 in July of 2020 (ONEI, 2016–2020).

It is important to note that while the Guidelines of 2011 only consider state enterprises as a socialist form of property and the cooperative as a social form of property, the 2016 Conceptualization went beyond that. This strategic document, in its article 159, established that cooperatives "form part of the system of socialist property . . . being an object of special attention" among the non-state-owned forms of properties (PCC 2016b, 10).

However, in practice, the CTIS have provoked much questioning and criticism. In July of 2017, Raúl Castro said: "We decided to form cooperatives; we tried some, and we immediately began forming dozens of construction cooperatives: Has no one analyzed the consequences that this brought and the problems it created?" (Castro Ruz, 2017). In 2019, a spokesperson for the Commission of the Implementation of the Guidelines stated:

The authorities recognize that the most favorable economic impact [of the CNAs] is in the activities of construction, personal and technical services and in industry. However, restrictions for its development continue, such as limited access to the wholesale market and its associated services. Also persisting are deviations in the management of some cooperatives, primarily associated with lack of discipline and violations of legality, which have distorted the principles of cooperativism. (Figueredo Reinaldo, 2019)

This could be associated with the fact that 77 percent of the cooperatives that were authorized were induced or originated from state-owned establishments, mainly associated with gastronomy, personal services, and construction. Depending on the ministry that sponsored them, they received little or no support, training or recognition.

New legal norms for the CNA cooperatives in Cuba were made public in September 2019, which insisted on the *experimental* character of the cooperatives, decreed that no new ones would be created and that all projects that were in the evaluation stage would be canceled. On the other hand, the education and training of members was established as a principle of cooperativism for the first time, and it became an obligation for cooperatives to create a fund from the net profits that would finance these activities (Figueredo Reinaldo, 2019).

However, the cooperatives themselves, as well as others in the non-state sector, considered the new norms discouraging for the CNAs; in fact, the approval of new applications is still suspended. Contrary to what was desired, new limits to the functions of existing organizations of this type were introduced. "This is a negative step and contradicts the current discourse of the Government, which speaks of liberating the productive forces," according to some entrepreneurs (Boza Ibarra, 2019).

In another change of direction—as we will see later—the strategy proposed in June 2020 for the post-COVID-19 economic recovery included the development of cooperatives with a view to their expansion, the elaboration of legal norms that would group both agricultural and nonagricultural, and the constitution of new cooperatives in prioritized sectors of the economy.

Indisputably, it is necessary for the state enterprises to lead the strategic sectors of the economy, and that government through planning is established at the different territorial and sectoral levels. And hence the importance of carrying out the necessary expansion of the nongovernmental sector (cooperative, associative, private) and recognizing the legal existence of the MSMEs and the cooperatives.

> In the first place, because they generate a large quantity of employment, which the public sector cannot maintain if it aims to be efficient. Secondly, because they guarantee certain products and services that could contribute especially to the growth of the economy which, as has been shown in historical evidence, the state-owned sector cannot produce efficiently. And third, because they allow internal (savings) and external (remittances) capital to be mobilized, capital which would otherwise be inactive or would not reach the country. (Carranza, 2020)

And to this should be added the need for a better use of endogenous resources—family and community—of the potential for public-private alliances and the capacity to be included in and contribute to local development strategies.

COVID-19 AND ITS SOCIAL IMPACT

And then came the double pandemic—COVID-19 and the worsening of the US blockade; the economic crisis linked to this manifests and deepens even more the social and economic inequalities. Facing difficulties with food distribution, those with more income can buy more and even hoard, while the "queue specialists" [*coleros*] who buy only to resell at higher prices have proliferated with the scarcity. Remittances, though reduced by the new restrictions and the economic downturn in the countries where family members reside, lighten the load for some and not for others. Owners of private vehicles can move without restrictions, but those who depend on public transport are limited. Access to the internet and the income needed to pay for it determines the possibilities for virtual shopping, knowledge of the market, and access to information. The possibilities for self-care, the use of free time, and even access to virtual classes for students are conditioned by the state of one's housing and habitat. The urban-rural gaps and those between different rural regions have become wider: at one extreme, those who are more productive and profitable, where the population has achieved increase in family incomes, while at the other extreme are the stragglers who wait for assistance.

The health crisis provoked by COVID-19 has had sweeping impacts on all sectors; in general, the degree of economic insecurity, employment, and health losses in the world has increased. Despite the fact that our government's management of the pandemic has been successful, Cuba cannot escape the dilemma of choosing between a reduction of risks and vulnerabilities and economic recovery. Cubans, women and men, entrepreneurs and workers, have felt the impact of this as risks to their lives, their families, their jobs and businesses—although the situation does not affect everyone equally.

The current crisis has had a very great impact on the private sector in Cuba which, at just a decade of existence, is still in development. Of a total of thirty-eight activities studied by the Auge Consultancy, 39 percent—mainly in activities related to tourism—suffered strong decline due to the crisis. In terms of employment, this represents 33 percent of the TCP workforce—198,000 workers—with doubtful perspectives for recovery in the short run. The effects of the pandemic have been prejudicial to more than 26,000 landlords, more than 500 Airbnb experiences and more than 52,000 involved in transport (Díaz Castellanos & Torres, Mayo 2020). On the other hand, some 13,000 workers in the private sector have benefited from the reduction of monthly license fees, while the country has failed to collect some 101 million pesos in taxes. There is a high probability that a percentage of the TCP activities will disappear, at least in the form they had before the crisis.

To all this must be added the people who are linked to the private sector but do not have labor contracts and fall into some type of informality. These are more prevalent in the groups earning the lowest wages, non-whites, and those living in *opaque* or disadvantaged regions.

Alejandro Gil, the Cuban Minister of Economy and Planning, declared: "It is a question of guaranteeing the vitality of the country, the food needs of the population, and that the economic impact be absorbed at the lowest possible social cost; that we distribute this burden among all Cubans in order to move forward" (Cubadebate 2020/07/16, 4).

So, how to do this with the distributive mechanisms that currently exist? What role can the economic, private, cooperative and governmental agents play to "distribute the burden," but, especially, to "guarantee the vitality of the country"?

According to economist Pedro Monreal:

> During the eventual economic recovery an equitable approach should be prioritized, that is, recognize that social inequality needs different actions in order to achieve results of social justice . . . ; it is not a question of an distributing the same to all, rather, of differentiated distribution. Social groups in situations of inequality—of any kind—should receive more benefits than the rest; otherwise the causes that are the origin of the inequality are not compensated for. (Monreal 2020, 4)

The aim cannot only be to distribute public income and aid in better and more equitable ways to individuals and social groups most in need. It is above all a question of putting everyone to work through the economic recovery of the country and relaunching the project of socialist construction, so as to resume the path of "updating the economic and social model."

A STRATEGY FOR CONSTRUCTION AND RECOVERY: KEY AREAS

Since the confirmation of the new coronavirus, the country adopted a Plan for the Prevention and Control of COVID-19, which contains 497 measures approved by the government, and which covers all the sectors of society. The priorities of this plan have been the health of the population, the social protection of the workers—both in the state and the non-state sectors—and restoring economic activity to prevent interruption of productive activities and essential services (MEP, July 2020).

The strategy proposed in June 2020 consists of two phases: the post-COVID-19 recovery and the strengthening of the economic activity of the country. It is structured through key areas related to the spheres of major impact in the national economy. It includes the development of cooperatives—with a view to their generalization—the elaboration of legal norms that would embrace all forms, and the creation of new cooperatives in prioritized sectors of the economy. Along these same lines, it proposes that steps be taken to establish MSMEs that could be private, state, and mixed. It also proposes to move toward the liberalization of self-employment by modifying the list of activities that would be permitted as well as the applicable taxation system, and by expanding the activities that can be exercised (MEP, Julio 2020).

A proposed program to recover and strengthen the Cuban economy—presented by a group of five prestigious Cuban economists—recommends a group of measures for the two phases of the economic program. For the nongovernmental sector, the gradual reopening of the TCP activities and the legalization of the MSMEs (differentiating them from individual self-employed workers) is proposed. It also favors the establishment of a new type of non-agricultural cooperatives: Cooperatives of Non-Agricultural Credits and Services (CCSNA in Spanish). It proposes extending the tax exemptions to TCPs; encouraging non-subsidized imports of goods that are exempt from or have reduced customs duties; and increasing internal sales of an expanded assortment of goods in freely convertible currency (MLC), which would also include capital goods and supplies (Pérez, Vascós, Carranza, Monreal, & Benavides, junio de 2020). It is important to note that there is no mention of business social responsibility as a defining element of this sector in socialism.

THE RELEVANCE OF SOCIAL AND SOLIDARITY ECONOMICS

The ethics of behavior in socialism is cooperation to transform human nature and the natural environment, in order to improve everyone's life. The distributive ethics of socialism is equality of opportunity for everyone. *Life's lottery* that allocates resources unequally to individuals, families, communities or territories should not determine the good and the bad in people's lives. Equality of opportunity means compensating those who are disadvantaged in the *lottery* through education, training and entrepreneurship, in addition to direct aid. In socialism, property relations should be aimed at ensuring equal opportunity—in the context of a mixed economy of socialism with a market—and reflect the ethics of cooperative behavior.

And here is where we can find the usefulness of appealing to Social and Solidarity Economics. SSE is about forms of economic activity that prioritize social and environmental goals and involve producers, workers, consumers and citizens that act collectively and in solidarity. It encompasses state-owned enterprises, joint ventures with foreign capital, cooperatives, public and private MSMEs, and self-employed workers. It is oriented toward the constitution of different social relations—based on horizontality and cooperation—decent working conditions, equitable division of earnings, and values of solidarity and responsibility. A social and solidarity economy whose core is not the reproduction of capital but the centrality of work in the reproduction of life.

Cuban socialism has historically been social and solidary. The purpose of a socialist economy is to satisfy the material needs of society and to support the process of social transformation—not to generate profit for its owners. The strategic objective of the Cuban model, as defined in the Conceptualization, is "to motivate and consolidate the construction of a prosperous and sustainable socialist society, economically, socially, and environmentally, committed to strengthening the ethical, cultural and political values forged by the Revolution, in a sovereign, independent, socialist, democratic, prosperous and sustainable country" (PCC 2016a, 6).

How has the social economy been perceived in Cuba up to now? Essentially as part of the socialist economy: driven by the central government, *from the top down*, and with a strong dominance of the state-owned business sector. Business social responsibility is implicit and normalized, but exercised without entrepreneurial autonomy and responding to mandates from above. Today, with the country much more diverse in its forms of property and management, it becomes a question of motivating an economy composed of state-owned, cooperative, and private economic agents, to explicitly assume—and as part of their economic functions of production, distribution, and consumption of goods and services—the principles of responsibility with society (family, workers, clients, and other stakeholders, as well as the community) and with the natural and the built environment (the patrimony), toward the goal of creating a prosperous, democratic, and sustainable socialism.

BSR refers to a group of social and environmental activities undertaken by businesses beyond their legal obligations (Betancourt, 2016). This applies not only to the large enterprises—in Cuba's case, state-owned businesses—but also the MSMEs, cooperatives, and social enterprises. BSR contributes to solving social and environmental problems; it can reduce the financial-regulatory burden of the state by assuming functions that typically are handled only by the public sector, and it is a key component in the creation of supply chains that lead to inclusive markets. In Cuba social responsibility, which must be assumed by all enterprises and institutions—public, private, cooperative, and associative—will not only contribute to solve problems and satisfy needs, but also promote socialist values in its workers, managers, associates, and owners—especially when these forge public-private alliances and help in the articulation of the different forms of ownership aimed at promoting local development. (Betancourt, Mayo-Agosto 2016).

In Cuba, the SSE Means Constructing Socialism from the Bottom Up

Why insist on encouraging SSE and the BSR in Cuba now? At least two factors point to the advisability of SSE in Cuba at this time. On the one hand, the diversification of the matrix of economic actors in Cuba today and the social changes that have taken place demand a productive and distributive perspective that is more decentralized, in which the various economic agents participate in a more responsible and articulated manner, in which the local development strategies led by the regional governments guide the development processes, and the public-private alliances empower resources and people. All these are elements that characterize the SSE. On the other hand, the country's response to COVID-19 has shown us the power of a strong and committed central government, capable of mobilizing the resources necessary to save the country. At the same time, the power of the private and community initiatives, allied with the public sector, has been demonstrated, as well as the creativity of farmers and private entrepreneurs to overcome the difficulties. Our public-private alliance is the base of the SSE.

The decline of tourism, the difficulties of access to world commerce and to foreign investments, and a US blockade that is ever stronger and far-reaching, oblige us to plan our economic growth based more on the local market, on our own endogenous resources—including the human ones—and on social commitment. The decentralization of economic activity is also a component of the SSE.

According to the United Nations, many enterprises and organizations of the SSE have responded to the COVID-19 pandemic in various ways. These include: restructuring their production according to the needs of the emergency, protecting the health of vulnerable groups, providing food and protective equipment, offering financial, cultural and artistic support, relocating supply chains, etc. (UN 2020).

The Cuban media has underscored the donations of agricultural products made by farmers and cooperatives to social institutions and health centers; among them: hospitals, senior residences and homes that shelter people vulnerable to COVID-19. Notable are the actions of a group of private and cooperative businesses which, in the middle of the COVID-19 pandemic, made adjustments so they could continue to operate with social commitment and in public-private alliances. Several examples show the high professional and technological level that was achieved by some private enterprises which have worked side by side with and for government centers of research, production and health (OASIS May 2020).

This does not mean that all enterprises in the private and cooperative sector have embraced the BSR in the time of the pandemic. But the variety of initiatives among these examples mentioned is an ode to the creativity of the Cuban private sector—even with its limitations—and rejects the false image that it only relates to businesses of low technology and professionalism, whose only objective is to generate profit for its owners. The nongovernment economy generates employment in traditional spheres, but also in emerging sectors.

How much more could be done through alliances between private workers and governmental institutions in a post-COVID-19 phase in Cuba?

In many countries, sustainable local food systems have seen a significant growth by including farm-to-table practices for restaurants and homes, with home delivery. In Cuba, interesting experiences are known from Pinar del Rio and Havana (Funes Monzote 2020). This dimension of the SSE, joined by producers in family and community gardens, would contribute to local food security. Another possibility would be the restructuring of the current agriculture market cooperatives (intermediaries engaged in retail trade of agricultural products)—which in the more than five years of existence have not offered a solution to the problems of access to products with higher quality and lower prices—into cooperatives of consumers-producers, which could result in food security for the Cuban family (Landa de Saá, 2017).

The full potential of the SSE enterprises for the recovery will depend on the will of the local governments to codesign and co-implement public policies and recuperation plans with a multi-stakeholder approach.

SOCIAL AND SOLIDARITY ECONOMICS
IN THE "NEW NORMAL"

As long as human interaction and social relations still entail threats to health, economic activity cannot responsibly consider returning to the old normal. In order to avoid contagion, people will be reluctant to congregate in restaurants and bars, attend events, and consume in public areas. What used to be considered normal is not possible at the moment and even if it were, it wouldn't be the same. Therefore, tensions are being generated that correspond to the new contradictions, which demand different and innovative tools and policies, for a new normal that preserves human health without sacrificing economic and social development (Betancourt 2020).

In Cuba we need to encourage social and environmental responsibility if we do not want capitalist ideology to flourish in the private and cooperative sectors. We need to strengthen and democratize state-owned enterprises; promote true cooperatives, civic social associations, and publicly funded institutions like universities; stimulate the scientific and technical development of all forms of property; and encourage alliances to carry out inclusive local development projects. We need new tools and to develop different actions in order to construct a new normal.

SSE acts as an engine of local development by articulating different forms of property, communities and knowledge hubs like the provincial universities and the Municipal University Centers, under the strategic direction of the local governments. Many of the SSE entities are rooted in their communities, where they play an essential role in sustainable development and local governance.

Social economy permits a better maximization of resources, increasing exports, reducing imports, restoring the environment, and augmenting local resilience and regional identity. SSE entities were pioneers in encouraging a circular economy by moving from products with high emissions and waste toward systems that use residuals and resources in a more efficient and sustainable way, while at the same time conserving natural resources and protecting ecosystems.

SSE is also key for developing innovative solutions to problems that are global and defy many communities in the entire world. By promoting shared knowledge, innovative solutions and good practices, the SSE is open to exchanges and shared learning. In these exchanges we have identified positive experiences, good practices, advances and resources in the different currents of SSE found in Latin America, North America, Europe and Asia, that can nurture our work (Betancourt 2018). There is proof of the possibility of increasing the impacts of SSEs through South-South and Triangular Cooperation, which are strategic instruments in support of innovative SSE practices that can be adapted to local possibilities and contexts in different parts of the world (Betancourt 2016).

CONCLUSIONS

The success of self-management is mediated by the supply of regional benefits and liabilities, resources, the ability to establish horizontal relations between regions and sectors, and the ways to solve the demands and the needs of the population. Social and solidarity economics can contribute in a well-organized manner. The central state and the regions can redistribute and channel resources in a different way toward territories in need and benefit communities and vulnerable groups through fiscal policies and favorable prices. Local development strategies can uncover opportunities and resources that are unknown or unexploited, put them in practice in an inclusive way, and mobilize external assets from sources not tapped until now. Local development projects should incorporate the social and environmental dimension, establish indicators, and apply the triple balance sheet to businesses: economic, social and environmental.

Changes in economic policies can contribute to the social and solidarity economy, but it is not necessary to wait for them to promote SSE at the local and community level. This requires moving away from prejudices associated with the different forms of property, to informed judgments; move from spontaneous solidarity to systematic social responsibility; transform production based on imports to the mobilization of endogenous resources; search for new export opportunities; go from the lack of investment capital to the mobilization of popular, community finances and of productive remittances. It is necessary to breach the watertight blocks associated with forms of property, move to state-owned-cooperative-private coordination in pursuit of an integral regional development.

The SSE entities create opportunities through collective actions; they offer protection through mutual aid and empower people and communities through the collective and participatory management of their members. The SSEs are key in the endeavor that *no one will be left behind* in our country.

We have analyzed how the measures to relaunch the economy in the negative conditions that are being imposed on us have as an undesired impact the worsening of the existing economic and social inequities. It has been demonstrated that, by assuming SSE and BSR consciously and in a coordinated manner, the country would have better tools at its disposal to confront the inequalities, and to encourage local inclusive economic development within the framework of the construction of socialism.

We need to be convinced that our individual and collective life projects can be constructed in Cuba, through socialism. In the current context, social and solidarity economics can contribute to achieve this.

NOTE

1. Editor's Note: MSMEs were finally authorized in September 2021. By the end of May 2022, a total of 3,460 private and 51 state-owned had been approved. (Redacción OnCuba, 2022) The new legislative package included expanding opportunities for

self-employment, MSMEs, and nonagricultural cooperatives (Ministerio de Justicia Republica de Cuba, 2021).

BIBLIOGRAPHY

Betancourt, R. "South-South and Triangular Cooperation Supports Social and Solidarity Economy in Cuba," *in Social and Solidarity Economy and South-South Cooperation: Fresh challenges and Lessons Learned—Compilation of Short Articles on South-South Cooperation*, 21–25. Costa Rica: CIF-ILO Social and Solidarity Economy Academy, November 2016. Retrieved from http://www.ilo.org /pardev/partnerships/south-south/WCMS_535081/lang--en/index.htm.

———. "Avances de la economía social y solidaria en áreas urbanas: lecciones para Cuba" [Advances of the Social and Solidarity in Urban Areas: Lessons for Cuba]. *V Taller de Estudios Sociales del Trabajo "Inclusión social y trabajo en la Cuba actual."* La Habana: CIPS, 2018.

———. "Social and Solidarity Economy and the Transformation of the Cuban Economic Model." *International Journal of Cuban Studies* 10(2): 209–29, 2018.

———. "El aporte de la Economía Social y Solidaria para construir socialismo en Cuba (I)" [The contribution of Social and Solidarity Economics for the construction of socialism in Cuba (I)]. *OnCubaNews*. July 7, 2020. Retrieved from https:// oncubanews.com/cuba/economia/el-aporte-de-la-economia-social-y-solidaria-para -construir-socialismo-en-cuba-i/.

———. "La Responsabilidad Social Empresarial en Cuba" [Business Social Responsibility in Cuba]. *Estudios de Desarrollo Social: América Latina y Cuba* 4(2), 34–43. May–August 2016. Retrieved from www.revflacso.uh.cu.

Boza Ibarra, G. "¿Qué les preocupa a los cuentapropistas cubanos?" [What concerns Cuban self-employed workers?] *EL TOQUE*, December 24, 2019. Retrieved from https://eltoque.com/que-les-preocupa-a-los-cuentapropistas-cubanos/.

Carranza, J. "La economía socialista no es la supresion del mercado" [The socialist economy is not the suppression of the market]. *Progreso Semanal*. May 21, 2020. Retrieved from https://progresosemanal.us/20200521/julio-carranza-la-economia -socialista-no-es-la-supresion-del-mercado/.

Castro Ruz, R. "Discurso pronunciado en la clausura del IX Período Ordinario de Sesiones de la VIII Legislatura de la Asamblea Nacional del Poder Popular" [Speech delivered at the conclusion of the IX Ordinary Session of the VII Legislature of the National Assembly of Popular Power]. *Diario Granma*. July 14, 2017.

Cubadebate. "Gobierno cubano informa sobre nuevas medidas económicas" [Cuban government announces new economic measures]. *Cubadebate*. July 16, 2020. Retrieved from http://www.cubadebate.cu/noticias/2020/07/16/gobierno-cubano -informa-nuevas-medidas-economicas-video/.

Díaz Castellanos, O., and R. Torres. *El emprendimiento privado en Cuba: Un paci-ente positivo a la COVID-19* [Private entrepreneurship in CUba: A patient postive for COVID-19]. La Habana: Auge Consultores, May 2020.

Feinberg, R. E. *Soft Landing in Cuba? Emerging Entrepreneurs and Middle Classes.* Washington, DC: Brookings Institution, 2013.

Figueredo Reinaldo, O. "Nuevas normas jurídicas para las cooperativas no agro-pecuarias en Cuba" [New legal norms for non agricultural cooperatives in Cuba]. *Cubadebate.* September 15, 2019.

Fonticoba Gener, O. "Cooperativas no agropecuarias. Camino a la actualización del modelo económico" [Non abgricultural cooperatives: Path to the updating of the copnomic model]. *Diario Granma*, December 11, 2012.

Funes Monzote, F. R. "Finca Marta. Proyecto agroecológico que ama y funda" [Marta's Farm: Agroecological project that loves and founds]. *Cubadebate.* June 12, 2020. Retrieved from: http://www.cubadebate.cu/especiales/2020/06/12/finca-marta-proyecto-agroecologico-que-ama-y-funda/#.XuOVv6SSk2w.

Landa de Saá, Y. "Cooperativas de consumidores: una propuesta para reducir los gastos de la familia cubana por concepto de alimentación" [Consumer cooperatives: A proposal for reducing the food costs of the Cuban family]. In R. e. Betancourt, *Construyendo socialismo desde abajo: la contribución de la economía popular y solidaria* (223–37). La Habana: Ediotorial Caminos. 2017.

Martínez Heredia, F. *En el horno de los noventa* [In the furnace of the nineties] La Habana: Letras Cubanas. 2005.

Martínez Hernández, L. "Trabajo por cuenta propia. Mucho más que una alternativa" [Self employment. Much more than an alternative]. *Diario Granma*, September 24, 2010.

———. "Ajustarse a la realidad e imponerse a ella con el trabajo" [Adapting to reality and surpassing it with work]. *Diario Granma,* May 5, 2020.

MEP. *Cuba y su desafío económico y social* [Cuba and its economic ans social challenge]. La Habana: Ministerio de Economia y Planificación, July 2020.

MINJUS. *Gaceta Oficial Ordinaria* No. 24. La Habana: Ministerio de Justicia Republica de Cuba, August 29, 2021.

———. *Gaceta Oficial Extraordinaria* No. 35. La Habana: Ministerio de Justicia Republica de Cuba, Diciembre 7, 2018.

Monreal, P. "Las colas cubanas en la era del COVID-19. Un caso de desempoderamiento ciudadano" [Queues in Cuba in the COVID-19 era: A case of citizen empowerment]. *El estado como tal*, Mayo 9, 2020. Retrieved from: https://elestadocomotal.com/2020/05/09/las-colas-cubanas-en-la-era-del-COVID-19-un-caso-de-desempoderamiento-ciudadano/.

OASIS. *Emprendedores responsables, un jaque a la COVID-19. Iniciativas de apoyo social. Ediciones I y II* [Responsible entrepreneurs: A check on COVID-10. Initiatives of social support. Editions I and II]. La Habana: Programa OASIS del Proyecto Cuba Emprende en alianza con la Consultoría Auge, May 2020.

ONEI. *RE,ME,CNoA.zip.* La Habana: Oficina Nacional de Estadíasticas e Información, 2016–2020.

———. *Anuario Estadístico de Cuba, 2019* [Statistical Annual of Cuba, 2019]. La Habana: Oficina Nacional de Estadística e Información de Cuba, 2020.

PCC. *Lineamientos de la Política Económica y Social del Partido y la Revolución* [Guidelines for the Economic and Social Policy of the Party and the Revolution]. La Habana: VI Congreso del Partido Comunista de Cuba. 2011.

———. *Conceptualización del Modelo Económico y Social Cubano de Desarrollo y Plan Nacional de Desarrollo Económico y Social hasta 2030* [Conceptualization of the Cuban Economic and Social Development Model and National Plan for Economic and Social Development until 2030]. La Habana: VI Congreso del Partido Comunista de Cuba, 2016a.

———. *Propuesta de Visión de la Nación, Ejes y Sectores Estratégicos* [Proposed Vision of the Nation, Strategic Lines and Sectors]. La Habana: VI Congreso del Partido Comunista de Cuba, 2016b.

Pérez, H., et al. "Propuesta de programa para recuperar y fortalecer la economía cubana." *El estado como tal*, Junio de 2020. Retrieved from: www.elestadocomotal .com.

Piñeiro Harnecker, C. *Diagnóstico preliminar de las cooperativas no agropecuarias* [Preliminary diagnosis of the nonagricultural cooperatives]. La Habana: Centro de Estudios de la Economía Cubana, Universidad de La Habana, May 2014.

Redacción OnCuba. "Cuba autoriza otras 104 Mipymes privadas" [Cuba authorizes another 104 private SMSEs]. *OnCuba News,* May 27, 2022. Retrieved from https: //oncubanews.com/author/oncuba/.

Romeo, L. "Nuevas modificaciones al Trabajo por Cuenta Propia buscarán frenar las ilegalidades existentes" [New changes in Self-Employment seek to stop current illegalities]. La Habana: *Cubadebate.* July 9, 2019. Retrieved from http://www .cubadebate.cu/noticias/2019/07/09/nuevas-modificaciones-al-trabajo-por-cuenta -propia-buscaran-frenar-las-ilegalidades-existentes/.

Tamayo, R., & Labacena, Y. "Así marcha el trabajo por cuenta propia" [Thus self-employment advances]. La Habana: *Juventud Rebelde,* February 10, 2019. Retrieved from: http://www.cubadebate.cu/especiales/2019/02/10/asi-marcha-el -trabajo-por-cuenta-propia-segun-juventud-rebelde/#.XGIPfHm8rIU.

Torres, R. "Aquí vamos otra vez" [Here we go again]. Miami: *Progreso Semanal,* August 17, 2017.

UN. *What Role for the Social and Solidarity Economy in the Post COVID-19 Crisis Recovery?* Geneva: United Nations Inter-Agency Task Force on Social and Solidarity Economy, 2020.

Chapter 3

The Social and Solidarity Economy

Integrating Bases, Experiences, and Possible Projections for Socialist Development in Cuba

Ovidio D'Angelo Hernández

For several years now, Cuba has faced a polemic with respect to social and solidarity economy (ESS in Spanish). This has prompted the organization of many scientific events, publications and field research projects, masters' and doctoral theses, etc. in the field of social sciences. However, different positions are still held regarding the real dimensions of the concept, its inclusiveness relating to the cooperatives—urban and agricultural—and other non-state enterprises.

The experiences of the nonagricultural cooperatives (CNA in Spanish), of some of the forms of agricultural cooperativism and of various forms of self-employment have not always been positive from the point of view of their social connotation, even though in all these cases a collection of practices has been fruitful for local community integration and development.

On the other hand, in the official discourse ESS it is not a recognized term, though it is accepted for the research field of the social sciences. In addition, starting from the classic Marxist thinkers, the topic of cooperativism—one of the important forms of ESS—has been treated as one of the main ways of building such a type of society from which a greater acceptance of its relations with the concept of ESS could result.

For this reason, this article will attempt to broach these issues—which have been presented by numerous national and international authors from their various viewpoints—based on the different dimensions attributed to the concept, starting from the nonlinear interpretation of some Cuban experiences and its range of possibilities within the socialist structure.

In this sense, we advocate for a reconceptualization that is adapted to our circumstances and to the historical context of the country, while at the same time sustaining its main foundational principles.

SOCIAL AND SOLIDARITY ECONOMY
IN ITS DIFFERENT VERSIONS

The definition of ESS that is used in Latin America and other regions of the world is still somewhat vague, and is alternatively used as a synonym of: social economy, popular economy, labor economy, the other economy, new cooperativism, associative forms, and popular self-managed enterprises. Some of the most frequent definitions (Cattani 2003; Coraggio 2003, 2007, 2013; Sarría y Tiriba 2003; Singer 2003) point to a range of possible actors: cooperatives of products and services, associations of producers (associated self-employed workers, public-private-community projects, and others), family groupings, consumer associations, social movements, etc.

Some authors consider that these possibilities include a group of productive enterprises or domestic units of a collective initiative, with a certain level of autonomy of management and internal democracy, equitable distribution of income, community projection, and sustainability. Their recognized sphere of action is preferably microsocial and of a local-community nature, many times as a survival technique of marginalized and vulnerable sectors.

The characteristics mentioned before are more appropriate to certain forms of cooperatives and self-managed firms than to all productive forms in the community. Because of this, Coraggio (2007, 2013) and others call this diversity of self-management forms a "popular economy." In fact, some Latin American authors call solidarity economy a social, economic, and political option (Sarría and Tiriba 2003), whose main characteristics are often called the "C Factor," which puts emphasis on cooperation, collectivity, community, and collaboration. This could be understood as the exercise of solidarity, participatory-decisive democracy, internal-external identity-belonging, and internal-external social projection.

In 1995 the International Cooperative Alliance (ACI in Spanish)[1] indicated the following as the principles that define the cooperativism movement: autonomy, solidarity, cooperation, confidence, mutual aid, reciprocity, equity, participatory responsibility, and care for the environment. (Alianza Cooperativa Internacional 1996)

On the other hand, the European concept of Social Economy (Laville 2001), or its denomination as the Third Sector—used by some theorists in order to include cooperative and solidarity enterprises, among others—suggests a certain equivalence with ESS, although this can hide the truly twisted relations that arise in various places between cooperative or self-management forms and socioeconomic capitalist relations.

In this sense, some Latin American authors refer to the concept of *new cooperativism*, in contrast to the cooperatives that have been assimilated or integrated into the areas of activity of the large capitalist or transnational enterprises and which work like their extensions. In our country, the field of cooperativism itself presents a diversity of forms: some are truly agricultural cooperatives (Agricultural Production Cooperative, CPA), others semi-cooperative like associations of private producers (Credit and Service Cooperative, CCS), or the most recent urban cooperatives (Nonagricultural Cooperatives, CNA). So there is a wide range of possibilities in using the concept of cooperativism and its relations with ESS, which will need some explanation.

For example, in relation to its scope, in this diversity of acceptances starting from concepts close to social and solidarity economy, Coraggio (2013) establishes a distinction between popular economy and social (solidarity) economy, which will be interesting to review in our reconceptualization. In the words of the Argentine economist:

> The plan of a social economy is not to broaden the popular economy—because the latter is a natural part of the capitalist system—but rather to surpass it, to develop its potential so as to make it into a social economy, a labor economy . . . , part of an emancipation project . . . , an economy that is socially conscious of the society it produces . . . , not at the service of the goal to accumulate capital or to accumulate power, but rather always at the service of the duplication in the situations of the daily life of all men and women. (Coraggio 2013)

SOCIAL AND SOLIDARITY ECONOMY IN SOCIALISM?

The topic of cooperativism, one of the foundational cores of the social and solidarity economy, has been addressed by classic Marxism on various occasions. Marx and Engels pointed out the potentials of cooperativism to convert social production into a unique, broad, harmonious, and free cooperative labor system, with the capacity to contribute to the transformation of society through the substitution of the authoritarian system of subordinating labor to capital (Marx 1973). And in his 1923 essay "On Cooperation," Lenin also emphasizes the importance of cooperatives as one of the premises for socialist transformation, and ends up affirming that socialism is a society of educated cooperatives, an instrument of the new socialist State structured by new arrangements of relationships, organization and social interaction (V. I. Lenin 1961).

However, in socialist practices, this point has had various derivatives. In the real socialism of the USSR there was a competition between the cooperatives (*koljoses*]) and the state agricultural enterprises (*sovjoses*), which tended to end up favoring the latter as being the most advanced socialization. Our country has gone through stages in which the relevance of one or the other form has alternated.

In the area of international debates, the determining role of cooperatives is a subject of discussion. The transformative potential of cooperativism and social economy is one of the central axes of the theoretical debate dealing with the capitalist structural system, although there are moments in which the possibilities of cooperativism as a transforming instrument of the economy and of society has been exaggerated by the creation of false expectations and delusions.

For Hesselbach (1978) and ACI (Alianza Cooperativa Internacional 1996), when the number of members reaches a certain level, it makes personal contact between directors and team members difficult. This situation can bring about a lack of control and of democratic participation at all levels; elements that enable the evolution towards a concentration of power in a technocracy that would end up choosing between its peers. This is true for some cases (Mondragón in Spain, Cruz Azul in Mexico, and other similar cooperative federations) which have established forms of cooperative structures that go beyond the local setting and, occasionally, beyond the national, including the rise of distortions of the original concept of cooperativism.

Based on the references mentioned before, we will review the concepts of Coraggio (2013) to discuss ESS "as a part of an emancipatory project . . . , an economy that is socially conscious of the society it produces . . . , not at the service of the goal of accumulating capital." A similar sense is found in the—even broader—proposal of Paul Singer (2007), who maintains that "the experiences of the solidarity economy are not only anti-capitalist; they are also expressions of socialism. Any democratic, egalitarian and self-managed enterprise—whether cooperative or not—is already socialist." For this author, the generalized self-management of the economy and of society is the economic and political program of socialism, although this would require the clarification of what is meant by processes of self-management and what is the role of the social and state institutions in this concept—questions to which we will refer later.

We could also ask ourselves about the view of the social role of the socialist state enterprise, whose function is considered key for the socialist structure in the most recent programmatic documents—Guidelines of the Social and Economic Policies of the Party and the Revolution (PCC 2011), Conceptualization of the Economic and Social Model of Cuba (PCC 2016), and the new Constitution of the Republic of Cuba (ANPP 2019). This issue leads us to consider the multidimensionality of the topic of ESS, which has recently been linked to the discussion on the need to give freedom to the productive forces in the Cuban socialist model that is under construction.

In our view, liberating the productive forces is part of a phenomenon of complex networks in economic, social, political, cultural, and judicial relations, and for this reason it cannot be dealt with as disconnected from the set of phenomena of social life, nor separate from the manifestations of the various socioeconomic forms. Therefore, an issue of major importance in the approach to this question is the consideration that everything in society is, in one way or another, linked to complex networks of institutional and social relations. What does appear to be clear, beyond the specific analysis of possibilities and tendencies, is that in this country the support is for a non-privatizing socialist model, along a noncapitalist path to development. In these circumstances, how far could the complementarity of economic forms reach? And how can we transform the state-managed enterprises from authoritarian-centralized forms to multi-stakeholder forms that include non-state forms? How can cooperatives and forms of management and private property be considered expressions of ESS?

CUBAN EXPERIENCES WITH THE SOCIALIST STATE ENTERPRISE AND THE NON-STATE MANAGEMENT FORMS, FROM THE ESS PERSPECTIVE

Marx clarified that when one is dealing with relations of production (and labor), it is always a question of *social relations*, and therefore also political, economic, judicial, etc. which, in contrast to the *classic* economy and to economic liberalism, express contradictory relationships between capital and labor,[2] which in turn leads us necessarily to the nature of the social labor relations that exist, with the resulting forms of alienation of the latter (and certainly not only economic).

What happens in our case? We would have to start from the current status of these social relations of production in the different existing forms of property in order to analyze to what point they fulfill their social role and in what way they could be expressed in ESS.

Difficulties of the Various Socioeconomic Forms
Current in Cuba

Without intending to be all-inclusive on the topic, we could say that there are currently contradictions and limitations in the different forms of property and management and their reciprocal relations which—given that the possible solutions would have to be different in each case—requires an approach to its current specificities. Judging by the economic processes of recent times, the retention and eventual growth of the non-state forms of business is anticipated, as well as an increase in the businesses under local control, foreign investment in the form of state-private property management, and a growing increase of autonomy in the management of state enterprises. These predictions present a more promising picture that the one now current, with views towards the socioeconomic development of the country. However, what is still pending is the continuation of progress in the intensification and breadth of other potential measures of social and organizational-economic character in the social articulation of the enterprises, internally and in the sphere of relations with communities and municipalities, as well as in the strengthening of its social role.

The Socialist State Enterprise

In the National Assembly of late 2019, the minister of the economy announced a series of twenty-eight initial measures that aim to encourage the operational flexibility of state enterprises, in progress towards a Law of Commercial Enterprises and Societies, with the objective of reorganizing the entire socioeconomic system in the current entrepreneurial diversity. However, among the persistent issues—presented in social research from the 1980s to now—the following may be found: low salary incomes compared to the non-state management forms, in spite of the compensatory measures that were implemented[3] and others soon to be; limited entrepreneurial autonomy compared to other forms of property and management, in spite of their own current limitations; the contradiction between the state property of the enterprises and the workers' and general citizens' feeling of being social owners; and the participation of the workers in the entrepreneurial decisions and benefits.

The contribution of the state enterprise in the country has made possible the financing of the social programs of health and education, as well as some measure of more or less equitable social redistribution of incomes through employment, and other guarantees such as Social Security, the financing of important parts of the whole economy and the life of the country.

However, from the analysis of the multiple organizational business forms that have been implemented during the revolutionary period, other alternatives have been proposed recently in the professional-public debate: forms of labor co-management and self-management; forms of leasing state enterprises to workers; secondary corporate branches—which are not yet found in the current spectrum of observable possibilities. In addition, emphasis has been made by official policy on the configuration of productive networks as value chains between different forms of property and economic management, as a way to interact towards a shared social purpose.

Cooperatives

The variety of existing cooperative forms in the country (CPA, UBPC, CCS, CNA)[4] has gone through different trajectories. While the agricultural cooperative forms are related to the National Association of Small Agriculturalists (ANAP), which includes private farmers, the CNAs—which have been subject to a probationary law over the past few years—still lack associative forms, which increases the problems of social management within the regional framework.[5]

As seen in government research and publications on the new experimental form of CNA, there are difficulties evident (instabilities in the revenue advances made to directors and members, lack of supplies, deficient productive and organizational links, little managerial autonomy, replication of management forms adapted from state enterprise), which have needed legal adjustments—some that are appropriate and others debatable—and have prolonged its experimental character by blocking new associations (Piñeiro 2011, 2014; D'Angelo et al. 2019; Henríguez 2017; Morillas Valdés 2018).

Other experiences in urban and agricultural cooperative forms have been more constructive socially, in some cases by offering community and social support and better conditions of income and life to their members. However, in all cooperative forms, a group of limitations has been identified. A true cooperative culture has not caught on at the social level. And this at the same time that, as we will elaborate later, the principles and values of cooperativism could constitute a flexible platform for the foundation of an entrepreneurial network of social and solidarity economy which would include the different management and property forms, with relations that are more humanizing.

Self-employed Workers

The broadening of the field of self-employed workers opened a larger space for the satisfaction of consumer goods, better and more varied product offers, better income benefits to sectors of the population, and in certain cases encouraging creative initiatives. The classification of self-employed workers cannot be reduced to one single form of homogenous management-property.

There are individual and family self-employed workers, those of subsistence level or restricted economies. In addition, there are also groups of those who provide services in rented localities, which function almost as a cooperative, together covering the costs of the rented space and its maintenance, and reach agreements. Also included are the small and medium-sized enterprises (SMSEs) of different sizes, with income levels that range from moderate to high, and which employ labor. The better and well-situated ones have high levels of income.

Other activities, informal or having the character of undeclared self-employment, are associated to some of these. It is worth noting that a number of self-employed workers (like some CNA and other forms of cooperatives) carry out functions with an entrepreneurial social responsibility that support vulnerable sectors or people of the community or contribute other benefits to their workers and residents. Among these emblematic cases is the Artecorte project in the capital.

Both the self-employed workers and the cooperative forms offer their employees sources of income that, as a general rule, are superior (even highly superior) to the state entrepreneurial forms. However, this sometimes happens at the expense of charging high prices for their products and services or the over-exploitation of labor—beyond the legal limits.

On the other hand, the associative (unionized) forms officially designed for the defense of the rights and other alternatives of labor justice create a double contradiction: title holders (owners) and employees participate within the same union; and this union is the same as the one to which state workers belong, but with different characteristics.

LIGHTS AND SHADOWS IN THE CURRENT
SOCIAL LABOR RELATIONS

The various socioeconomic entrepreneurial forms of the country demonstrate potentials and various levels of limitations and distortions of humanizing labor relations. With recent measures and others that are in preparation, the state enterprise seems to be moving towards formats of greater equity and sense of belonging.

In the same manner, one idea that was recently expressed by the minister of the economy refers to the need to bring the workers in the various forms of property and management closer together, in order to avoid the flight of the qualified workforce in the state sector. This would close the gap that currently exists, to the extent in which the global economy and international relations—particularly the onerous US economic blockade—would allow for that. However, in the field of labor relations it would be possible to move toward forms of social organization by way of the participation of workers in the making of decisions (micro- and macrosocial) and in other areas.

The situation is diverse and contradictory in other forms of socioeconomic management and property. As an example we mention the dysfunctions of the cooperatives, the massive employment of salaried workers, the over exploitation of work in some private SMSEs (currently self-employed),[6] the concept of an inequitable distribution of the capital gains obtained and of group decisions made with the workers in some of its variants.

ALIENATION OF LABOR, LEVELS OF ENRICHMENT VS. SOCIAL EQUITY

The current challenges of our society, as seen from the economic and sociopolitical labor and property conceptions, should take into account different alternatives in order to accomplish that society as a whole can progress towards more reduced forms of alienation of labor—this being the fundamental activity of the life of the free and receptive citizen—which is a historical ideal of socialism. There was recently a summons, and actions were taken on the key topic of fostering chains of production—with their implications for local and national development—which can be a measure of progress in the socioeconomic expression of the different forms of property and management, though not far enough given what is possible.

Many issues remain pending in order to achieve an appropriate synergy, in the social and the economic spheres, in the design for a multi-varied, solidarity, and participatory economy. Therefore, we shall retake the issue of labor—and social—alienation as related to an understanding of the self-management process in both spheres of social relations.

The topic of labor alienation is closely related to the forms of the exercise of economic and sociopolitical power (Marx 1961; Foucault 2003). In both directions, the organizational forms of the social relations determine their nature. In the area of economic enterprises, the processes of participation in the decisions and profits, in the determination of the working and living conditions, are factors that—when properly applied—can contribute to reduce labor alienation in the various socioeconomic forms. This establishes a transformation in the current conception of the various forms of management and property by emphasizing the processes of labor and social self-management on the road to socialist development. We will make some proposals on this topic later on.

In our case, we understand self-management to be a model that is applicable to all human agencies in society, at all levels, but whose frame of action needs to be harmoniously linked to the state functions.

As Texier (2002) states: "Only through seeing an economy as a whole, the problem of self-management and of the forms of property must be examined so as to allow the planning to take into account the economic totality and its equilibriums." (Texier 2002) This involves the economic sphere, in the sense of the desired market and the agreement of the agents involved. It establishes the problem of the limits and benefits of the small private, the mixed and other properties, in addition to the social role of the citizens themselves in the economic management; as well as the different kinds of participation in the social structure from its community and organizational foundation.

This scenario would mean the possible reduction of alienation of inter-personal and social relations, and institutional transparency based on shared commitments and powers. Such a situation also directly establishes the problem of social management, particularly self-management as a form of balancing central and local, individual, group, and institutional powers as compensation, diversification, and contribution to ideas that are creative toward the centralized state powers, in the social, economic, juridical spheres and that of political participation.

Therefore, self-management, understood in such a way, is not exclusive of the socioeconomic sphere of labor but rather, from the perspective of the socialist development, spaces of coordination with the exercise of citizenship in the local sphere would be needed. This would complement a view of social and solidarity economy as an expression of the entire society.

SOCIAL SELF-MANAGEMENT: A WAY TOWARD SOCIAL TRANSFORMATION?

The topic of *local self-management* has acquired more relevance recently. Not only because it is linked to new perspectives and practices of socioeco-nomic relations, but also from the position of the organizational and political praxis of society. In both cases, of course, it is seen from different theoretical perceptions—sometimes contradictory—which go from reformist and con-servative positions to radical and emancipatory viewpoints.

In one of its most important variations, social self-management is expressed through different forms and mechanisms of local self-government; also, and in a broader outlook, it implies the expression between popular self-government and the local institutions and spaces. Therefore, it is a form of articulating the Gramscian distinction between civil society and political society (Acanda 2005), and the complex articulation between state and social relations (including the economic ones).

The topic of social subjectivity and the daily practices associated with the new frames of organizing local-social self-management establishes an important challenge based on the theory and on its implications for the social network and the forms of social citizen participation, as well as for the expression between different socioeconomic forms, state agencies, and the participatory and vital democracy of the people.

SOME POSSIBLE PROJECTIONS OF THE ESS CONTEXT FOR THE DEVELOPMENT OF SOCIALISM IN CUBA

Even in the current multi-stakeholder and varied contexts, success can be achieved through non-alienating principles, principles of solidarity, of social cooperation, of workers' self- and co-management, which have nourished authors of socio-critical currents and of solidarity economy.

In our country the possibilities of ESS have been seen as a key focus in the projection of the socialist economy (Piñeiro 2011). This last author establishes that "Cuban ESS is potentially the union of the three spheres—public, business and private—composed of a group of economic stakeholders—state, associative and autonomous—who assume the principles of responsibility with society and the environment" (Betancourt 2015, 65). These two aspects (social and environmental responsibility) are important in any consideration of the topic. In our research we agree with the possibility of broadening ESS to all socioeconomic forms, and we even propose extending its holistic appreciation to the entire society (D'Angelo 2015).

The implementation of ESS in the various socioeconomic sectors, in management and property forms also requires an effort in the creation of a governmental organization of multi-stakeholders, in which the building of public-private solidarity and participatory alliances performs an important role, together with the initiatives at community and local levels—an issue that was dealt with in our research (D'Angelo et al. 2020). Moreover, the economic and social relations are articulated in complex frames that could make possible the highest range in the participation of ESS in the entire society (D'Angelo 2010; D'Angelo et al. 2019, 2020).

Addressing these criteria and with the viewpoint of its constructive broadening toward other sectors of the economy—ever more present in our country—the use of the social and solidarity economy concept could be reformulated in order to be able to apply its principles to the different sectors and forms of property and management of the economy, in a differential and flexible manner.

Among other modalities that specialists could propose on these topics, this flexibility can refer to the following:

- Various scales of the redistribution of capital gains among the workers, with a margin for the gradual recuperation of the initial investment (from the owners in the TCP-SMSEs and also in state enterprises), as well as fulfilling the labor legislation and the relative equity in the internal distribution of income;
- Different modalities of participation by the worker collectives in projections and decisions of the non-state forms and the state enterprises; a broadening of the fields of social investment towards all forms of property and management and to its productive links, as per the previously mentioned considerations;
- More space for the local self-managed forms, especially those of a collective nature, with a positive impact on resolving local needs;
- Application of tax rates that would reduce the proportion for the smaller self-employed workers and would fix progressive rates according to the size and the volume of income (without stifling the stimulation of their growth) of private, cooperative or mixed state-private forms of SMSEs (as practiced in some capitalist developed countries);
- Certain social and fiscal benefits corresponding to the exercise of social entrepreneurial responsibility-commitment in all forms of property and management;
- Redesign of the labor union functions as a constructive and participatory compensation, appropriate to the type of property and management.

The formation-diffusion of the socioeconomic solidarity values and the possible measures of their appropriation by the citizens requires the multidimensional and prioritized encouragement of a culture of human relations at a new level—a challenging task that involves sustained and profound courage. It also requires the building of a broad social consensus, like a new social pact that would express the understanding and acceptance of the roles, limits and social possibilities of all the socioeconomic forms.

Conditions of poverty, but also individualistic ambitions generate human misery of many different kinds. Both need to be halted so as to avoid that the potential freedom from poverty generates a greedy social conscience instead of an appropriate equilibrium, approved in a collective manner, of the distribution of wealth, of individual and collective prosperity. This progress would involve the encouragement of a culture of *being* versus *having*, a vision of frugality as the way of a personal-collective development toward a solidarity conscience and practice.

At the micro level, the empowerment of the social stakeholders is the formative way toward the achievement of the self-management performance, while the social spaces should promote it, starting from the decentralization and flexibility of participation, the possibility of the expression, and the reflexive positioning of the stakeholders themselves. This question relates to the concession of power of the institutions and representatives of the State to the stakeholders, who are autonomous and responsible for the social collectivity, builders of the social consensus. One of our interests in the analytic dimension of empowerment for development through socialism is the introduction of the category of integrative autonomy (D'Angelo 2005, 2007, 2010; D'Angelo et al. 2014, 2019), which articulates various social processes, considered in a cross-sectional way, to advance into a hologrammatic view of development. From this category, the self-organizing processes need to be taken very seriously.

In addition, the measures and adjustment of socioeconomic coherence, with a view towards the ideal of an economy of greater social integration, need new participatory, deliberative and dialogic methods of multi-stakeholder and citizens agreement, which would take into account the general final aims and some of the interests, with options of group receptivity and the creation of constructive alternatives relating to the socialist ideals perspectives.

NOTES

1. The principles and values of international cooperativism were set by the Rochdale Society of Equitable Pioneers [sic] from the middle of the nineteenth century, thus forming the international cooperative movement and the modern concept of social economy (Monzón, 1989). It was the Declaration of Manchester that defined its essential characteristics starting from its values and principles, the search for the satisfaction of the needs of the members and the community, rather than the capital, the collective character of property, and democratic functioning.

2. Capital as an economic power in capitalism, which acquires a hegemonic character and can metamorphose through other powers, like the state.

3. Payment according to results obtained, salary reforms for the budgeted sector, and other compensations.

4. CPA: Cooperativas de Producción Agropecuaria [Agricultural Production Cooperatives]; UBPC: Unidades Básicas de Producción Cooperativas [Basic Units of Cooperative Production]; CCS: Cooperativas de Créditos y Servicios [Credit and Services Coopera5tives]; CAN: Cooperativas no Agropecuarias [Non-Agricultural Coperatives].

5. N.E. In August 2021, the Cuban government passed the Decree-Law 47/2021 On the Non-Agricultural Cooperatives (Consejo de Estado 2021), which established permanent new norms for constituting and operating CNAs which ended the experimental nature established in 2018.

6. N.E. In August 2021, the Cuban government passed the Decree-Law 46/2021 On Micro, Small and Medium-sized enterprises (Consejo de Estado 2021) which for the first time allowed for the creation and operation of private enterprises with legal

status. Self-employed workers with more than three employees will be required to become SMSEs.

BIBLIOGRAPHY

Acanda, J. L. 2005. *Traducir a Gramsci.* La Habana: Editorial Ciencias Sociales.

Alianza Cooperativa Internacional. 1996. *Los principios cooperativos para el siglo XXI.* Fondo Nacional Universitario.

ANPP. 2019. *Constitución de la República de Cuba.* La Habana: Asamblea Nacional del Poder Popular. http://www.granma.cu/file/pdf/gaceta/Nueva%20Constituci%C3%B3n%20240%20KB-1.pdf.

Betancourt, Rafael. 2015. "La economía social y solidaria y la actualizacion del modelo económico cubano." *Blog Catalejo de la Revista Temas.* http://temas.cult.cu/blog/?p=2071#more-2071.

Cattani, A. 2003. "A Outra economia Definições essenciais." In *A outra economia*, by A. Cattani, 23–30. São Paulo: Editora Veraz. https://www.economiasolidaria.org/sites/default/files/Laotraeconomia.pdf.

Consejo de Estado. 2021. "Decreto-Ley 47/2021 De las Cooperativas No Agropecuarias." *Gaceta Oficial No. 94 Ordinaria de 19 de agosto de 2021.*

Coraggio, J. L. 2013. "Cómo construir otra economía." In *Desafíos para cambiar la vida Economía Popular y solidaria. Cuadernos de solidaridad no 6*, by C. López. La Habana: Editorial Caminos.

———. 2003. "Economía del trabajo." In *A outra economia*, by A. Cattani, 151–63. São Paulo: Editora Veraz. https://www.economiasolidaria.org/sites/default/files/Laotraeconomia.pdf.

———. 2007. "Introducción." In *La economía social desde la periferia. Contribuciones latinoamericanas*, by J. L. Coraggio, 17–57. Buenos Aires: UNGS-Altamira. ttps://coraggioeconomia.org/jlc/archivos%20para%20descargar/ECONOMIA%20SOCIAL%20DESDE%20Periferia.pdf.

D'Angelo, O. 2006. "¿La autogestión local como vía para la transformación social?" *Revista Temas* (37).

———. 2005. *Autonomía integradora y transformación social: El desafío ético emancipatorio de la complejidad.* La Habana: Publicaciones Acuario. http://biblioteca.clacso.edu.ar/Cuba/cips/20120822100925/angelo.pdf.

———. 2007. *Contextualidades complejas y subjetividades emancipatorias.* Ponencia, La Habana: Seminario Internacional de Complejidad.

———. 2015. *Economía solidaria y autogestión social: algunas proyecciones y desafíos en nuestra realidad actual.* Biblioteca Virtual CLACSO.

———. 2013. "Economía solidaria y autonomía integradora." In *CD Caudales*. La Habana: CIPS.

———. 2011. "Economía solidaria: Reconstrucción urbana y ciudadanía integradora Aproximaciones y proyecciones en nuestra realidad actual." *X Encuentro Internacional de Manejo y Gestión de Centros urbanos.* La Habana: Oficina del Historiador de La Habana.

———. 2010. "La subjetividad social. Desafíos para su investigación y transformación." In *Cuadernos del CIPS. Experiencias de investigación social en Cuba*. La Habana: Publicaciones Acuario.

D'Angelo, O., et al. 2019. *Alianzas Público-Privadas con Prácticas Solidario-Participativas APPSP para la gestión del desarrollo local, desde la autonomía integradora Centro Habana, 2017-2019-2021*. La Habana: Programa Nacional de Desarrollo Local, CITMA-CIPS.

———. 2014. "Economía Solidaria en la Transformación Comunitaria: Proyecto Santo Ángel por Dentro." La Habana: Biblioteca CLACSO.

———. 2020. *Resultados de investigaciones sobre fomento de APPSP en escalas de Gobierno de Centro Habana*. La Habana: CIPS.

Foucault, M. 2003. *El sujeto y el poder. Trabajo original publicado en 1982*. Santiago de Chile: Escuela de Filosofía, Universidad Arcis. http://148.202.18.157/sitios/catedrasnacionales/material/2010a/martin_mora/3.pdf.

Henríquez, P. 2017. *Participación social de los miembros de la cooperativa Model Centro Habana*. Tesis de Maestría, La Habana: Universidad de La Habana.

Hesselbach, W. 1978. *Las empresas de la economía de interés general*. México: Siglo veintiuno editores.

Laville, J. L. 2001. "La Economía Social en Europa." *Otra Economía* (Red Latinoamericana de Economía Social y Solidaria (RILESS)) 1 (1). www.riless.org/otraeconomia.

Lenin, V. I. 1973. "Sobre la cooperación (Trabajo original publicado en 1923)." In *Obras Escogidas en tres tomos*, 414–17. Moscú, URSS: Editorial Progreso.

———. 1961. *Obras escogidas en tres tomos. (Trabajo original publicado en 1921)*. Moscú, URSS: Editorial Progreso.

Marcelo, L. 2022. "Los tipos socioeconómicos en la fundamentación de las políticas futuras sobre el universo empresarial cubano," *Tesis presentada en opción del grado científico de Doctor en Ciencias Económicas, pendiente del acto de defensa*.

———. 2014. *Tipos de propiedad económica y transición socialista en Cuba*. La Habana: Instituto Nacional de Investigaciones Económicas INIE.

Marx, C. 1973. *Fundamentos de la crítica de la Economía Política. Trabajo original publicado en 1939*. La Habana: Editorial Ciencias Sociales.

———. 1961. "Manuscritos económico-filosóficos de 1844. Trabajo original publicado en 1844." In *Escritos económicos varios*, by C. Marx, edited by Traduccion y recopilacion W. Roces, 25–125. Editorial Grijalbo.

Monzón, J. L. 1989. *Las cooperativas de trabajo asociado en la literatura económica y en los hechos*. Madrid: Ministerio de Trabajo y Seguridad Social España.

Morillas Valdés, F. D. 2018. *Estrategias empresariales de las Cooperativas No Agropecuarias para su inserción y sostenibilidad en el entramado socio-productivo local*. Resultado de Investigación CIPS., La Habana: CIPS Grupo de Creatividad para la Transformación Social.

PCC. 2016. "Conceptualización del Modelo Económico y Social Cubano de Desarrollo y Plan Nacional de Desarrollo Económico y Social hasta 2030." La Habana. VI Congreso del Partido Comunista de Cuba.

———. 2011. "Lineamientos de la Política Económica y Social del Partido y la Revolución." *VI Congreso del Partido Comunista de Cuba.* La Habana.

Piñeiro, C. 2011. *Cooperativas y Socialismo: una mirada desde Cuba.* La Habana: Editorial Caminos.

———. 2014. *Diagnóstico preliminar de las cooperativas no agropecuarias en La Habana, Cuba.* La Habana: Centro de Estudios de la Economía Cubana (CEEC), Universidad de La Habana.

Sarría, A., and L. Tiriba. 2003. "Economía Popular." In *A outra economía*, edited by A. D. Cattani. São Paulo: Editora Veraz. https://www.economiasolidaria.org/sites/ default/files/Laotraeconomia.pdf.

Singer, P. 2003. "Economía solidaria." In *A outra economia*, edited by A. D. Cattani. São Paulo: Editora Veraz. https://www.economiasolidaria.org/sites/default/files/ Laotraeconomia.pdf.

———. 2007. "Economía solidaria. Un modo de producción y distribución." In *La economía social desde la periferia*, edited by J. L. Coraggio. Buenos Aires: Contribuciones latinoamericanas. UNGS-Altamira. https://coraggioeconomia .org/jlc/archivos%20para%20descargar/ECONOMIA%20SOCIAL%20DESDE %20Periferia.pdf.

Texier, J. 2002. "Socialismo, democracia, autogestión." *Revista Marx Ahora* (Instituto de Filosofía) (14).

Chapter 4

The Foundations of Popular and Solidarity Economics as Fulfillment of the Social Property of All People in the Socialist Transition

Luis del Castillo Sánchez

Among the positions taken in the Conceptualization of the Cuban Economic and Social Model, (PCC, 2016) which was submitted to debate in mid-2016, the affirmation that the socialist state should concentrate on the complex tasks appropriate to it stands out. The state should separate itself from the immediate management or administration of specific activities that require a high level of independence, autonomy and responsibility; without specifying that the state should not fulfill business functions, but the functions that are specific to its role of being the representative of the social property, the inspiration, regulation and control. Therefore, businesses should not be responsible for the obligations of the state, nor should the state be responsible for the enterprise system. Thus, the traditional concept of state-as-entrepreneur should not have a place in the model for the state enterprise system, otherwise, the public functionaries would not resign nor be replaced, nor would the state enterprises collapse, because there would always be reasons—from one or another of its roles (representative of the property and manager at the same time), for neither to happen.

Among the principles for the good governance of the state enterprise we note that the nomination and election process of the directors of the state enterprise should guarantee the selection of professionals at the highest level, since it is the managers of the upper-level administration who motivate the changes—in an integrated manner, with the participation and responsibility of the labor collective—to achieve the fulfilment of the objectives. To the extent to which the state guarantees a better level of business leadership, it will be in a better position to achieve success. The need for a professional business direction and management for the socialist state enterprise is essential to its nature. It is derived from the democratic corporate process itself, which encourages an entrepreneurship with committed leaders who have a high professional level related to the experience and aptitudes of business management. Lenin's advice, that "not everything derives from political power, but rather in knowing how to direct, how to place people appropriately" (Lenin 1990, 115), is significant and valid.

Moreover, the need for a non-state sector—in particular a private sector composed of micro, small and medium enterprises (MSMEs)—including the traditional cooperative form, is recognized, both as related to ownership and for the management system. However, the assertion that is made regarding private property also fulfilling a social function needs at least a foundation, which is missing in the document. And another issue is to note that, through the economic, labor and environmental regulation of the private sector, the possible negative impacts on the social interest should be avoided or mitigated, as well as emphasizing the need to encourage public-private alliances and the mixed sector of the economy, among other ways. All this was always included in the traditional and original ideas of socialist transition, in particular when it was specified that this transition did not begin in the most developed countries.

Reducing the MSMEs to the private sector is inexplicable, because the classification of such enterprises responds to their size, as per the number of workers and the level of billing. Since the 1980s and 1990s, studies and proposals have been made on the MSME sector within the entrepreneurial structure of the socialist economy; however, none were approved or implemented, as has been the case with other essential economic issues.[11] Maintaining the identification of the socialist corporate sector exclusively with the large enterprises or with the large groups of enterprises—without any technical, economic or competitive foundation—goes against the need of the natural cycle of the flourishing and development of the business, of the nature of the enterprise, the innovation and the requirements of the new technologies. Should such unfounded criteria be maintained, we would leave innovation, entrepreneurship, and competitiveness exclusively to the private sector, and however much control we may have over the means of production, the enterprise system of social ownership would be downgraded, lagging behind, supplanted, and leaning toward extinction.

We cannot determine a priori that, because we are in the construction stage of socialism, any economic relation has a socialist character, not even in the state sector. In our case, things are actually even more complicated, since a distinction must be made between the initial phase of the transition, which inherits different socioeconomic forms, and the contemporary phase, in which the effects of mistaken economic conceptions and policies are manifested—and applied with authority—which do not solve the set of contradictions between the different levels of socialization and the necessary forms of ownership and management. On the other hand, in the classic Marxist conception, the elimination of private property based on labor is not recognized as a task of the socialist transition, since it is the conditions of capitalist development themselves that lead to their transformation or termination. With a better foundation, in the processes of socialist transformation coming from underdevelopment, the pre-socialist duties are merged with the tendencies of the new production relations. In that way, mixed, combined, and integrated forms should prevail, to contribute to the development objectives, without having to hasten the establishment of artificially pure and arbitrary economic forms of socialism. In reference to this, Lenin remarked the following in 1921:

> We will not allow ourselves to be dominated by a *socialism of feeling*. . . . It is all right to make the most of all types of economic forms in the transition, and given the need for them, one should know how to use them, in order to strengthen the links between the farmers and the workers, in order to boost the national economy without delay, in a country that is ruined and exhausted, in order to encourage industry, to facilitate further, broader and more profound measures. (Lenin 1961, 668)

It is necessary to indicate that the economic forms of transition do not refer to the temporary and interim character of any of them, but rather to a mediation of the contradiction, as an intermediate link that would contribute to its resolution by taking the best of each and reduce the negative effects, so as to obtain the objectives that are being sought. We need to take into consideration that the risk of the individualism of private property and that of state corruption can be fully interwoven, which is expressed in the fact that the freedom to decide and choose is linked to the need for market freedom, through the principle of free supply and demand. However, when there are conditions of imperfect markets, scarce resources, monopolist power in the assignments of key raw materials; without appropriate counterweights such as institutions in defense of competition, of the rights of consumers against marketing abuses of power, together with the inefficiency, corruption, and gaps left by the distortions of the economic state sector, a rationale of speculative and parasitic capital will be imposed over the one of associative labor.

The smaller a country and its internal market is, the greater are the possibilities for one or another form of property and management the establish marketing power on the remaining production and commercialization agents. In this way, adverse effects are generated relating to the satisfaction of needs; among them the imposition and speculation of prices, the direction of the supply only toward the sector of middle to high income levels, the encouragement of intermediary networks without any real contribution of value, the accumulation and concealment of the production, the high rates of commercial margins without resulting in a better quality or benefit, and the lack of protection for the consumer. With the historical experience of the fall of *real socialism*, it would be interesting to delve deeper into who had the greater freedom and power of decision to rapidly appropriate the goods and resources that were *the property of all the people*, as these societies reiterated insistently in the program documents that proclaimed them to be socialist. This is the fundamental danger if we have the construction of a new society as an objective. All this seems to deny the sacrifice of generations who have resisted all external aggressions, as well as all deformations, improvisations, and internal errors in leading the country—in particular as related to running and managing the economy.

The essence of social ownership over the means of production is not determined by its state form of property but resides in the process of a gradual transformation of the salaried worker to an associated producer who needs to fulfill the functions of social production, at the level of and for the whole society; and this includes the processes of running, managing, and participating in the decision making. The worker and the workers' collective should be able to assume the responsibility of these tasks under the conditions of management autonomy and responsibility. Therefore, the nature of being associated producers is what determines being a joint proprietor, as the acquisition of wealth is determined by their performance as efficient and effective producers in the creation of this wealth. The job determines the social position of the individual, and not simply being an owner, since absolutizing this latter situation leads to egalitarian and private income tendencies, and even to considering themselves an *individual owner* in the misappropriation of the society's resources. In this respect, there are systematic practices being developed of putting together organized actions and links—which are not achieved in the productive forms—to divert and appropriate any kind of resource that can generate income without labor. This is more acute in conditions of chronic shortages, while the working class itself is deformed in a broader sense, from management at any level, down to the person who takes care of a warehouse or transports the goods.

Associating the salaried worker with the connotation of *owner*, as people wish to do, has not achieved the desired effects, not even in the case of cooperatives that have been stimulated by the state sector. The quality of salaried worker does not always—nor directly—determine a responsible participation in the making of joint decisions on production and results, because individual and collective interests that are external to the labor contributions and the outcome of the work can prevail. The central contradiction is related to how to educate and train the worker or the labor collective as associate producers from the original condition of salaried workers, without having to wait for higher stages of development. When this cannot be resolved adequately, the trends to private individual or collective formats prevail as the effective solution by way of the relations between private owner and contracted worker, since the incentives of private property become stronger than those related to social property. It is one thing for the private sector to coexist with social ownership, and another for the first to extend toward and impose itself on the second, by not providing an adequate management of the effective transformation process of social property in its business implementation. In this management, various administrative forms and models of corporate business need to be encouraged, such as: administrative contracts with national and foreign management, hiring, franchise systems, subcontracting, tenders, temporary employment, telework, a technologically based management model, among others. In addition, linking with other forms of ownership and private and cooperative management is encouraged.

Strictly speaking, on the one hand, the socioeconomic role of the State in relation to social property is based on exercising its power in order to mediate the opposition between the salaried worker and the need to transform him/ her into an associate producer. Therefore, it needs to integrate its functions in order to encourage, facilitate and support all forms and ways that would allow the learning and training of the functions of the worker and the collective as associate producer. On the other hand, it must be a coercive system in order to guarantee the quantity of work and consumption in the conditions in which work prevails as a way of life. It is in this sense that the state character of the social ownership enterprise needs to be understood, so as not to confuse its form with the essential content. Thus, when Lenin indicated in 1921 that socialism is the system of educated cooperators (Lenin V. I., 1961), he meant that the democratic principles of the cooperative association should be a characteristic of the social enterprise property in its state form, and that it is never limited to a specific size of enterprise. In the same way, Marx (1867) indicates that in capitalism the cooperative factory of the workers themselves constitutes a new form, an expression of other relations of production, in which antagonism has been abolished (Marx, 1973).

There is no doubt that Leon Trotsky defined an essential aspect of the state nature of social property when he indicated that:

> In order for private property to become social, it has to pass inevitably through nationalization, in the same way that a caterpillar, in order to become a butterfly,

needs to go through being a chrysalis. But a chrysalis is not a butterfly. Myriads of chrysalises die before becoming butterflies. State property is no more *that of all the people* than to the extent that social privileges and differences disappear, and that therefore the State loses its reason for being. Said another way, State property becomes socialist to the extent that it ceases to be State property (Trotsky, 2010, p. 177).

Such an expression calls into question the identification of the *non-state* sector only with the private sector—be this at an individual or group level—as well as reducing it to a complement of the socialist state sector. To refer to the non-state public aspects could be seen as a contradiction for those who limit the public sector strictly to the State. It could also be seen in this way for those who assume that non-state is necessarily private and thus subject to the sphere of personal sovereignty and of market regulations. At their extremes, these two options have represented the positions that have characterized the discussions during the last thirty years of the twentieth century, by assigning to the State or to the market the roles of exclusive organizers of social life (Cunill Grau, 1997).

The projects, enterprises and associative forms should also be seen as property of all the people, from the local or community dimension, non-profit, or the processes of innovation and technology-based business enterprises generated by universities and research centers. This is why it is important—from the social property standpoint—to define those which, as related to the strategic means of production, respond to the state form, and to incorporate the associative community dimension linked to the recognition of the Popular and Solidarity Economy (EPS in Spanish).

On the other hand, an ideal, homogeneous place cannot be assigned to *the whole society*, or attribute to it an intrinsic virtue, because it is characterized by a heterogeneous structure of needs and interests. Relations of solidarity and equity coexist with expressions of socio-economic inequalities, tendencies toward the encouragement of private egotism, different attitudes toward work, exclusion, and manifestations of an abusive marketing power facing a deficient regulation of the market.

Alvaro García Linera stated the following:

As a structure of new economic relations, socialism cannot be a state construction, nor an administrative decision, but rather, and above all, the widely held, creative and voluntary work of the working classes themselves, which will bring the experience of new ways of production and managing wealth into their own hands. (García Linera 2017, 86)

EPS allows the economic strengthening of popular power and serves as a counterpoint to the private sector, and thus popular power + popular economy translates into building socialism from the bottom up.

The reasons for validating the principles of EPS in the promotion of business ventures in our current conditions are based on the formation of the values of socialism starting from the individual, family and community level. The economy can be democratized and we can empower the local agents without having to encourage only individual or collective private property. It has to do with setting associativity before individualism in private property, solidarity before egotism, labor rationales before capital and speculative rationales, promoting the development of the individual to be a consequence of the development of his/her community, and not the opposite.

In the analysis of the experience of EPS in Latin America—which is sometimes marred by errors and political issues—it is important to emphasize that it does not only come about as an alternative to the effects of neoliberalism, but also as a response to the deformations that led to the failure of the so-called *real socialism.* Among others, José Luis Coraggio refers to an idea that claims to go beyond the option between a capitalist market—which he associates with the economy *as is*—and a state that centralizes and regulates the economy—which he associates with the deformed variants of a bureaucratic socialism (Coraggio, 2011). The centralized state should be improved because it withdraws power from society and assumes the representation of a national common good; it acts as a delegate which, in the absence of a substantive democracy, easily falls into the temptation to obey the interests of the most concentrated economic groups, to make an unjust and socially inefficient system *governable.*

We can draw the conclusion that the model of the countries that began to build socialism is characterized by propelling economic and social development, but also by yielding to the enormous weight of the state bureaucracy, which ends up making central planning a tool of fatal immobilization for society. Therefore, it cannot be seen only as a project for the poor, but rather for the whole society, and which can only be valid as an alternative to the effects of the neoliberal policies.

The popular and solidarity economy is the assembly of resources, capabilities and activities, and of institutions that, according to solidarity principles, regulate the appropriation and disposition of these resources in the implementation of activities of production, distribution, circulation, financing and consumption organized by the workers and their families, by community or associative self-managing forms (Coraggio, Arancibia, and Deux 2010). It is considered that neither the individual nor the family enterprises by themselves are included in this definition, unless they are associated in solidarity with other similar ones; for example, a network of joint provisioning of homes, or one that commercializes small producers.

EPS is linked to the socialist project to the extent that it has the human being as its center of development; it seeks to satisfy the common needs of the population; it is at the service of society, as serving the community members is its primordial organizational commitment; it recognizes different forms of social organization for production, in which the society of people takes precedence over that of capital. It also constitutes an opportunity for the workers who become available as a result of the restructuration process of the state sector, because in the absence of an inclusive financial system, it turns out to be impossible to promote a personal venture for the worker who has depended exclusively on his employment income.

Taking into account the scientific-technical potential that has been created in this country, the tendency of the popular economy ventures cannot only be associated with the survival of the vulnerable sectors—as is the case in Latin America—but to innovative projects and those based on technology. For this reason, possibilities are opened for technological parks at a local and national level, as well as university-business foundations, to encourage qualified jobs, to generate capitalization levels and personal incomes that raise the quality of life and contribute to the development of the community. And all this without having to be subordinate to one or another sectorial ministry, within a central state structure, since contradictions have become evident by leaving the approval of local projects and initiatives to that level when, because of the magnitude of the resources and the impact, it is not a priority interest for the national economy. However, they are of vital importance for a determined locality or community; in particular when these are excluded from the centers of national or sectorial development, as well as for the initial technology-based ventures with a high level of risk.

By promoting different types of organizations—like *start-ups*, *spinoffs*, solidarity cooperatives, associations, popular economic units, community sectors, revolving funds, communal banks, networks of cooperation, and commerce at fair prices—new socio-productive models are being encouraged from the different areas on the basis of associativity and self-management, from the joint direction of the local governments and other organizations, with an institutional model supported at a national level. For that to happen it is essential to be able to count on a public non-state institution or agenda for the local development initiatives and popular economy, which would regulate the promotion, judicial recognition, control and supervision of the EPS ventures or projects, as well as other forms of property and management of local interest. This should be complemented by the role of local governments in the design, implementation, and evaluation of the public policies that will allow for the organization of the local agents and the integration into national, sectorial, and regional interests, to make the most of endogenous resources.

Considering the chronic deficiency of some state functions—like inter-institutional coordination, promotion and encouragement in the design of economic policies to solve socioeconomic problems—non-state nonprofit public entities should be created that would allow for the development of such functions with greater efficiency and flexibility, compared to the ministerial-state environment. This relates to public entities that function with operational autonomy and are of similar management to the private sector. They can be financed by direct subsidies from the central government, by transfers through taxes whose complete or partial objective would be legally associated with their financing, or by the generation of their own resources linked to the sale of goods and services. In addition, they should be subject to a double control: state and social; they should break with the sectorial perspective; they should facilitate the integration of the agents, the productive chains, the socialization of the specialized experience and the flexibility of the organizational structure. They can assume different organizational forms such as agencies, associations, foundations, endorsement and motivational entities, institutions, etc.

In summary, this deals with the issue of the economic system of socialist transition, based on the social property of all the people as the main form of property, having to start from the principle that the state should not monopolize its representation, nor implement it in an absolute way. Therefore, it is necessary to enable the development of virtuous circles linking the state, the market, and society, which, from the economic point of view, means renewing the concept of the socialist state enterprise and recognizing the economic system of EPS as the expression of the community-associative dimension of social property. Together with this, the set of public non-state entities should be developed so as to ensure the public interest in the implementation of the State functions. Addressing the issue of institutionalization may favor the satisfaction of needs from and for society and, from there, also from there to exert pressure for the State sphere to be truly and effectively of all the people—meaning that it would be open to the participation and engagement of all.

NOTE

1. Editor's Note: The legislation passed in 2021 that legalized MSMEs does authorize private, state, and mixed enterprises (Consejo de Estado, 2021).

BIBLIOGRAPHY

Consejo de Estado. Decreto-Ley 46/2021 Sobre las micro, pequeñas y medianas empresas [Law-Decree 46/2021 On micro, small and medium-sized enterprises]. (GOC-2021–777-O94). La Habana: *Gaceta Oficial* (94), August 19, 2021.

Coraggio, J. L. *Economía social y solidaria. El trabajo antes que el capital* [Social and solidarity economy. Labor before profits]. Quito, Ecuador: Ediciones Abya-Yala, 2011. Retrieved from: https://www.coraggioeconomia.org/jlc/archivos %20para%20descargar/economiasocial.pdf.

Coraggio, J. L., Arancibia, M. I., & Deux, M. V. *Guía para el Mapeo y Revelamiento de la Economía Popular Solidaria en Latinoamérica y Caribe* [Guide to Mapping and Revealing the Popular Social Economy in Latin America]. Lima: Grupo Red de Economía Solidaria del Perú (GRESP), 2010. Retrieved from: https://base .socioeco.org/docs/gu_a_para_mapeo_y_relevamiento_eps_en_lac.pdf.

Cunill Grau, N. *Repensando lo público a través de la sociedad: nuevas formas de gestión pública y representación social* [Rethinking the public by way of the society: New forms of public management and social representation]. Buenos Aires: Editorial Nueva Sociedad, 1997. Retrieved from: http://sitp.pichincha.gob.ec/ repositorio/diseno_paginas/archivos/Repensando%20lo%20p%C3%BAblico%20a %20trav%C3%A9s%20de%20la%20sociedad.pdf.

García Linera, A. *¿Qué es una revolución? De la Revolución Rusa de 1917 a la revolución en nuestros tiempos.* Quito: Vicepresidencia del Estado de Bolivia, 2017. Retrieved from: https://rebelion.org/docs/234964.pdf.

Lenin, V. I. *Obras completas* [Complete Works]. Moscú, URSS: Editorial Progreso, 1990. Originally published in 1922.

———. *Obras escogidas en tres tomos* [Selected works in three volumes]. Moscú, URSS: Editorial Progreso, 1961. Originally published in 1921.

Marx, C. *El Capital* [Das Kapital]. La Habana: Editorial Ciencias Sociales, 1973. Originally published in 1867.

PCC. *Conceptualización del Modelo Económico y Social Cubano de Desarrollo y Plan Nacional de Desarrollo Económico y Social hasta 2030* [Conceptualization of the Cuban Economic and Social Development Model and National Plan for Economic and Social Development until 2030]. La Habana: VI Congreso del Partido Comunista de Cuba, 2016.

Trotsky, L. *La Revolución Traicionada* [The Revolution Betrayed]. Caracas: Ministerio del Poder Popular para la Educación Universitaria de Venezuela, 2010. Originally published in 1937. Retrieved from https://koha.cenamec.gob.ve/cgi-bin/ koha/opac-retrieve-file.pl?id=6b7a2a8cd6ad8ad33c35f72744cf5.

Chapter 5

Participatory Budgeting

A Management Tool for Local Development in Cuba, Seen from the Experiences of the Office of the Historian of the City of Havana

Orestes J. Díaz Legón and Maidolys Iglesias Pérez

The improvement of the municipal government and the mechanisms of participation, as well as the encouragement of local development constitute courses of action in the frame of the administrative and economic reforms that are happening in our country. (PCC 2017; PCC 2016; PCC 2016b) The Constitution of the Republic of Cuba, proclaimed in 2019 (ANPP 2019) refers to the recognition of the principle of municipal autonomy and the acceptance of new forms of participation in the local sphere (Articles 168 and 200), which are examples—at least from the formal perspective—of the strengthening of the role the Cuban assumes in the political, economic, and social framework of the country.

In this sense, the following article has as its objective to propose guidelines for the introduction of practices of participatory budgeting (PB) in the Cuban environment, starting from the methodology and lessons learned in an experiment developed in the Historical Center of Havana. This is based on the possibilities that the new constitutional text grants to the municipalities and the population, and on how necessary it is for transparency, accountability and popular participation to support local budgetary procedures in Cuba, as a formula to link the citizens to the taking of far-reaching decisions in municipal life.

BRIEF NOTES ON PARTICIPATORY BUDGETING

In relation to popular participation much has been said and written. Political experts, sociologists, lawyers—among others—have devoted innumerable efforts to the study of this category. In these, popular participation is presented as one of the terms that can kindle the most heated debates, has such great support, and its scientific attraction is such that there is always justification to go back to it, all the more so if there is a question of its articulation at the local (municipal) level.

Decades ago, the focus of attention relating to local democracy centered on citizen participation in the election and organization of the local authorities. Currently there is a broader understanding relating to popular participation, both as associated to doctrine (González Quevedo 2010; Méndez y Cutié 2012), and to legal regulations (República Bolivariana de Venezuela 1999, Art. 70). The holding of local elections and participation understood as representation is not enough. Local democracy implies popular participation to its greatest extent; that is to say, the possibility of the residents of a municipality to directly influence the issues that are relevant to them, as well as to intervene in the preparation, approval, implementation and control of the local public policies. This being so, channels of interaction have taken on importance, like strategic planning, consultative councils, local management units, open town councils, and public hearings. Within this list, PB also stands out, as a mechanism that involves popular participation and social control.[1]

The experience of PB appeared in Brazil in the 1970s, in the municipality of Lages. In the 1980s, numerous cities adopted popular participation in the preparation of the budgetary law, as was the case in Vila Velha, Angra dos Reis and Porto Alegre. PB, as it is conceived today, came about in 1989, motivated by the Partido de los Trabajadores [Labor Party] when it acceded to the Prefecture (Seabra de Godoi y Oliveira S. de Rezende 2019). In Porto Alegre the quest was for the radicalization of democracy through participatory formulas which placed the municipality at the center of the political struggle, in order to achieve transparency, decrease corruption and strike down poverty. Based on these premises, PB was born, as a way to influence the forming, execution and control of local public decisions. During the first five years of the twenty-first century, the Brazilian experience with participatory budgeting had been adapted and adopted in Latin American and European cities (Alcaldía de Porto Alegre 2005). For El Troudi, Harnecker and Bonilla-Mollina, PB "is the process by which the population participates in defining the levels of the revenue and expenses of the municipal public budget to be invested in the localities, and indicates in which spheres investments should be made and what should be the work to be prioritized" (El

Troudi, Harnecker y Bonilla-Molina 2005, 79). Benjamin Goldfrank, in turn, maintains that PB "is a process by which the citizens, individually or through civic organizations, can contribute in a voluntary and consistent manner to the making of decisions on the public budget, by means of annual meetings with the governmental authorities" (Goldfrank 2006, 4).

There exists a wide range of experiences and methodologies collected by authors such as Acevedo, Mejía y Matamoros 2004; Castillo 2004; Lencina 2004; Matías 2004; Montecinos 2006; Francés García y Carrillo Cano 2008. Generally speaking, one can say that the natural environment of the PB is the municipality, being the political-regional organization that is closest to the citizens and the place in which they display their immediate needs. PB constitutes a public space in which local authorities and citizens interact in a direct way, which comes to life in different stages. At the time when the expenses to be undertaken are decided, the residents of a municipality will be asked—through PB—to determine what their problems are, to organize them hierarchically so as to constitute a standard for performing the governmental and administrative activities. If in the municipal budgets the disbursements are divided into common expenses and investment expenses, PB principally works in the latter (be it in part or completely), and therefore these are the ones that have a direct impact in the increase in the quality of life of the citizens.

PB aims for the democratization of the budgetary procedure at the municipal level. It should not be forgotten that:

> if it is the people who should find the satisfaction of their needs and hopes in the municipalities, if it is the people who should receive the public services directly, through governmental and administrative actions, it is without any doubt the people's thinking that is the first element to be taken into account in the technical—and therefore also the democratic—activities of the municipalities. (Carmona Romay 1955, 31)

LEGAL FOUNDATIONS FOR PROMOTING PARTICIPATORY BUDGETING IN CUBA

The Cuban Constitution of 2019 (ANPP 2019) regulates principles, rules, and rights that act as foundations for the fulfillment of the experiences of PB as a democratic practice. For example:

- The recognition of Cuba as a socialist state of social rights and justice, organized with all and for the good of all (Article 1);
- The consideration that sovereignty inalienably resides with the people, from whom all State power emanates (Article 3);

- The obligation of the State organizations, their executives, functionaries and employees to respect, look after and respond to the people, to maintain tight links with them and submit to their control (Article 10);
- The right of people to ask for and receive truthful, objective, and appropriate information from the state, and to have access to the information that the organizations and entities of the state generate (Article 53);
- The right of the Cuban citizens to participate in the formation, exercise, and control of the power of the state, which, among other matters, means participation in elections, plebiscites, referenda, popular consultations and other forms of democratic participation (Article 80, sub d);
- The development of initiatives aimed at the use of the local resources and possibilities by the state organizations (Article 101, sub d);
- The acting by the state organizations, their executives and functionaries with rightful transparency (Article 101, sub h).

In the same manner, the constitution confers to the municipal authorities the foundation of the authority necessary to develop self-transformative proposals having the character of citizen participation in its territorial limits. This, to the extent that the structure of the municipality rests, among other components, on the attribution of "legal autonomy and personality" to achieve the satisfaction of the "local needs," the recognition of "self-employment income" the faculty to "decide on the utilization of the resources," and the possibility to "order the normative dispositions" necessary for the exercise of its faculties (Articles 168 and 169).

It is necessary to add to the foregoing the ways that—as relating to the "guarantees of the rights to popular local petition and participation" (Article 200)—the Constitution supports the active involvement of the citizens in decision-making and control over government actions. For example:

- The call for popular consultation by the Asamblea Municipal del Popular Power [Municipal Assembly of the People's Power (AMPP, in Spanish)] on issues of local interest;
- Attention given to the proposals, complaints, and requests of the population;
- The right of the people of the municipality to propose to the AMPP the analysis of topics related to their area of responsibility;
- The right of the people to have an appropriate level of information on the decisions of general interest that are adopted by the organizations of Popular Power.

In addition, in the Cuban legal sphere, other positive elements for the design and implementation of the PB can be found at the constitutional or at regular legislative levels.

On the one hand, there is the recognition of the Popular Councils as organizations of the local Popular Power, which function on the basis of encouraging the people's participation and local initiatives toward their attainment. In the current municipal institutional structure, the Popular Councils are the appropriate space to "identify the problems and needs of the region . . . and their possible solutions," which leads to their revalorization as an area to promote the PB (ANPP 2019, Art. 199; MINJUS 2020, Art.194 b).

On the other hand, there exists a tax intended for the sustainable development of the municipalities. The establishment of the Contribución Territorial para el Desarrollo Local [Regional Contribution for Local Development (CTDL in Spanish)] constitutes one of the sensible innovations of Law 113/2012 (MINJUS 2012, Art. 305–315) with regard to local development in the Cuban territory. Currently, speaking in a budgetary way, this tax acts like revenue that is relinquished by the municipal budget; in the future it should form part of the baskets of self-employment revenues recognized by the Constitution. At the time of defining taxable issues, the previously mentioned Law 113–2012 (Article 305) expects that "a Property Tax will be established towards the sustainable development of the municipalities."

Special mention should be made for Decree no. 33, "For the strategic action for the regional development", approved on March 2021, as support for the implementation of the PB in Cuban municipalities. This decree is consistent with Guideline 17 of the Economic and Social Policy for the 2016–2021 period (PCC 2017); the Strategic Axis called "Socialist Government, effective, efficient and socially integrative" of the Foundations of the National Plan of Economic and Social Development until 2030 (PCC 2016); Article 168 of the Constitution (ANPP 2019); and the Policy to encourage regional development.

It should be noted that Decree no. 33 states that:

> The Administrative Municipal Council proposes to apply methods of participatory budgeting to the Municipal Assembly of the People´s Power by using funds from Regional Contribution for local development or any other financial resource [...], in order to promote the people´s participation in the promotion of local development. (MINJUS 2021)

In this way, the PB finds political institutional backing and legal status in the sphere of local democracy in Cuba, in concordance with the constitutional proposals. The existence of a financial component in the municipal budget—CTDL [sic] in this case—allows for the adjustment of the project as per the finances available to the region, and guarantees a stable source of financing. It thus contributes to minimizing the risk of making participation conditional on future funds, with the subsequent irregularity in the process, and the risk of losing confidence in the benefits of participation.

It is clear that the introduction of PB in the municipal structure systemically and coherently produces several challenges. Among these, the idea can be considered that for the implementation of PB an effective interinstitutional cooperation is required. The AMPP and the Municipal Administration Council, from their respective areas of responsibilities, should establish a road map—to include deliberate, causal, planned, coherent and systemic actions—that would allow for the use of the funds obtained through CTDL, based on popular participation. And for this, the identification, involvement and coordination of other formal or informal key stakeholders in the region is also needed, such as municipal university centers, which could contribute to guide the views of the residents of a community.

The design and approval of the municipal development strategy in each of the country's municipalities is a requirement of Decree no. 33 and an essential point for the PB. This tool will contribute to setting the priorities for the municipality, and will thus be the basis for the PB.

The preparation of the bases and indications for the PB by the ministries of Economy and Planning and of Finance and Pricing—in their respective spheres of competence, and without putting at risk municipal autonomy and citizens' initiatives—should be a presupposition. A true PB will not be created if there is a reduced sphere of decision-making for the municipality and ample facilities for organization and control by the higher levels. In the same manner, achieving the synchronization of the preparatory stages of the economic plan with those of the municipal budget, under the protection of the PB, will be another issue to be taken into account.

In summary, to be able to rely on the residents of a municipality is an ethical requirement of the Cuban political and social model. The incorporation of the citizens into the budgetary procedures at the municipal level can be a reality.

"POR TU BARRIO": PARTICIPATORY BUDGETING IN HAVANA'S HISTORICAL CENTER

The privileges granted to the Office of the Historian of the City of Havana (MINJUS 2001; MINJUS 2011; MINJUS 2014; MINJUS 2019)—especially its autonomy for regional planning and the management of the budget it administers—its responsibilities to encourage coordination with the agencies of the Popular Power, and its commitment to integral development, all made the historical center of Havana a propitious setting to carry out a PB experience, even if the national legal frame did not establish this apparatus in the management of the public budget.

In this context, PB was seen as an effective local management tool to consolidate the integral management model of the historical center of the capital, to raise transparency in public management, promote the integration between the regional governmental institutions, encourage an environment of confidence between the population and the public managers, and strengthen the social network. The exercise tested the management and capacity to bring people together, on the part of the OHCH [Oficina del Historiador de la Ciudad de la Habana—Office of the Historian of the City of Havana] and of the municipal government. Both institutions would take on the challenge of managing an innovative process, in a specific region, while taking into account their spheres of action, functions, and structure.

For their part, the citizens—accustomed to both agencies determining and resolving regional priorities—were called on to raise their active role in public management, sharing the solutions to the issues and the orientation of public resources with the local government, in addition to familiarizing themselves with the procedures of management and carrying out the public budgets. In other words, from being passive beneficiaries the citizens became protagonists in the decision-making process. All this involved a great deal of dialogue, agreement, and transparency in the management of the financial resources.

Given these premises, in 2014 the Master Plan of the OHCH—after a thorough study on the subject, visits by specialists in charge to Latin American experiences with PB and arranging training workshops on the topic—developed the "Por tu Barrio" [For your Neighborhood] project in the Catedral Popular Council of Old Havana, as per the principles and methodology postulated in the PB. The foregoing was done in the frame of the project Gestión participativa local de la rehabilitación del Centro Histórico de la Habana [Local participatory management of the rehabilitation of the Historical Center of Old Havana (GEPAC in Spanish)], sponsored by the Swiss Agency for Development and Cooperation (COSUDE in Spanish).

For this, the coordinating group set up a methodological process that is described in the arrangement carried out in the Master Plan of the Office of the Historian (Plan Maestro. Oficina del Historiador de la Ciudad de La Habana 2019), with the explanation and methodological recommendations corresponding to each stage of the project.

After fulfilling each of the steps of the process, the election of the Consejo Popular Catedral [Popular Council of the Cathedral] was elected with the relevant evaluation for carrying out the pilot project. It was successful, due to the organizational level of the structures of the Popular Power and the leadership of its formal and informal representatives, the sense of belonging and sensibility of the population, and the prestige and confidence in the responsible organization, that is, the OHCH. All this guaranteed the constant articulation and feedback between the leaders of the Popular Council and the coordinating group.

The communication strategy, the coaching and the methodologies of participation that were used in the grassroots meetings—spaces in which the population participated directly not only in the identification of the regional problems but also in the proposals for their solution—were keys to the success. We need to recognize that during the process, the punctuality of the participants, the quality of the interventions and the lucidity of the proposals triumphed. The capacity and sensibility of the population for proposing solutions of collective benefit beyond individual needs was also manifest.

In all of this, the experience of the institutions that collaborated in the process was also important, such as the Centro de Intercambio y Referencia de Iniciativa Comunitaria [Center for Exchange and Guidance of Community Initiatives (CIERIC in Spanish)], Centro de Estudios del Desarrollo Local y Comunitario [Center of Local and Community Development Studies (CEDEL in Spanish)], and the Martin Luther King Memorial Center (CMLK in Spanish).

From the experience of the "Por tu Barrio" project in Old Havana, the learnings by its coordinators, collaborators, and stakeholders can be sketched out. In the case of Cuba, taking these into account can result in a success factor when the time comes to replicate participatory budgeting in other regions as an instrument of participatory management for local development. The following are the lessons learned:

- The regions with a greater participatory culture have a higher probability of success in the application of PB. Participation should be seen as a cultural process, complementary to daily life. PB should not be developed in places where the importance of collective management is unknown. Every citizen should understand that s/he is a key stakeholder in the construction of a collective project, that it is his/her right and duty, and s/he should therefore be motivated and willing to express opinions on the issues, to decide on their solutions and participate in their implementation. Those regions that have had some experience that generated confidence in the authorities, and the perception that citizens' criteria are being taken into account, have an advantage over those which have not.
- The regions that are able to set up multidisciplinary teams have a good starting point for the application of PB. If there are professionals trained in key institutions, with academic support and formal and informal leaders who have prestige among the population, this facilitates the

coordination of the process. The absence of these players can create a lack of confidence in the citizens, and a questioning of their legitimacy.

- The existence of legal and technical standards which protect PB is important, although it must be taken into account that it does not guarantee the participation of the stakeholders, nor the success of the process. When legal foundations have been set for PB, and there is a strategy for citizen participation in the municipality, coordination and articulation between the different levels of government are facilitated.
- The conformity of the government authorities at the different levels is key. The process should not be initiated until there is evidence of the recognition of this consensus by the government authorities at all levels; it is important that it has been approved by the relevant government organizations, and be documented as an institutional agreement.
- PB should be developed in a form that is coordinated with the other public management instruments and the process of local development. The Strategies of Municipal Development, the regional land use plans, the investment strategies, the definition and execution of the municipal budget and its articulations with the Economic Plan are fundamental for guaranteeing its successful realization.
- PB should be coordinated by a public organization, with authority, knowledge and abilities to approve and manage the budget of the region. The AMPP faces the challenge to establish itself as the head of the process, by leading the intervention of the different stakeholders, and therefore it is essential to promote the abilities of the coordinating group and the officials at the various decision-making levels.
- The presence of diverse stakeholders in the PB supports the legitimacy of the process. The public institutions, the enterprises, the academic sphere, social organizations, private entrepreneurs, formal and informal leaders and the different collectives that constitute the population should feel themselves to be participants and coauthors of the project; they should remain convinced that the project really belongs to the municipality and not to the municipal authorities. The plurality of the stakeholders legitimizes the consensus that is required in all stages of the process, increases the commitment, and therefore the ability to respond to the obstacles and possibilities for the proposals to be implemented satisfactorily.
- The recognition of the usefulness of the PB is a key factor for the success of its implementation. The citizens will be encouraged if they see that the process is useful when it accepts and contributes to the solutions of their demands, and strengthens citizen empowerment and the shared exercise of authority. By no means should the PB be organized when the authorities have already decided which intervention to undertake. The participants should be able to influence the final result of the process.

- The social, economic, political, and historical context determines citizens' participation, so knowledge of the region is essential in order to develop a successful process. Idiosyncrasy, beliefs, sociodemographic characteristics, and the participatory culture determine the model and planning of the process: responsible institution, timing, members of the coordinating group, stakeholders involved, communication strategy, and even the areas and techniques of participation.
- Planning the steps of the PB, from a diagnosis to the evaluation of the process, is fundamental for the development of a successful process. The PB process requires intense hours of dedication on the part of the coordinating group and the citizens in general. For this reason, the participants and the resources required in all stages of the process should be clearly defined. The timetable of the PB should be detailed and included in the working agendas of the participating stakeholders. Under no circumstance should the stages and scheduled steps be disrupted for the sake of hastening the process or achieving results that are foreign to it. However, it should be a flexible timetable that envisages adjustments so as to deal with possible contingencies. Meticulously planning and designing a strategy of prevention gives the process authenticity and protects the work of the coordinating group. In this way prolonged interruptions or the suspense of the process because of contingencies—with the subsequent loss of confidence in the apparatus and the institutions—can be avoided.
- Locations and mechanisms for participation are essential for the success of the PB. The participatory processes need areas for coordination, meetings, reflection and dialogue between the stakeholders. The PB can take over the known and recognized locations and mechanisms of articulation and citizen participation, or it can generate its own. The choice depends on the characteristics of each region, on the effectiveness and confidence that the existing locations have produced in the community. There should be permanent areas for the coordination and monitoring of the processes and the interaction with the citizens. In both cases, in-person meetings and virtual platforms need to be explored in order to approve the opportunities that information and communication technologies offer.
- A strategy of communication is fundamental to guarantee the success of the PB. Participation will be greater if the objectives of the process and its benefits are clearly visible, and all those involved in working together towards a shared vision of the well-being of everyone are summoned. In the same way, the limits and the risks should be communicated, clearly and with realism, so as to avoid creating false expectations and the subsequent frustration of the citizens. It is also indispensable to guarantee

transparency at every stage: information must be clear, relevant, appropriate and multiple; this facilitates the accountability and the technical and social control of the process. In addition, the media (printed and digital press, radio, television, word of mouth) and the communication materials (folders, banners, signs), should be coherent with the context in which the experience is developed, in order to avoid unnecessary expenses for ineffective strategies.

• The PB process does not end with the accomplishment of the project selected by the citizens; it should involve the evaluation of the impact of its implementation. It is necessary to define measurable markers, both for management control—which are useful in the monitoring of the efficiency of the process and the fulfillment of the planned activities—as for the evaluation of the impact—necessary to determine its effectiveness. The stakeholders, and especially the beneficiaries, should participate in the monitoring and evaluation of the achievements, for which they will require access to the information and feedback mechanisms so as to channel their criteria. In this way a participatory apprenticeship is achieved, errors and risk factors are identified, which favors the design of more efficient and effective processes in the future.

The exercise of PB in the Historical Center of Old Havana has strengthened the institutional framework of public organizations, increased the knowledge of authorities and citizens on the tools of participatory management, and delved deeper into the reality of the region, its problems and needs. In the same manner, it encouraged the study and validation of the applicability and usefulness of the exercise in the Cuban reality.

FINAL POINTS

FIRST: The Conceptualization of the Cuban Economic and Social Development Model; the National Plan for Economic and Social Development until 2030 and the Guidelines for the Economic and Social Policy for the 2021–2026)— as governing political documents—call for the improvement of popular participation, which suggest the possibility of proposing PB practices in Cuba. In harmony with the foregoing, the PB has explicit recognition in the Decree no. 33 to encourage regional development in Cuba.

SECOND: In the framework of the Constitution of the Republic of Cuba (ANPP 2019), the PB is established as a viable mechanism for the residents of a municipality to influence the purpose of local financial resources, as related to the implementation of the joint project of development that they decide.

THIRD: In the institutional sphere in Cuba, elements can be identified that are favorable for the realization of PB. Submitting to debate a part of the revenue collected by CTDL allows for a refreshing of municipal activity, and converts the municipal budget into a trustworthy instrument of local public planning and management, based on popular participation.

FOURTH: The exercise of PB provides the region with a suitcase full of projects which in many cases depend for their execution on the articulation of stakeholders and actions that do not require financing, with more importance, because they respond to problems identified by the very same citizens, who in addition propose their solution.

FIFTH: The *Por tu Barrio* exercise, developed in the area of the Historical Center of Havana, constitutes an example of how much can be done in the efforts to link citizens in a meaningful way, and become a guide for the deepening and realization of PB practices in the Cuban reality.

NOTE

1. The International directives on the decentralization and strengthening of local authorities recommend: "With regards to consolidating the civic commitment, local authorities should have as their objective the adoption of new forms of participation, such as councils of neighbors, of the community, on-line democracy, the preparation of participatory budgets, civic initiatives and referendums as they apply to the specific context" (ONU-Habitat 2009, 9).

BIBLIOGRAPHY

Acevedo, J., S. Mejía, and A. Matamoros. *Construyendo ciudadanía: Los Presupuestos Locales, un espacio que garantiza la efectividad de la participación ciudadana en Honduras* [Building citizenship: Local Budgets, a space that guarantees the effective participation of citizens in Honduras]. San José: Fundación Arias para la Paz y el Progreso Humano, 2004.

Alcaldía de Porto Alegre. *Presupuesto Participativo y finanzas locales* [Participatory Budgeting and local finances]. Porto Alegre, Brasil: Alcaldía de Porto Alegre, 2005.

ANPP. *Constitución de la República de Cuba* [Constitution of the Republic of Cuba]. La Habana: Asamblea Nacional del Poder Popular, 2019. Retrieved from: http://www.granma.cu/file/pdf/gaceta/Nueva%20Constituci%C3%B3n%20240%20KB-1.pdf.

Carmona Romay, A. G. "La autonomía financiera municipal a la luz de la Escuela Sociológica del municipio" [Municipal financial autonomy in light of the Sociological School of the municipality]. *I Congreso Iberoamericano de Municipios.* Madrid, 1955.

Castillo, J. et al. *El presupuesto municipal participativo. Guía metodológica. La experiencia de Villa González* [The participatory municipal budget. Methodological guide. The experience of Villa Gonzalez]. Santo Domingo: Fundación Solidaridad, 2004.

El Troudi, H., M. Harnecker, and L. Bonilla-Molina. "Herramientas para la Participación" [Tools for Participation]. Caracas: 2005.

Francés García, F., and A. Carrillo Cano. *Guía metodológica de los Presupuestos Participativos* [Methodological Guide to Participaroty Budgeting]. Alicante: Colectivo Preparación, 2008.

Goldfrank, B. "Los procesos de Presupuesto Participativo en América Latina: éxito, fracaso y cambio" [Participatory Budgeting processes in Latin America: success, failure and change]. *Revista de Ciencia Política* 26 (2), 2006.

González Quevedo, J. *Bases jurídicas, desde la participación ciudadana, para el empoderamiento político. Estudio de los actuales modelos constitucionales de Venezuela, Bolivia y Ecuador* [Legal bases, from citizen participation,for poltical empowerment]: Study of the constitutional models of Venezuela, Bolivia and Ecuador]. Masters' Thesis. La Habana: Universidad de La Habana, 2010.

Lencina, M. V. *Presupuesto participativo: la experiencia de Poder Ciudadano 2001–2003.* [Participatory budgeting: The experience of Citizen Power 2001–2003]. Buenos Aires: Fundación Poder Ciudadano, 2004.

Matías, D. "Presupuesto Participativo y Democratización" [Participatory Budgeting and Democratization]. Santo Domingo: Programa de Apoyo a la Reforma y Modernización del Estado, 2004.

Méndez, J., and D. Cutié. "La participación popular y los derechos. Fundamento y contenido del nuevo constitucionalismo latinoamericano" [Popular participation and rights. Basis and content of the new Latin American constitutionalism]. In *Estudios sobre el nuevo constitucionalismo latinoamericano*, by R. Viciano Pastor (Ed.). Valencia: Editorial Tirant lo Blanch, 2012.

Ministerio de Economía y Planificación. "Política para impulsar el desarrollo territorial" [Policy to promote regional development]. La Habana, 2020. Retrieved from: https://www.mep.gob.cu/sites/default/files/Documentos/POLITICA-PARA -IMPULSAR-EL-DESARROLLO-TERRITORIAL.pdf.

MINJUS. Decreto 33/2021. Para la gestión estratégica del desarrollo territorial" [Law Decree 33/2021 For the strategic action for the regional development]. Gaceta Oficial de la República de Cuba, Edición Ordinaria, No. 40, La Habana: Ministerio de Justicia, 16 de Abril, 2021.

MINJUS. "Decreto Ley 143/1993. Sobre la Oficina del Historiador de la ciudad de La Habana" [Law-Decree 143/1993 On the Office of the Historian of the city of Havana]. *Gaceta Oficial de la República de Cuba, Edición Ordinaria, No. 14, de 4 de noviembre de 1993*, La Habana: Ministerio de Justicia, 30 de octubre, 1993.

———. "Decreto-Ley 283. Modificativo del Decreto-Ley No. 143/93 Sobre la Oficina del Historiador de la Ciudad de La Habana" [Law-Decree 283 Modifying Law-Decree 143/93 On the Office of the Historian of the city of Havana]. *Gaceta*

Oficial de la República de Cuba, Edición Extraordinaria, No. 24, La Habana: Ministerio de Justicia, 22 de Junio, 2011.

———. "Ley 132/2019. De organización y funcionamiento de las asambleas municipales del Poder Popular y de los consejos populares" [Law 132/2019. On the organization and functioning of the municipal assemblies of Popular Power and the popular councils]. *Gaceta Oficial de la República de Cuba, Edición Extraordinaria, No. 5*, 1 16. La Habana: Ministerio de Justicia, 2020.

———. "Decreto-Ley No. 325. Modificativo del Decreto-Ley No. 143 Sobre la Oficina del Historiador de la Ciudad de La Habana" [Law-Decree No. 325. Modification of Law-Decree No. 143. On the Office of the Historian of the city of Havana]. *Gaceta Oficial de la República de Cuba, Edición Extraordinaria, No. 52, de 12 de diciembre de 2014*, 10 16. La Habana: Ministerio de Justicia, 2014.

———. "Decreto-Ley No. 216. Modificar los límites establecidos en el Artículo 1 del Decreto-Ley No. 143 de 30 de octubre de 1993 en lo que respecta a la Zona Priorizada para la Conservación." [Law-Decree No. 216. Modifies the limits established in Article 1 of the Law-Decree 143 of October 30, 1993, with respect to the Priority Conservation Zone]. *Gaceta Oficial de la República de Cuba, Edición Ordinaria, No. 12*, 1 30. La Habana: Ministerio de Justicia, 2001.

———. "Decreto Ley No. 368. Modificativo del Decreto-Ley No. 143 'Sobre la Oficina del Historiador de la Ciudad de La Habana,' de 30 de octubre de 1993" [Law-Decree No. 368. Modifies Law-Decree No. 143 On the Office of the Historian of the city of Havana]. *Gaceta Oficial de la República de Cuba, Edición Ordinaria, No. 24, de 3 de abril de 2018*, 12 17. La Habana: Ministerio de Justicia, 2019.

———. "Ley 113/2012. Del Sistema Tributario" [Law 113/2012. Of the Tax System]. *Gaceta Oficial de la República de Cuba, Edición Ordinaria, No. 53*, 11 21. La Habana: Ministerio de Justicia, 2012

Montecinos, E. "Descentralización y democracia en Chile: análisis sobre la participación ciudadana en el presupuesto participativo y el Plan de desarrollo comunal" [Decentralization and Democracy in Chile: Analysis of citizen participation in the participatory budget and the Plan for Comunal Development]. *Revista de Ciencia Política*, Santiago de Chile: 2006.

ONU-Habitat. *Directrices internacionales sobre descentralización y fortalecimiento de las autoridades locales* [International directives on decentralization and strengthening of local authorities]. Programa de las Naciones Unidas para los Asentamientos Humanos. 2009. Retrieved from: https://unhabitat.org/books/directrices-internacionales-sobre-descentralizacion-y-fortalecimiento-de-las-autoridades-locales.

PCC. *Conceptualización del Modelo Económico y Social Cubano de Desarrollo y Plan Nacional de Desarrollo Económico y Social hasta 2030* [Conceptualization of the Cuban Economic and Social Development Model and National Plan for Economic and Social Development until 2030]. La Habana: VI Congreso del Partido Comunista de Cuba, 2016a

———. *Conceptualización del Modelo Económico y Social Cubano de Desarrollo y Plan Nacional de Desarrollo Económico y Social hasta 2030* [Conceptualization of the Cuban Economic and Social Development Model and National Plan for Economic and Social Development until 2030]. La Habana: VI Congreso del Partido Comunista de Cuba, 2016

———. "Objetivos de Trabajo del Partido Comunista de Cuba [OTPCC]" [Work Objectives of the Communist Party of Cuba]. *Cubadebate*, Enero 29, 2012. Retrieved from: http://www.cubadebate.cu/wp-content/uploads/2012/02/tabloide _objetivos_conferencia.pdf.

———. PCC. *Lineamientos de la Política Económica y Social del Partido y la Revolución* [Guidelines for the Economic and Social Policy of the Party and the Revolution]. La Habana: VI Congreso del Partido Comunista de Cuba, 2011

———. *Propuesta de Visión de la Nación, Ejes y Sectores Estratégicos* [Proposed Vision of the Nation, Strategic Lines and Sectors]. La Habana: VI Congreso del Partido Comunista de Cuba, 2016

———. *Lineamientos de la Política Económica y Social del Partido y la Revolución* [Guidelines for the Economic and Social Policy of the Party and the Revolution]. La Habana: VII Congreso del Partido Comunista de Cuba, 2017

Plan Maestro. Oficina del Historiador de la Ciudad de La Habana. *Sistematizaciones realizadas a los Instrumentos de Gestión Participativa* [Systematizations applied to the Instruments of Participatory Governance]. La Habana: GEPAC, 2019.

República Bolivariana de Venezuela. *Constitución de la República Bolivariana de Venezuela,* [Constitution of the Bolivarian Republic of Venezuela]. 1999

Seabra de Godoi, M., and E. I. Oliveira S. de Rezende. "O Orçamento Participativo em Belo Horizonte: avanços e desafíos" [Participatory Budgeting in Belo Horizonte: Advances and challenges]. In *B. Nascimento de Lima, L. de Alvarenga Gontijo y M. Ferreira Bicalho (Org.). Cuba-Brasil diálogos sobre democracia, soberanía popular y derechos sociales.* Belo Horizonte.: Editora D'Plácido, 2019.

Chapter 6

The Inclusion of Vulnerable Groups as Subjects of Development

Proposals from the Viewpoint of the Solidarity Economy

Geydis Fundora Nevot and Reynaldo Miguel Jiménez Guethón

The updating of the Cuban model is a process conceived for the common good; however, not all people have participated in the same way in the opportunities and benefits. Development in socialist thinking should not start with the idea of a uniform society, since this would establish itself with biases that would block any effort toward social justice.

One of the transformations intended for the improvement of society in general was the diversification of the property system and the forms of economic management, but not everyone has embraced it in the same way. As can be seen below (Graph 1, Table 1), women and Black persons are underrepresented in the private and cooperative areas.

The official data do not show a cross section of these factors of social disadvantage, but several qualitative studies do. A study of more than three hundred research projects on inequalities, as part of the project Participatory Social Policies: Keys to Equity and Sustainability,[1] revealed a profile of vulnerability mostly referred to Black and mulatto women who are heads of single-parent homes or highly dependent large families, homemakers, middle-aged adults and seniors, longtime residents in unhealthy neighborhoods or socially disadvantaged regions with a low or middle educational

Figure 6.1. Women in the cooperative and self-employment spheres (in %).
Source: ONEI. Anuario Estadístico de Cuba, 2019 [Statistical Annual of Cuba, 2019]. La Habana: Oficina Nacional de Estadística e Información de Cuba, 2020.

Table 6.1—Participation in Socioeconomic Spheres, by Skin Color (%)

	Black (10.9)	Mestizos (26.8)	White (62.3)
Base Unit of Cooperative Production (UBPC)	9.4	33.0	57.7
Agricultural Production Cooperative (CPA)	7.8	26.7	65.4
Small farmer, associated or no to a Credit and Services Cooperative (CCS)	4.2	20.5	75.3
Land usufructuary, associated or no to a CCS	7.9	28.5	63.6
Private Sector	9.0	22.9	68.1

Source: CEPDE. El censo según color de la piel [Census according to skin color]. La Habana: Oficina Nacional de Estadísticas e Información. 2016

level. There are also the informal female workers whose illegal activity makes them criminally liable and who have fewer possibilities of labor mobility and migration; in particular, young Black and mulatto women who are more vulnerable while migrating and less likely to get a job in a recipient community (Zabala 2020).

The aforementioned project also looks at the relationship between policies approved during the ten-year period 2008–2018 and at the closing or opening of gaps in equity (Fundora 2020a), which reveals that more homogeneous access does not lead to fair outcomes. It emphasizes that the new economic opportunities have mostly favored families and individuals with marketable tangible and intangible assets and capital (houses and cars for rent, buildings for services, services that can be provided in the self-employed or informal sectors, etc.). At the same time, those opportunities constitute limitations for groups and families that do not have such assets.

Therefore, the gender gap in the development of private enterprises persists, as the sociodemographic profile of the owners is limited to adult white men with a middle to high educational level (Munster 2010; Echevarría and Lara 2012; Zabala 2015; Luis 2015).

It should be emphasized that low-income families—as associated with gender (female), skin color (Black) and region—take less advantage of employment and income generation opportunities (Voghón 2008; Zabala 2015). In this sense, there is persistent and increasing skin-based inequity in the socio-occupational and classist structure. Black and mulatto people prevail in jobs that require lower qualifications and fewer assets, which replicates placement in disadvantageous positions on the socio-occupational scale (Voghón 2008; Espina, Núñez, et al. 2010; Zabala 2015).

There are also persistent gender gaps for lack of balance in the individual's family, work and private life, both in the state enterprises and budgeted entities and in the non-state sector: men with more personal time and favorable conditions to access the labor market in the state, cooperative (agricultural or otherwise) and self-employment sectors; a tendency toward the presence of women in more precarious jobs and low productivity sectors; and women having greater difficulties to access multi-employment modalities (Munster 2010; Echevarría 2013; Bombino 2015).

It is worth noting that research on the perceptions of Black women in Havana (Fundora 2016) identified the main changes that have impaired their access to economic resources and good working conditions. They include reduction in employment opportunities, the extension of the retirement age, the approval of a labor code with no integral focus on equity, delayed approval of cooperatives, price rises in all kinds of markets (formal and informal), the loss of the purchasing power of money, and the drop in the supply of subsidized products, among others.

All of this reveals the importance of considering the mobility processes of groups in vulnerable situations, especially Black women of a low socio-economic level, who are also known to enjoy social protection. The system of free and subsidized social services in Cuba guarantees the same rights to all; in addition, there are social assistance funds for families with basic needs as yet unmet.[2] However, for a woman, receiving a subsidy or payment for informal activities is not the same as being a business manager, a farm owner, a cooperative member—who has a say, voting rights and dividends—an owner of a rental business or a coordinator of a municipal initiative of local development.

The causes of this phenomenon go back in time and transcend both governmental institutions and family reproduction. Involved in this artificial adversity are racist, sexist and classist practices that crystallized for years until they became natural throughout society, even to the very people who suffer from them.

Evidently, when we design agendas for development, we must take into account both the successful profiles and the socially disadvantaged ones. Not all opportunities that come from a Plan or Strategy for development have the same potential.

DEVELOPMENT OPPORTUNITIES AND INEQUALITIES

Understanding the updating process can be a window of opportunity to work with vulnerable sectors. That is, the configuration of a context to promote changes based on the convergence of factors favorable to transformation (multiple trends): streaming problems or ideas (conversion of an item into a well-identified public problem), streaming solutions (circulation of old and new ideas to solve problems, policy references, the image of a reality that needs changing) and political circumstances (events such as elections, campaigns, wars, and economic, legal and administrative reforms, etc.) (Kingdon 1984; Harguindéguy 2015)

As has been stated previously, not all groups take similar advantage of a window of opportunity. In order to understand this phenomenon, the category of opportunity hoarding is useful. The sociologist (Pérez Sainz 2014) draws inspiration from Weber's concept to study the capacity of some individuals or groups to appropriate wealth and well-being produced by others or generated collectively and the structuring or institutionalization of inequality through the replication of this unequal appropriation.

This is one of the explanations of why some groups remain at a social disadvantage, but it is not the only perspective. (Gutiérrez 2011) brings a key viewpoint to this issue. The author focuses on the geographic and social (subjective) distance between the socially disadvantaged population and the opportunities that arise by using the instruments of social reproduction (strategies and micro-practices) available to the recipients of the policies. This approach is closely related to the concept of assets defined by (Katzman 2018), who ascribes social vulnerability to the lack of assets (material and immaterial resources on which individuals and homes have control and whose mobilization allows for the improvement of their well-being, prevents the deterioration of their living condition or reduce their vulnerability).

By this logic, it is appropriate to include the concept of assets that explains those material and immaterial barriers that prevent the use of opportunities or the accumulation of assets by households. They may have to do with disabilities, ethnic origin or sexual orientation in discriminatory contexts, stereotyping, conditions of marginalization, violence, etc.

The relations that structure inequality in opportunity hoarding and the assets and liabilities that decide the welfare of groups in a vulnerable situation[3] make it possible to rethink the processes of individual and collective empowerment of these people.

The recent creation of the Consejo Técnico Asesor [Technical Advisory Council] of the Ministry of Labor and Social Security (August 2020) became a strategic framework for innovative strategies, policies and programs of Prevention and Social Work. The insertion of these population sectors into the different forms of economic management is a key objective contingent on training, the strengthening of the social networks, information, participation and the access to development funds for initiatives to overcome welfarism and the reproduction of poverty and vulnerability. However, for what kind of socio-economic relations should these people be trained as part of their social integration and development?

SOCIAL WORK AND THE ENGAGEMENT OF VULNERABLE GROUPS IN DEVELOPMENT; BUT FOR WHAT KIND OF DEVELOPMENT, WHAT KIND OF ECONOMY?

In response to the economic changes of the updating process, there were initiatives to qualify actors who would make a better use of this opportunity.[3] Different viewpoints on development and social equity underlie these initiatives, including:

- Developmental and economistic approach to individual mobility: Training of entrepreneurs (without regard to their identities, conditions, positions, starting points and social standing).
- Developmental approach to individual mobility with social responsibility: Training of diverse entrepreneurs (with or without regard to their social characteristics), choosing self-transformation processes (which can include socially disadvantaged people) and at the same time promoting the ability of the entrepreneurs to support others with redistributive actions, which may be related to welfare or not.
- Developmental approach to structural mobility: Training of promoters and educators so they will have an influence on the transformation of a context (community, region, sector, environment). Other economic practices are encouraged (based on solidarity and cooperation) as a tool for collective development and the transformation of individualistic, unsustainable, predatory, authoritarian, inequitable, discriminatory and other practices. The trained persons develop pedagogical and methodological skills to multiply knowledge and tools on the expressions of solidarity economy. It does not exclude actions of social responsibility.
- Emancipatory approach to personal transformation and structural mobility: Training of people whose work is based on the values of

cooperativism to improve their material and spiritual living conditions, and at the same time transforming the system of relations in
which they are placed (from social responsibility to the elimination of
relations based on the appropriation of other people's work, promotion of new businesses, production linkages, etc.). Steps are taken to
make sure that these are people with difficulties to seize opportunities
because they go through cycles of violence and reproduction of poverty
and have little economic and political capital and a dysfunctional cultural, social, and symbolic capital in successful socioeconomic spaces.
Educators, promoters, and consultants are also trained who multiply the
solidarity economy approach to transform communities, networks, and
other spaces.

Given these alternatives, taking an ethical and political stand is very important. A central position in the work with vulnerable groups and the social
structures that reproduce their disadvantages needs a profound analysis of
what types of intervention would alleviate an urgent problem or allow the
rupture of this asymmetry. Given the social responsibility of the successful
actors, is it better to train these people to do business as private entrepreneurs
or cooperative members or to restrict them to being recipients of goods, services and benefits? What would these options mean for the development of
these groups?

One possible option is to increase the social responsibility of cooperatives
and self-employed workers based on a redistribution toward vulnerable sectors. Cuba uses this option by distributing free food to soup kitchens, maternity and senior citizen homes and daycare centers; helping with home repairs
and the shopping basket of the poorest families; providing equine-assisted
therapy for disabled children; offering free repair services; setting preferential
or subsidized prices for goods and services; organizing activities for children;
celebrating important dates; repairing public works and spaces and, to a lesser
extent, creating some jobs, training courses, etc.[4]

These activities have improved the temporary access of these groups to
goods and services of a better quality, with a perspective more centered on
age and generational equity, disablement and poverty. To a lesser extent, the
gender gaps are also addressed. A welfare-oriented approach prevails in these
activities (except in the case of training and in some jobs) which hinders the
independence, autonomy and empowerment of sectors otherwise capable of
handling them. They can also reproduce individual stigmatization and vic-
timization. Class- and race-based inequalities are not addressed despite their
prevalence in the profiles of vulnerability, as was indicated before.

This is not about disqualifying these initiatives, but seeing them as temporary measures that should come with others if we expect to make more profound and lasting transformations.

Another proposal under discussion is to train vulnerable sectors to start their own business, either as self-employed or small entrepreneurs. This trend is prevailing at a global level, promoted by international organizations, development agencies and different countries. They are based on the idea of holding poor people responsible for their own hardship because of their lack of initiative, resources or abilities. In general, socio-classist relations leading up to inequalities (exclusionary or marginalizing dynamics in markets, production process, distribution of wealth, political spaces, etc.) are not challenged.

Cuba has also fostered private business, not as centered on the perspective of poverty reduction as on the diversification of forms of economic management and the provision of more jobs to people affected by the processes of rationalization of the public sector and to those engaged in informal activities. In general, the resulting diversification of the socio-labor structure has been successful, with 21.1 percent for people employed in the private sector by 2018 (ONEI, 2019). However, this option is still debatable from the perspective of overcoming the poverty and vulnerability of economically disadvantaged Black women, given the unequal distribution of the assets needed to set up a business and the continuing presence of sexist and male chauvinistic models that prevent the long-term success of their initiatives and their participation in the labor market.

Research has identified the existence of poverty and vulnerability among the self-employed workers (Espina 2015; Zabala 2015); gender- and skin color-based inequalities in terms of business ownership; and an increase in the number of workers with fewer labor rights in the private sector. This is because the law does not provide for indefinite work contracts and the rules governing labor hired by an individual employer are only temporary and valid for one project, which leaves these workers at the mercy of their employer and tampers with job security and family income (Peña Farías and Voghón 2013; Martín 2015; Izquierdo and Morín 2017).

Other problems are the reinforcement of the informal economy or black market in the labor category of self-employment, with the existence of exploitative relations that affect much more the workers without a formal contract (Peña Farías and Voghón 2013; Espina 2015). On the other hand, the nonrecognition of small and medium enterprises (SMEs) as legal entities makes it easier for private entrepreneurs to misappropriate other peoples' work (Galtés 2016).

The other option to consider is the social and solidarity economy (SSE) and the popular and solidarity economy (PSE) to promote the participation of vulnerable groups in cooperatives or other forms of collective employment.

Since the number of poor women in many Latin American countries has been on an upward trend because of marginalization, there is emphasis on the promotion of economic relations based on the popular economy (Fundora, Dixon and Vázquez 2017).

Popular feminism (Korol 2016) has revealed the emancipatory and transformative nature of various solidarity economy strategies for poor, Black, aboriginal, mulatto, and peasant women. Family and community agriculture, collective vegetable gardens, the organization of community kitchens, the creation of economy and production networks, and the socialization of caregiving services with the creation of toy libraries, training areas, community laundries, etc. stand out among the associative strategies.

Since 2009, the cooperatives in Central America are consolidating feminine inclusion through the Alianza de Mujeres Cooperativistas de Centroamérica [Alliance of Women Cooperative Members in Central America]. In Tirol, Argentina, cooperative work led to the social inclusion of a group of unemployed women in the twenty to fifty age-group in industrial jobs mostly taken by men. In 2013, Costa Rica arranged for the consideration of equality by all decision-making organizations at the highest level of the cooperative movement and their obligation to comply with the gender equality and equity policy of that sector,[56] as well as for the strengthening of the Comité Nacional de Mujeres Cooperativistas (CONAMUJER) [National Committee of Women Cooperative Members]). Colombia established the Gender Equity and Equality Policy for Associated and Working Women and a Gender Committee to ensure its compliance (Coomeva 2017).

Until now, the percentage of Cubans employed in the cooperative sector grew from 4.17 percent in 2011 to 10.48 percent in 2018 (ONEI 2019), but with underrepresentation in terms of gender and skin color. However, these figures do not include other experiences of cooperative management in production, services, and consumption organized at the community level by economically disadvantaged people.

The bureaucratic obstacles to set up cooperatives have not prevented their members from developing new models of management based on cooperation and solidarity principles in spite of their legal status as self-employed (an easier-to-get permit). Among these initiatives are the shoe store "La Oportuna" and the workshop "¡Atrévete, eres más!" [Go for it, you can do it!] in Marianao; the daycare center "El Amor" in Párraga; the beauty shop "Swing Cubano" for women with Afro hair styles in El Cerro; the shoe, leather, and doll shop "La Muñeca Negra" [The Black Doll] in La Lisa; "Hilarín" in Alamar; the "Oddara" coffee shop in Marianao; the Integral Farm "Las Torcas" for the care of seniors; the bakery and candy store "La Exquisita"; the hairdressing and barbershops "Belleza con Swing" and "Un paso adelante" [A step forward], and others.

While their impact has been limited to the regional, legislative, institutional, and political levels, the greater relevance of this proposal is to tackle inequality where gender, social class, and skin color intersect. Cooperative management has helped these types of women to become professionals in their fields, redefine what they do, have their own resources and exercise full control over them, manage their free time better, improve their living conditions, recognize their personal ability and potential, broaden their experiences, contribute to transform their families and communities, develop equitable relations, change their world view, modify the distribution of household chores, build networks, and identify themselves as people with economic, sexual and reproductive rights (González, Lisbet Caballero and Sardá 2018).

As they said in interviews carried out by the Talleres de Transformación Integral del Barrio [Integral Neighborhood Transformation Workshops], doing associative business has produced a favorable outcome: "The advantage is in the training, learning, the roles and comradeship . . . because there are more people and therefore more production and profits than if it were done individually." . . . "One advantage is that, from an economic viewpoint, we distribute both the profits and expenses in equal shares, which makes the burden lighter; we are not experts, but each one has their own specialty." . . . "As to social and spiritual matters, when one of the members has a problem we help them find a solution; another advantage is that we try to agree on things even if we all think differently." . . . "We encourage one another." . . . "We can meet, plan for future steps, and share the responsibilities, failures, problems and prejudices" (González, Lisbet Caballero, and Sardá 2018).

This type of inclusion, based on the principles and practices of the Solidarity Economy, is key to contribute to the personal mobility of disadvantaged individuals, as well as to undo the patriarchy, racism and the classist stratification of the property system, the production and management systems of the socioeconomic fields in Cuba and the distribution and redistribution structures.

CHALLENGES OF SOCIAL WORK WITH VULNERABLE GROUPS FROM THE SOLIDARITY ECONOMY PERSPECTIVE

The Solidarity Economy approach is considered a suitable way of changing inequality in which gender, class and skin color intersect. Collective power has provided a support to confront the pressures caused by the top business competitors; the traditional control that partners or other close males socialized in hegemonic masculinity expect to have; discrimination or disparagement; violence; lack of time because of household and caregiving duties; the obstacles to access bank credits and other resources; the high mortality rate of the small enterprises; difficulties to access information networks, credits, advertising space, trade opportunities, production linkages, etc.

Hence the need for a greater involvement of trainers, social workers, project managers, etc., in capacity building to start this type of business and to organize, work, participate and reproduce life. Not all pedagogical proposals are suitable to train socially disadvantaged groups and promoters of a gender-responsive solidarity economy. There are differences between training entrepreneurs for the private and for the cooperative sector. Even if elements of business management, accounting systems, bodies of laws, communication, and social responsibility concur, emphasis should also be placed on other elements, such as the way to understand the economy, power, politics, the domination-emancipation relation, and inequality. It is also important to increase the number of alternatives to exercise the solidarity economy (production, service, credit, housing and consumer cooperatives; solidarity finances; fair trade; solidarity kitchens and vegetable gardens; mutual benefit societies) based on practical national and international models.

There are differences between the training in solidarity economy for socially disadvantaged people and for other kinds of actors. It is important to start not only from their knowledge about solidarity economy, but also from the positive and negative practices of popular economy (cooperation to commit illegal acts and get involved in the informal economy). It is essential to attach value to their own experiences, merits, skills and codes without decontextualizing their training.

With regard to social work with the associative participation of women, feminist authors have revealed how, historically, the system of domination has created strategies for division and confrontation, according to Varcacel (1997, as quoted in Lagarde n.d.):

> Starting from meetings and conflicts, from false beliefs in the natural solidarity of women, it is clear that relations between women are complex and riddled with difficulties derived from different powers, hierarchies and supremacies, competition and rivalry. [These are] political mechanisms sprung from the exclusionary social fragmentation that surrounds us and from gender standards designed to maintain male supremacy over those of us women who are estranged from one another. From this comes the awareness of the need for the unity of women in order to increase our influence and, on the other hand, for the elimination of the misogynous confrontation between us women, which makes us grow further apart and weaker and depreciates every one of us. (Lagarde n.d., 125)

In the case of social work with Black people there are other challenges in contexts in which subjective racism persists. Encouraging associative links in business can be influenced by the fact that Blacks and mulattoes attach less value to solidarity as a virtue than to other qualities. According to (Romay 2015), the tendency toward individualism as a social attitude can be explained by the lack of confidence in the effectiveness of group solidarity or the recognition of the social fragility of the person's relevant (racial) group.

Some contextual challenges to keep expanding this idea are: the invisibility of inequality and its root causes; the twisted idea of the dichotomy of state and non-state; the small space that the Solidarity Economy has in the public and the media political agendas; a greater social tendency toward the development of self-employment rather than cooperativism; legal loopholes and lack of an institutional structure to promote this form of economic management; and scarcity of resources, among others.

NOTES

1. Coordinated by Dr. María del Carmen Zabala of FLACSO-Cuba with the cooperation of its researchers and academics from CEEC (Centro de Estudios de Economía Cubana) [Cuban Economy Studies Center], CIPS (Centro de Investigaciones Psicológicas y Sociológicas [Psychological and Sociological Research Center], the Schools of Law, Economy, Communication and Geography and CEDEM (Centro de Estudios Demográficos) [Demographic Studies Center], of the University of Havana.

2. These include preferential treatment by the Ministry of Labor and Social Security (2012), the Procedures Manual for Preventive Labor, Assistance and Social Work.

3. A configuration resulting from an imbalance between the availability and the ability to mobilize assets (expressed as individual or family attributes, defined at micro level) and the requirements to access opportunities (expressed structurally and defined at macro level), which generates a tendency to a decreasing mobility or a clear difficulty for individuals or households to sustain social positions (Fundora 2020a; Katzman 2018; Filgueira, 2001, as quoted in Zabala, Fuentes, et al. 2018, 101).

4. Between 2014 and 2020, FLACSO-Cuba has participated in several systematized and analyzed training courses on cooperativism, entrepreneurship and social economy together with the University of Havana, the Martin Luther King Memorial Center, the Escuela Andaluza de Economia Social (EAES), the Instituto Panameño Cooperativo (IPACOOP), the Consejo Nacional de Cooperativas de República Dominicana (CONACOOP), the Talleres de Transformación Integral del Barrio (ITTIB), the Grupo para el Desarrollo Integral de la Capital (GDIC), the Instituto Nacional de Ciencias Agrícolas (INCA) with its Programa de Innovación Agrícola Local (PIAL) and the Centro de Intercambio y Referencia Iniciativa Comunitaria (CIERIC). The design of this analytical proposal stemmed from these activities (Fundora 2020b).

5 Data taken from the documentaries *Razones* [Reasons] (2013) and *Los poderes vitales del éxito* [The vital powers of success] (2017) by Casa Productora de Audiovisuales Palomas, and *El oficio de crecer* [The profession of growing] (2018) by

the Production Group *Son del Barrio*. Documentary memoirs of the Workshop *El Negocio* [The Business] in the context of the course "Emprendimientos en Cuba," [Entrepreneurship in Cuba] organized by the University of Havana in 2014.

6. Dossier No. 18.199, *Democratización de las Diferentes Instancias de Decision del Movimiento Cooperativo* [Democratization of the Different Decision-Making Entities of the Cooperative Movement].

BIBLIOGRAPHY

Bombino, Y. "Oportunidades y desafíos del proceso de actualización para la inserción laboral de la juventud rural en Cuba" [Opportunities and challenges of the updating process for the employability of rural youth in Cuba]. In *Los correlatos socioculturales del cambio económico*, edited by M. Espina and D. Echevarría, 179–97. La Habana: Ruth Casa Editorial y Editorial Ciencias Sociales, 2015.

CEPDE. *El censo según color de la piel.* [The Census by skin color]. La Habana: Oficina Nacional de Estadísticas e Información, 2016.

Coomeva. *Cooperativas y el desafío de la inclusión femenina.* [Cooperatives and the challenge of female inclusion]. COOMEVA, 2017. Retrieved from: http://espacios .coomeva.com.co/publicaciones.php?id=46768.

Echevarría, D. "Procesos de reajuste en Cuba y su impacto en el empleo femenino: dos siglos y repetidas desigualdades" [Readjustment processes in Cuba and their impact on female employment: two centuries and repeated inequalities]. In *Miradas a la Economía cubana,* edited by O. E. Pérez and R. Torres, 129–46. La Habana: Editorial Caminos, 2013.

Echevarría, D., and T. Lara. "Cambios recientes: ¿oportunidad para las mujeres?" [Recent changes: Opportunities for women?]. In *Miradas a la economía cubana,* edited by O.E. Perez and R. Torres. La Habana: Editorial Caminos, 2012.

Espina, M. "Reforma económica y política social de equidad en Cuba" [Economic reform and social policy for equity in Cuba]. In *Los correlatos socioculturales del cambio económico*, edited by M. Espina and D. Echevarría, 239–72. La Habana: Ruth Casa Editorial y Editorial Ciencias Sociales, 2015.

Espina, M., L. Núñez, L. Martín, V. Togores, and G. Ángel. *Sistematización de estudios sobre heterogeneidad social y desigualdades en Cuba. 2000–2008* [Systematization of the studies on social heterogeneity and inequalities in Cuba]. Research Report. La Habana: CIPS, 2010.

Fundora, G. "¿Educación para qué y para quiénes? Universidad, desarrollo inclusivo y economía solidaria" [Education for whom? University, inculive development and solidarity economics]. *Revista Estudios del Desarrollo Social Cuba y América Latina* 8 (No. Especial): 272–294. 2020. Retrieved from: www.revflacso.uh.cu.

———. "Mujeres negras cubanas: Entre la renovación del modelo socioeconómico y la reproducción de la configuración cultural" [Black Cuban women: Between the renovation of the socioeconomic model and the reproduction of the cultural configuration]. *Revista Estudios de desarrollo social: Cuba y América Latina* 4 (4) 2016. Retrieved from: www.revflacso.uh.cu.

————. *Políticas sociales y sus efectos en las desigualdades. Análisis del contexto cubano 2008–2018* [Social policies and their effect on inequalities: Analysis of the Cuban context 2008–2018]. La Habana: Editorial Acuario, 2020.

Fundora, G., E. Dixon, and E. Vázquez. "Pensar y vivir en cooperativa: un espacio educativo para el empoderamiento femenino" [Thinking and living in cooperative: an educational space for female empowerment]. *Revista Estudios de Desarrollo Social: Cuba y América Latina* 5 (2): 24–37, 2017. Retrieved from: www.revflacso .uh.cu.

Galtés, I. "Aportes para un rediseño de la política salarial en el contexto de la actualización del modelo económico cubano" [Contribution to a redesign of the salary policy in the context of the updating of the Cuban economic model]. PhD dissertation, Universidad de La Habana, La Habana, 2016.

González, L., I. Lisbet Caballero, and T. Sardá. *Gestión cooperada entre mujeres. Un reto desde los Talleres de Transformación Integral del Barrio* [Cooperated management among women: A challenge from the Neighborhood Workshops for Comprehensive Transformation. La Habana: Editorial Caminos, 2018.

Gutiérrez, A. "Estrategias de reproducción social. Las microprácticas y la política social. Capital y redes sociales" [Strategies of social reproduction. Micropractices and social capital. Capital and social networks]. In *América Latina y el Caribe. La política social en el nuevo contexto*, edited by J. Valdés and M. Espina, 107–34. Uruguay: UNESCO-FLACSO, 2011.

Harguindéguy, J. B. *Análisis de políticas públicas* [Analysis of public policies]. Madrid: Editorial TECNOS, 2015.

Izquierdo, O., and J. Morín. "El modelo económico y social de desarrollo socialista y los actores laborales no estatales" [The socialist model of economic and social development and the non-state actors]. In *Trabajo decente y Sociedad. Cuba bajo la óptica de los estudios sociolaborales*, edited by O. Izquierdo and H. Burchardt, 133–64. La Habana: Editorial Universidad de La Habana, 2017.

Katzman, R. "Enfoque AVEO." *Conferencia presentada durante el Seminario Permanente de políticas sociales* [AVEO Approach: Conference presented at the Permanent Seminary on social policies]. La Habana: FLACSO-Cuba, 2018.

Kingdon, J. W. *Agendas, Alternatives and Public Policies.* Glenview, IL: Scott, Foresman and Company, 1984.

Korol, C. "Feminismos populares. Las brujas necesarias en los tiempos del cólera" [Popular feminisms. Necessary witches in times of cholera]. *Nueva Sociedad* (265): 142–52, 2016.

Lagarde, M. "Pacto entre mujeres" [Pact beteen women]. *Sororidad.*, n.d. Retrieved from: www.celem.org.

Luis, M. J. "Las transformaciones laborales realizadas en Cuba entre los años 2010 y 2014, su repercusión en los jóvenes" [The transformation of labor in Cuba between 2010 and 2014, its repercussion for young people]. *Revista Estudios* (18): 42–53, 2015.

Martín, J. L. "El toro por los cuernos: La necesaria transformación de las relaciones de trabajo en el país, como asignatura pendiente de la actualización del socialismo cubano" [The bull by the horns: The necessary transformation of work relations in the country, unfinished business for the updating of Cuban socialism]. In *Los correlatos socioculturales del cambio económico*, edited by M. Espina and D. Echevarría, 92–116. La Habana: Ruth Casa Editorial y Editorial Ciencias Sociales, 2015.

MTSS. *Manual de Procedimiento para el Trabajo de Prevención, Asistencia y Trabajo Social.* [Procedures Manual for the Work of Prevention, Assistance and Social Work]. La Habana: Ministerio de Trabajo y Seguridad Social (MTSS), 2012.

Munster, B. *Empoderamiento económico de las mujeres cubanas. Escenarios de incertidumbres e impactos en el actual proceso de reorganización económica del país.* [Economic empowerment of Cuban women. Scenarios of uncertainty and impacts on the current process of economic reorganization of the country]. Informe de investigación, CIEM, La Habana: CIEM, 2010.

ONEI. *Anuario Estadístico de Cuba, 2019* [Statistical Annual of Cuba, 2019]. La Habana: Oficina Nacional de Estadística e Información de Cuba, 2020. Retrieved from: http://www.onei.gob.cu/sites/default/files/07_empleo_y_salarios_2019.pdf.

Peña Farías, A., and R. Voghón. *La reconfiguración de la Política de Empleo y Seguridad Social: horizontes para pensar la relación igualdad-ciudadanía en el contexto cubano actual* [Reconfiguration of the policy of Employment and Social Security: horizons for thinking about the relation equality-citizenship in the current Cuban context]. Informe de investigación, La Habana: Universidad de La Habana, 2013.

Pérez Sainz, J. *Mercados y bárbaros. La persistencia de las desigualdades de excedente en América Latina* [Markets and barbarians: The persistence of inequalities of surplus in Latin America]. San Jose: FLACSO, 2014.

Romay, Z. *Cepos de la memoria. Impronta de la esclavitud en el imaginario social cubano* [Memory traps. Imprint of slavery in the Cuban social imaginary]. Matanzas: Ediciones Matanzas, 2015.

Voghón, R. "La transmisión intergeneracional de la pobreza: entre el cambio y la reproducción" [Intergenerational transmission of poverty: between change and reproduction]. Masters' Thesis, Universidad de La Habana, La Habana, 2008.

Zabala, M. C. *Análisis interseccional de las desigualdades en Cuba 2008–2018.* [Intersectional analysis of inequalities in Cuba, 2008–2018]. La Habana: Editorial Acuario, 2020.

———. "Equidad social y cambios económicos en Cuba: retos para la atención a la pobreza y las desigualdades" [Social equity and economic changes in Cuba: Challenges for dealing with poverty and inequalities]. In *Los correlatos socioculturales del cambio económico*, edited by M. Espina and D. Echevarría, 35–56. La Habana: Ruth Casa Editorial y Editorial Ciencias Sociales, 2015.

Zabala, M. C., et al. "Referentes teóricos para el estudio de las desigualdades sociales en Cuba: reflexiones sobre su pertinencia" [Theoretical references for the study of social inequalities in Cuba: reflections on their pertinence]. *Revista Estudios del Desarrollo Social: Cuba y América Latina* 6 (1): 86–118, 2018.

Chapter 7

Population, Value Chains and Social and Solidarity Economy

Epistemological Alignments

Dianné Griñan Bergara

Population studies focus on the reproduction, distribution, and growth of the population from three theoretical-methodological perspectives: demography, economy, and the relation between population and development. Hence the open approach to interdisciplinary methods and the recognition that the size, structure, and dynamics of the population are related to social processes of various types (Bueno 2003).

From the middle of the twentieth century to the present time, the topic of the design and implementation of population policies is fundamental in the sphere of demography because of the persistence and worsening of social problems that cannot be hidden in the face of growing levels of poverty in environments of profound inequalities. This was debated during the International Conference on Population and Development held in Cairo in 1994, as was the relation between these phenomena and the state and dynamics of the population. At this conference, a demographic panorama that no population projection had anticipated became noticeable: the accelerated drop in fertility led to a substantive decrease in growth rates. However, this was not the case for mortality rates. Specialists in the field concluded that the accelerated decrease in growth rates did not only respond to the drop in fertility but also to the worsening of social problems reflected in the behavior of the demographic variables.[1] As a result of this demographic evolution, the age structure of the population changed more rapidly: the proportion of people under fifteen years of age decreased, and that of people of sixty and over increased (Miró 1999).

These facts determined the need to integrate population policies into the development models in order to overcome conditions of poverty, social inequalities, unemployment, and underemployment, as well as the problems of economic growth and their impact on family income. The existing obstacles to women's participation in economic activities were discussed, as were the migration of professionals seeking better job opportunities and its relation with the disqualification of the labor force and the link between unequal access to education and its effects on the structure of the labor force—gender, age, educational level. Likewise, women's chances to obtain well-paid jobs and contribute to economic growth; the need to create jobs for young people; and, in other respects, the consideration of demographic aging as an opportunity to have a larger labor force without neglecting the socioeconomic conditions that influence its engagement.

While population studies have historically responded to more traditional demographic perspectives, mainly the one intended to clarify the relation between population growth and economic growth,[2] their focus in the last decades of the twentieth century moved toward the relation between population and development. Thus, this problem became the center of attention of various topics on the political and scientific agenda, and intersecting topics were gradually incorporated to facilitate the understanding of this relation. Through international cooperation, practices and studies in Cuba have been introduced that contribute to making this perspective better known.

Between 2015 and 2018—as part of a cooperation agreement with the United Nations Population Fund (UNFPA) and the United Nations Development Programme (UNDP)—the Centro de Estudios Demográficos de la Universidad de La Habana (CEDEM) developed a study that incorporated a gender-responsive population dynamics to an experiment carried out in the bean belt of central Cuba through the international cooperation project AGROCADENAS, coordinated by UNDP and the Ministry of Agriculture (MINAG).[3] The results of this study led to the Country Programme of UNFPA (2014–2018),[4] documented in the area of population dynamics in the United Nations Development Assistance Framework (UNDAF).[5]

This research led to the systematization of the theories on value chains and other similar experiences in Latin America with the aim of designing a methodological strategy that would allow the incorporation of the population-development relation to a project on agro-industrial chains in the country. This text summarizes the main analyses that resulted from the revisions made and establishes a relation between these perspectives and the proposals for a social and solidarity economy. Since they are closely related to the latest theoretical approaches of some of the prime promoters of the value chains, they share points of view in the current debates on development at different levels and restore the role of the local actors in the processes and strategies aimed at developing a more favorable scenario for the elimination of inequities.

POPULATION AS OBJECT AND
SUBJECT OF DEVELOPMENT

The data on the state and dynamics of the population are input material to design and implement public policies aimed at socioeconomic development. Perhaps in no other field is it so important to establish the links that exist between population and development as in the planning of human resources for activities that produce goods and services (Elizaga 1971). Along the same lines, in 1978 the United Nations declared that:

- As a demographically identifiable category, the role of the labor force is to produce goods and services to meet people's needs.
- The size and proportion that the labor force represents in the population has undeniable repercussions on the productive capacity of the economy and on the attainable level of per capita income.
- As a whole, the demographic characteristics of the labor force (gender, age and other attributes such as educational level, experience and ability of the workers, motivation, etc.) are primary determinants of the productive power. (Naciones Unidas. 1978)

We should add that the demographic characteristics of the labor force are primary determinants of the productive power in relation to their institutional, cultural, socioeconomic and work context. These environments and their different links intervene in the structure, dynamics and distribution of the labor force, its performance and its changes (Griñan 2019). Just like other components addressed by demography, gender and age influence popular participation in economic activity as differential attributes in the behavior of labor force indicators. All countries still register lower participation rates among women than men, indeed a consequence of the persistence of gender gaps as yet unconquered. Maternity, conjugal circumstances, family care, and a lower retirement age have an influence on women entering into and leaving economic life, as well as on the differences between their participation and that of men.

The increase or decrease of the economically active population (EAP) is also closely related to the changes in the socioeconomic structure of societies: schooling, income, women's participation, techno-productive transformations, etc. Therefore, the EAP grows or shrinks depending on the demographic and socioeconomic changes that take place in specific periods—a situation that can be interpreted in a positive or negative way. This is not necessarily because of the characteristics of the state and the dynamics of the population,[6] but rather on the characteristics of the social policies and the incidence of production factors that account for and take into account the changes in the demographic structure and dynamics (Elizaga 1979).

For example, as part of the process of demographic transition[7] there is a period during which the EAP grows in a sustained manner and faster than the proportion of dependent people and an age structure known as "demographic bonus" is observed. Although this offers opportunities for economic growth—as stated before, given the favorable concurrence of production factors—their use involves various socioeconomic challenges that imply a trade-off between immediacy and long-term planning. Different experiences show that it is not enough to count on the demographic bonus. The economic and social structures, the policies and other sociohistorical determinants are processes that have an impact on the production capacity of an economy and on the degree of absorption of the labor force, regardless of the size of the population and the EAP (Griñan 2019).

Studies on the topic (Faus 2002; Ortega, y otros 2016) find various challenges related to the demographic bonus in countries that went through their first demographic transition. They highlight the need to restore investment in education and in innovative training, research and development programs, as well as in the creation and strengthening of productive jobs and policies that favor the consolidation of linkages. These studies reveal an obvious pattern related to the positive impact of the labor force on economic growth based on the impact of policies on the production structures, the institutional environment, labor relations, qualifications, and training. Good practices and research related to this issue are based on the idea that the demographic bonus does not directly lead to economic growth; thus, they go beyond the traditional view of the labor force as input for the production system. Therefore, the demographic dynamics does not work in isolation, nor does it resolve by itself the topic of productivity (Griñan 2019).

DYNAMICS OF THE VALUE CHAINS
AND THE CREATION OF VALUE

The theories that introduced the perspective of linkages in the academic and productive scenario evolved during the time in which the debates on development became famous—especially those on economic development. The emergence, evolution and subsequent momentum of these perspectives shared the same context as the discussions on the relationship between population and development.

The perspectives on linkages have been the result of a theoretical debate that started in the 1950s and grew with the contributions of various authors during those years who adopted different approaches to understand the production structures (agglomerations, clusters, productive chains, value chains, etc.). Two views can be identified which, in general, bring together those different contributions: a business perspective, marked by the outstanding role of a figure like Michael Porter, and another one seen from the perspective of industrial and sectorial organization, embraced by Gary Gereffi, John Humphrey, Hubert Schmitz, and Peter Gibbon, among others (Anaya 2015).

The value chain is essentially a form of analysis of entrepreneurial activity by disaggregating an enterprise into its constituent parts in order to identify sources of competitive advantage in those businesses that generate value and in their interrelations. To this end, the enterprise develops and streamlines the activities of its chain more cheaply and better than its competitors (Chávez 2012). `The connections between the different links of the chain are produced at the same rate as value is created in each stage of the production and marketing process of a product or service for its acquisition.

"The value chain of a business is an interdependent system or network of activities related by linkages. Linkages are relationships between the way one value activity is performed and the cost or performance of another" (Porter 1990, 74). It is assumed that there is some sort of cooperation and that the activities included in the linkage depend on the type of product or service. For example, there can be linkages in the textile, mining, agricultural or other industries. "In a value chain, the products move between interdependent businesses that work together in a vertical coalition" (Iglesias 2002, 5–7).

According to Michael Porter (1985), even if the structural characteristics of the linkages depend on the economic sector, two types of activities can create value and competitive advantage based on the premise of business cooperation. These are primary activities (including logistics, operations, marketing, sales and service) and supporting activities (including enterprise infrastructure, human resource management, technology development and procurement). Therefore, if a value chain is essentially a form of organizing business through the disaggregation of the enterprise into value-adding activities and the identification of those that can be sources of competitive advantage, the enterprise can seize those opportunities depending on its capacity to develop such decisive activities throughout the value chain (Anaya 2015).

This is important, since not all activities add value, only those that make a positive difference between the revenue from the sale of the product or service and the manufacturing cost (producing large volumes in an efficient way) and those that distinguish the enterprise in the competitive environment (creation of a product or service perceived as unique in the market) (Chávez 2012).

After his *Competitive Advantage* (1985), Porter and his followers developed other elements that incorporated a perspective on value chains that were more committed to their development context. The chains were analyzed not only from the logic of their performance—exclusively oriented toward success in business—but also with a leaning toward the communities. In this way, the theoretical corpus on the topic began gradually to include other concepts, such as corporate social responsibility and shared value[8]—both closely related to the social and solidarity economy proposal. This is possibly because, while the value chains seemed to be a very successful structure for production (although, as we will see, not in all cases), the conditions for development in many areas of the world, on the other hand, were becoming increasingly unbalanced.

THEORETICAL INTEGRATION OF THE POPULATION-DEVELOPMENT PERSPECTIVE, THE CHAIN APPROACH AND THE SOCIAL AND SOLIDARITY ECONOMY PROPOSAL IN LATIN AMERICA

The potential of the chain approach for the definition of public policies has influenced its growing introduction in Latin American countries, with greater or lesser success during the last few years. Political instability has been a determining factor in the realization of strategies that favor the development of chains and, in addition, aim for social efficiency in the labor processes. On the other hand, the characteristics of the reception of theoretical-methodological production have also had their influence, because the efforts to replace the North American and European paradigms are still insufficient. Regional scholars hold that replacing the use of theories of limited scope imported from other realities by a discussion of its bases and by alternative proposals, as opposed to labor organization practices and models uncritically taken from other contexts, is still an unresolved matter (Dombois y Pries 1994; De la Garza 2005).

A logic based on the outsourcing of costs from large to medium-sized enterprises with a clear disproportion of powers in weak institutional contexts has been observed in the chains established in Latin America. This explains the difficulties related to product quality and enterprise efficiency and the problems linked to job insecurity. For this reason, the bases of the efficiency criteria that underlie the development of the production structure have been questioned, inasmuch as the distribution of competences along the chain suffers from great inequalities and a growing lack of coordination between technological modernization and occupational qualification (Abramo y Riveros 1997).

For these reasons, theoretical and methodological contributions which recognize the social problems that currently affect the population—and its various subgroups—have been identified in the region, as well as the fact that the development of chains does not always produce the results expected in social and economic terms. As the delegate of the CODESPA Foundation in Ecuador said in an interview in 2016 about the development of linkages in the continent:

> The economic impact is evident and influences the improvement in the income of the producing families and their associations. The fact that this economic impact influences the improvement of the quality of life of the families entails the insertion of cross-sectional labor strategies based on gender, food security, education, etc. . . . As a result of failures in financial intermediation that still exist in Latin America, a large number of people and areas are deprived of financial services, especially the rural areas and people engaged in agricultural work. Even when it comes to the development of chains, the access to funds by small producers is not only essential to increase production, but also a basic element to access working capital and invest in assets so that the small associative enterprises or SMEs can grow and consolidate. . . . Cooperation among the public and private sectors and the associations of producers and local and international NGOs is key to tackle the problems that we have today. (Gelis 2016)

How can we connect the role of the population-development approach, the theory of value chains, and the proposal for the social and solidarity economy in order to help overcome inequalities in development? Some studies on value chains show a way that could shed light on this issue, based on the design of participatory diagnostic and action tools that we can summarize under the following principles (Anaya 2015):

- Economic: create or strengthen business networks; increase the competitiveness of a product at national or international level; capitalize on market opportunities or unfulfilled demands; create jobs.
- Social: make the market accessible to producers; create jobs; increase the income of the participating actors (especially the small producers) and their percentage of the profits; promote gender equity.
- Environmental: reduce the environmental damage caused by the development of a specific economic activity; promote clean productive technologies and the use of renewable energy sources.

As per the words of the author previously quoted: "The fundamental weakness of these kinds of actions taken by cooperation agencies is that once their period of intervention has ended, there is not always a guarantee that the results achieved are sustainable" (Anaya 2015, 38) Other proposals explain how to approach this issue by taking into consideration the social efficiency and sustainability currently needed to strengthen Latin American chains, in which the problems of food security and the rural context have become a regular issue. They hold that the sustainable development of the chains should tally with increased income and food security for the poor and the small producers, together with steps to facilitate the acquisition of surplus value by the poor in rural areas so that they can meet their needs, taking into account the market structure (Betancourt 2015; Arguello y Olivero 2015; Correa 2017; Téllez y Rivera 2017; Howland, et al. 2019).

Another line of research includes social equity and participation approaches as the organic basis to design the chains (Chavarría y Sepúlveda 2001; Fernández, y otros s.f.; González y Van der Heyden 2004; Stoian y Donovan 2004). Below are its main general points:

- Limitations of the value chains to redress the concentration processes that contribute to spatial and social inequality by recognizing the behavior of social and demographic dimensions in specific spaces and their historical record regarding the economic dimension (productive specialization, business density, the complexity of their structure).
- Inconsistencies between the discourse processes constructed by public institutions to encourage linkage development and the capacities of the socioeconomic and demographic nodes to reverse the processes of regional density and inequality.
- Living conditions of the population and their (dis)qualifying characteristics.
- Inability of the public and private sectors to develop and consolidate effective concepts to strike a balance between subsistence-oriented and profit-making activities in rural households.
- Life strategies in the presence of external and internal conflicts; promoting the evolution of business initiatives toward competitive rural enterprises.
- Noneconomic factors (external and internal) that determine the competitiveness of agro-industrial chains. Outstanding among them are the agroecological conditions; a new institutionalism that guarantees competitiveness, equity and sustainability; cultural and demographic environment; tools and policies to increase the competitiveness of the most backward actors and improve their quality of life.

The social and solidarity economy proposal is in line with the above views and issues. In accordance with the analysis integrated into the population-development relation and value chain approaches, it is pertinent to highlight the following ideas and principles of the social and solidarity economy (Coraggio 2013):

- It proposes to develop an alternative economic system as an to relations based on competitiveness.
- It defends the principles of solidarity, redistribution, reciprocity and legitimation of the common good.
- It is based on identifiable solidarity components within the various sectors of the economy; for example, participatory budgeting and public services, non-governmental organizations, foundations, enterprises with co-management systems, labor unions, ethnic communities, social enterprises (which can be part of the private sector), cooperatives, etc.
- It tends to favor the most vulnerable people to overcome the welfarist approach and promote their reintegration into the economy.
- It recognizes the interrelation among economy, politics and culture.
- It demands a thorough debate on the role of the state, the operation of the market, the forms of property and appropriation, the role and control of money, and the degree of labor commercialization.
- It considers a different distribution of the existing wealth and a revision of the rules of appropriation and use of the means of production through the transformation of the production structures.
- It recognizes the existence of social inequalities, noticeable in the growth of the economies and the increase of poverty.

In the specific context of the value chains, this perspective reinforces the idea that the population should be at the center of the development processes as producer and beneficiary, in the understanding that neither geographic boundaries nor business scopes define the operating range of a chain. On the contrary, it is in the social context—as the historical space constructed through social relations (Viales 2010)—where the value chains develop, interact, and gain practical and symbolic significance.

As part of the relational logics that concur throughout a value chain, we can identify a wide variety of actors—enterprises, scientific and economic institutions, governments, etc.—some of which relate directly to production, distribution and marketing activities, whereas others develop within their environment but interrelate constantly. It is precisely in the interaction among these actors in the social space where we find horizontal and vertical alliances with common risks and benefits and which need to share as well a social assignment resulting from the links of the productive context with their communities.

By assuming that enterprises of a different kind in terms of structure, size and form of management can design a value chain, the social and solidarity economy approach makes them co-responsible for the processes of local development together with other actors engaged in this social space based on relations established through linkages. This can support the creation of quality jobs, the harmonic incorporation of small and medium enterprises into the existing network of socioeconomic relations, the efficiency of the small producers, the management of participatory processes in decision-making, the resolution of conflicts and the building of consensus to influence the causes of the main problems of regions and localities, the assistance provided to the most vulnerable groups, etc. All this requires coordinated actions among the actors, facilitating and sensitizing strategies and, above all else, an institutional network sufficiently consolidated to be able to create the conditions that make this possible.

To this end, the chains cannot be oriented toward competition in order to succeed in business, but toward the development of a scenario that favors the reproduction of the population as a sociodemographic system, especially the population that produces goods and services in an equitable environment. According to the perspective of population-development relation and to the social and solidarity economy approach, this can be possible if the work done is economically profitable as a means of self-sustenance, if the workspace favors self-realization based on a set of learned (or desired) skills, be they professional or self-taught, and if there is stability and development in both directions.

Just like in business relations, the reproduction of the population happens in the social space and on a daily basis; therefore, the interdependence between the public and the private contexts defines the conditions for such reproduction. It is a well-known fact that the wage relation by itself is not enough to reproduce the labor force's means of sustenance. There must be accessible opportunities for all population subgroups and the service infrastructure must respond to the needs of daily life. In conclusion, the cost of the reproduction of the population should be a joint responsibility of the family, the governments—and their institutions—and the enterprises.

FINAL THOUGHTS

The proposal that this text presents aims at the integration of the population-development approach, the theory of value chains and the perspective of the social and solidarity economy in order to contribute to the debate that these topics are producing in the region. The first assumption underlying this objective is that the population that produces goods and services, i.e., the labor force, is a productive force, but also a consumer population. Both dimensions are closely related, a fact to be considered in every analysis, methodology and project, to which end, production, knowledge and the use of population data are essential.

On a theoretical level, it is necessary to recognize the labor force as a unit of analysis—with a definite place in the structure and dynamics of the chains—in the relations between the actors and in the activities related to production and marketing, with emphasis on the product´s role as a factor and object of production. The labor force[9] is part of both the structure and dynamics of the actors inherent in a value chain and the relations and transformative actions of a product.

In other words, the labor force—given the conditions of its reproduction in a value chain—takes part to a greater or lesser extent in the competition to optimize the economic benefits, not only of the chain and its links but also its own, by recognizing that it is one of the actors involved and that it plays an important role in the substantive processes of the said competition.

Although the value chain approach boasts a solid development and practical experience, it is still the object of modeling and discussion. The intention in this case is not to define what a value chain is, but to include in its present concepts the approach of the population-development relation, together with that of the social and solidarity economy. In this connection, our viewpoint brings the labor force to center stage as a demographically identifiable category within the substantive processes of business competition that the value chain approach brings about. It also promotes the approach to equity and to the participation of the different population subgroups. The social and solidarity economy proposal relates to this objective, strengthens the perspective of the population-development relation and complements the view on the role of the enterprises in local and regional development. The principles laid down in this text confirm this assertion.

The approach of the population-development relation becomes stronger and broadens its capacity to explain the labor force as a population subgroup—its characteristics, the conditions in which it produces development and benefits or not from this process—through the integration of socioeconomic and demographic variables. The interpretative framework proposed herein can contribute to this goal even if the balance between the natural and economic resources and the demographic behavior of the population and its living conditions reveals an interrelation that deserves more in-depth studies. To this end, an effective planning of development based on the information about the status and dynamics of the population becomes essential as valuable knowledge for the decision-making processes at local and regional level.

NOTES

1. However, some Latin American countries registered low mortality levels, expressed by a life expectancy at birth similar to those of countries with greater social and economic development. This was the case in Cuba, a situation which has been maintained until the present.

2. This issue had as its principal exponent Thomas Robert Malthus, as reflected in his "An essay on the principle of population" (1798).

3. With the support of the European Union (EU) and the Swiss Agency for Development and Cooperation (SDC).

4. Results: endorsement of development programs to improve the integration of population, gender, generation and specific regional dynamics, and efforts directed to capacity building in the institutions that provide statistical and academic information to incorporate the population dynamic in the development programs.

5. Project AGROCADENAS was directed to the strengthening of agri-food chains at local level. In 2016, it presented a report recognizing the need to strengthen its management and improve the scope and quality of its results through the incorporation of the population perspective. Intersections were identified which had a direct influence on the design and implementation of the different initiatives of the project. For this reason, the coordination of AGROCADENAS mobilized to broaden the spectrum of institutional alliances with the inclusion of CEDEM through UNFPA.

6. Otherwise, the problem would seem to lie in the dynamics and structure of the population and not in the social system in which it develops.

7. A process of declining birth and mortality rates in time as a result of the development of society in its broadest sense, with the industrialization process as the main driving force of this development.

8. This approach appears in several of Michael Porter's works, which became popular as of the nineties. Other advocates of the value-chain approach and business scholars analyzed and enriched them since then. Among Porter's most widely known publications on this subject are *America's Green Strategy* (1991), *The Competitive Advantage of Corporate Philanthropy* (2002), *Strategy and Society: The Link between Competitive Advantage and Corporate Social Responsibility* (2006), and *Creating Shared Value: Redefining Capitalism and the Role of the Corporation in Society* (2011).

9. Its structure and composition by gender, age, educational level, years of work experience, suitability, and other attributes; its mobility inside and outside the enterprises or economic sectors; its interactions with formal and informal social institutions; the acquisition of its own output; and the living conditions and possibilities of consumption that result from this acquisition.

BIBLIOGRAPHY

Abramo, L., Riveros, L. *Las reformas sociales en acción: empleo* [Social reforms in action: employment]., Santiago de Chile: CEPAL, 1997.

Anaya, B. *Articulación de cadenas de valor hortofrutícolas para la satisfacción de demandas. El caso de la cadena del mango en Santiago de Cuba* [Articulation of fruit and vegetable valur chains for the satisfaction of demands. The case of mango in Santiago de Cuba]. Tesis de doctorado, La Habana: Facultad de Economía de la Universidad de La Habana, 2015.

Arguello, A., Olivero, M. *Café Convencional en Nicaragua: Análisis de la Cadena de Valor del Café Convencional en Nicaragua período 2012–2013* [Conventional coffee in Nicaragua. Analysis of the value chain of conventional coffee in Nicaragua, period 2012–2013]. Tesis de doctorado, Managua: Universidad Nacional Autónoma de Nicaragua, 2015.

Aroca, I. "Diagnóstico de proyectos productivos y soberanía alimentaria en comunidades. Caso Rocafuerte" [Diagnosis of productive projects and food security in communities. The case of Rocafuerte]. *ECA Sinergia*, 7(1), 95–106, 2016.

Betancourt, M. "Política de seguridad alimentaria nutricional (SAN) y desarrollo territorial en Colombia" [Food and nutritional security (SAN) policy and regional development in Colombia]. Tesis de doctorado, Madrid: Universidad Complutense de Madrid, 2015.

Bueno, E. *Población y desarrollo. Enfoques alternativos de los estudios de población* [Population and development. Alternative approaches in population studies]. Zacatecas: 2003.

Chavarría, H., Sepúlveda, S. *Competividad de la Agricultura: Cadenas Agroalimentarias y el Impacto del Factor Localización Espacial* (No. INFOAGRO) [Competition in Agriculture: Agro-food chains and the impact of the Spatial Localization Factor]. Instituto Interamericano de Cooperación para la Agricultura, 2001.

Chávez, J. C. *Cadena de valor, estrategias genéricas y competitividad* [Value chain, generic strategies and competition]. 2012. Retrieved from: http://www.eumed.net/libros-gratis/2013b/1345/index.htm.

Coraggio, J. L. "Las tres corrientes de pensamiento y acción dentro del campo de la economía social y Solidaria" [The three currents of thought and action within the field of the social and solidarity economy]. *Revista Brasileira de Estudos Urbanos e Regionais* 15(2): 11–24, 2013.

Correa, G. "El deber ser en los agronegocios" [What agri-businesses ought to be]. *Revista de la Universidad de La Salle, 2017*(72), 253–274, 2017.

De la Garza, E. "Epistemología de las teorías sobre modelos de producción" [Epistemology of the theories on models of production]. En *Los retos teóricos de los estudios del trabajo hacia el siglo xxi*, 2005. Retrieved from: http://bibliotecavirtual.clacso.org.ar/clacso/gt/20101102030444/6toledo.pdf.

Dombois, R., and L. Pries. "¿Necesita América Latina su propia Sociología del Trabajo?" [Does Latin America need its own Sociology of Work?] En *Economía y Sociología del Trabajo. La Sociología del Trabajo en América Latina*. Ministerio del Trabajo y Seguridad Social, Madrid: 1994.

Elizaga, J. C. *Aspectos demográficos de la mano de obra en América Latina* [Demographic aspects of the labor force in Latin America]. Santiago de Chile: CELADE, 1971.

————. *Dinámica y economía de la población* [Dynamic and economy of the popula-
    tion]. Santiago de Chile: CELADE, 1979.

Faus, M. *"Potencial demográfico y mercado de trabajo"* [Demographic potential and
    labor market]. *Scripta Nova, 117*(64), 2002.

Fernández, V. R., Cardozo, L., Gesualdo, G., Seval, M. *Aglomeraciones producti-
    vas y desarrollo regional: una perspectiva contextualizadora y multidimensional*
    [Productive clusters and regional development: a contextual and multidimensional
    perspective]. (s./f.).

Gelis, F. "Las Cadenas Productivas: concepto, elementos y barreras" [Productive
    chains: concept, elements, and barriers]. *RedEAmérica.* 2016. Retrieved from:
    https://www.codespa.org/inicio.

González, M., Van der Heyden, D. *Metodología de análisis de cadenas productivas
    con equidad para la promoción del desarrollo local* [Method of analysis of produc-
    tive chains with equity for the promotion of local development]. SNV. 2004.

Griñan, D. "El potencial demográfico como categoría analítica para el diagnóstico de
    cadenas de valor" [Demographic potential as an analytical category for the diagno-
    sis of value chains]. Estudio de caso. *Novedades en población, 15*(30), 164–177,
    La Habana: 2019.

Howland, F., Le Coq, J., Martínez-Barón, D., Tapasco, J., Loboguerrero, A., Sandoval,
    J. M., Villamil, M. *Hacia una política de crecimiento verde para el sector agro-
    pecuario en Colombia* [Towards a policy of green growth for the agricultural sector
    in Colombia]. 2019.

Iglesias, D. *Las cadenas de valor como estrategia: las cadenas de valor en el sector
    agroalimentario* [Value chains as a strategy: value chains in the agri-food sector].
    Argentina: EEA-INTA, 2002.

Miró, C. América Latina: la población y las políticas de población entre Bucarest y El
    Cairo [Latin America: population and population policies between Bucharest and
    Cairo]. *Papeles de población, 5*(20), 1999.

Naciones Unidas. *Factores determinantes y consecuencias de las tendencias
    demográficas* [Determining factors and consequences of the demographic tenden-
    cies]. New York: 1978.

Ortega, L., De la Fuente, J., Quintero, K., Rivera, J. M. "Bono demográfico:
    retos y oportunidades para favorecer el desarrollo en el Estado de Guanajuato"
    [Demographic bonus: challenges and opportunities for favoring development in the
    State of Guanajuanto], Mexico: 2016. Retrieved from: https://www.researchgate
    .net/publication/311454311.

Porter, M. *La ventaja competitiva de las naciones* [Competitive advantage of nations].
    Buenos Aires: 1990.

Stoian, D., Donovan, J. "Articulación del mundo campesino con el mercado: inte-
    gración de los enfoques de medios de vida y cadena productive" [Articulation of
    the farming sector with the market: integration of the approaches of way of life and
    productive chains]. *Memorias de la Semana Científica,* 14–16, 2004.

Téllez, G., Rivera, A. "Producción Agrícola: La cadena productiva del arroz en
    Nicaragua y su enfoque en la seguridad alimentaria en el ciclo 2012–2013"
    [Agricultural production: The productive chain of rice in Nicaragua and its

approach toward food security in the cycle 2012–2013]. Managua: Universidad Nacional Autónoma de Nicaragua, 2017.

Viales, R. "La región como construcción social, espacial, política, histórica y subjetiva." [The region as a social, spatial, political, historical and subjective construction]. *Geopolítica(s)* 1(1): 157–72, 2010.

Chapter 8

Do Public-Private Partnerships Have Room in the Present Cuban Context?

Notes from a Practical Experience

Mirlena Rojas Piedrahita

We light the oven so that everyone may bake bread in it.

—José Martí

In the last ten years, the sphere of labor has been reconfigured in the Cuban context, characterized in general by forward and backward steps, as well as by tension and consensus.[1] Not only does the diversification in forms of property and management provide a heterogeneous and changing setting, it also gives rise to a context in which the state has admittedly ceded some of its responsibilities to individual and family management by Cuban men and women. Since then, certain specific spaces have gained strength and legitimacy where public-private partnerships and a de facto market can find some room.

This context unfolds on a programmatic platform based on the Guidelines of the Economic and Social Policies of the Party and the Revolution for 2016–2021 (PCC 2017), the Bases of the National Economic and Social Development Plan for 2030: Vision of the Nation, Central Points and Strategic Sectors (PCC 2016) and the Conceptualization of the Cuban Economic and Social Model of Socialist Development (PCC 2016). Add to this the recent Special Publication, Cuba and its Economic and Social Challenges. Summary of the Economic and Social Strategy to promote the economy and tackle the world crisis caused by COVID-19 (MEP Julio 2020).

What are the main theoretical foundations regarding public-private partnerships? Which aspects contain these types of links and what are the main responsibilities of each party? Is it safe to say that the bases for the development of public-private partnerships in the Cuban context are in place? Can the communities strengthen their potential through public-private partnerships as a function of development and social welfare?

Such questions will guide the present article in the pursuit of answers from a theoretical-conceptual and a practical viewpoint. The experience described herein is part of the project "Strengthening environmental transformations for adaptability to climate change in Cuban communities,"[2] coordinated and directed by the Cuban NGO Centro Félix Varela. The purpose is to socialize the potential of public-private partnerships in our context based on a practical experience in Yarual, a community of the Bolivia Municipality in the Cuban province of Ciego de Ávila.

The relevance of this topic in a context of socialist construction such as that of Cuba responds not only to the pressing need for both complementarity among the various economic actors and spaces, but also to the search for avenues for development based on the innovation and creativity of its people. That is why it is important to give visibility to practical experiences likely to *change the lives* of the human beings as the main force at the root of the Cuban socialist project.

ON THE PUBLIC-PRIVATE PARTNERSHIPS: SOME THEORETICAL STARTING POINTS

Nowadays, the connection established between the public and the private has several meanings. It is known as coordination, relation, association, partnership, cooperation, etc., as there is no single definition of the term.[3] It is therefore important to take into account that this lack of a common definition has implications, most of which depend on the political, economic, cultural and social context of the country where they occur.

The theoretical origin addressed as one of its first lines (Pliscoff y Araya 2012) justifies this kind of relation as the public action resulting from the debate that took place in the late 1980s and early 1990s around the school of New Public Management (Hood 1991). In particular, this school of thought conceives public-private partnerships as *management techniques* that facilitate a better use of the state's scarce resources.

In this respect, Savas (1990) uses the analysis of privatizations to include public-private partnerships as a form of market interference in the public sector. This debate assumed that there are certain areas in which the state has neither resources nor capacities to intervene and, therefore, it is necessary to reach an agreement with the private sector. This view is very similar to the one presented by Williamson (1988), who holds—based on his transaction cost theory—that a different agreement would be necessary to reduce transaction costs depending on the type of targeted activity. This type of justification for public-private partnerships refers mainly to an efficiency-based argument rather than a cooperation proper (Donahue y Zeckhauser 2011).

From the Latin American perspective, the realistic need to consider the creation and development of public-private partnerships is related to the lack of financial resources of the state administration as a result of neoliberal policies markedly intended to reduce the state's role to a minimum by restricting various public policies on social matters (Bresser 1999, quoted by Pliscoff y Araya 2012). This is one of the main factors leading up to the emergence of public-private partnerships, intended to improve the performance of public policies and their impact on society.

Pursuant to this context, these are some of its definitions:

- A partnership for cooperation is a work strategy based on the collective work of actors who participate as equal partners and for a common goal. This entails sharing responsibilities and risks, as well as improving their capacity, resources, and contributions to achieve greater impacts or results (Fundación DIS 2008, as quoted by Oleas 2017).
- A cooperative effort between two or more organizations from the public and the private sector (including civil society organizations) based on a strategic and voluntary commitment to common goals to promote development (though they may have different interests) and share risks, benefits, and responsibilities through the equitable distribution of power (Cardona y Sariego 2010).
- Voluntary cooperation through which individuals, groups or organizations agree to work together to fulfill an obligation or carry out a specific initiative, sharing both the risks and the benefits involved, and to review their relationship regularly if necessary (Oleas 2017).
- An agreement between the public and the private sector, in which the private sector takes over some services or works incumbent on the public sector through a clear agreement on shared objectives to provide for the public service or its infrastructure. It combines the skills and resources so that they share the risks and responsibilities (Grupo Banco Mundial 2019).
- Recognized as a multi-actor interrelation that includes both production sectors and different social organizations expected to work together with a view to local community development (D'Angelo y Morillas 2019). Its

authors make specific reference to public-private partnerships based on principles of solidarity and joint participation that bring them closer to a socialist rationale.

Since sustainable development has taken center stage in these matters recently, the 2030 Agenda of the United Nations acknowledges the importance of this type of relation based on its goals. International organizations such as CEPAL (Economic Commission for Latin America and the Caribbean), UNDP (United Nations Development Program), and the World Bank have taken a stance on this issue, trying to come up with a distinct definition of its goals, the actors involved and their roles, and how to measure the fulfillment of the expected results. Likewise, they addressed the nature and scope of their cooperation, its possible value-adding components, sustainability and impact, and the laws governing this kind of relations (PNUD Cuba 2019).

For the purposes of this chapter, public-private partnerships are links that entail a contractual relationship between the parties involved (legal forms of management and property, NGOs, international cooperation agencies, etc.) based on due joint responsibility and multi-actor partnership (economic, social, political, and popular actors). The aim is to guarantee the development of the process in place and the equitable distribution of power as a function of shared economic and social management.

According to (Oleas 2017), public-private partnerships give rise to certain expectations:

1. Value-added contributions of each actor and synergy between the actors, related to the effective ability of the organizations involved in the partnership to add substantial elements to the collective purpose of development. The principle would be that the outcome of the joint effort is more than the sum of the individual results without cooperation.
2. Sustainability and impact, which means that the outcome of the partnership should be sustainable and make a proven impact. This raises hopes that the said partnership will have long-lasting results as the number of beneficiaries grows unlimitedly and outplay other punctual, limited solutions to long-term problems.
3. Active participation of the parties and combination of the invested assets so that each organization involved can play an effective role in every development process of the partnership that contributes to their collective experience and capacity.
4. A common vision of development that respects the interests of the parties on equal terms. This leads to the search for concrete and consensual results based on common strategies of all organizations engaged in the partnership, in the conviction that, in the same way, the long-term

success of the partnership will depend on the respect for and concern about the interests of all parties.

5. Effectiveness and efficiency of the development solutions derived from the partnership. This makes sense insofar as the establishment of a partnership has associated transaction costs that are justifiable as long as the proposed solution is effective in terms of the cost-benefit ratio and efficient to achieve better development results (Loro, 2014, as quoted in Oleas 2017) and meet social goals.

Some types of public-private partnerships mostly based on the responsibilities of each form of management (Pliscoff y Araya 2012; Robinson et al. 2010) are also recognized.

While these models depend on the characteristics of each sector, it is recognized that such partnerships connect with the strategies related to the business social responsibility of the different forms of management and the way that their organizational, legal, social, economic, and environmental actions reflect in their design the execution, monitoring, and impact of its practical operations.

Other references use different terms, in this case related to the reforms of socialist models such as the one in China. For example, integration of private enterprises, political absorption of private entrepreneurs, and institutional embeddedness. The advantage of these terms is that they do not refer to relations between *equal* actors, which makes it possible to make a realistic assessment of the political economy of a kind of reform used by the Communist Party of China to absorb what that country officially calls representatives of the advanced productive forces (Monreal 2020).

This topic should be studied in greater depth from the standpoint of political economy, given the need to clarify the concept so that it reflects at least three essential elements. First, the way that the political nature of the partnership leads to links based on political understanding and the acceptance of the strategy to be followed. Second, the formulation and implementation of any given strategy should guarantee a degree of sustainability such that it will facilitate an economic transformation based on consensus and collective bargaining among the various actors engaged in the partnership. Last but not least, there is a need to coordinate private analyses within the socialist logic in Cuba for the benefit of the whole society, which involves addressing the social nature of labor and the alienation of the workers.

Table 8.1—Types of Public-Private Alliances (PPA)

Type of PPA Model	Responsibilities of the public sector	Responsibilities of the private sector
Operate and maintain	An existing (planned, designed, built and financed) asset owned by the public sector. The monitoring and regulation of the financial aspects are maintained.	The private sector administers the asset by operating and keeping it in a specific condition and receives payment for its operation, maintenance, or administration.
Rehabilitate, operate, and transfer	An existing asset owned by the public sector is transferred to the private sector. The planning and specification of the service or the asset is done by the state.	The rehabilitated private sector (which includes the modification of the design, its construction according to parameters, the requirements of the public sector, and the financing). It administers the asset by operating and maintaining the site according to certain parameters for a fee until it is returned to the public sector.
Design, construct, operate, and maintain	Planning (specification of requirements for the asset or service), financing the cost of the asset, monitoring and regulation of the performance of the asset or service.	Design of the site (as per the requirements of the public sector), construction, operation and maintenance of the asset (and financing of the operating costs for a fee).
Design, construct, and operate	Planning (specification of requirements for the asset or service); acquisition of the asset for a previously agreed price. Monitoring and regulation of the asset; the financial management services are maintained.	Design of the site (as per the requirements of the public sector), construction, operation and maintenance of the asset for a fee.

| Design, construct, finance and operate | Planning (specification of requirements for the asset or service), payment for the availability or use of the asset (and the services) through a unitary payment. Monitoring and regulation of the financial management services are maintained. | Design of the site (as per the requirements of the public sector or specifications based on results), financing, construction, operation and maintenance of the asset. The property and the risks associated with the transfer of the assets to the public sector at the end are maintained. Collect a fee based on the capital investment and the operational costs. |

Source: Adapted from Robinson, Carrillo, Anumba, and Patel (2010), Governance And Entrepreneurial Knowledge For Public-Private Partnerships. *UK: Wiley-Blackwell.*

PUBLIC-PRIVATE PARTNERSHIPS IN THE CUBAN CONTEXT

This is a relatively new topic in Cuba. Taking 2010 as the turning point, a new era began, based on the implementation of a number of transformations formally specified in the Guidelines for the Economic and Social Policy approved in 2011 (PCC 2011) and ratified in 2017 by the 6th and 7th Congresses of the Cuban Communist Party (PCC 2017), respectively. All of the above takes place in a context known as Updating of the Cuban Economic and Social Model.

A process of labor reorganization is under way in the country ever since, in which the transformations related to the expansion of non-state forms of property and management are essential. Among these, the following stand out:

1. Land leased in usufruct to individuals or legal entities through Decree-Laws 259/2008, (MINJUS 2008), 300/2012 (MINJUS 2014) and 312/2013 (MINJUS 2017).
2. Larger number of activities that self-employed workers (TCP in Spanish) can perform.[4]
3. Experimental creation of nonagricultural cooperatives.

Several actions are directly or indirectly linked to services such as room or home rentals; food and drink establishments—from cafeterias to restaurants; passenger carriers who use a variety of means—from cars to bicycle taxis; trading in handicrafts, and lodging management.

Ever since their conception, the first clause of the Guidelines of 2011 recognizes that:

G1—"The socialist planning system shall continue to be the main management tool of the national economy and shall in turn adjust its methodological and organizational provisions to accommodate new forms of management."

G2—"In addition to the socialist state enterprise as the main entity of the national economy, the management model must recognize and promote joint ventures, cooperatives, the leasing of land in usufruct, rental of establishments, self-employment and other forms that could contribute to increase the efficiency of social work" (PCC 2011).

In 2017, the conceptualization of the model recognized economic actors of a private nature as a complementary element that facilitates economic welfare and streamlines the potential for production for the benefit of national socioeconomic development. It also recognized the small and medium enterprises (SMEs)—albeit not legally yet—as an instrument to promote the development of productive, commercial and service activities that favor production linkages and local development by prioritizing the food industry, construction, social and personal services, repair and maintenance work, complementary tourism offers, handcrafted goods, transportation, communications, and community services, among others. There is no doubt that these developments have a local impact and pose new challenges to the planning, management and regional control at urban and strategic level (PCC 2016).

According to Soto (2019), in July 2018, as part of the process to improve the legislation regulating private employment, Cuba issued a new package of legal regulations which were then modified just days before they were supposed to come into force. One of the main features of the new legislation is that it set on 123 the number of authorized private activities. The intention was not to eliminate some of them, but to group them into more compact categories and the licensees more integrated. It also entails the emergence of new figures, more specific causes for withdrawing a license, the possibility to keep a license operational despite the temporary absence of its holder, and the extension to legal entities of the right to provide room and home rental services.

The forms of non-state management (self-employment, small private enterprises or nonagricultural cooperatives) open new possibilities for individual and collective initiative. On the one hand, they foster production or service activities more in line with the demands and needs of the population and less dependent on central government guidelines, as well as a more diversified supply. On the other hand, they facilitate the collection of tax revenues with a view toward investment and the generation of more income for many sectors of society hitherto subject to limited salaries in state sectors or illegal black market activities, to the detriment of the national resources (D'Angelo y Morillas 2019).

In this connection, Cuban specialists (Tabares, Pérez y Cárdenas 2019) believe that the public–private partnerships are not an easy contract option for the public sector, nor do they offer a universal solution. However, they do provide a flexible framework to mobilize specialized personnel and the resources of the private sector in order to provide, in the right circumstances, better and more lasting and cost-effective public services, which definitely entails social benefits.

The said authors consider that in no case should this relation be idealized. There are different interests and purposes involved, hence the need to identify a joint project, to define the stakeholders and their specific goals and prepare a contract that clearly describes, among other matters, the scope and specific objective of the partnership. This produces benefits, but also potential risks that the public administration can by no means overlook. It could happen that the development, tendering, and other expenses—incurred during a given project—exceed the cost of the traditional public contractual processes. Some projects may be easier to finance; some only yield profits in local currency, and others become a source of foreign currency.

July 2020 saw the publication of the Special Tabloid Cuba and its Economic and Social Challenges. Summary of the Economic and Social Strategy to promote the economy and tackle the world crisis caused by COVID-19 (MEP Julio 2020), presented by Alejandro Gil, minister of Economy and Planning, in the television program *Mesa Redonda* of July 16, 2020 (*Mesa Redonda* 2020).

In essence, this document refers to the consolidation of the non-state sector based on the establishment of SMEs in state and non-state sectors, the replacement of the index of activities approved for self-employment with a list of those forbidden to them and the promotion of nonagricultural cooperatives and wholesale markets to supply them. Likewise, it highlights the need to level the playing field for all actors of the economy and it states the need to conceive the integral engagement of various actors in the Cuban economic model by devising general rules applicable to all of them without distinction (MEP Julio 2020).

In particular, the minister pointed out the need to:

- Protect domestic production and get rid of our harmful import mentality that made us fall into the habit of bringing a ship from abroad with the solutions to our scarcity and thus the need to raise the hard currency to pay for the shipment.
- Regulate the market, mainly by indirect methods. This is totally in line with our economic model and our guidelines. We have to let the market act and regulate it in terms of the goals of our planning process, using mostly indirect instruments rather than purely administrative measures

likely to make a certain positive impact in the short run but hardly effective as economic management tools. We need to make progress in this respect.

- Complementarity of the economic actors. Our model provides for various economic actors. We have to find the way to make them link and intertwine with one another, together as one, because we are all Cuba. Let us all, the self-employed, the state and the non-state sectors, the cooperatives, the state enterprise, come together as a function of this goal. We have to find this complementarity to defend ourselves against aggressions, keep moving forward and bring prosperity to our people (*Mesa Redonda* 2020).

The above proves that the official discourse recognizes the need to establish connections and interlace the different economic actors of the country, as various scholars have already noted, as well as the relevance of regulating activities based on planning, but without centralist excesses and administrations that hinder development. In this respect, the need to take stock of the inequalities that could emerge between private and state property is still an unresolved matter in the interrelation of the different forms of property and management.

According to the Cuban economist Juan Triana (2020), public-private partnerships can be a way to reduce Cuba's imports and dependence on foreign capital and to create jobs (especially in unprotected sectors). They can also help improve the life of many people and become a resource to promote the equality that we need for development, and which should be the *sought-after* outcome of this process.

By way of example, Cuba has in place programs, initiatives, and projects aimed at the consolidation of public-private partnerships. That is the case of the Joint Program in Support of new initiatives of decentralization and production incentives in Cuba (Núñez, Cobarrubias y Delgado 2013), financed through the Development and Private Sector window of the SDG fund. Its main challenge was to promote new types of relations between state and non-state forms of management with a view to creating partnerships and allocating resources to municipal development.

In this regard, it became essential to broaden the productive capacity of the non-state sector and provide municipal governments with methodological tools to design and implement regional development strategies. This process, new to Cuba, led to a systematization exercise centered on the coordination of the state and non-state sectors and intended to extract and socialize the main lessons learned and good practices, both for those who participated in the program and for other actors willing to replicate what they learned in similar experiences.

Another example is the experience of the Havana Historical Center and its process of comprehensive management for development, based on specific values, cultural legacy, and economic, political, and social aspects—which make this site unique and exclusive. With an eye to add the new forms of non-state management to its development plans, this zone of exceptional values that earned it National Monument and World Cultural Heritage status set out to include in the design of its main planning and management tools a number of policies and actions to strengthen and organize the role of private enterprises and their development, taking into account the interests and general objectives of development in the area and the different economic actors involved in its daily life.

Some experiences in this regard have to do with international cooperation and the establishment of nonagricultural cooperatives such as *Forja* (blacksmiths) and *Vitria* (glaziers)—both made up of graduates of the School Workshop of the Office of the Historian of the City of Havana (OHCH)—and *El Carruaje* (coachmen). No less known is the experience of *Callejón de los Peluqueros* [Hairdressers Alley] thanks to the emergence of many businesses triggered by the Project *ArteCorte* [Art of haircutting] in the Santo Angel neighborhood of the Catedral Popular Council (Iglesias 2017). This experience includes a partnership established with the OHCH to launch a community project that offered new opportunities for the development of various enterprises—from hostels and restaurants to art galleries and studios—that in turn coordinate their work to make the project sustainable. Furthermore, the experience of Vélo Cuba—where the State not only leases premises from but also contributes public investment for private bicycle rental services—is another example of this type of partnership.

While the official discourse promotes the complementarity of economic actors in today's Cuban society, now more than ever the nature of these relations should be intentionally defined through the elimination of the obstacles to the deployment of new initiatives and the provision of special regulations that avoid the reproduction of socioeconomic differences. The multi-actor links that promote a local economy—rather than the excessive subordination to the state mechanisms—need to spread its productive forces and expedite their coordination so that, once a linkage is created, they can make the most of Cuba's current potential.

THE PRODUCTION OF HANDMADE ARTICLES
WITH GUANO CANO (CUBAN HAT PALM)
AND ITS POTENTIAL FOR THE PROMOTION
OF PUBLIC-PRIVATE PARTNERSHIPS

The community of Yarual belongs to the municipality of Bolivia in the province of Ciego de Ávila. It borders on the Bay of Jigüey to the north, the Miraflores Popular Council to the south, the municipality of Esmeralda in the province of Camagüey to the southeast and, to the southwest, on the urban Bolivia urban Popular Council located in the Great Wetland North of Ciego de Ávila, a Ramsar site since 2001. Its construction started in 1981 and finished in 1984. The aim of this community was to increase the labor force in the sugarcane fields of the old sugar mill Bolivia.

A diagnosis carried out by members of the Management Group established in this community[5] as part of the NGO Felix Varela Center's project "Strengthening environmental transformation for adaptability to climate change in Cuban communities," revealed the current situation of its residents. The private sector of the economy is not represented in any of its forms of management. The majority of the people do not have capital assets such as bank accounts, fishing vessels, or their own means of transportation. The men (Yarual is 84 percent men and 16 percent women) hold the best-paid jobs, compared with other local occupations. These jobs are in the Cayo Coco construction enterprise, the UBPC agricultural cooperative, and the rice fields.

One of the aggravating circumstances in this area is the water situation. The community has to pump water from a distance of 16 kilometers through a pipe in poor condition, collect it in a cistern, and distribute it to the buildings. The deterioration of the piping system prevents some residents from getting any water, and the groundwater is brackish owing to an increase in salinization. From the economic viewpoint, these facts disclose gaps related to the lack of resources such as access to water tank trucks or containers to store the water. Ninety-five percent of the population is in this situation.

The Yarual Workshop, made up for the most part of women weavers of guano cano (the plant they use as raw material), is one of the community's main strengths. It belongs to the Provincial Enterprise of Local Industries, whose social object is to manufacture and sell nonfood products.

Officially, the enterprise is engaged in eleven branches of production of goods and services in small numbers or made-to-order to maximize the regional potential, improve the quality and creativity of the artisans, guarantee production efficiency, and make a profit for the economy and society. It is also in charge of marketing its production.

However, the work of those directly engaged in production suffers limitations and inefficiency. In an interview with these women weavers, one said, "these products are mainly sold to the Fondo Cubano de Bienes Culturales (Cuban Stock of Cultural Assets) tourist stalls in hotels and Plan Turquino entities," although the local residents are also their customers. The main hope of those who weave Guano Cano is to be able to market their output directly and make more money.

The Workshop has a total number of 13 female employees whose production target is 326 bags per month, each priced at CUP 6.50. Among their main products are baskets of different sizes, bathroom bins, ornaments, and brooms. These workers get a bag of toiletries twice a year. In this respect, they receive no other benefits than those allocated to their daily and mass production targets. Another important fact of their current situation is that the main provider of Guano Cano is the municipal Forestry Base Enterprise Unit (BEU), which sells the raw material to the local industry.

This reality suffers from many difficulties found at the root of the system. There is no connection with industrial development at local or regional level, so it would be useful to take advantage of the existing potential with a view to streamlining the links between the various forms management and property. The lack of an organized system in tune with regional interests and objectives draws a veil over the existing potential for development.

Therefore, a proposal designed to establish public-private partnerships is likely to facilitate local development and make it more dynamic, based on the sustainable exploitation of Guano Cano for local production purposes. The objective would be to foster public-private partnerships through the production of handmade articles with guano cano, a distinct product in the region and the country.

It is important to point out that right now this workshop operates in a building that is public property and therefore an asset under state control. In this respect, a partnership with the private sector can pave the way for a more efficient management, maintenance and operation of the building. This also means that the Workshop could become—in a socially responsible manner—a nonagricultural cooperative, which would lead to the creation of jobs by hiring labor to fill certain vacant positions. Likewise, another benefit of the partnership is that it can facilitate the establishment of vocational study circles to teach local children and teenagers to weave with this plant and to preserve it in places with salinized soil such as Yarual, which would favor links with grassroots organizations.

This article presents a proposal for the establishment and implementation of a public–private partnership in three steps or stages—design, organization, and monitoring and evaluation—that share some key elements that the authors have identified in the community.

Design Stage

Conception of the idea, the main objective, and the type of partnership established, while recognizing the link between two or more actors. This stage is based on a horizontal structure with greater autonomy, reaching a consensus and signing an adequate contract between the parties.

The key stakeholders in the Yarual community are the Guano Cano Forestry UEB, the Provincial Enterprise of Local Industries, women entrepreneurs who can obtain licenses in non-state employment activities (and form a nonagricultural cooperative), local government bodies, the NGO Centro Félix Varela, Plan Turquino, the rice-growing enterprise, and the population in general. Regardless of which actor starts the process to establish a public-private partnership, what is certain is that there are common guidelines on the relations between the actors depending on where their partnership originates.

This is also where mechanisms can be set up for dialogue and agreement between the actors with the support of the Centro Félix Varela and its previous experiences with Regional Dialogue (Centro Félix Varela 2020). In addition, links with other institutions such as the Center for Studies on the Cuban Economy (CEEC) and its teachings on the conception of a Business Plan for local initiatives are very useful.

Organization Stage

Raise awareness of the need for more resources and less bureaucratic barriers to reach certain goals. The involvement of particular strategic actors is crucial in this stage, irrespective of the previous survey of economic and social actors. A *project* should be formulated for the development of the partnership as such. In this way, a horizontal relationship makes it possible to understand the structural configuration of a process with the various forms of management—state and non-state—at the center of the initiative under study.

It is important to understand some of the principles underlying this structure. The 2018 Peoples' Summit (Confederación Latinoamericana y del Caribe de Trabajadores Estatales 2018) laid down the Social and Solidarity Economy principles found at the root of the type of partnerships addressed in this article, namely:

1. Equality: promotion of equality in all relations and of the balanced fulfillment of the interests of all people engaged in these activities.
2. Employment: promotion of employment opportunities, most specially for the disadvantaged, who must be guaranteed decent working conditions and salaries and the possibility to develop as human beings.

3. Interaction with the environment: all production methods and actions of the organization must respect the environment and contribute to its protection.
4. Cooperation: the aim is to facilitate cooperation among the members of the organization and between the latter and its surrounding environment.
5. Absence of profit motives: the benefits derived from the processes must be used in nonprofit solidarity initiatives or cooperation projects.
6. Commitment to the environment: there must be an all-out commitment to the social environment and to the cooperation with other organizations that live on it.

The suggested name of the initiative is Mujeres tejedoras del Guano Cano (Women Weavers of Guano Cano)[6] and its goal to market handmade articles of Guano Cano through the promotion of public-private partnerships aimed at local development. This initiative would be essentially directed toward the local population with a view to creating jobs and working in harmony with the strategies of the regional development plan identified by the municipal government.

The above will lead to the empowerment of the women producers and other local women engaged in this process, customer diversification, payment without intermediaries for marketed goods, and the provision of services at affordable and differential prices for low-income groups, single mothers, and socially disadvantaged families.

Monitoring and Evaluation Stage

Indicators are determined according to the expected service to be provided, the development achieved during the organization process and the binding contract previously signed. These indicators must meet the above-mentioned solidarity principles. In this stage, the participation of the various actors, both public and private, focuses on the use of new mechanisms. It is a question of following up on the accomplishments, obstacles, lessons learned, and future projections.

These stages are just a contribution to the strengthening of public–private partnerships in the community of Yarual. From the achievement of a local development project and the coordination of various economic actors recognized in Cuban society will come a product capable of revitalizing the current situation and seizing the existing potential according to the available opportunities.

FINAL CONSIDERATIONS

- The public-private partnerships need a conceptual definition tailored to the current arrangement of the Cuban social and labor structure. An interpretation based on political economy may bring to light the need to reach a political understanding and a strategic definition of the binding nature of these relations.
- Some actions are under way with a view to public-private partnerships; the official discourse explicitly recognizes the complementarity of economic actors and there is knowledge about a number of related good practices. However, they have not managed yet to organize a participatory form of management at grassroots level or an *intentional* multi-actor structure to promote initiatives of this kind that could connect in turn with the existing regional development strategies. The necessary conditions to build this kind of relations are either not yet in place or insufficient in number.
- The communities should use their potential to strengthen their role and meet the most pressing needs of their residents using existing local and provincial strategies. They still fail to take advantage of existing capacities or use them for the benefit of their residents.
- The experience of Guano Cano is a potential resource for the community of Yarual. The coordinated development of its productions, the economic and social recognition of its producers and the real possibility to create jobs by encouraging a harmonic and sustainable link with nature can pave the way for, among others, the replacement of imports and the promotion of social equity using the opportunities that the Cuban Government offers them.

NOTES

1. With acknowledgment of and appreciation for Ania Mirabal Patterson's contribution to the analysis.

2. The objective of the project is to contribute to increase the resilience of the chosen communities based on strengthening the environmental transformations for adaptability to climate change in local development processes. It covers the period from 2020 to 2022.

3. For the purposes of this article, the terms relations, alliances, partnerships, cooperation, and coordination are used interchangeably, depending on the views of the authors cited.

4. Resolution 33/2011 of the Ministry of Labor and Social Security centered on the process of organization and control of the self-employed workers (TCP) and

established their duties and the steps to register their activity. This document served its purpose, but Resolution 41/2013 of the same Ministry, which stipulated Regulations for self-employment, eventually revoked it. This Resolution authorizes new activities for self-employment, together with their scope and the entities that allow their exercise. Resolution 42/2013 of the Ministry of Labor and Social Security extends to 201 the number of activities authorized for self-employment (Soto, 2019).

5. The Management Group is made up of several residents of the community and its coordinator is Ana Manzano, an official of the Ministry of Science, Technology and the Environment.

6. Two residents of the community who attended a workshop on business planning models suggested this name. Its acceptance in the community should be a collective decision agreed by those who are engaged in the initiative.

BIBLIOGRAPHY

Cardona, R., and L. Sariego. *Guía metodológica para la formación y gestión de alianzas público-privadas para el desarrollo.* [Methodological guide to the formation and management of public–private partnerships for development]. Fundación para la Sostenibilidad y la Equidad ALIARSE 2010.

Centro Félix Varela. "Fortalecimiento de transformaciones ambientales para la adaptabilidad al cambio climático desde comunidades cubanas " [Strengthening environmental transformations for adaptability to climate change in Cuban communities]. La Habana: Centro Félix Varela, Documento de proyecto, 2020.

Confederación Latinoamericana y del Caribe de Trabajadores Estatales. Declaración final de la Cumbre de los Pueblos [Final Declaration of the Summit of the Peoples], 2018. Retrieved from: http://clate.org.

D'Angelo, O., and F. D. Morillas. "Gestión de alianzas multiactorales, intersectoriales y subjetividades-prácticas para una cultura solidaria del desarrollo local-comunitario" [Managing multi-stakeholder, inter-sectoral alliances and practical subjectivities for a solidary culture of local-community development]. La Habana: Simposio Internacional CIPS, 2019.

Donahue, J. D., and R. J. Zeckhauser. *Collaborative Governance: Private Roles for Public Goals in Turbulent Times.* Princeton University Press, 2011.

Grupo Banco Mundial. Acerca de las Asociaciones Público-privadas [On public-private partnerships], World Bank, 2019. Retrieved from: https://ppp.worldbank.org/public –private-partnership/es/asociaciones-publico-privadas/acerca.

Hood, C. "A Public Management for all seasons?" *Public Administration.* (69): 3–19, 1991.

Iglesias, M. "La Economía Social y Solidaria en la Gestión Integral del Centro Histórico de La Habana" [Social and Solidarity Economics in the Comprehensive Management of the Historical Center of Havana]. Oficina del Historiador de la Ciudad de La Habana, Plan Maestro, 2017.

MEP. Cuba y su desafío económico y social. Síntesis de la Estrategia Económica y Social para el impulso de la economía y el enfrentamiento de la crisis mundial provocada por la COVID-19 [Cuba and its economic and social challenge. Synthesis of the Economic and Social Strategy por stimulating the economy and tackling the global crisis caused by COVID-19]. Tabloide Especial, La Habana: Ministerio de Economía y Planificación, Julio 2020. Retrieved from: https://www.mep.gob.cu/es /documento/cuba-y-su-desafio-economico-y-social.

Mesa Redonda. "Palabras del ministro de Economía y Planificación" [Words of the Minister of Economics and Planning for Cuban TV]. 16 July 2020. Retrieved from: https://www.youtube.com/watch?v=NSlCPjr2KaA.

Ministerio de Trabajo y Seguridad Social. "Resolución 33/2011 Reglamento del ejercicio del trabajo por cuenta propia" [Resolution 33/2011 Regulations for the exercise of self-employment]. La Habana: Gaceta Oficial No. 29 Extraordinaria de 7 de septiembre de 2011.

———. "Resolución 41/2013 Reglamento del ejercicio del trabajo por cuenta propia" [Resolution 41/2013 Regulations for the exercise of self-employment]. La Habana: Gaceta Oficial No. 27 Extraordinaria de 26 de septiembre de 2013.

———. "Resolución 42/2013 Actividades que se pueden ejercer como trabajo por cuenta propia" [Resolution 42/2013 Activities that can be carried out by self-employed workers]. La Habana: Gaceta Oficial No. 27 Extraordinaria de 26 de septiembre de 2013.

MINJUS. "Decreto Ley 300/2012. Sobre la Entrega de Tierras Estatales Ociosas en Usufructo, de 20 de septiembre de 2012" [Law-Decree 300/2012 On the allocation of fallow lands in usufruct]. La Habana: Gaceta Oficial de la República de Cuba, Edición Extraordinaria, No. 9, Febrero 6, 2014.

———. "Decreto Ley 312/2013. Régimen especial de la seguridad social de los creadores, artistas, técnicos y personal de apoyo, así como de la protección especial a los trabajadores asalariados del sector" [Law-Decree 312/2013 Special social security treatment for performers, artists, technicians and support personnel, as well as special protection for salaried workers in the industry]. La Habana: Gaceta Oficial de la República de Cuba, Edición Extraordinaria, No. 14, de 7 de abril de 2017.

———. "Decreto Ley 259/2008. Sobre la Entrega de Tierras Ociosas en Usufructo, de 10 de julio de 2008"[Law-Decree 259/2008 On the allocation of fallow lands in usufruct, July 10, 2008]. La Habana: Gaceta Oficial de la República de Cuba, Edición Extraordinaria, No. 24, 11 julio de 2008.

Monreal, P. "¿Hacia una alianza estratégica público-privada en Cuba?" [Strategic public-private alliance in Cuba?]. *Rebelión*, 2020. Retrieved from: https://rebelion .org/hacia-una-alianza-estrategica-publico-privado-en-cuba/.

Núñez, R., K. Cobarrubias, and T. Delgado. "La articulación entre el sector estatal y no estatal: Con todas las manos" [The articulation between the state and non-state sectors: All hands on deck].In Programa conjunto PNUD. Fondo para el logro de los ODM, 2013.

Oleas, D. "Alianzas público-privadas y desarrollo territorial" [Public–private partnerships and regional development]. Serie Territorios en Debate, no. 6. (Consorcio de Gobiernos Autónomos Provinciales del Ecuador (CONGOPE), 2017. Retrieved from: https://biblio.flacsoandes.edu.ec/libros/digital/57081.pdf.

PCC. *Conceptualización del Modelo Económico y Social Cubano de Desarrollo y Plan Nacional de Desarrollo Económico y Social hasta 2030* [Conceptualization of the Cuban Economic and Social Development Model and National Plan for Economic and Social Development until 2030]. La Habana: VI Congreso del Partido Comunista de Cuba, 2016a

———. "Documentos del 7mo Congreso del Partido aprobados por el III Pleno del Comité Central del PCC" [Documents of the 7th Congress approved by the III Plenum of the Central Committee of the PCC]. Partido Comunista de Cuba, 2017.

———. *Lineamientos de la Política Económica y Social del Partido y la Revolución* [Guidelines for the Economic and Social Policy of the Party and the Revolution]. La Habana: VI Congreso del Partido Comunista de Cuba, 2011

———. *Lineamientos de la Política Económica y Social del Partido y la Revolución* [Guidelines for the Economic and Social Policy of the Party and the Revolution]. La Habana: VII Congreso del Partido Comunista de Cuba, 2017

———. *Propuesta de Visión de la Nación, Ejes y Sectores Estratégicos* [Proposed Vision of the Nation, Strategic Lines and Sectors]. La Habana: VI Congreso del Partido Comunista de Cuba, 2016b.

Pliscoff, C., and J. P. Araya. "Las alianzas público-privadas como gatilladoras de innovación en las organizaciones públicas: Reflexiones a partir de la situación chilena." *Revista Chilena de Administración Pública* 19: 173–98, 2012. https://revistaeggp.uchile.cl/index.php/REGP/article/view/21180.

PNUD Cuba. "Objetivos de Desarrollo Sostenible y el Sector Privado" [Sustainable Development Objectives and the private sector]. 2019. Retrieved from: https://www.cu.undp.org/content/cuba/es/home/sustainable-development-goals.html.

Robinson, H., P. Carrillo, C. J. Anumba, and M. Patel. *Governance and Entrepreneurial Knowledge for Public-Private Partnerships*. UK: Wiley-Blackwell, 2010.

Savas, E. "Taxonomy of Privatization Strategies." *Policy Studies Review* 18 (2): 110–28, 1990.

Soto, L. "Sector privado y contrato económico: reflexiones en el marco de la actualización del modelo económico cubano" [Private sector and economic contract: reflections on the framework for updating the Cuban economic model]. La Habana: *Revista Estudios del Desarrollo Social: Cuba y América Latina* (7), 2019.

Tabares, L., C. M. Pérez, and O. Cárdenas. "Papel de la administración pública en la relación público-privada" [Role of public administration in public-private relations]. *Folletos Gerenciales* 23 (2): 117–26, 2019. Retrieved from: https://folletosgerenciales.mes.gob.cu/index.php/folletosgerenciales/article/view/208/219.

Triana, Juan. "Lo público, lo privado y el bienestar" [The public, the private and well-being]. OnCubaNews, 2020. Retrieved from: https://oncubanews.com/opinion/columnas/contrapesos/lo-publico-lo-privado-y-el-bienestar/.

Williamson, O. "The Logic of Economic Organization." *Journal of Law, Economics, & Organization* 4 (1): 65–93, 1988.

Chapter 9

Business Social Responsibility of the State Enterprise

The Experience of the Center of Molecular Immunology

Jusmary Gómez Arencibia and Mirlena Rojas Piedrahita

During the past several years the Social Labor Studies Group [Grupo de Estudios Sociales del Trabajo (GEST)] of the Cuban Psychological and Sociological Research Center [Centro de Investigaciones Psicológicas y Sociológicas (CIPS)], has focused its research on the topic of business social responsibility—BSR (RSE in Spanish). This activity is collected in the results of the research carried out during the last few years (M. Rojas, J. Gómez and H. Piedra, et al. 2016) (M. Rojas, J. Gómez, et al. 2019).[1]

RSE has progressed from a philanthropic and economistic view toward the incorporation of social and ecological dimensions. It is a multidimensional concept in which ethical, legal, social, economic, participatory, and environmental components play a fundamental role. In turn, this change of paradigm is related to the new perspectives developed within the social, economic, juridical, and business sciences during the second half of the twentieth century and so far in the twenty-first. This definition is set within a grid that includes other topics: business, stakeholder groups,[2] local development, public policies, business and environmental sustainability, judicial systems, and political will.

The topic of RSE gains ground and evolves with the dynamics imposed by the globalization processes, the acceleration of economic activities, and the emerging development of an ecological awareness facing an increase in environmental issues. Also influencing the issue are the upsurge of new information technologies and telecommunications, the economic and social crisis, the prominence assumed by the territories within the strategies of local development, the deterioration of productive and labor activities, the transformation of labor relations. and the exacerbation of inequality and social exclusion processes.

Cuban academics (M. Rojas, J. Gómez and H. Piedra, et al. 2016) consider that there is a mechanical association made between *being socialist* and *being socially responsible*. They also propose that there is a tendency to naturalize RSE within the social system—that RSE is dislocated from the business activity—and within the existing regulations.

The fundamental objective of this article is to reveal the achievements and the challenges of RSE in Cuba, with particular emphasis on the Center for Molecular Immunology (Centro de Inmunología Molecular—CIM). This entity is a Cuban state enterprise under the Organización Superior de Desarrollo Empresarial (OSDE)[3] BioCubaFarma. Together with other organizations, it constitutes part of the knowledge-based sector of the Cuban economy (Rojas and Gómez 2011).

The chapter is organized in two sections: the first puts forward the theoretical assumptions of the topic; the second presents this reality at CIM. The contribution of this chapter is particularly centered on revealing the good practices of RSE that are implemented at CIM, as well as its areas of improvement. Some reflections on the achievements and the limitations of this reality in Cuba will serve to enhance these pages.

CONCEPTUAL BASES OF BUSINESS
SOCIAL RESPONSIBILITY

This section aims to present the main trends in the theoretical approach to RSE, both in the international and in the national context. Other notions which contribute to the conceptual map of RSE are also connected.

The International Context

The concept of RSE has several meanings and has its base in various theoretical suppositions. We are taking as a reference the works of (Garriga and Melé 2004) who identify four groups of theories that are the foundation of the topic addressed:

- Instrumental theories: these associate the development of RSE activities in businesses to actions linked to obtaining better economic benefits for their shareholders. In this way, they establish a direct relation between

RSE and the creation of wealth (Friedman 1970; Murray and Montanari 1986; Porter and Kramer 2002).

- Integrative theories: these explain the development of RSE activities through the desire to integrate various social needs, like the compliance with laws and public policies, and balanced management of the specific benefits to the stakeholders (Carroll 1979; Jones 1980; Vogel Winter 1986; Wilcox 2005).
- Theories with a political slant: these emphasize the social power that the entity acquires, as it finds itself inserted into a society. They explain the existence of a social relation or contract between the enterprises and the community, resulting from the power and influence that each enterprise has on the economy (Davis 1960; Donaldson and Dunfee 1994; Wood and Lodgson 2002).
- Theories on ethics and morality: these study the development of RSE activities as a response to the compliance with universal rights[4]; they consider business activities which pay attention to the progress of the present as well as that of future generations (Freeman 1983; Kaku 1997; Annan 1999; Chomali and Majluf 2007).

From the perspective of a critical analysis, these theories have not progressed because of their disjointed and restricted view on the topic. What currently predominates is the need for a systemic viewpoint of RSE, based on the sustainability of corporate actions. Some studies (Korin 2011; Instituto Ethos 2016) recognize the lack of knowledge about RSE from a standpoint that encompasses this view. In these studies, one can see the tendency to business voluntarism (donations, welfare, philanthropy), but the models linked to good practices, the full exercise of rights, economic, social, and cultural inclusion in value chains are scarce. The preceding does not include the sustainability of socially responsible actions, and therefore it is more a question of short-term amenability than of obtaining medium and long-term benefits.

Backing a systemic viewpoint in the treatment of RSE takes us to the understanding of the term from a perspective centered on the sustainability of business actions. In this sense, RSE provides a vision of business with responsible citizenship integrated into the business strategy beyond the legal obligations (Villalobos Grzybowicz 2011). This issue directs us to a 180-degree turn in the perspective that points to *business sustainability.* According to Betancourt (May–August 2016), the change of the wording corresponds to the progress of a conservative corporate climate that avoids the association of the words *social* and *corporate*, while *sustainability* becomes more acceptable as it suggests the environmental dimension, as long as *the social* is included, but not explicitly.

The foregoing implies a metamorphosis in the paradigm of the ways of seeing and doing by the people who create businesses, confronting the ways of directing, managing, and including systemic viewpoints of RSE into their internal and external scope of activities. These systems occupy the economic, social, ethical, environmental, legal, cultural, and participatory aspects. Their essence is defined in the relationship with their workers, with the surrounding community and the different stakeholders with which they interact.

Various authors (Vives and Peinado 2011), institutions (Instituto Ethos, Brazil; Fundación Avina, Argentina; Consorcio Ecuatoriano de Responsabilidad Social; PROhumana, Chile), and international organizations—the Interamerican Development Bank (IDB), the International Organization of Labor (ILO), the UN Economic Commission on Latin America and the Caribbean (ECLAC), the Organization for Economic Cooperation and Development (OECD)—focus on the topic of RSE from a systemic viewpoint, and they are the main sources for identifying some of its details. These could be summarized by the following concepts: centered on the sustainability of the activities of social responsibility; multidimensional character; anchored in a strategic and business management perspective; encourages the interrelation of the enterprise with its stakeholders; influences both consumers and investors; offers transparency in its corporate activities and carries out a responsible management of the working conditions and of occupational safety and health.

In their formulation, the relation between the enterprise and the community acquires another nuance. The businesses in a particular area constitute an important stronghold and one of the key movers that can contribute to local development. The enterprises should contribute to the satisfaction of the needs of their workers and of the surrounding population. This can be achieved through the creation of jobs, social security, and maintenance and protection of the surroundings. Adopting this valuation can have substantial consequences, and the scope of their actions may be significant, hence the importance of undertaking a responsible behavior in and from the enterprise itself.

The contemporary debates mainly concentrate on the need to establish boundaries between the natural resources and the requirements that societies impose on the enterprises. They recognize the importance of having a strategic vision of the business practices associated fundamentally with eco-efficiency, with the triple approach between the economic, the social, and the environmental, as well as with inclusive business practices. Emphasis is placed on the importance that businesses have in the area of the community, where their actions should include raising the quality of life, not only of its employees but also of the community because of their influence on it and as an active part of it.

In an effort to making RSE visible, several initiatives have been developed that promote business activities focused in this way: the declaration related to the fundamental labor principles and rights, established by the ILO (1998); the Global Compact (2000)[5] established by the United Nations; the creation of the Consejo Estatal de RSE [RSE State Council] in 2015, affiliated to the Government of Spain's Ministry dedicated to matters of public policy for the stimulation and development of RSE.

Currently, the function of RSE is acquiring increased relevance in the efforts to clarify what its role should be as a preventive antidote of irresponsible business or institutional behaviors. It allows the identification of what measure it could contribute to finding consistent solutions to the crisis, with the purpose of establishing the foundations for refurbishing the rules of the game. These should be based on an ethical management, a greater and better accountability, and an amplification of the confidence and credibility of the stakeholders (enterprises, governments, unions, and representatives of civil society), strengthened by an authentic legitimacy (Jiménez Araya 2019).

In spite of these advances, in the Latin American region action focused on charity and philanthropy based on the expansion of the private sector takes precedence. The development of these *welfare activities* allows businesses and their owners to enjoy the benefits of exemptions, bonuses, and other tax advantages (Drucker and Maciarello 2008). In this way, RSE becomes a business strategy that is of benefit to the owners, in detriment to the stakeholders with which they interact.

For the countries of Latin America and the Caribbean, this is the time to prepare or improve public policies, instruments for strengthening and supporting RSE initiatives, and then go beyond a passive governmental position to elaborate an RSE agenda; one that involves all sectors of the economy, from the small and medium businesses to the multinationals; and that will enable a synergy between all the stakeholders in this new process. From this region several institutions[6] can be recognized that break with the foregoing. These contribute to the legitimation of socially responsible businesses and to the retrieval of the good practices, strategies and management models of RSE that can be replicated.

In spite of the benefits and the advantages that RSE offers, we need to remember that it emerged from the capitalist context. It started as a way to clean up the image of the exploitative business which, as part of its *marketing* incorporates actions (inventory, documentation) of charitable work toward the community, and this image serves as an instrument to achieve a more advantageous positioning in the market (Reyes 2018). A facade as a *socially responsible enterprise* is repeatedly peddled in order to acquire the backing of its stakeholders, which causes the image of what is generally known as RSE to be devalued and discredited.

Signs of the development of a socially responsible consciousness appear as being contradictory when the characteristics of the contemporary world are analyzed: environmental deterioration, persistence of poverty and of situations that generate social inequality, unemployment and underemployment, salary gaps (relating to gender, age, skin color, ethnicity, religious beliefs, geographical areas) and financial crisis—just to mention some of the problems. We need to ask about the socially responsible activities of the large transnationals that direct and control the global economy, about their sustainability paradigms and their commitment to future generations.

It is obvious that the changes and transformations that can be implemented—through RSE strategies—are not by themselves enough, nor can they be left to the *business will*. It is necessary to make agreements on public-private alliances, to be included in the agenda of public policies, to ensure that the steps to be taken not be of benefit to some few people or to the businesses, but that they promote equity and social justice.

An Approach to RSE from the Cuban Context

Until the end of the last century, the theoretical debate on RSE was absent from the national scientific productions. Even as measures were implemented and transformations were institutionalized that contributed to the development of a socially responsible awareness, conditions were not ripe for the development of an academic debate on the subject. The environmental topics, the community projection, labor rights, the social importance of businesses beyond their profitability, formed part of the preceding era, but it was not until the end of the 1990s that the subject began to be broached by the national scientific community.

In the last few decades the topic reached new heights in the country because of the activities of several institutions.[7] Even if it is difficult to identify tendencies within these approaches, it is possible to find some homogeneity in their attitude: the link of the enterprise with its stakeholders (the community, the environment), its contributions to local development, its naturalization within the Cuban socialist system, its emphasis on the management and participation processes, as well as its multidimensional character present in its conceptual implementations (M. Rojas, J. Gómez, and H. Piedra, et al. 2016).

Steps are being taken that contribute to the articulation of the contributions of studies on the topic supported by various centers at the national level. However, its absence in the business environment—the parceling up of the good practices of RSE, without integrating or systematizing them— has caused the outlines to become blurred. The same is happening with the absence of this topic in the national legislative context; its lack of visibility in the programmatic documents that today rule the process of Updating of the

Cuban Economic and Social Model—and the proof of that is the nonexistence of laws that protect or promote it.

These absences are the result of the concentration and verticalization of the power of the Cuban state with few ideas of RSE, of the limitations in incentives for stimulating enterprises, the resistance to separate and decentralize the management mechanisms in state enterprises, as well as the zeal to legislate business success. The impacts that businesses generate in the regions are not recognized, and there is a lack of knowledge on how to manage in a socially responsible manner, with practices that take into account the interests of the different stakeholders. A lack of training and education on these topics and on the ways to integrate RSE in the strategies of municipal development can also be observed. Moreover, an excessive centralization in the decisions regarding financing of investment—especially long-term—are also noted, which makes it impossible for all organisms and sectors involved to participate (Cruz, et al. 2015).

Based on the review of the chronologies (M. Rojas, J. Gómez, and H. Piedra, et al. 2016), and the systematizations (Korin 2011; Instituto Ethos 2016) within the framework of these pages, we accept the following definition of RSE:

> A form of business management with a multidimensional character (ethical, social, economic, legal, environmental, participatory) which includes the commitment to generate value in coherence with the development of sustainable, verifiable and intentional practices. It is expressed in the interaction of the enterprise with its stakeholders in a particular context, aiming for equity and social justice. (M. Rojas, J. Gómez, and H. Piedra, et al. 2016)

Even if this concept, expressing our theoretical commitment, is adopted by the research group, in the current Cuban context it is seen as requiring a greater emphasis on the social aspect—within its multidimensional perspective. The fundamental contribution of the Cuban socialist system should concentrate its attention on the participation of the workers as the main owners of the means of production.

Several analytical dimensions can be gleaned for the topic that is of interest here, which serve as an objective examination for the practical experience implemented at CIM. From this definition (M. Rojas, J. Gómez, and H. Piedra, et al. 2016, 13), the following dimensions of RSE can be identified:

- Ethical: a group of values, standards and principles reflected in the culture of the enterprise in order to share them with its stakeholders from a humanistic perspective.

- Social: activities directed toward guaranteeing the quality of life at work, from the perspective of equity and well-being, at the individual, group, organizational, community, and social levels, and taking into account the diversity of the stakeholders.
- Legal: current judicial regulations on structure and functioning, both as related to the internal and external sides of the enterprise, of obligatory fulfillment, in a particular context.
- Economic: the generation of assets, in harmony with the development of sustainable, verifiable, and intended practices.
- Participatory: the degree of involvement and participation of the workers in decision-making within the working environment, and their reflection in the interrelations of the enterprise with its stakeholders.
- Environmental: the sustainable use of natural resources and materials, preservation of biodiversity, prevention and control of undesirable effects of human actions.

The dimensions of RSE have a dual and crossover character. These are shown both internally and external to the enterprise. And these characteristics make it difficult to set limits to their presentation.

THE CENTER OF MOLECULAR IMMUNOLOGY AS A SOCIALLY RESPONSIBLE ENTERPRISE

This section is aimed at presenting the good practices of RSE as developed at CIM. To start with, we provide a brief characterization of CIM, which serves as an opening to the presentation of the socially responsible activities of this enterprise.

The Center for Molecular Immunology (CIM)

CIM is a biotechnological enterprise, property of the Cuban state, belonging to the OSDE BioCubaFarma (2013).[8] It is devoted to the research, production, and commercialization of biotechnological medications. It presents sustainable investigative and economic results, the result of the investment policies and the development of its scientific potential.[9]

It has a solid foundation of intellectual property, consisting of more than sixty inventions and more than seven hundred foreign patents, of which four hundred have been granted. It has twenty-two medications in production— sixteen of which are protected by patents issued in Cuba (seven are registered, ten in clinical trials, and five in a preclinical phase). These results gradually and continuously require its growth both in infrastructure and in personnel.

The center has a director general and a vertical organizational structure. It is set up in five categories: Quality, Commercialization, Research and Development, Industrial Operations, Administration, and Services. Its work strategy is based on a management and processes approach.[10]

The technology on which the research and production processes are based follows international standards. Work is done individually and by research groups, especially those devoted to scientific activity. The center has a total of 1,108 workers—among whom women and young people are the majority—and of these, 44 have a PhD and 150 have a master's degree.

The stakeholders of the center are identified in the CIM *Manual of Communications Management* (Centro de Inmunología Molecular 2012):[11]

- Internal: directors, specialists, administration and services.
- External: suppliers, buyers, hospitals and national oncology centers, spokespersons of national and international research centers, patients and families, students (university and secondary schools), communications media, governing organisms, the community and the general public.
- Mixed: centers of production and commercialization, interns or students working on their thesis, collaborators from other centers.

The social objective of the unit, as approved by Resolution 786, is stated as:

The investigation, production, development and commercialization of monoclonal antibodies and other recombinant proteins used for the diagnosis and the treatment of cancer and other diseases related to the immune system. To introduce them into the Cuban Public Health system and make the scientific-productive activities sustainable, so that they become economic contributions to the country. (Centro de Inmunología Molecular 2020)

The Center's mission is specified as:

Obtaining and producing new biopharmaceuticals destined for the treatment of cancer and other non-transmissible chronic diseases, and introduce them into the Cuban Public Health system. Making the scientific and productive activity sustainable by contributing to the economy of the country. (Centro de Inmunología Molecular 2017)

The vision established in its strategic project is:

Within a short period, we can become an organization that generates resources for the country, with a tangible impact in [rates of] cancer survival in Cuba, operate scientific-productive institutions in Cuba and in other countries, in a sustainable manner for the economy, as well as for the quality of the products. (Centro de Inmunología Molecular 2017)

The enterprise has a responsibility toward its suppliers, consumers, and clients. As related to the first group: to appropriately fulfilling its contracts and commitments, and informing them of its values and code of conduct, while motivating them to develop a positive attitude, of respect and effective compliance with the rights of their workers. At the same time, the responsibility toward clients and consumers is exercised by the permanent concern for developing trustworthy products and services which reduce to a minimum the health risks of the population by providing the appropriate information on the potential risks of the products.

The human being is the ultimate objective of these products, and so their health, quality, of life and well-being must be at the center of the target. Because of this, there is persistence in motivating the change of mentality toward a scientific dialogue and toward the permanent search for possible errors in the hypotheses before undertaking any R+D+i [research, development, and innovation] which does not comply rigorously with the required scientific results (Delgado Fernández 2017).

Is CIM a Socially Responsible Enterprise?

Responding to this question is difficult because the discussions around this topic are filled with inconclusive controversies. Without denying the importance of the areas with clear need for improvement, it is considered that CIM is an enterprise that has a socially responsible projection, that develops activities that go beyond what is required, and which achieves impacts in its environment and in its interaction with its stakeholders. It is possible to identify a group of good practices that can be systematized and applied to other entities of this and other sectors. On the other hand, CIM does not escape from the national reality. Its socially responsible activities do not enjoy complete integration or feedback. The confusion about the topic, the legal gaps, the lack of a system that integrates RSE and the fact that it forms part of the entrepreneurial strategy are constantly lurking.

As a Cuban state enterprise, and through the very fact of being inserted in a system that is socialist in character, the revenues generated are distributed by the state, for the benefit of the whole society. This is a key factor that allows for the understanding that the economic profits generated by the enterprise are not bestowed on a particular person or group, but that they fulfill a social function with a broad scope and more equitable aims.[12] In such a delicate sector as health, where high profits are the order of the day internationally—because of which the ethics of the pharmaceutical sector are often in doubt—in this case there is greater transparency where the human being is the prime beneficiary. Public health in Cuba has universal accessibility and is free, which allows for everyone to benefit from the contributions of this entity. Research is aimed at improving the quality of life of men and women, regardless of their social class, religion or culture, skin color, or age (M. Rojas, J. Gómez, et al. 2019).

In the 2016 General Report, the director stated that about 9,000 Cuban patients and 150,000 patients of other countries had benefited from the results of the center, while at the same time he noted the vaccine against lung cancer. The sales of that year were over 230 million Cuban pesos, with exports to thirty countries (Delgado Fernández 2017).

The socialist state enterprise, and particularly CIM, has the social task to produce goods and services to be equitably distributed by the state, a basic principle of the Cuban nation. RSE, linked to the social state responsibility, questions itself about the manner in which it constitutes *an entity* that is ever more vulnerable, both from the economic and from the social point of view. This translates into the fact that the social strategic responsibility of the enterprise is not sufficient without support from the state, referring to the real possibility of autonomy and entrepreneurial management with other strategies, also of management, as is the case with the territory, of suppliers and clients.

From the legal point of view, CIM is required to comply with the provisions of the national and international regulatory agencies.[13] The foregoing have as their objective the regulation of the labor and productive processes. The reason for the strict compliance of the regulations resides in the very nature of the activity being exercised. The products being manufactured cannot be dangerous to those to whom they are directed, and who already have serious health problems. The medications that are produced have to be secure, above all. The workers at CIM are aware of the importance of their labor (M. Rojas, J. Gómez, et al. 2019).

The biotechnological sector has to comply with the good practices of production, laboratory, engineering, storage, and distribution, with the International Conference on Harmonization of Technical Requirements for Registration of Pharmaceuticals for Human Use, and the biosecurity regulations of the World Health Organization (WHO). To these are added the integration of the pharmaceutical regulatory agencies, developed within the framework of the Alianza Bolivariana para las Américas [Bolivarian Alliance for the peoples of America]. Meetings of regulatory focus, of regulatory committees between health agencies bring new instructions that must be followed. In 2013 CIM became a social state enterprise, which required its compliance with what had been established for these enterprises.

The development and training of its workers is an element classified under the good RSE practices exercised by the center. Labor competencies in the organization are reflected in the job profiles, which in their turn concur with the elements required by the regulatory agencies. These elements are assembled in the G12PNO-1135 Profile of job titles (Centro de Inmunología Molecular 2018).

The organization has a Training Plan for Good Productive Practices for all students linked to the key processes of the development, production and commercialization cycle. This early association of the students with the center has resulted in their completing their qualifications in less time, which has an effect on the sustainability of the labor productivity and on the satisfaction of the demands of the Cuban and foreign regulatory agencies.[14]

The modalities established for training are: in person, virtual, and remote. These activities are characterized by being permanent, differentiated, or stratified, according to the requirements of each job and its exercise (M. Rojas, J. Gómez, et al. 2019). They implement an external training plan that is free of charge for workers of the collaborative network. Student tutoring, both undergraduate and postgraduate, is another important element within this process.

Inside the biotechnology enterprises, workers are exposed to numerous risks.[15] The ways to prevent these are fundamentally related to the compliance with good practices in production and laboratories, to having the necessary equipment to carry out specific activities, and the identification of danger zones because of high temperatures and because of exposure to dangerous substances. CIM has a low rate of work accidents, recording an annual average of three incidents (M. Rojas, J. Gómez, et al. 2019).

At CIM there are procedures both for moral and material motivation as well as for monetary remuneration. The motivational program is supported by a budget that is established annually and is controlled through indicators that specify their efficiency and efficacy, from both the organization and the workers' sides. The moral motivation is based on the encouragement of a climate of recognition of those who meet the relevant goals and results. It is an instrument which allows the strengthening of the links between the workers and the organization. It contributes by raising the sense of belonging, and the motivation of the people toward satisfactory result in the exercise of the labor, improvement, innovation and emulation.

The salaries at the center have increased in response to specific demands, as a mechanism to retain the strength of qualified labor, and reduce labor fluctuation. It is precisely in a closed-circle enterprise—which needs qualified workers and whose training takes very long—where salary should be a stimulus for constant improvement and permanence in the organization. In Cuba there are no salary differences associated with gender or skin color.

CIM has a harmonious relation with the community, which is the result of working together and of complying with the established standards and regulations. The enterprise is located in an area of very low population. The fact that it is under national control makes its municipal role invisible. One form that this relation takes is through the interactions it has with the "Mártires del Corynthia" primary school.[16] In the local museum there is an area dedicated to the display of the history of the enterprise.

The Union of Young Communists at the Center promotes and carries out various activities: an exchange between HIV patients and scientists of the center; activities in the Pediatric Oncology halls; sponsoring the Orphanage for Children without family support in Playa municipality; science fairs that encourage the exchange of students; and support for seniors' homes of the municipality. It is the responsibility of the union and the direction of the enterprise to link retired people and the families of the workers to the activities of the enterprise, and take responsibility for their health. In addition, the enterprise also arranges and implements vacation plans for its workers.

In the literature it is indicated that the impact of this kind of enterprise on local development is low, because of its international reach, which is why they should concentrate mainly on the saving of energy and water supplies,[17] on the creation of jobs that are attractive to people with high qualifications,[18] on the insertion in the value chains of the products they develop, and on the links with educational institutions in the region as well as with local service organizations.[19]

Internationally, and likewise in Cuba, the biotechnology sector does not have an upward curve in the creation of jobs, because it is for the most part an automatized sector. The tendency is for inward development, an interconnection between the production and the value chains. The result of this linkage would generate new jobs which in their turn would support the biotechnological production, and would reduce their costs.

These enterprises are contaminating agents par excellence, although it is necessary to note that the biotechnological industry is not the greatest consumer of energy, nor the one that generates the greatest amounts of waste. This slows down their economic output and decreases the quality of life of the community residents. It is essential to reverse these elements in order to promote local development. CIM has a Security, Health, and Environmental Policy, which is implemented based on the requirements established in the current legislation. The organization continuously identifies the dangers and vulnerabilities, develops a process of evaluation and control of the risks, and has water filters and solar panels. Measures are implemented to save energy and there are activities aimed at the recycling and recuperation of raw material.

Externally, the socially responsible enterprise must be in a condition to identify the environmental impacts of its activities, with a view to reducing them. The development of its projects must consider the necessary compensations for use of natural resources and its environmental impact. The care for the environment must be present in all areas of the enterprise and in each product, process or service.

Participation is a category that interconnects with all dimensions of RSE. The socially responsible enterprise favors the organization of its workers, aims to harmonize interests, and establishes a link and transparent communication with the union on common objectives. At the same time, it offers its workers an opportunity to share the challenges of the enterprise, to get involved in the problem solving, in the achievement of jointly established goals and in personal-professional development. This year payments for patent copyrights will be started; this new law is a recognition of the participation of workers in the achievements.

In the Cuban entrepreneurial context, areas of worker participation are common, like the discussion and approval of the workers' collective agreement, the agreements on the hours of work and of rest, the analysis and the approval of regulations for the distributions of profits, the systems of the material stimulation of the workers and of the social development funds of the collective, the improvement of working and living conditions, solutions to the technological problems of production and services (the group of innovators and streamliners), emulation among workers, etc. (Rodríguez, Caballero, and Rojas 2016).

The areas for worker participation that currently exist in this organization lack a real and solid integration and interconnection among them. These fundamentally develop at the information and consultancy levels and are not aligned with the organizational strategy; this reflects a transformation that does not quite reach the essential level but rather the formal one. The participatory practice dominates at their basic levels. This determines that the fundamental strategic and tactical decisions that are related to entrepreneurial topics are essentially taken within the main collective authorities of the management, by its corresponding executives.

The center has a communication strategy in line with the general strategy of the organization and of integrated human capital management. Different communication channels[20] are used to transmit and share information and values with the workers, clients, and the surrounding area. They also use face-to-face communication, morning meetings, seminars, mailboxes (digital and conventional), and the procedure for the management of rumors as a communicative element of importance.

The current entrepreneurial management model opts for the decentralization, initiative, and self-responsibility of the enterprise—factors that can be achieved only through a system of participatory management. This system should crystallize and institutionalize the democratization mechanisms of the social relations system of the work in the socialist state enterprise, so that they cannot be damaged in their attributions and principles.

The link between centralization and decentralization in business management has a great relevance for the development and growth of this sector in the country. The high-technology industries require a decentralized management because they depend greatly on grassroots initiatives, as well as on the continued exploration of opportunities of their niche markets and the capacity of the organization to respond rapidly to them. On the other hand, the economic plan should foresee investment resources, as well as the strengthening of the productive and service chains in the country, which can consolidate and reinforce the growth of biotechnology as a sector for export and high productivity (Chico 2017).

The enterprise that is the object of this study maintains a positive cash flow that can finance its production and research and generate profits. At the same time, it adjusts fiscal commitments to the dynamics of its income and expense cycles, without violating its annual commitments. It is possible to establish reserves in national currency from its positive balance. Its financial management is centralized, with bank accounts (in national and foreign currencies) and access to credit.

CIM has the responsibility to generate profits through the value added of its products, the complete coverage of the distribution plan for the national health network, and clinical trials mostly directed toward the treatment of cancer, inside and outside the country. The foregoing does not achieve an economic balance that spills over into other social aspects that could produce new benefits in this sense (Chico 2017).

It is known that at CIM, RSE practices are carried out that are directed toward sustainable development, which is emphasized in the ethical and moral values that the enterprise presents toward their various stakeholders. Even if a complete balance is not achieved among the social, economic, and environmental components because of the limitations that have been mentioned, the desire of the center in this sense is acknowledged. There is also an awareness of the need for strategically conceiving a way for workers, for the enterprise, the community and specific structures of the society to act through collective relations based on a win-win philosophy. This is a question of supporting common sense, which starts with the enterprise but involves diverse stakeholders.

The changing circumstances and context are the scenario in which all these elements unfold and build. They shape the people involved, or the so-called stakeholders, as essential subjects who can modify and transform their reality. The real requirements and universally established rights are often decisive of the entrepreneurial management style which is sought as an inescapable human principle.

CONCLUSIONS

RSE is a topic disconnected from entrepreneurial activities. Even if it can be identified within business strategies and policies, it lacks an independent expression. It tends to be naturalized within the core of the Cuban social system, which results in making the opportunities it contributes invisible from both existing legislation and entrepreneurial practices.

Grouping current laws that applaud business social responsibility [RSE] with the aim of envisaging a judicial framework that would establish the foundations for the development and implementation of socially responsible activities.

CIM is a socially responsible enterprise. It does not elude the effects of the national and international context and circumstances in which it finds itself. However, its special assignment, its economic contributions and its development in the international and national markets, the ethical principles with which it copes, its constant searches to generate spaces for dialogue and participation toward the different levels, attest to its socially responsible actions.

The lack of autonomy of the enterprise, the excessive controls and regulations, the desire to legislate entrepreneurial success, the *regulation* of the participation on the part of certain channels, block the development of the social relations of socialist production.

There is still a need for the management of RSE to be inserted in the business strategy in an explicit manner. RSE at CIM is being managed empirically, without a basis of training or legal framework that would encourage it.

NOTES

1. With acknowledgment of and appreciation for Idania Caballero Torres's contribution to the analysis.

2. In the literature the interest groups are called stakeholders. In the context of this paper they are understood to be individuals, groups and organizations that interact directly or indirectly with the enterprise—for example entrepreneurs, suppliers/providers, workers, consumers, clients, community, region, government, mass organizations (PCC, Labor Union, UJC)—re the possibility for social change (M. Rojas, J. Gómez y H. Piedra, y otros 2016).

3. Roughly translated as "Higher Organization of Business Development," OSDEs are consortiums or business groups of public enterprises in a specific sector and owned by the same state ministry or agency.

4. Such as the respect for human rights, the rights of the workforce, the respect for the environment, the concern for sustainable development.

5. According to (Jiménez Araya 2019), up to now the [United Nations] Global Compact has signed up more than 12,000 enterprises, and around one fifth of these

have had to resign because they did not comply with some of its principles. The Compact was ratified and renewed through successive Declarations of the World [Business] Leaders' Summit, in which priority is assigned to new incentives to generate confidence and new productive models that are environmentally sustainable, because never before has there been such great need for responsibility and leadership.

6. Instituto Ethos, Brazil; Instituto Argentino de Responsabilidad Social Empresarial (IARSE); Consorcio Ecuatoriano de Responsabilidad Social (CERES); Centro Mexicano para la Filantropía (CEMEFI).

7. Centro Félix Varela; Centro de Investigaciones Psicológicas y Sociológicas (CIPS); Facultad de Economía y Centro de Estudios de Técnicas de Dirección (CETED), Universidad de La Habana; Universidad de Pinar del Río; Plan Maestro de la Oficina del Historiador de La Habana; Red Cubana de Economía Social y Solidaria y Responsabilidad Social Empresarial (ESORSE [sic]).

8. The Decree 302 creating the OSDE is dated December 2012, although CIM officially became a business enterprise July of 2013.

9. CIM has obtained 35 awards from the Cuban Academy of Sciences and has shared this distinction on 12 occasions with other entities from its Business Group (OSDE). Prize awarded by the World Organization of Intellectual Property (2002; 2015) and the experts of the Cuban Office of Property.

10. The Center has ten management processes that help it function better: formulation and control of the principal objectives, financial administration and internal control, direction of the productive and commercial activities, supervision of quality, attending to mixed businesses and the negotiations, management of projects and products, direction of the scientific activities, supervision of the clinical research, administration of the services and investments, the permanent development of the human capital.

11. This responds to the group of Cuban Standards 3000 and to Resolution 60 (which is the Governmental Accountability Office of the Republic of Cuba, 2011).

12. The redistribution, a process that is centralized by the State, brings up a critical point of the debate. At the moment of deciding on the use of its profits, in social investments at the local or community level, the enterprise finds a path to follow; at the same time this redistribution could be more tangible, palpable, for its own workers.

13. The regulatory agencies are the following:
Cuba: Centro Estatal para el Control de los Medicamentos (CECMED)
Brazil: Agencia Nacional de Vigilancia Sanitaria (ANVISA)
United States: Food and Drug Administration (FDA)
European Union: European Medicines Agency (EMEA)
Canada: Health Products and Food Branch (HPFB)

14. These capacities include students of the Polytechnic School of Industrial Chemistry "Mártires de Girón," and university students in Havana and of other provinces.

15. Among the most common risks are: chemical, chemical-biological, ergonomic, physical, electrical, by falling, fires and explosions, muscular-skeletal.

16. The programs include competitions, and recreational activities with children; they also carry out literary workshops.

17. A low energy rate and high fixed operational costs which requires the avoidance of breaks in productivity because of lack of raw material or noncompliance of Good Practices.

18. Vocational training, decrease in emigration and raising the retirement age.

19. In particular: recycling, children's daycare facilities, seniors' residences, repairs of equipment and homes, etc.

20. The communication channels of the center are: telephone, mail, internet, manuals, and murals (digital and conventional).

REFERENCES

Annan, K. 1999. "UN Global Compact." UN Press Release SG/SM/6881. World Economic Forum in Davos, Switzerland. https://www.un.org/press/en/1999 /19990201.sgsm6881.html.

ANPP. 2019. *Constitución de la República de Cuba.* La Habana: Asamblea Nacional del Poder Popular. http://www.granma.cu/file/pdf/gaceta/Nueva%20Constituci %C3%B3n%20240%20KB-1.pdf.

Betancourt, R. Mayo-Agosto 2016. "La Responsabilidad Social Empresarial en Cuba." *Estudios de Desarrollo Social: América Latina y Cuba* (FLACSO UH) 4 (2): 34–43. www.revflacso.uh.cu.

Carroll, A. 1979. "A Three-Dimensional Conceptual Model of Corporate Performance." *Academy of Management Review* 4 (4).

Centro de Inmunología Molecular. 2020. "Convenio Colectivo de Trabajo." Documento Inédito, La Habana.

———. 2017. "Informaciones del Centro de Inmunología Molecular." La Habana.

Centro de Inmunología Molecular. 2012. *Manual de Gestión de la Comunicación.* La Habana: (G12MGIC-01).

———. 2018. *Perfil de puesto de trabajo.* La Habana: G12PNO-1135.

———. 2013. "Programa de Entrenamiento de Buenas Prácticas. Aseguramiento de la calidad." La Habana.

Chico, E. 2017. "Conectando gestión y automatización en el CIM." *Revista Nueva Empresa* 7 (1): 12–16.

Chomali, F., and N. Majluf. 2007. *Ética y Responsabilidad Social en la Empresa.* Santiago de Chile: Editorial El Mercurio-Aguilar.

Cruz, M., N. Garbizo, C. González, Y. Acosta, and F. Gómez. 2015. "Metodología para la implementación de un Sistema de indicadores de Responsabilidad Social Empresarial, en los entornos locales." *Memorias del Simposio Nacional CIPS.* La Habana: Centro de Investigaciones Psicológicas y Sociológicas.

Davis, K. 1960. "Can Business Afford to Ignore Social Responsibilities?" *California Management Review* 2 (3).

Delgado Fernández, M. 2017. "Enfoque para la gestión de la I+D+i en la Industria Biofarmacéutica cubana." *Revista Cubana de Información en Ciencias de la Salud* 28 (3).

Donaldson, T., and T. Dunfee. 1994. "Toward a Unified Conception of Business Ethics: Integrative Social Contracts Theory." *Academy of Management Review* 19 (2).

Drucker, P. 1987. *La gerencia. Tareas, responsabilidades y prácticas.* Buenos Aires: ibrería El Ateneo.

Drucker, P., and J. A. Maciarello. 2008. *Management. Revised edition.* New York: HarperCollins.

Freeman, E. 1983. "Stockholders and Stakeholders: A New Perspective on Corporate Governance." *California Management Review* 25 (3).

Friedman, M. 1970. "The Social Responsibility of Business Is to Increase its Profits." *New York Times Magazine.*

Garriga, E., and D. Melé. 2004. "Corporate Social Responsibility Theories: Mapping the Territory." *Journal of Business Ethics.*

Instituto Ethos. 2016. *Los indicadores Ethos de responsabilidad social empresarial.* Brasil: Conexión ESAN. https://www.esan.edu.pe/apuntes-empresariales/2016/08/los-indicadores-ethos-de-responsabilidad-social-empresarial/.

Jiménez Araya, T. 2019. "Responsabilidad social empresarial y derechos humanos. Innovación versus Statu Quo: Retos y Oportunidades para Cuba."

Jones, T. 1980. "Corporate Social Responsibility Revisited, Redefined." *California Management Review* 22 (3).

Kaku, R. 1997. "The path of Kyosei." *Harvard Business Review* 75 (4).

Korin, M. 2011. *El camino de la Responsabilidad Social Empresarial en América Latina y la contribución de la Fundación Avina.* Buenos Aires, Argentina: Avina Foundation.

Martin, J. L. s.f. "La Participación en la economía. Algunas reflexiones para el debate." In *Participación social en Cuba*, edited by A. J. Pérez García. Editorial Ciencias Sociales.

MINJUS. 2014. "Código del Trabajo." *Gaceta Oficial de la República de Cuba, 29 (Extraordinaria),* 6–17.

Murray, K., and J. Montanari. 1986. "Strategic Management of the Socially Responsible Firm: Integrating Management and Marketing Theory." *Academy of Management Review.* 11 (4).

Porter, M., and M. R. Kramer. 2002. "The Competitive Advantage of Corporate Philanthropy." *Harvard Business Review.*

Reyes, A. 2018. *Reflexiones sobre la Responsabilidad Social Empresarial ante contradicciones del cuentapropismo y la empresa estatal en Cuba.* Tesina para el Diplomado Sociedad Cubana, La Habana: Fondos biliográficos del CIPS.

Rodríguez, F., I. Caballero, and M. Rojas. 2016. "El sistema de dirección participativa como soporte de la estrategia de la empresa estatal socialista cubana." *Economía y Desarrollo* (2).

Rojas, M., J. Gómez, H. Piedra, L Cabello, and Barrera, S. 2016. *La Responsabilidad Social Empresarial desde espacios estatales cubanos. Aproximación a una propuesta de modelo de gestión.* Resultado de Investigación, La Habana: Fondo bibliográfico del CIPS.

Rojas, M., J., Gómez, Y. González, A. Reyes, J. C. Campos, and I. Caballero. 2019. *La Responsabilidad Social Empresarial en el Centro de Inmunología Molecular.* Resultado de Investigación, La Habana: Fondo bibliográfico del CIPS.

Rojas, M., and J. Gómez. 2011. "La Responsabilidad Social Empresarial y el Desarrollo Local: una visión complementaria." *XXVIII Congreso ALAS Fronteras Abiertas de América Latina.* Recife, Brasil.

Villalobos Grzybowicz, J. 2011. "La RSE en México." *Conferencia Internacional Responsabilidad Social Empresarial, Cooperativismo y Desarrollo Local.* La Habana.

Vives, A., and E. Peinado. 2011. *La Responsabilidad Social de la Empresa en América Latina.* Fondo Multilateral de Inversores. Publicación del Banco Interamericano de Desarrollo.

Vogel, D. Winter 1986. "The Study of Social Issues in Management: A Critical Appraisal." *California Management Review* 28 (2).

Wilcox, D. 2005. *Responsabilidad social empresarial (RSE), la nueva exigencia global.* Estudios 2005, documento de trabajo 13, Chile: Universidad Viña del Mar.

Wood, D., and J. Lodgson. 2002. "Business Citizenship: From Individuals to Organizations." *Business Ethics Quarterly*, Ruffin Series, No. 3.

Chapter 10

Cooperatives in the Restarted Reforms

Some Proposals for a Law of Cooperatives

Camila Piñeiro Harnecker

After more than five years of delay,[1] it seems that relatively soon Cuba will finally have a legislation for cooperatives.[2] This was mentioned as part of the new measures that were announced which seek to overcome the current economic crisis, aggravated by the COVID-19 pandemic and the intensifying US sanctions against Cuba.[3] This is great and very much awaited news! However, for those of us who understand the philosophy of cooperativism and its potentials for rescuing Cuban socialism, it is at the same time a source of concern.

At times of such great challenges and emergencies, measures ought to be adopted promptly and with a cold, realistic understanding that the best scenario might not be possible. However, as explained before, the best intentions, when badly carried out, can have results that are contrary to those expected (Piñeiro 2012). The experience with cooperatives that has been gained from the beginning of the Revolution until now—among many important lessons, some of which will be mentioned later—shows us that cooperatives cannot be created hastily and that they can become distant from cooperative values and principles if the legal and regulatory frame is not appropriate.

From an integral view of the economic, social, cultural, and environmental problems that threaten us, it is clear that we need true cooperatives, the ones which will really contribute to the solutions. Otherwise, the pendulum will again swing against cooperatives, and the cooperative model will be blamed for deficiencies for which it is not really responsible. And this would really fit the bill for those who, in their adoration of private enterprise, do not understand cooperatives and see them as a "waste of time"—as they probably also see the socialist transformation—and would prefer to expand private enterprise into all activities, without the "disloyal" competition that cooperatives would give to private businesses. Or for those who would prefer that cooperatives do not demonstrate the lack of efficiency of many—and note, I'm not saying all—of the state enterprises, and thus threaten their jobs and—in some cases, we must admit—their ability to continue wasting resources that belong to all of us.

There is a lot of ground to cover, because cooperatives do not operate in a vacuum and our intention should be that they contribute to the consolidation of the achievements of the revolution and to perfecting our socioeconomic model, seen integrally. But here we will concentrate on the most urgent issues. We provide five proposals—presented in five separate sections— which we hope are taken into consideration in the process of drafting a Law of Cooperatives:

1. The proposal for a Law of Cooperatives should be drafted with the participation of cooperative leaders, and receive feedback through a process of consultation within the cooperatives.
2. The Law of Cooperatives should establish the institutional ecosystem necessary for the development of the cooperative sector, which should carry out the functions of promotion, supervision, representation and coordination of public policies.
3. The Law of Cooperatives should recognize the cooperative principle of autonomy of the cooperatives, and therefore, agreements between cooperatives and broader social interests should be sought through negotiation and not imposition.
4. The Law of Cooperatives should allow the creation of higher-tier cooperatives and multi-stakeholder cooperatives.
5. The Law of Cooperatives should facilitate that any group of people that complies with the requirements established in the Law can create a cooperative within a reasonable time frame.

These suggestions are based on lessons learned from Cuba's own experience with cooperatives and that of other countries in which legislators have seen cooperatives as a way to come closer to more prosperous and just societies.

1. THE PROPOSAL FOR THE LAW OF COOPERATIVES SHOULD BE DRAFTED WITH THE PARTICIPATION OF COOPERATIVE LEADERS, AND RECEIVE FEEDBACK THROUGH CONSULTATION PROCESSES WITHIN THE COOPERATIVES

Why is this crucial, and why should it be the starting point of any conversation on a legislation for cooperatives? Because doing it in any other way would be antidemocratic and not respectful of the cooperatives that have existed in our country for so many decades. It would also lose the advantages of the participation of the law subjects in the legislative process, beginning with the quality of the rules as such, and the willingness of current cooperative members to adopt the behaviors that the law aims to encourage.

To not do what is proposed—that the cooperative sector participate in the drafting and analysis of the legislation that should rule them—would go against the participatory rationale behind the drafting and consultation process that took place before the establishment of the *Guidelines of the Economic and Social Policy of the Party and the Revolution* (PCC 2011) and of the *Conceptualization of the Cuban Economic and Social Model of Socialist Development* (PCC 2016).[4] It would also contradict with past consultation processes around legislation for agricultural cooperatives, in which the National Association of Small Farmers (Asociación Nacional de Agricultores Pequeños—ANAP) played a key role in organizing the discussions and articulating feedback to legislators. Finally, it would also go against international practice, in which cooperatives—through their representative organizations, either by their own initiative or by invitation of the relevant public authorities—prepare a draft or participate in the drafting of cooperative legislation.

In the case of Cuba, where there truly are no representative organizations of the cooperatives (a point which will be analyzed below), cooperative leaders from a diversity of strong cooperatives should be invited. It is these leaders, more than the functionaries of state entities, legal or academic experts, who really know which elements of the current legislation need improvement, and what needs to be added for the cooperatives to consolidate and expand in our country while contributing to the satisfaction of the needs of our people. To not invite the cooperative leaders to participate in the drafting of a law for cooperatives and its corresponding rules, or to not have at least a consultation process with the members of the cooperatives, would be to disrespect the thousands of agricultural cooperatives that have been functioning for decades in our country, as well as the hundreds of industrial and service cooperatives that have between five and ten years of experience.

Having the proposed participatory legislative processes would contribute to Cuban cooperatives comprehending their rights and responsibilities. It would make them feel part of the vanguard of this economic struggle that we are waging; which as we know it is not only economic. It would also ensure that a quality law and its rules are produced and thus there is no need to modify them within a short time. In fact, we believe that the main reason for there being so many setbacks and imprecisions in the 2019 regulations for cooperatives (Consejo de Estado 2019a, 2019b), is because they were prepared without the cooperatives, and the sector was not consulted either, not even experts.

2. THE LAW OF COOPERATIVES SHOULD ESTABLISH AN INSTITUTIONAL ECOSYSTEM NECESSARY FOR THE DEVELOPMENT OF THE COOPERATIVE SECTOR, WHICH SHOULD CARRY OUT THE FUNCTIONS OF PROMOTION, SUPERVISION, REPRESENTATION AND COORDINATION OF PUBLIC POLICIES.

When the results of the assessment of the experiment with the nonagricultural cooperatives were announced in August 2017, it was explained that the main deficiencies were related to the control of the new cooperatives by the different ministries and provincial administrative councils responsible of it (Puig 2017). This was not unexpected because these state and local government entities have neither the capacity or—in many cases—incentives to effectively supervise cooperatives.

They have too many more imperative tasks to be able to control effectively that dozens or hundreds of cooperatives comply with all regulations, which is difficult for them to do even with their own enterprises (Figueredo 2019). In addition to bandwidth, they lack preparation to do so because many don't really understand how cooperatives are different from both state and private businesses.

Moreover, in some cases, the success of cooperatives goes against some state and government entities' institutional or corporate interests and those of their functionaries, because it will eventually put at risk that they will continue to be entrusted with the responsibility—and the resources attached to it—of some of the activities that cooperatives could carry out more effectively. For example, cooperatives, if allowed to thrive in agriculture, could demonstrate the ineffectiveness of many public agribusinesses that are responsible for supplying production inputs and services, and for the commercialization of agricultural outputs.

The Guidelines mention the need for a public or "government entity that conducts the sector."[5] In reality, as the international experience demonstrates, more than that is required. There is a need of an ecosystem (or a group of inter-related entities) for the development of the cooperative sector, which should cover the functions of promotion, supervision, representation and coordination of public policies, at the national and local levels. If we really intend to implement what is currently established in the Guidelines, Conceptualization, and 2019 Constitution stating that cooperatives are to be dominant within the non-state sector, it is fundamental to establish this ecosystem. Therefore, it is essential to reflect it in a law of cooperatives, in which it should be made clear which entity is responsible for each of these four functions.

The different ministries and Central State Management Entities (Organismos de la Administración Central del Estado—OACE) should supervise, from a methodological point, the compliance with the technical standards relative to the specific activities that the cooperatives carry out (food safety, buildings' safety, labor safety), just as these are regulated currently and how it should be done with all enterprises. However, the supervision of compliance with cooperative legislation should be charged to an entity that specializes in this field, that understands the cooperative difference (i.e., the peculiarities of this organizational format), and that will do it in a pedagogic manner—raise the alert on time, help to correct and avoid dissolving cooperatives that could be saved. This specialized supervision entity—which in many countries is called Superintendence (Superintendencia)—is even more important in order to avoid fake cooperatives, which are more likely if legislation and public policies grant them preferential treatment; as it should, given cooperatives' greater responsibilities and contributions to the communities and to the country.[6]

Although in some countries the functions of supervision and promotion of the cooperatives fall to the same entity, the international trend is to separate them, meaning that there is one entity in charge of promotion and another of supervision. In this way, contradictory incentives are avoided—that the functionaries put a brake on authorizing new cooperatives because it would cause them more work, or that they do not supervise appropriately because they are more interested in the growth of the sector than in its quality (compliance with principles and behaviors established in the legislation).

The entity in charge of the promotion of the cooperative sector should, at least partially, be financed by the cooperative sector. Given that cooperatives currently pay—as it should, per rationale mentioned above—a lower taxation rate than private enterprises, and that it is a way to materialize the sixth universal cooperative principle of cooperation among cooperatives, it would be logical for the promotion entity to be financed at least in part through a small tax on cooperatives' net revenues and that—if necessary—the state would cover the rest of its budget, basically by way of the taxes it charges the cooperatives. Therefore, the organization or organizations that represent the cooperative sector should participate in some way in its board of directors. There are different ways of doing this, but the important thing is that the cooperative sector must be taken into account, through institutional ways, when the time comes to select the person or persons who will be in charge of the entity charged with promoting or advancing cooperatives.

This cooperative promotion entity, which in many countries is called an Institute (Instituto de Cooperativismo o Cooperativas), is vital to facilitate services related to cooperative education, to the emergence or "incubation" of new cooperatives, to strengthening or "accelerating" those who could reach higher productive rates, to coaching or "accompaniment" of those who need it for associative or economic reasons, to mediation of conflicts, to advancing cooperation among cooperatives, to inserting cooperatives in local or regional development strategies, to the authorization to constitute a cooperative, to the formal registration of a new cooperative, to the management of cooperatives' records, to facilitating access to credit that is consistent with the cooperative difference, to ensuring cooperatives are not left out of public policies, among others. These are services that are specific to cooperatives or that need to be adapted to their organizational particularities, therefore the need for an entity specialized in promoting cooperatives. These services are crucial both to start-up and well- established cooperatives, for them not just to be successful but also to fulfill their potential to a more inclusive, equitable, and solidaristic society. The cooperative promotion entity would not need a large bureaucracy, but it would work in alliance with educational, consulting, and research centers.

In addition to promotion and supervision, the cooperative sector also needs an organization that articulates or "integrates" them and represents them vis-à-vis the state and other national and international actors. This cooperative representation organization is as or perhaps more important than any other entity, since in some countries in which the state does not have cooperative promotion policies it is the cooperative representation organization that takes on the promotion and supervision functions.

In Cuba, there are quite a few self-employed people who have organized themselves to make claims before the state when legislation has affected them; and they have been successful in being taken into account in some aspects. Cooperatives should be able to raise their concerns to state entities. And it should be possible to do so in an institutionalized way, and not just through letters or individual meetings; not by representing just a few cooperatives, but the majority of the sector.

If cooperatives are expected to be the second most important business form in Cuba's socioeconomic model, there should be a way for them to communicate with the state. This national-level organization of representation of all cooperatives—which in many countries is called League (Liga) or Confederation (Confederación)—should be constituted by organizations of cooperative integration at territorial (municipal or provincial), as well as sectorial (agriculture,[7] gastronomy, construction, transportation, etc.) levels. It would be financed by the cooperative sector and its leadership, elected at the base level.

Considering Cuba's true condition of being a besieged nation because the US government and its lackeys use all imaginable forms to sabotage our revolutionary process including planting undercover agents in key organizations, state security must ensure that nominees for positions at this cooperative representation organization are not agents serving foreign states, as is the case for all organizations of civil society. In addition, the directors of the cooperative promotion entity appointed by the state could be given veto power or the power to preselect candidates nominated from the cooperatives.

From its local branches to its national level office, this cooperative representation organization could exercise other functions in addition to representation, such as the exchange of knowledge and good practices between cooperatives, the management of funds to support cooperatives that face temporary emergencies and—perhaps most important for our country—the coordination of municipal development programs and plans. In the following sections, different ways in which cooperatives can be useful tools of local development will be indicated; if cooperatives could count on having a spokesperson in the local government, this would be of great assistance to them.

Lastly, it would be advisable to also have a space for coordination of public policies relevant to the cooperative sector, in which all previously mentioned entities (promotion, supervision and representation) could participate together with key pertinent OACEs and provincial governments. This ad hoc space for policy coordination could be an Interinstitutional Committee (Comité Interinstitucional), presided by the commission of the National Assembly in charge of—among other topics—promoting cooperatives, the Council of Ministries, the cooperative promotion entity, or whichever institution is considered most relevant.

3. THE LAW OF COOPERATIVES SHOULD RECOGNIZE THE COOPERATIVE PRINCIPLE OF THE AUTONOMY OF THE COOPERATIVES; AGREEMENTS BETWEEN COOPERATIVES AND BROADER SOCIAL INTERESTS SHOULD BE SOUGHT THROUGH NEGOTIATION AND NOT IMPOSITION.

Let's begin by clarifying what is meant by cooperatives' "autonomy." A cooperative's autonomy is measured by the capacity of its members, or—if allowable—those delegated by them, to make decisions that are both operative and strategic, both economic in nature (procurement, sales, investments, production goals, etc.) as well as associative (internal rules, election of directors, entry or exit of members, etc.), and independently, meaning without interference of external agents who are not invited by the cooperatives. This implies that the cooperative can relinquish or delegate some decisions—never the most important ones like those related to the election of its directors, internal rules, and the criteria to recompense members and distribute net revenues—but this entrustment must be approved in a general assembly.

It is important to note that no social organization in the world is completely autonomous, because they generally establish commitments with other organizations, and their options are always to some extent conditioned by the environment and historical context in which they operate. This also applies to businesses that operate in *free* or nonregulated markets, which are limited by the imperative to reach or maintain a certain position in the market, to grow or be caught by the competition, to reduce and externalize its costs, by the uncertainty about overproduction cycles or demand contractions, etc.

Let us stop here to think about why autonomy is important for the success of cooperatives. Autonomy is essential for cooperatives because it is a fundamental condition for having a democratic management. Can there be a democratic management when an external agent—be it a state entity, a stockholder or someone else—imposes certain decisions?

Legislation—like the Law Decree 365/2018 and the Decree 354/2018 of the agricultural cooperatives (Estado 2019a, Consejo de Estado 2019b)—that imposes a *connection* or a relationship (be it of subordination or not) on the cooperative with some other organization (be it state or not), beyond the control and regulation entities, infringes on the principle of autonomy. Similarly, legislation—like those just mentioned—which bestows to entities external to cooperatives the powers of deciding on when they fuse or split (divide), and even on when they expire (close), without explanatory grounds as established in the legislation, also infringes on the principle of autonomy. The universal cooperative principle of autonomy should not fail to be mentioned in any cooperative legislation.

Just as with autonomy, cooperative legislation should also endorse the seventh universal cooperatives principle of commitment to the development of the communities, which goes beyond narrow social responsibility, i.e., understood as complying with legislation, paying taxes and generating jobs. The cooperatives should not be separated from the communities in which they operate. In order to contribute to local development, cooperatives can enter into agreements with state entities, local governments, community organizations and other organizations that represent social interests, so as to co-finance and co-implement strategies for local development, or in order to orient their activities toward the satisfaction of social needs. Moreover, for those activities of profound social impact which deserve it—especially in our society, in which cooperatives are expected to be guided by broader interests than those of the people that constitute their membership—the cooperatives that so decide should be able to include representatives of those social interests when taking certain decisions. As we will see in the next section, some legislation allows for them to invite representatives of social interest groups to participate in certain decisions—if this is what the members autonomously desire.

All this is to say that Cuban legislators should know that it is possible to have cooperatives respond to broader social interests—beyond their memberships' interests—without sacrificing their autonomy. To impose mandates on cooperatives is the easiest way, but not the most effective. Cooperatives cannot be *tied* to a plan, but rather its members must be convinced by material and/or moral incentives, and—not less important—through the hegemony or dominance of a solidarity and egalitarian culture in which embracing the needs of others—especially of those whom we affect with our activities and those who need it the most—will be the natural, rational and responsible thing to do.

If what is sought is that agricultural cooperatives earmark part of their production for "social consumption,"[8] this can be achieved by "social responsibility clauses" in contracts for leasing or usufruct usage of lands, and/or in contracts for supplying of productive inputs, technology and services at cost-price, and/or in agreements to reduce taxes on agricultural land ownership or on surpluses (i.e., profits), among other material incentives. In addition, moral incentives such as public recognitions for their social contributions are also important and very effective particularly in small communities; although insufficient only by themselves, and more so when there is the possibility to sell to others at much higher prices.

By the same token, it is important to note the prices of sales by cooperatives to the state should provide them with some margin of surplus which the cooperatives can use to invest in improving their members' working and living conditions. Subsidies should not be given to cooperatives so they can produce at lower prices, but rather to the public entities that provide for social consumption. The state should fulfill its payment commitments too, so that it can also demand from the cooperatives.

There should not be any legislation establishing that the prices at which cooperatives sell their products (goods or services) to the state or to the population be in accordance with "demand and supply," as it is currently stated. But rather, cooperatives ought to set fair prices agreed on by the parties involved. Cooperatives, even if they do not exist to "lose money" because they must be self-sustainable, also do not exist just to make profits because their objective is not to maximize profits or surpluses but to maximize the satisfaction of the needs of their members and communities. They should therefore not abuse their position in a market that is undersupplied (i.e., scarcity) and set the highest prices they can, but charge prices that will allow them to have a favorable surplus rate and are the most affordable possible.

Price-gouging regulations do exist—as part of competition laws—even in countries with highly unregulated markets, to ensure that the prices of some basic products don't rise or fall too rapidly without there being justifying circumstances. Nevertheless, it should be made clear that price controls are not an effective mechanism to ensure fair prices in the medium and long term. Therefore, in order to sustainably accomplish a decline in the current high prices that the population has to pay for some basic goods and services, the state should implement policies that promote production and manufacturing, be it with greater productivity and/or new enterprises; particularly for businesses that are be better prepared to respond to social interests such as state, cooperative or community enterprises.

Consequently, if we would like families to have access to agricultural products at fair prices, without subsidies, then agricultural cooperatives should be allowed to organize as second-tier cooperatives (i.e., cooperatives whose members are cooperatives formed by persons or by legal entities), so that they take on distribution and commercialization, in a direct way through their own stores, or through stores administered by consumer cooperatives, both of which are very common in the world. As we will explain in the following sections, these higher-tier cooperatives are better prepared in organizational terms (incentives, organizational flexibility, etc.) to offer their member cooperatives all the services they need to produce and commercialize greater volumes at higher quality. In this way, they could reduce the very large and painful output losses by the state agricultural enterprises that are the result of inefficient management. To the degree that there is better agricultural production, controlled by the producers themselves and not intermediaries, the cooperatives will need fewer material incentives in order to be motivated to sell at fair prices and to contribute to mass consumption, so that they will come to see the sales to the state as a benefit which offers them buying security for their products.

It is in this manner, through higher-tier cooperatives of production cooperatives in dialogue with the state and with the consumption cooperatives, that agriculture is organized in countries like Uruguay, Norway, France, and Japan, where both consumers and producers receive benefits from agricultural production, and also how it was organized in developed countries in times of crisis—as in the case of the greater part of Europe during the last years of World War II and the decades that followed, and in the United States during the Great Depression—where demand exceeded supply. Although some will deny this and will call for *freeing* more the markets, agricultural products are non-replaceable goods—i.e., people will buy food even though prices rise—and therefore in under-supplied markets the final sellers are always going to be able to impose prices to the consumers. On the supply, since agricultural products are highly perishable, producers will find themselves forced to sell even though it may be at low prices, in order not to lose everything. Therefore, as the experience of countries with the most advanced agricultural industries demonstrate, commercialization of agricultural products should be controlled by the producers or the consumers, and not by intermediaries, whether they be private transporters, state enterprises or worker cooperatives who manage agricultural markets. This is even more true when our domestic production is insufficient to satisfy the demand, and there is a lack of adequate storage and processing facilities.

Beyond agricultural production, for cooperatives that offer services of social impact (like transportation, elderly care, childcare, etc.) to do so at a reasonable cost and respecting certain technical or methodological standards and coverage commitments (i.e., offering their services in distant and low-income communities) these desired behaviors could be established in social responsibility clauses in operation licenses and contracts for leasing spaces from the state; and could be promoted via material and moral incentives like the ones already mentioned. However, in no case should it be mentioned in the legislation that a cooperative is obligated to do this; it should be a decision made by the members.

In a more general way, if we are interested in cooperatives materializing their great potentials to be engines of local development (Piñeiro 2020) and to contribute directly to satisfying social needs, then it is essential to create spaces for coordination between local governments and cooperatives and all businesses interested—known as democratic planning—so that they can become acquainted with local development priorities, establish synergies, and become part of local development strategies. Cuban agricultural cooperatives have shown how much they can do for their communities, even if they could do much more, because of this coordination with local governments and institutions. Many nonagricultural cooperatives regret not having been able to do more for their communities precisely because most local governments have kept them at a distance.

In summary, the cooperative law should respect both universal cooperative principles of autonomy and of commitment to the communities. It should guarantee cooperatives' autonomy while at the same time facilitating their ability to respond to social interests via agreements with representatives of these social interests—ideally reached through democratic planning and not just required social responsibility clauses in contracts—or, when appropriate, through multi-stakeholder cooperatives. Obviously, they should be permitted to be in better conditions to produce the necessary goods and services, and to commercialize directly with consumers or users, be these people, public institutions or enterprises.

4. THE LAW OF COOPERATIVES SHOULD PERMIT THE CREATION OF HIGHER-TIER COOPERATIVES AND MULTI-STAKEHOLDER COOPERATIVES

A higher-tier cooperative is one formed by cooperatives: second-tier or secondary cooperatives are formed by first-tier or primary cooperatives—simply known simply as cooperatives—which are formed by natural persons (i.e., people) or legal persons (i.e., businesses and other entities); third-tier cooperatives are integrated by second-tier cooperatives; and so on (Piñeiro, 2015: 25–29). For Cuban cooperatives to be in better conditions to produce what is necessary and satisfy social needs, it is crucial that higher-tier cooperatives can be created so they supply their member cooperatives in a timely, consistent and cost-effective manner with the production inputs and services they need.

Cooperation among cooperatives (i.e., inter-cooperation) constitutes the sixth universal cooperative principle; meaning that it is key for the success of these socioeconomic organizations. In fact, it is precisely in the regions of the world where cooperatives are strongest and there is a great number of them—northern Italy, the Basque country, Quebec, Uruguay—where mechanisms of inter-cooperation, and especially higher-tier cooperatives, have been established.

Inter-cooperation is fundamental for the success, resilience, and sustainability of cooperatives, because together they can more effectively ensure the goods and services their members need, they can plan and implement development strategies of greater scope, can ensure access to cooperative education, innovation, research, and development, and can also to a certain extent avoid the negative effects of operating through mercantile relations.[9] In addition, it is an important lever for them to be able to really contribute to local development.

Higher-tier cooperatives are the most advanced form of inter-cooperation, because it allows their members to not only share resources and reduce risks over longer periods of time, but also to count with governing bodies that facilitate joint decision-making over future resources and risks. The rationale that leads to the creation of first-tier cooperatives is the same that leads to higher-tier cooperatives—cooperation instead of competition.

Among the main services that higher-tier cooperatives provide to their members are the following: joint purchase of raw materials and other production inputs at lower cost; contracting of production services (equipment rental, transport, logistics, etc.) at better prices; adding value to members' outputs by means of processing or better quality (post-sale services, marketing, etc.); bulk sales to clients that demand greater volumes; improving living conditions of the cooperatives' members (building homes, childcare, retirement pensions, stores, etc.); obtaining financing for investments at lower costs and under better terms; establishing joint funds for investments from members' savings; reallocating redundant members from cooperatives that face low demand; redistributing surplus among cooperatives so that those facing losses because of market cycles, volatility, or other conditions out of their control can overcome them with the help of this temporary (for a few years maximum) solidarity surplus from successful cooperatives, and therefore income among cooperatives and their members are less unequal; among others. In brief, higher-tier cooperatives offer the advantages of cooperation in a similar way as primary cooperatives: to enjoy the advantages of production at a greater scale, secure production inputs and services, pool and share resources, reduce risks, better serve members' social needs, and help each other because together more can be achieved than separately.

A socialist economy cannot be conceived with cooperatives working in isolation, without cooperating among them. In the socialism that was conceived by Marx, Engels, and Lenin—as well as by other, more recent Marxists—cooperatives play an important role and operate in an articulated manner in higher-tier cooperatives, which allows them to take full advantage of cooperation and materialize cooperative values both internally and in their external relations (Piñeiro, 2011: Part II). Given that cooperatives cannot be *tied* to centralized and vertical planning mechanisms—because, as explained before, they would no longer be cooperative—it is vital that they are able to orient their activities toward broader social interests. Higher-tier cooperatives can play a key role also articulating members' interests and aspirations and facilitating that they "internalize" broader social interests. Moreover, higher-tier cooperatives allow member cooperatives to establish coordinated plans and mechanisms to achieve greater equity and opportunities for self-realization among members—which are central goals of socialism.

In fact, it is worth adding that:

> the analysis of the experience at Mondragón [a fifth-tier cooperative] suggests that cooperatives are willing to cede autonomy on strategic and even management decisions, if the decision-making process is in the hands of democratic organisms in which they can represent their interests and participate (directly or indirectly) in these decisions. Wage scales, the percentage of (non-member) employees that is permitted, criteria for the use of its surpluses, major investments, are decided by the Congress of all the Mondragón cooperatives. Moreover, directors of the second-tier and third-tier cooperatives participate in the board of directors of the member cooperatives. In this way, and without aiming to do so, Mondragón contributes to clarifying questions on the possibility to combine entrepreneurial autonomy and planning, which is so transcendental in socialist debates. (Piñeiro 2011, 12)

One of the principles that the current cooperative legislation establishes is "collaboration among cooperatives," but the way in which it can occur is limited to contracts, agreements, exchanges or other documents (Consejo de Estado 2019b, Articulo 8; Consejo de Estado 2019a, Articulo 6). It is worrisome that the possibility to create second-tier cooperatives, even as it appeared in Law Decree 305/2012 (Consejo de Estado 2012, Articulo 5)—and with which began the experiment of non-agricultural cooperatives, but which was never legalized—it does not appear in the new Law Decree 47/2021 for nonagricultural cooperatives (Consejo de Estado 2021), nor in the one relating to agricultural cooperatives. Although Guideline No. 15 in the updated (2017) Guidelines still mandates explicitly "beginning the process of constituting second-tier cooperatives" (PCC 2017, No. 15), they have disappeared from the official discourse and do not appear in other official documents.

We understand—or would like to—that the cause for this delay or hesitation is a misunderstanding of higher-tier cooperatives. Therefore, it should be noted that higher-tier cooperatives are not a form of concentration of property. A second-tier cooperative's capital or assets is not the total sum of the assets of the member primary cooperatives; but it is as great or as small as the member cooperatives decide to contribute to the higher-tier cooperative's capital; and in general, after providing the resources that were agreed on, the surplus returns to the member cooperatives. Therefore, higher-tier cooperatives should not be seen as enterprises that add the member cooperatives together, but rather as new enterprises that are at the service of the member cooperatives. On another hand, if the cause of the hesitation is that some second-tier cooperatives may displace agricultural state enterprises that have been put in charge of providing production inputs and services to agricultural cooperatives, that is not acceptable. If these state enterprises offer their services effectively, then second-tier cooperatives could just facilitate contracting with them. Otherwise, cooperatives—and the population—should not have to endure the consequences of their lack of effectiveness.

It should also be noted that, just as with primary cooperatives, higher-tier cooperatives cannot be imposed—a cooperative cannot be forced to create or become a member of a higher-tier cooperative. Cooperatives only decide to join higher-tier ones voluntarily, because these offer the services that are needed by them and they recognize the advantages of inter-cooperation. This does not mean that the decision to join cannot be encouraged. Generally, when primary cooperatives are strong, and especially in their associative or social component, it is natural that they seek to join forces with other cooperatives.

On another hand, the law for cooperatives should not restrict first-tier or primary cooperatives only to worker or producer cooperatives; it should also allow the creation of multi-stakeholder cooperatives. Before presenting the usefulness and importance of this innovative and trendy type of cooperative, we will explain what these consist of.

Until now, we have referred to primary cooperatives, in which all members are of the same type or kind of *stakeholder*: workers, producers, or consumers. Multi-stakeholder cooperatives, sometimes known as hybrid cooperatives, are those composed of more than one kind of stakeholder. In practice, they refer to multiple forms of co-management between workers, producers, consumers and—in some cases—representatives of broader social interests such as local governments and community organizations, among others. They can bring together all different combinations of these four types or kinds of stakeholders (Piñeiro 2015, 30–31).

The first and most common multi-stakeholder cooperatives are consumer cooperatives that decided to include their employees as members and in such a way so that their interests as workers can be taken into consideration. Not just as consumer-members, whose interests are mostly to access quality and affordable goods and services, but as worker-members, whose main interests are to achieve dignified working conditions and a fair recompense for their work.

In these cases, in which there are consumers and workers in a multi-stakeholder cooperative, both stakeholders could have their general assemblies in which they would decide on issues that are relevant only to them, and they would elect their delegates to the board of directors of the multi-stakeholder cooperative, which would be composed of delegates of each general assembly—the proportions being their decision. In some multi-stakeholder cooperatives, they don't have separate general assemblies but ensure representation of all stakeholders in the board of directors.

Why would cooperative members be interested in creating more complicated governance structures in their cooperatives? Because it's necessary in order to make sure that all stakeholders interests are taken into account, and those most affected by the cooperative activity have an opportunity to participate in decision-making. Also, because it allows a people with different interests to find a compromise that benefits all.

For example, in a consumer and worker multi-stakeholder cooperative, consumers would be expected to try to cut costs and maybe reduce workers' incomes, while workers would be expected to try to raise their incomes. Even though this could seem like irreconcilable positions, the truth is that both sides know they need to find a middle ground that makes the cooperative viable, sustainable and socially responsible.

This kind of innovative cooperative makes it possible to confront several problems. First, it allows for the creation of cooperatives of consumers or producers who do not exploit wage labor, because employees are turned into worker-members. Secondly, it is very useful to tackle many of the main problems that most communities face where some participation of local governments in a cooperative's decision-making—even if minimal—is needed; for example, cooperatives in the care industry (children, seniors, and people with differentiated capacities), communal services (cleaning and maintenance of public spaces, recycling from the homes, etc.), and utility provision.

It also constitutes a way to organize some community development projects in a transparent manner, so that participation of all interested parties in the taking of decisions is assured, and so that the representatives of the local government or of community organizations may be included. Because of the need to protect cooperatives' autonomy, these aforementioned stakeholders (local government and community organizations), normally only have a very limited participation in the board of directors: just speaking privileges, a veto on decisions related to social issues, strategies and production plans, distribution of utilities or other strategic decisions in which it is important that the community interests be taken into account—or however the cooperative assembly should decide.

In brief, a law of cooperatives should not be limited only to the types of cooperatives that already exist in Cuba, but it should permit the creation of other types. Most importantly, second-tier cooperatives, which are fundamental for the development of primary cooperatives, and multi-stakeholder cooperatives, which would allow cooperatives to truly contribute—as is hoped—to local development and the planned development of our economy.

5. THE LAW FOR COOPERATIVES SHOULD FACILITATE THAT ANY GROUP OF PEOPLE THAT COMPLIES WITH THE REQUIREMENTS ESTABLISHED IN THE LAW CAN CREATE A COOPERATIVE WITHIN A REASONABLE TIME FRAME

The procedures established in the current legislation for the creation of agricultural cooperatives are still extremely centralized and top-down, and authorization is also vulnerable to the narrow interests or lack of understanding about cooperatives on the part of public functionaries and mass organizations (Consejo de Estado 2019b, Articulo 14.1). For nonagricultural cooperatives, with the passing of Law Decree 47 in 2021, the authorization process is finally straightforward and open to any groups of people. However, there are still practical hurdles and limits to some activities it is not clear if cooperatives can or cannot do.

Cooperative conversions (i.e., when a cooperative is created out of an existing business by at least some of its former workers) are an easier and generally more viable way of creating cooperatives than cooperative startups. If the goal is still to transfer a significant number of state business units to the non-state sector with a preference for cooperative conversions, then the state should define the economic activities and the criteria to decide if it is appropriate to convert a given state business unit into a cooperative. To ensure that these conversions are really voluntary and not imposed on state workers, the decision should be to authorize conversions only in those units where the majority of workers have expressed interest in managing them organized as cooperatives (Piñeiro 2015). The procedure for cooperative conversions from state business units should be revised considering this and the fact that there is a new legislation for nonagricultural cooperatives.

As was mentioned in the second part of this paper on the ecosystem necessary for the development of cooperatives, the authorization for the creation of cooperatives should be under the authority of an institution or entity tasked with cooperative promotion. The authorization to create cooperatives cannot be under the control of state entities, enterprises or mass organizations whose functionaries could feel threatened by the success of the cooperatives, as is currently the case with agricultural cooperatives. Mass organization or labor unions—although they could have basic organizing units (or nucleus) within the cooperatives if members decide to join—should not intervene in the processes of authorization. If the leaders or members of a cooperative that is in the process of starting up or already functioning demonstrate unethical or antisocial manners, it should be their fellow members who decide to expel them from the cooperative for not complying with the cooperative values;

and if the behavior results in illegal actions, it should be legal sanctions that would prevent them from participating in the cooperatives.

While it is recommended in most cases that cooperatives coordinate their activities with representatives of social interests—both sectoral (OSDE or ministries) and regional (municipal or provincial administrative councils, as per their scope)—cooperatives should not be hostage to the interpretations and insecurities of certain state functionaries. Those responsible for authorizing cooperatives should evaluate whether a proposal complies with the established requirements, as is currently occurring with nonagricultural cooperatives.

The Cuban private sector has grown continuously for more than two decades, while membership in cooperatives has decreased. Before the pandemic, the number of workers in the private sector had reached more than 600,000, thus exceeding the fewer than 500,000 people that are members of cooperatives (ONEI 2019). Some point to this fact in order to argue that the private sector has a greater capacity to generate jobs than the cooperative sector. Conveniently, they do not mention the fact that the creation of agricultural cooperatives has been very top-down since the initial years, and until 2021 nonagricultural cooperatives were only created during approximately one year (between 2013 and 2014) and under a hyper-centralized authorization process. It can be estimated that around nine hundred proposals were not authorized or did not get evaluated during that time period (Piñeiro 2020).

The participation of the different business forms or types of property in employment is fundamental to define the social relations that predominate in a given country, and therefore the values or anti-values and behaviors that are being internalized by people. This is basic Marxism or dialect materialism. In a country committed to building socialism there should be small and even medium private capitalist enterprises—to the extent that these respond to social interests and even if they exploit wage labor—but these should not have a greater participation in employment than cooperatives or state enterprises. Currently, even though the state sector has the greatest participation in employment, given the inefficiency and bureaucratism in a large part of state enterprises, it is the private sector which is achieving a cultural hegemony in Cuba's social relations.

If we are still hoping for the more "socialized" or socialistic social production relations to predominate, and that therefore the cooperatives really become the second most important entrepreneurial form after state business (as established in the Conceptualization), it should be not only allowed but possible for any group of people interested in creating a viable cooperative—which, obviously, complies with the established requirements—to do so.

In these times of pandemic, many countries are encouraging the development of cooperatives, not because they are interested in building socialism but rather because they recognize what the evidence has demonstrated: that cooperatives, in comparison with its private counterparts, have greater resilience to economic crises, a greater commitment to local development and a greater capacity to satisfy social needs (CECOP-CICOPA 2012; ILO 2014; Burdin 2014). In cooperatives, the attitude toward their members and communities does not depend entirely on leaderships but is the result of their organizational principles. Fundamentally, because it is a collective property, managed in a democratic manner to satisfy the needs and aspirations of its members, a cooperative therefore does not look for a maximization of profits. Thus, during economic crises, cooperatives maintain jobs, redistribute surpluses or losses equitably, and reorient their activities toward the satisfaction of social needs. Moreover, as was defended in the previous section, inter-cooperation and especially higher-tier cooperatives can be used as powerful mechanisms of self-protection for the cooperatives and its communities in periods of crisis.

Another advantage of cooperatives is that their growth does not constitute concentration of property, wealth or income. In these socioeconomic organizations, profits or surpluses are distributed among members according to their contribution of labor—or of production or consumption, for the cooperatives of producers and consumers, respectively—and, therefore, they are more equitable. Moreover, cooperatives are much more responsible in their tax contributions, because of their greater transparency.

Important questions around the final 2021 opening to micro, small, and medium private enterprises (MSMEs) have not been discussed in Cuba's public debate—What is going to happen to the medium private enterprises once or if they become *large*? Or in other words: are we willing to accept that the MSMEs grow without limits? It is known that private enterprises tend to grow, because profits are concentrated in the owners, and they generally decide to reinvest in order to make the business grow and receive yet more profits. Taking this into account, as well as inequality and other negative effects resulting from the concentration of income and wealth, economists like Thomas Piketty (Piketty 2019) and socialist politicians like Bernie Sanders (Sanders 2019) have proposed adoption of public policies that would compel private businesses—starting at a certain size—to grant workers the right to participate in decision-making.[10] Sanders also proposes that workers become co-owners of these large businesses through their shared ownership of collective funds created and nurtured from profits, as Swedish economists proposed in 1975 in what has been called the Meidner Plan. The original plan of the 1950s—presented and defeated in the mid 1970s—proposed that enterprises of more than fifty workers should assign 20 percent of the profits to these collective funds (Meidner 1978). So therefore, why not envision public policies in Cuba that motivate private enterprises to convert themselves into cooperatives?

As some authors have noted (Betancourt 2020; Torres 2020), the growth of the private MSMEs will worsen the growing inequality in Cuba, and will have negative impacts on the social groups with the highest vulnerability: people without remittances or savings, women, people with differentiated capacities, young people. The promotion by municipal governments of cooperatives formed by people in vulnerability could contribute significantly to move forward on two fronts simultaneously: the expansion of a non-state sector that offers collective solutions to problems that affect these communities, and the specialization of our social security system toward one that empowers people and doesn't reduce them to passive beneficiaries—something that we mentioned before as having greater importance in times when the country finds itself obliged to resort to again a pseudo-dollarization, and poverty and inequalities grow.

Cooperatives formed by people in vulnerability will not appear spontaneously, as the majority of these persons do not feel themselves able to be the owner of an economic organization. It is therefore essential that people be informed and sensitized and that they be given the opportunity to develop the necessary skills and attitudes to become effective members of cooperatives. In fact, the international experience suggests that cooperatives of historically marginalized people generally arise from incubation processes, with accompaniment during the first two to five years. The establishment of a cooperative promotion entity would be definitely crucial to really materialize this potential of cooperatives in Cuba.

CONCLUDING REMARKS

In conclusion, we hope that these proposals for a law of cooperatives—which we hope is in the process of been prepared—will take into consideration what we as experts on the topic have proposed for several years, through established channels and by articles such as this one. We have suggested some key elements and processes for drafting cooperative legislation, for the constitution of cooperatives, and for the public policies and institutions necessary to encourage a cooperative development such that it contributes to community and national development. While a greater opening toward cooperatives would always be welcome, not every legal and institutional framework will result in what is expected from cooperatives. Once again, we say that it would be preferable to do things properly.

NOTES

1. The law of cooperatives [Ley de Cooperativas] was announced in 2012—at the start of the experiment with the nonagricultural cooperatives—with the promise that it would be approved in 2015, a date that was then postponed. It was not mentioned again until, after the approval of the new Constitution of the Republic of Cuba in 2019, some of the laws that were planned be approved in the near future were named.

2. When this chapter was written, we were hoping the legislation could be a general law of cooperatives, for all different types of cooperatives. It was later proven that the legislation was reduced to worker and producer cooperatives outside of agriculture—finally expanding the "experiment" with "nonagricultural cooperatives."

3. Declarations of Economic Minister Alejandro Gil in the Round Table [Mesa Redonda], July 16, 2020.

4. The Guidelines (see PCC, 2011) and Conceptualization (see PCC, 2016) are documents that were widely debated and approved by the Cuban National Assembly and by the Cuban Communist Party (PCC, from its Spanish acronym), which—in different ways—lay out the main characteristics of the society that Cubans are hoping to build, and identify cooperatives as the second most important business model form after the public/state business model.

5. Guideline No. 16 states: "The legal norm on cooperatives will regulate all types of cooperatives and must ratify that as collective property, they will not be sold or transferred their possession to other cooperatives, to non-state management forms or to natural persons. Propose the creation of the government entity that conducts the sector."

6. In Cuba, as in other countries, and as suggested by the United Nations (ONU, Resolution 64/136 of 2019), cooperatives are charged lower taxes, are given priority in the leasing of state buildings, in the contracting of goods and services by the state, and discounts—without subsidies—in the purchase of production inputs, etc.

7. Given that the National Association of Smallholder Farmers (Asociación Nacional de Agricultores Pequeños—ANAP) does not really represent the cooperatives in the agricultural sector—because it does not include members of UBPCs and because farmers who are not linked to any form of cooperative are also members of it, and moreover since it is also a kind of a trade association of individual or collective landowners—it would be necessary to create an entity that represents all agricultural cooperatives. Nevertheless, as the members of the UBPC (and of other nonagricultural cooperatives) could maintain their membership in their respective labor unions, the members of the agricultural cooperatives (CCA and CPA) could maintain their membership in ANAP. These are two kinds of different organizations that represent different sets of interests: the organization or entity of cooperative integration represents the interests of cooperative members at the cooperative level, and the unions and mass organizations like the ANAP represent the interests of cooperative members and others at the individual level.

8. This term generally refers to what is being commercialized through the basic food basket—that which is offered through the "Ration Card" ["Libreta"] and other highly regulated and subsidized sales—and what is consumed in schools, hospitals,

and work centers. The establishment of "state commitments" [encargos estatales] with state businesses and cooperatives, is one of the ways the state has to obtain the necessary goods to provide for social consumption.

9. The negative effects of operating through mercantile relations include the externalization of costs (pollution and other negative impacts of its economic activity), internalization of benefits (the use of qualified labor, infrastructure and other public goods and services without compensation or contribution), and its inability to respond to social interests that are not linked to "effective consumption" (i.e., what people can afford to pay).

10. Both are inspired by the successful German codetermination experience, which started in the 1950s and was generalized in 1976. Codetermination establishes the possibility of creating workers' councils in enterprises of any size, and that, in enterprises of more than five hundred workers, workers elect representatives for their board of directors, reaching 50 percent of the votes in enterprises of more than two thousand workers. See: *The Codetermination Bargains: The History of German Corporate and Labour Law* (2016) 23(1) *Columbia Journal of European Law* 135 LSE Legal Studies Working Paper No. 10/2015. http://eprints.lse.ac.uk /61593/1/The%20codetermination%20bargains%20the%20history%20of%20german %20corporate%20and%20labour%20law.pdf.

BIBLIOGRAPHY

ANPP. *Constitución de la República de Cuba* [Constitution of the Republic of Cuba]. La Habana: Asamblea Nacional del Poder Popular, Febrero de 2019. Retrieved from: http://www.granma.cu/file/pdf/gaceta/Nueva%20Constituci%C3 %B3n%20240%20KB-1.pdf.

Betancourt, R. "El aporte de la Economía Social y Solidaria para construir socialismo en Cuba (I)" [The contribution of Social and Solidarity Economics for the construction of socialism in Cuba (I)]. OnCubaNews. July 7, 2020. Retrieved from https:// oncubanews.com/cuba/economia/el-aporte-de-la-economia-social-y-solidaria-para -construir-socialismo-en-cuba-i/.

Burdin, G. "Are Worker-Managed Firms More Likely to Fail than Conventional Enterprises? Evidence from Uruguay." *Industrial and Labor Relations Review*, 202–38, 2014.

CECOP-CICOPA. "The resilience of the cooperative model. How worker cooperatives, social cooperatives and other worker-owned enterprises respond to the crisis and its consequences." 2012. Retrieved from: https://issuu.com/cicopa/docs/report _cecop_2012_en_web.

Consejo de Estado. "Decreto Ley 305/2012. De las Cooperativas No Agropecuarias" [Decree-Law 305/2012. On Nonagricultural Cooperatives]. *Gaceta Oficial de la República de Cuba, Edición Extraordinaria, No. 53*, diciembre 11, 2012.

———. "Decreto Ley 368. Modificativo del Decreto-Ley No. 143 Sobre la Oficina del Historiador de la Ciudad de La Habana de 30 de octubre de 1993" [Decree-Law 368. Modifies Decree-Law No, 143 On the Office of the Historian of the City of

Havana of October 30, 1993]. *Gaceta Oficial de la República de Cuba, Edición Ordinaria, No. 24, de 3 de abril de 2018*, diciembre 17, 2019.

———. "Decreto 354/2018. De las Cooperativas Agropecuarias" [Decree-Law 354/2018. On Agricultural Cooperatives]. *Gaceta Oficial de la República de Cuba, Edición Ordinaria, No. 37*, mayo 24, 2019.

———. "Decreto 356/2019. De las Cooperativas No Agropecuarias" [Decree-Law 356/2019. On Nonagricultural Cooperatives]. *Gaceta Oficial de la República de Cuba, Edición Ordinaria, No. 63*, agosto 30, 2019b.

———. "Decreto Ley 366/2019. De las Cooperativas No Agropecuarias" [Decree-Law 366/2019. On Nonagricultural Cooperatives]. *Gaceta Oficial de la República de Cuba, Edición Ordinaria, No. 63*, September 30, 2019c.

———. "Decreto 354/2018. De las Cooperativas Agropecuarias" [Decree-Law 354/2018. On Nonagricultural Cooperatives]. *Gaceta Oficial de la República de Cuba, Edición Ordinaria, No. 37*, mayo 24 2019d.

———. 2021. "Decreto-Ley 47/2021 De las Cooperativas No Agropecuarias" [Decree-Law 47/2021. On Nonagricultural Cooperatives]. *Gaceta Oficial No. 94 Ordinaria de 19 de agosto de 2021.*

Cubadebate. "Gobierno cubano informa sobre nuevas medidas económicas" [Cuban government announces new economic measures]. *Cubadebate*. July 16, 2020. Retrieved from http://www.cubadebate.cu/noticias/2020/07/16/gobierno-cubano -informa-nuevas-medidas-economicas-video/.

Figueredo, O. "Contraloría detecta pérdidas y daños económicos millonarios en empresas de La Habana" [Comptroller's Office detects millionaire losses and damages in Havana enterprises]. *Cubadebate*, 24 enero, 2019. Retrieved from: http: //www.cubadebate.cu/noticias/2019/01/24/contraloria-detecta-perdidas-y-danos -economicos-millonarios-en-empresas-de-la-habana/#.X17.

ILO. *Resilience of the cooperative business model in times of crisis. Sustainable Enterprise Programme/Responses to global economic crisis.* International Labour Organization, 2014. Retrieved from: https://www.ilo.org/wcmsp5/groups/public/-- -ed_emp/---emp_ent/documents/publication/wcms_108416.pdf.

Meidner, R. 1978. *Employee Investment Funds.*

MINJUS. *Gaceta Oficial de la República de Cuba, Edición Ordinaria, No. 63*, 30 agosto, 2019.

ONEI. *Anuario Estadístico de Cuba, 2019* [Statistical Annual of Cuba, 2019]. La Habana: Oficina Nacional de Estadística e Información de Cuba, 2020. Retrieved from: http://www.onei.gob.cu/sites/default/files/07_empleo_y_salarios_2019.pdf.

ONU. 2019. *Resolución 64/136. Las cooperativas en el desarrollo social* [Resolution 64/136. Cooperatives in social development]. Organizacion de las Naciones Unidas. Retrieved from: https://www.un.org/es/ga/64/resolutions.shtml.

PCC. *Lineamientos de la Política Económica y Social del Partido y la Revolución* [Guidelines for the Economic and Social Policy of the Party and the Revolution]. La Habana: VI Congreso del Partido Comunista de Cuba, 2011.

———. *Lineamientos de la Política Económica y Social del Partido y la Revolución* [Guidelines for the Economic and Social Policy of the Party and the Revolution]. La Habana: VII Congreso del Partido Comunista de Cuba, 2017.

————. *Conceptualización del Modelo Económico y Social Cubano de Desarrollo y Plan Nacional de Desarrollo Económico y Social hasta 2030* [Conceptualization of the Cuban Economic and Social Development Model and National Plan for Economic and Social Development until 2030]. La Habana: VI Congreso del Partido Comunista de Cuba, 2016a.

Piketty, T. *Capital e ideología* [Capital and ideology]. Madrid, España: Grupo Planeta, 2019.

Piñeiro, C. "Ahora que sí van las cooperativas, vamos a hacerlo bien. Roles de las cooperativas en el nuevo modelo económico cubano" [Now that cooperatives are coming, let's do it well. Role of cooperatives in the new Cuban economic model]. *Temas Catalejo*, 2012. Retrieved from: http://www.temas.cult.cu/catalejo/economia/CamiBila_Pineiro.pdf.

————. *Introducción al Cooperativismo. Ideas Básicas para la Práctica* [Introduction to cooperatives. Basic Practical Ideas]. La Habana: Editorial Caminos, 2015.

Piñeiro, C. "Las cooperativas no agropecuarias y su contribución al desarrollo local" [Nonagricultural cooperatives and their contribution to local development]. *Economía y Desarrollo* 164(2), 2020. Retrieved from: http://scielo.sld.cu/scielo.php?script=sci_arttext&pid=S0252-85842020000200010.

————. "Las cooperativas y los pensadores socialistas" [Cooperatives and socialist thinkers]. *Rebelión,* 2011. Retrieved from: https://rebelion.org/docs/125970.pdf.

Puig, Y. "Autoridades explican nuevas medidas respecto a cooperativas no agropecuarias" [Authorities explain new measures related to nonagricultural cooperatives]. *Cubadebate*, agosto 9, 2017. Retrieved from: http://www.cubadebate.cu/noticias/2017/08/09/autoridades-explican-nuevas-medidas-respecto-a-cooperativas-no-agropecuarias/.

Sanders, B. "Corporate Accountability and Democracy." 2019. Retrieved from: https://berniesanders.com/issues/corporate-accountability-and-democracy/.

Torres, A. "¿Nadie quedará desamparado?" [Nobody will be left defenseless?]. OnCubaNews 2020. Retrieved from: https://oncubanews.com/opinion/columnas/sin-filtro/nadie-quedara-desamparado-i/.

Chapter 11

The Cooperative as an Energizing Agent of the Social and Solidarity Economy Model in Cuba

Yamira Mirabal González and Iriadna Marín de León

NOTES ON THE SOCIAL AND SOLIDARITY ECONOMY

The social and solidarity economy (ESS in Spanish) is being seen today as an opportunity to face the inevitable economic, social, and environmental challenges that afflict the global community, with the support of each of the socioeconomic agents[1] that participate in it, in the search for and application of initiatives, solidary vocation, and entrepreneurial spirit aimed at the common good. Particularly for Cuba, it also responds to the needs and norms set out in the Conceptualization of the Economic and Social Development Model (PCC 2016), by endorsing a more equitable, inclusive, and participatory development.

ESS has been studied and defined by different authors and regulatory documents (see Roitman 2016; Labrador, Alfonso and Rivera 2017; Provincia de Mendoza 2012).

Among the components that define the concept, it is worth mentioning the following:

These elements build an economy whose core is not the reproduction of capital but the centrality of labor in the reproduction of life.

In this context, with the aim to broaden the characteristics of the definition of ESS, the International Labor Organization (OIT in Spanish) proposes the following defining criteria (OIT 2010):

- It is centered on people.

- Its organizations are of a hybrid nature, meaning that they combine profitability—which is not primary—, social change and social values.
- They operate on the basis of negotiated rules and guaranteed reciprocity, especially through social control.
- They function within the frame of an economic democracy.
- Among their objectives, they include the conservation of social bonds.
- They can also have as their objective the search for a reduction of the gap between individuals and authorities (in the community associations).

The principles that sustain ESS at the international level are the following (see Rivera et al. 2012):

1. Solidarity, cooperation, and democracy as a way of life and human coexistence—a standard that every person and labor and entrepreneurial organization that forms part of the solidarity economy sector must follow.
2. The supremacy of labor over capital—with which the origin of economy and human development is found again, and the respect for labor is rescued from the slavery that capital exercises.
3. Associative labor as the fundamental foundation of the organization of enterprises, production, and economy—which replaces salaried labor as a capitalist institution, the main cause of unjust distribution of wealth, marginality, and poverty.
4. Social ownership of the means of production, in which workers, as the direct producers, are the owners and managers of the enterprise, full beneficiaries of the economic results—with which the exploitation of human beings by human beings, of human beings by the state, and the fundamental cause of class struggles are eliminated.
5. Self-management as the superior form of worker participation in entrepreneurial management, in the economy, and in the leadership of the society and the state—with which marginality is eliminated and real democracy is built and consolidated.

With respect to the case of Cuba, Betancourt and Gómez Arencibia (2019) have offered a definition of ESS, understood as the economic form that is centered on social protection and equity, leading to the creation of quality employment, fair growth, the progress of the foundational democracy and sustainable development, and in which the role of the local governments is fundamental. It is a way of operating the economy that organizes the production, distribution, circulation, and consumption of goods and services in an associative or cooperative manner. It is not based on the pursuit of profit in an individualistic way, but rather on resolving needs, on seeking high-quality ways of life for all those who participate in it, their families and communities, in collaboration with other communities, while at the same time establishing fraternal and solidary social ties in a self-managed and democratic way in the decision-making process, by assuming the management of the natural resources and the respect toward future generations, without exploitation of foreign workers—and all in a responsible manner.

As part of the conception of the ESS model in Cuba, the following principles that rule its development and constitute the base of the integration of the various sectors and forms of property and management of the economy are defined: Solidarity, social community responsibility, participative democracy, distribution of income, the articulation of the public-private sector and of social community agents, as well as of self-managed membership that promote productive social networks as self-managed or co-managed forms, for the benefit of labor and of an emancipatory citizenry (D'Angelo 2015).

In Cuba, according to the progress reached on the topic of ESS, and in agreement with what was established in the Constitution that was recently approved, the socioeconomic agents correspond to the forms of ownership approved in Article 22, and defined as: socialist of all the people[2]; cooperative; owned by political, mass, and social organizations; private; mixed; owned by institutions and associative forms; and personal (ANPP 2019).

Based on the analyses that were done, it is necessary to recognize the cooperative as an agent of economic, productive, and social development that has been consolidated as one of the main protagonists of the ESS sector, supported by the contributions it brings to the socioeconomic sector to raising its efficiency and efficacy levels, and of the quality of life of its members and of society—which reaffirms its role as a key agent in local development.[3]

The Constitution of the Republic of Cuba (ANPP 2019) defines the cooperative ownership form as that supported by the collective work of its owner-members and by the effective exercise of the principles of cooperativism. This definition breaks with the heretofore agrarian character of the cooperatives in our country.

Cooperatives can be distinguished from other socioeconomic agents, starting from their conception and operation and depending on their specificities, through four factors, according to (Rivera, y otros 2012):

1. In the first place, the cooperatives, and the different associative forms in general, start from a framework in which the values of justice and solidarity determine the way economic and social benefits are obtained. In general, the enterprises that function according to the system of these principles develop the opportunity to work in better conditions and they are more efficient and effective, which constitutes a strength for the cooperative administration.

2. In second place, the democratic administration. The highest authority of the government of the cooperatives is the General Assembly of Associates (AGA in Spanish), which constantly tries to reproduce its social capital and hold the confidence of the members, the workers, family, the community, and society in general. Therefore, society plays an essential role in the decision-making process.
3. The third element is the form of distribution of the income and profit, in which the tendency is more toward equality and equity.
4. And as the fourth and final element, the importance of the social responsibility[4] that the cooperatives have toward their members and workers, their families, and the community, in which the economic aspect (the base), and its social aspect (the purpose), link together.

These factors require that the administrative processes generated in them be given their own method, with the additional aim of tackling the problems that exist in the cooperative enterprises. Specifically, the deficient structure of the relations between the State and the cooperatives as it has been broached up to now, constitutes one of the problems that affects their management from an external point of view—a topic that also suffers from insufficient support, which is not only theoretical but also practical.

In the Cuban context, ESS should contribute to the integration of the different socioeconomic agents based on the use of its potentials, as well as contribute to local development, within the framework of the updated economic and social model. It constitutes an ideal space for the materialization of the municipal ESS as a fundamental organization with the necessary autonomy, with a sustainable nature, with a solid economic-productive base using endogenous and exogenous resources, and the interagency, interregional and multilevel articulation. This aim recognizes the strategic role of the cooperative sector and, through the productive chain, its link to the other forms of state and non-state management, as a contribution to the construction of socialism in Cuba.

COMMON ASPECTS BETWEEN THE PRINCIPLES OF THE CUBAN SOCIALIST SYSTEM AND ESS

The Constitution of the Republic of Cuba establishes a set of fundamental principles which converge with the principles of ESS and which allow for the analysis of its relevance to Cuba by guaranteeing the interrelation of the different forms of management through local sustainable development.

Below we offer the aspects considered to be shared principles of the Constitution and those on which ESS is based.

Table 11.1.—Analysis of the Constitutional Principles and Those of the ESS Sector

Fundamental principles of the Constitution of the Republic of Cuba	Principles of ESS	Shared aspects
ARTICLE 1. Cuba is a socialist state of social rights and justice, democratic, independent and sovereign, organized with all and for the good of all as a unitary and indivisible republic, founded on the labor, dignity, humanism and ethics of its citizens for the enjoyment of liberty, equity, equality, solidarity, well-being, and prosperity.	Solidarity, cooperation, and democracy as a form of life and human coexistence; a rule that every person, labor organization, and enterprise that forms part of the solidarity economy sector has to follow.	• Practicing human values • Equality of rights and duties • Cooperative labor as the basis for individual and collective well-being and prosperity
ARTICLE 13. The state has the following as its essential objectives: a) to channel the efforts of the country in its construction of socialism and to strengthen national unity; b) to maintain and defend the independence, integrity and sovereignty of the nation; c) to conserve national security; d) guarantee effective equality in the enjoyment and exercise of rights and in the fulfillment of the duties consecrated in the Constitution and the laws; e) promote sustainable development that will assure individual and collective prosperity and obtain higher levels of equity and social justice, as well as conserve and augment the achievements attained by the Revolution; f) guarantee the full dignity of the people and their integral development; g) reinforce the ideology and the ethics inherent to our socialist society; h) protect the natural, historic, and cultural patrimony of the nation, and i) assure the educational, scientific, technical, and cultural development of the country.	The supremacy of labor over capital, with which the source of the economy and of human development is found again, and labor and its dignity is rescued from the condition of slavery exercised by capital. ————————————— Associative labor as the fundamental base of the entrepreneurial organization, production and economy, replacing salaried labor as a capitalist institution, as well as the main cause of the unjust distribution of wealth, marginality and poverty.	• Supremacy of labor over capital. • Recognition of labor as the basis of development. • Contribution to individual and collective development. • Enjoyment of rights and fulfillment of duties. • Existence of a regulatory frame. • Encouragement of sustainable development. • Promotion of integral development based on scientific research.

ARTICLE 18. In the Republic of Cuba there prevails a system of socialist economy based on the ownership by all the people of the fundamental means of production as the principal form of property, and the planned direction of the economy, which takes into account, regulates, and controls the market as per the interests of society.	Social ownership of the means of production in which the workers, as the direct producers, are the owners and managers of the enterprise, and full beneficiaries of the economic results. With this concept, the exploitation of man by man and of man by the state is avoided—the fundamental cause of class struggle.	• Recognition of social ownership over the means of production. • Recognition of the rights and duties of man as a social being. • Democratic and participative management.
	Self-management as the highest form of participation of the workers in the management of the enterprise, the economy, and in directing society and the State, with which marginality is eliminated and real democracy is built and consolidated.	

Note: Table based on the Constitution of the Republic of Cuba (ANPP 2019) and Rivera Rodríguez, C. A., O. Labrador Machín, J. L. Alfonso Alemán, L. Ojeda Mesa, Y. Mirabal González, and I. Marín de León. 2012. Cooperativismo, gestión y desarrollo social. Santo Domingo: Editora Corripios S.A.S.

The points in the principles of the ESS sector that coincide with those in the Cuban socialist social system invite the promotion of the institutionalization of this sector in the country, so that it can contribute not only to solving problems and satisfying needs, but also to the promotion of values, to the articulation between the different forms of management and to the use of the abilities and resources, both endogenous and exogenous, toward a local sustainable development.

The Guidelines of the Economic and Social Policy of the Party and the Revolution—which were approved in the VI Congress of the Cuban Communist Party in 2011 (PCC 2011), and updated later, in the VII Congress in 2017 (PCC 2017a)—as well as in the Conceptualization of the Economic and Social Development Model (PCC 2016) and the Bases of the National Plan of Economic and Social Development until 2030: Proposal for a Vision of the Nation, its Strategic Core and Sectors (PCC 2017b), clearly show the determination of the Cuban government to encourage the socioeconomic development of the country, in which the diversification of the forms of ownership and non-state management and their interaction with the state enterprises occupies a fundamental role.

The Guidelines (2011; 2017) present objectives that contribute to the achievement of these proposals, among which the following can be noted:

- To continue updating the Planned Management of the Economic and Social Development, which includes the agents of all forms of property and management, increasing efficiency and efficacy. To guarantee the integral nature of the system and the interrelation of the different agents.
- To continue progress in the application of fiscal stimuli that would promote the systematic development of the non-state management forms.
- To expand labor in the non-state sector as a further employment alternative, dependent on the new organizational forms of production, and the new services to be established.
- To continue the transformation of the management model, in agreement with the greater presence of non-state forms of production, in which the agricultural state enterprise will constitute the main director of the technological development and of the production and commercialization strategies. To use the monetary-mercantile relations in an effective manner and to consolidate the autonomy conferred on the producers in order to increase efficiency and competitiveness.

In 2017, within the main transformations that are the basis of its updating, the Conceptualization of the Economic and Social Development Model (PCC 2016) reiterated the consolidation of the primordial role of the "socialist ownership of all the people"—state-owned enterprises—over the fundamental means of production, and the recognition and diversification of the different forms of appropriately interrelated ownership and management.

Related to this, a group of features are revealed, among which the following stand out:

- The relations of ownership over the means of production define the nature of any socioeconomic system, given that the dominant form of ownership determines the relations of production, distribution, exchange and consumption in society. This is why the main role of socialist ownership by all the people over the basic means of production constitutes a fundamental principle.
- The existence of non-state forms of ownership and management has as its objective to enable the state and the government to concentrate on their own complex tasks, to contribute to the integral efficiency of the economy, generate jobs, roll out initiatives, boost the productive forces,

increase public revenues for the State budget and contribute to the well-being according to the objectives of socialist development.

- The system of entrepreneurial entities includes all ownership forms that the law allows: State-owned enterprises, cooperatives, mixed and private enterprises, as well as enterprises owned by political, mass, and social associations, and other entities of civil society. All entrepreneurial entities interact to the benefit of economic and social development; they function according to similar conditions in the markets and must conform to the regulatory structure and the control as defined by the law.
- The state and government management includes the actions they undertake for the administration of all types of resources, as well as for the coordination between the economic agents. It promotes an effective and efficient performance and interaction of the economic agents through the cooperation, integration and complementarity of the production systems, which are composed of various forms of ownership and management. Based on the intended goals, the forms of association and the articulation of productive chains are diversified between the economic agents, which contributes to the increase of the services and of the national production, their efficiency, quality and competitiveness.

The Bases of the National Plan of Economic and Social Development until 2030: Proposal for a Vision of the Nation, its Strategic Core and Sectors (PCC 2017b) also establish guidelines based on the integration of the state and non-state management forms, through objectives such as:

- Implementing a diversified strategy toward international inclusion, which would include both final products as well as processes and activities—a strategy aimed at opening up opportunities for enterprises and other Cuban entities according to their characteristics, technological level, and diversity of management forms.
- Raising and stimulating the diversity, efficacy, efficiency, quality, investment, and productivity capacity of the different forms of non-state management.

The view and conception of the Cuban state on the diversification of the non-state management forms and their interrelation with the state sector favors the proposal of an ESS model that would guarantee the integration of all socioeconomic agents based on the progress of the country. In addition, it would establish the role that these agents would have in the design and management process of the development strategies at the municipal and provincial levels, in an inclusive, sustainable, and participative manner.

The political aim of the Cuban government—which, by orienting its objectives toward the social benefit and the improvement of the people's quality of life, places the human being, their needs, abilities, and labor at the center of the economic system—is in harmony with the core of ESS, which in this context is called on to play a fundamental role in social transformation.

THE COOPERATIVE AS ENERGIZING ELEMENT IN THE ECONOMÍA SOCIAL Y SOLIDARIA IN CUBA

The development of the cooperative sector in the country has gone through four stages which, in the case of the first three, respond to the emergence of the non-state organizational forms of agricultural production that we have today: the Credits and Services Cooperatives (CCS in Spanish), which started in 1961; the Agricultural Production Cooperatives (CPA in Spanish), created in 1975; the Basic Units of Cooperative Production (UBPC in Spanish), begun in 1993; and, in the case of the fourth stage, the establishment of the Nonagricultural Cooperatives (CNA in Spanish) in other sectors of the economy, starting in 2012.

Today there are 4,828 agricultural cooperatives in the country, with 447,235 members; 2,463 of these are CCS, 869 CPA and 1,496 UBPC (ONEI 2020). For their operations, the CCS, CPA, and UBPC cooperatives are currently directed by the Law Decree 365/2018 "On Agricultural Cooperatives."[5]

As a part of the updating process of the economic model that is underway in the Cuban economy, and derived from the Guidelines of the Economic and Social Policy of the Party and the Revolution approved in 2011 (PCC 2011), the creation of CNAs has begun in Cuba in industrial and service sectors of the economy.

The process of approval of CNAs began in December of 2012, supported by the Law Decrees 305 and 306, both from the Council of State (Consejo de Estado 2012), and Decree 309 of the Council of Ministers (Consejo de Ministros 2012), as well as Resolutions 570 and 427, both from 2012, from the Ministry of Economy and Planning and of Finances and Prices, respectively (Ministerio de Economía y Planificación 2012; Ministerio de Finanzas y Precios 2012). Based on the information provided by the Commission on the Implementation of the Guidelines of the Party and the Revolution—and reflected in various press media, printed and digital—there have been 498 CNAs authorized; of these, by their own decision, ten were not created, 46 were eliminated or are in the process of being eliminated, and 46 were revoked; all of which shows that there are actually 396 functioning CNAs. Of the 498 cooperatives that were authorized in the country, 77 percent were of state origin, meaning that they were created from the State Entrepreneurial

Units, which means that only 23 percent came from grassroots initiatives (Granma 2019).

In order for the cooperatives to really become a stimulating element within the ESS sector in Cuba, its management should be improved based on the solution of an assembly of problems or limitations they present, which are grouped according to the elements that relate to their process of organization and functioning (see Table 2). These elements are the following:

1. Conceptualization: it considers the limitations and proposals related to concepts and definitions based on the economic-productive and social management of the cooperatives.
2. Judicial code; it reflects the limitations and proposals that require modifications in the documents that regulate the legal framework of the cooperatives functioning.
3. Education, training and cooperative information: it mentions the problems and proposals related to training and workshops to contribute to the improvement of the economic-productive and social management of the cooperatives.
4. Constitution, functioning and elimination: based on the limitations that were identified, the proposals which are reflected as part of this element are aimed toward the processes of constituting, functioning and elimination of these organizations.
5. Cooperative management: it expresses the limitations and proposals appropriate to the cooperative management process.
6. Institutional environment: it reflects the proposals based on the internal relations and relations with other organisms and institutions, based on the limitations identified in this respect.
7. Control of the cooperative management: it shows the limitations centered on control within the management process.

Based on the implementation of the proposals mentioned and of other contributions that will be made related to these matters, the improvement of the cooperative sector management aims to strengthen self-management and social projection, as well as compliance with the policies and strategies of public management, as related to the recognition and consideration of the cooperative enterprise as a key agent of ESS in Cuba.

The validity that the cooperative enterprises have in the nature of enterprises is indisputable, taking into account their representation in the production of goods and services, in addition to their social commitment—being essential agents of development.

The cooperative constitutes an energizing entity within the group of agents that are involved in the economic and social life recognized in the

Table 11.2 - Proposals for the improvement of cooperative management.

	Limitations	*Proposals*
1. Conceptualization		
1.1	The regulation of the cooperative does not reflect its essence	Define the cooperative as an association of people who practice the values of cooperativity; its purpose is to satisfy the needs of its members, the community and society in general, through an enterprise of collective ownership managed according to universally recognized principles.
1.2	There is a difference between agricultural and non-agricultural cooperatives, based on their conception and judicial code.	Unify and harmonize the functioning of the cooperative sector in Cuba based on its conception and judicial code.
1.3	The cooperatives do not interact in similar conditions to the rest of the economic agents.	Adapt the practice and judicial code so as to achieve that all economic agents interact in similar conditions.
2. Judicial code		
2.1	Based on the conception and judicial code of the cooperatives, their socioeconomic essence is distorted as their characteristics are confused with those of other forms of management.	Prepare a general Law of cooperatives that will unify and harmonize the cooperative sector according to its identity.

(Continued)

3. Education, training and cooperative information

3.1	Absence of a systematic process of education, training and workshops on cooperativity, which has a negative impact on the development of the cooperative.	Establish a system of cooperative training that would allow for the growth and development of the cooperative movement and the training of human capital at the different levels of teaching.
		Design and implement a national strategy of communication for the promotion of the cooperative culture, aimed at the public goals that are identified.
		Create a program on Cuban television, oriented toward the dissemination of good practices related to cooperativity and toward promoting a general and integral culture on the topic.
		Incorporate content associated to the promotion of the cooperative culture in the educational programs of primary, secondary, pre-university schools and in higher education.
		Design and implement a national program on cooperative education, training and workshops aimed at state and cooperative directors, members and contract workers.
		Recommend that the University, in conjunction with the Asociación Nacional de Economistas y Contadores de Cuba [National Association of Economists and Accountants] (ANEC), coordinate the process of cooperative training and workshops, taking into account the needs of each one.
3.2	The consultation that is offered to the cooperatives does not respond to the particular characteristics of this type of enterprise. Rather, it reproduces patterns of other forms of management.	Encourage processes of training for consultants specialized in cooperative topics, with priority on aspects of accounting, both financial and legal.

4. Constitution, functioning and elimination

4.1	The establishment of forced cooperatives transgresses the cooperative principle of voluntary participation, which should be the natural starting point for the creation of these entities.	Encourage the creation of cooperatives based on the principle of voluntary participation. In economic or productive activities, or of services administered by the State—which are not considered primary—the decision on the form in which this activity is managed (state, private or cooperative mipymes [sic]), should be subject to the principle of voluntary participation of its workers.
4.2	The statutes include issues that are not essential to the functioning of the cooperatives. These issues, because of their potency, need constant revision, which carries the consequence that the statutes will need frequent modification and submitted to a long process of legalization, which has an impact on the legal security of the members.	Recognize the relevance of the Reglamento Interno de la Cooperativa in the Law as a manifestation of the self-regulation of this form of management, in order to relieve the statutes of contents that are complementary or of low importance.
4.3	The cooperative legislation does not specify the requirements that the member charged with the control and auditing function must fulfill.	Establish that, in order to be the member charged with the control and auditing of the cooperative, appropriate training as a cooperative member and knowledge of accounting and similar activities is required.

5. Cooperative management

5.1	The regional scope of the approved activities in the social objective of the cooperatives limits the use of its productive capacities; moreover, the regions are affected because they cannot contract CNA services for their needs from other provinces.	The cooperatives should be able to offer their products or services in the entire national area if they have fulfilled the local contractual obligations based on the collective labor of its members and without resorting to the use of the contractual workforce.

(Continued)

5.2	The lack of availability of sufficient supplies and materials in the retail and wholesale network becomes an obstacle to the management process, which has an impact on the product and service prices offered by the cooperatives.	Improve the logistics of the resupply market so that it guarantees stability in the supplies, materials, and equipment necessary for the vitality of the socioeconomic activity of the cooperative sector.
5.3	There is no efficient mechanism that facilitates access to imports by the cooperatives that have their own financing.	Create logistical and banking mechanisms so that the cooperatives can realize imports with their own financing in foreign currency through a state enterprise. This would mean creating and managing accounts in foreign currency in the name of the cooperatives.
5.4	Even when the principle of Social Responsibility—which supports the functioning of the cooperative sector—is established in the legal framework, there are no mechanisms that would guarantee their implementation and assessment.	Implement Social Responsibility as a principle inherent to the cooperative, and encourage its compliance. Authorize the Consejos de la Administración Municipal (CAM) to reduce by 50 percent the regional contribution to local development to be provided by nonagricultural cooperatives that offer budgets for supporting programs of Responsabilidad Social Directa.

6. Institutional environment

6.1	Insufficient institutionalization for relations between the state and the cooperatives.	Carry out the institutionalization of the cooperative sector based on the creation of the Instituto Nacional de Cooperativismo, whose actions would contribute to the autonomy, growth, consultancy, and control of the sector.
6.2	Absence of self-organization structures of the cooperative movement.	Move ahead experimentally in the creation of structures related to the cooperative sector, based on internal collaboration and articulation, which would contribute to the growth of productive chains and the representativity of the sector (cooperatives of second level, federation and confederation).

6.3	The cooperatives are not recognized by the CAMs and the banking system as agents authorized to present project proposals of local development.	Establish that the cooperatives can present project proposals of local development in their different classifications to be approved and financed by the CAMs. The projects could come from the same cooperative or as the result of its inter-cooperation with one or more cooperatives or state and private management forms, as long as they contribute to the Estrategia de Desarrollo Municipal (EDM) and the Estrategia de Desarrollo Provincial (IEDP), and that they be approved by CAM or by the Provincial Council.
6.4	Insufficient areas and mechanisms for the articulation of the municipal and provincial governments with the cooperatives.	Strengthen the areas and mechanisms of articulation between the municipal and provincial governments with the cooperatives.
6.5	Starting with the banking system, there is a lack of specialized mechanisms that would contribute to the stimulation of the development of cooperatives.	Design a banking policy that stimulates the development of the cooperative sector in Cuba. Create a communication strategy of the existing banking services, based on the development of the cooperative enterprises.

7. Control of cooperative management

7.1	The standards that regulate the accounting and financial activity of the cooperatives are seen as lacking focus and specificity.	Systematize and publish the standards that regulate the accounting and financial activity of the cooperatives.
7.2	Lack of a Guía de Control appropriate to the characteristics of the cooperatives.	Design and implement a Guía de Control that contributes to efficiency in the management of the cooperatives, and reinforces their identity. Such a guide should also constitute a base for the preparation of the self-control instruments.

Note: Table based on the diagnostic of the management of the cooperatives in Cuba.

governments; the community[6]; the Entities of the Central Administration of the State (OACE); other institutions; the productive sector and that of state and private services. The relations that are established among these agents should be supported by a respect toward the autonomy of the management of cooperative enterprises, as well as by the recognition of the Cooperative Social Responsibility and the necessary integration and conciliation of sectorial and local interests, as shown in Figure 1 below.

However, in the absence of a model of ESS, the potential that each of the socioeconomic agents offers from their integration do not achieve a coherent articulation in the current Cuban context. Given these circumstances, it is therefore a question of finding a new approach by government policy, which would stimulate the integration and the development of the various forms of entrepreneurial management, in particular the cooperatives, so that the humanizing, innovative and strategic perspective in the management processes are strengthened. One of the challenges that ESS faces in our country is demonstrating its viability as an economic form, and its impact on the people—from the promotion of values and principles that are centered on their needs and those of their communities—in a spirit of voluntary participation,

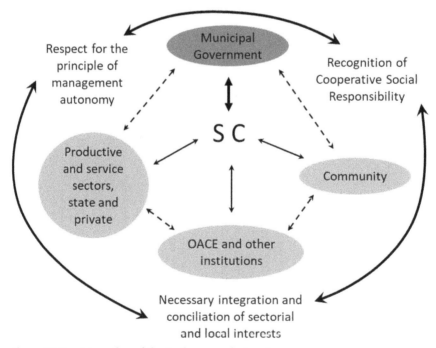

Figure 11.1. Integration of the Socioeconomic Agents.

Source: Based on Marín de León, I. 2016. "Modelo de gestión pública para el sector cooperativo a escala municipal." Tesis de doctorado en Ciencias Económicas, Universidad de Pinar del Río, Pinar del Río.

self-help, and independence, and through the enterprises and organizations that would guarantee a balance among economic success, equity, and social justice at a local scale.

CONCLUSIONS

1. Cooperatives relate to each other, and to the other economic and social agents, through actions of cooperation and collaboration. Their aim is centered on the satisfaction of the needs of its territories, such as: public services, housing, food, education, and training. Moreover, they generate income and jobs as a contribution to local sustainable development. For these reasons, it is worth supporting a social economy that favors social inclusion and that also shows itself to be a path toward the construction of collective agents and socioeconomic networks inserted into productive groups and local and regional value chains.

2. The articulation between the fundamental principles of the Republic of Cuba and the principles of ESS allows for the recognition of the value of an ESS model for the country that contributes to the interrelation of the different forms of management and to the development and consolidation of the Cuban economic and social model.

3. The proposals for the improvement of the economic-productive and social management of the cooperatives, based on their contribution to local sustainable development, with a systemic and strategic perspective, constitute a contribution to the theoretical, methodological and practical analysis of its management process, which establishes the bases for the institutionalization of the ESS model in Cuba, and the recognition of cooperatives based on the use endogenous and exogenous resources and the articulation with the regional governments and other agents.

NOTES

1. Government; state, private, and cooperative enterprise system, academic and scientific research institutions, professional, mass, and social organizations, among others.

2. Editor's Note: Refers to state-owned enterprises.

3. A process of social construction and structural change which, based on an innovative regional environment, develops local capacities to manage public policies, strategies, programs, and projects that are aimed at using native and foreign resources and to harmoniously articulate national, sectorial, and regional interests

that encourage economic, social, natural, and political transformations—institutional changes in the areas with sustainable bases and with an active and protagonist citizen participation—so as to raise the quality of life of the population (Torres, Gómez, González, Ares, Cardoso, Flores, 2018).

4. Cooperative Social Responsibility: the obligatory and conscious commitment that the cooperative has to contribute to the development and the improvement of the quality of life of its members and workers, its families, the community, and society in general, based on efficient and efficacious economic processes (Alfonso Alemán 2013).

5. This was superceded in 2021 by Decreto-Ley 47/2021 "De las Cooperativas No Agropecuarias" (Consejo de Estado 2021). See Cubadebate (2021).

6. Conceived as the environment in which it is located and with which it establishes a direct social commitment as part of its social responsibility.

BIBLIOGRAPHY

Alfonso Alemán, J. L. "Responsabilidad, gestión y balance social en las empresas cooperativas" [Responsibility, management and social balance in cooperative enterprises]. *Cooperativismo y Desarrollo* 1 (2): 248–63, 2013.

ANPP. *Constitución de la República de Cuba* [Constitution of the Republic of Cuba]. La Habana: Asamblea Nacional del Poder Popular, Febrero de 2019. Retrieved from: http://www.granma.cu/file/pdf/gaceta/Nueva%20Constituci%C3%B3n%20240%20KB-1.pdf.

Betancourt, R., & Gómez Arencibia, J. *Sinopsis de la Red Cubana de Economía Social y Solidaria y Responsabilidad Social ESORSE* [Synopsis of the Cuban Network of Social and Solidarity Economics ESORSE]. La Habana: Centro de Investigaciones Psicológicas y Sociológicas CIPS. 2019.

Consejo de Estado. Decreto Ley 365 y 366/2019. De las Cooperativas No Agropecuarias" [Decree-Law 365 & 366/2019. On Non-Agricultural Cooperatives]. *Gaceta Oficial de la República de Cuba, Edición Ordinaria, No. 63*, September 30, 2019.

———. "Decreto-Ley 47/2021 De las Cooperativas No Agropecuarias" [Decree-Law 47/2021. On Nonagricultural Cooperatives]. *Gaceta Oficial No. 94 Ordinaria de 19 de agosto de 2021.*

———. "Decreto Ley 305/2012. De las Cooperativas No Agropecuarias" [Decree-Law 305/2012. On Nonagricultural Cooperatives]. *Gaceta Oficial de la República de Cuba, Edición Extraordinaria, No. 53*, diciembre 11, 2012.

Consejo de Ministros. "Decreto No. 309 Reglamento de las Cooperativas No Agropecuarias de Primer Grado" [Decree No. 309 Rulebook for First Degree Nonagricultural Cooperatives]. *Gaceta Oficial No. 053 Extraordinaria de 11 de diciembre de 2012*, diciembre 11, 2012.

Cubadebate. "Aprueba Consejo de Ministros perfeccionamiento de actores de la economía cubana" [Council of Ministers approves improving actors of the Cuban economy]. junio 11, 2021. Retrieved from: http://www.cuba.cu/economia/2021-06

-02/aprueba-consejo-de-ministros-perfeccionamiento-de-actores-de-la-economia
-cubana/56162.

D'Angelo, O. *Economía solidaria y autogestión social: algunas proyecciones y desafíos en nuestra realidad actual* [Solidarity Economics and social
self-management: Some projections and challenges for our current reality]. La
Habana: Biblioteca Virtual CLACSO, 2015.

Granma. "Nuevas normas jurídicas que actualizan y perfeccionan la legislación
sobre las Cooperativas no Agropecuarias" [New legal norms that update and
improve the legislation onNon-AGricultural Cooperatves]. *Granma*, Agosto 29,
2019. Retrieved from: http://www.granma.cu/cuba/2019-08-29/nuevas-normas
-juridicas-que-actualizan-y-perfeccionan-la-legislacion-sobre-las-cooperativas-no
-agropecuarias-29-08-2019-21-08-37.

Labrador, O., J. L. Alfonso, and C. A. Rivera. "Enfoques sobre la Economía Social y
Solidaria" [Points of view on Social and Solidarity Economics]. *Cooperativismo y
Desarrollo, 5(2),* 137–146, 2017.

Marín de León, I. "Modelo de gestión pública para el sector cooperativo a escala
municipal" [Public management model for the cooperaive sector at the municipal
scale]. Tesis de doctorado en Ciencias Económicas, Universidad de Pinar del Río,
Pinar del Río, 2016.

Ministerio de Economía y Planificación. "Resolución No. 570/2012." *Gaceta Oficial
No. 053 Extraordinaria de 11 de diciembre de 2012.*

Ministerio de Finanzas y Precios. "Resolución No. 427/2012." *Gaceta Oficial No.
053 Extraordinaria de 11 de diciembre de 2012.*

OIT. 2010. *Economía social y solidaria: Construyendo un entendimiento común.*
Documento de trabajo. CIF-OIT, Turín: Organización Internacional de Trabajo.

ONEI. *Anuario Estadístico de Cuba, 2019* [Statistical Annual of Cuba, 2019]. La
Habana: Oficina Nacional de Estadística e Información de Cuba, 2020.

PCC. *Bases del Plan Nacional de Desarrollo Económico y Social hasta 2030* [Bases
for the National Plan for Economic and Social Development until 2030]. La
Habana: VII Congreso del Partido Comunista de Cuba, La Habana, 2017.

———. *Conceptualización del Modelo Económico y Social Cubano de Desarrollo y
Plan Nacional de Desarrollo Económico y Social hasta 2030* [Conceptualization
of the Cuban Economic and Social Development Model and National Plan for
Economic and Social Development until 2030]. La Habana: VI Congreso del
Partido Comunista de Cuba, 2016a.

———. *Lineamientos de la Política Económica y Social del Partido y la Revolución*
[Guidelines for the Economic and Social Policy of the Party and the Revolution].
La Habana: VI Congreso del Partido Comunista de Cuba, 2011.

———. *Lineamientos de la Política Económica y Social del Partido y la Revolución*
[Guidelines for the Economic and Social Policy of the Party and the Revolution].
La Habana: VII Congreso del Partido Comunista de Cuba, 2017.

Provincia de Mendoza. *Provincia de Mendoza Ley de Promoción de la Economía
Social y Solidaria núm. 8435* [Province of Mendoza Law for the Promotion of
the Social and Solidarity Economy No. 8435], 2012 Retrieved from: https://base
.socioeco.org/docs/ley_8435_ess_mza.pdf.

Rivera, C. A., O. Labrador, J. L. Alfonso, L. Ojeda, Y. Mirabal, and I. Marín. *Cooperativismo, gestión y desarrollo social* [Cooperatives, management and social development]. Santo Domingo: Editora Corripios S. A. S., 2012.

Roitman, R. D. "¿De qué hablamos cuando hablamos de economía social?" [What are we talking about when we say social economy?], 2016.

Torres, C. C., G. Gómez, M. González, E. Ares, R Cardoso, and Flores, J. "Modelo para la gestión de políticas territoriales de desarrollo local a escala municipal en Cuba" [Model for the management of regional policies of social development at the municipal level in Cuba]. *Anales de la Academia de Ciencias de Cuba*, 2018. http://www.revistaccuba.cu.

Chapter 12

Participation in the Strategies and Social Management of Nonagricultural Cooperatives in Centro Habana Municipality

Francisco Damián Morillas Valdés

CONSIDERATIONS ON THE ROLE AND IMPLEMENTATION OF COOPERATIVE PRINCIPLES

From its origins, the cooperative movement has questioned the ethical and social values of business management for being often oriented to the maximization of economic benefits. In this connection, efforts are currently under way to find more just and equitable ways of building an economy other than based on the domination of capital. In the specific case of the cooperative enterprises, their principles and values are stepping stones to the development of attitudes or willingness to act according to the objectives of this *other economy*, in which the human beings and their progress and well-being are at the root of all economic and business management.

With the 1995 ICA (International Cooperative Alliance) revision,[1] the doctrinal principles of the cooperative movement established the following:

1. Voluntary and open membership: Joining a cooperative is a free choice, so no one can be forced to become a member.
2. Democratic member control: This has to do with the value of participatory democracy and assumes that all partners are equal regardless of how much they contribute to the organization or who participates more actively in the policy- and decision-making processes. These

  characteristics may vary according to the statutes or regulations of the
  cooperatives (Esteller 2002).
3. Member economic participation: Members contribute equitably to the
  capital of their cooperatives. They perform their economic activities
  through their own efforts and mutual help, for the benefit of the community and their own, which in turn contributes to good discipline, better
  results, personal motivation, and stronger solidarity.

In reference to participation, several authors (Hesselbach 1978; ICA
1995; Laville 2001; Da Ros 2005; Monzón 1989) argue that the members
should take part in making decisions and resource planning, management,
and control, as well as in the decisions of institutions, programs, and actions
involving the interests of the participants. It is about engagement in certain
activities, ranging from signing a petition to voting on certain appointments.

Hesselbach (1978) indicates that putting into practice the cooperative principles and the single vote is not sufficient to guarantee the democratization
of internal management. According to this author, the assemblies sometimes
have a certain number of members who make personal contact between the
managers and the managed, which may favor the empowerment of some and
a lack of control and of democratic participation. These behaviors lead to
the concentration of power on a technocracy that would eventually elect its
managers from among its peers, as well as to wrong decisions and inequality
of opportunity and development among the members.

As an essential condition to promote legitimacy and individual commitment to collective work, participation has a major impact not only on the
community where the subject lives but also on society as a whole. Without a
doubt, the cooperatives are instruments of citizen participation inasmuch as
they gather a group of individuals who have common concerns or interests
and wish to work together to find solutions and make good use of some
people's initiatives, other people's prudence and everybody's opinions (Da
Ros 2005).

1. Autonomy and independence: Cooperatives are autonomous, self-help
  organizations controlled by their members. If they enter into agreements
  with other organizations, including governments, or raise capital from
  external sources, they do so on terms ensure democratic control and
  maintain their autonomy (Esteller 2002).
2. Education, training, and information: Cooperatives provide education
  and training for their members so they can contribute effectively to the
  development of their organizations. This education covers both the doctrinal elements of cooperativism and technical knowledge depending on
  the partnership's sphere of activity (Esteller 2002).

3. Cooperation among cooperatives or inter-cooperation: In order to serve their members and communities most effectively, the cooperatives work together through local, national, regional, and international structures as well as through agreements between those different levels.
4. Concern for community: Cooperatives must contribute to the development, social transformation, and well-being of their communities. They are particularly responsible for ensuring the sustainable development of their communities from an economic, social, and cultural viewpoint and for the protection of their physical and biotic environment.

Lenin (1923) warned that we must not be so naive as to ignore the risks facing cooperatives due to society's political and ideological orientation. Specifically, in capitalist societies, cooperatives can become "a specific type of enterprise dominated by the logic of the market" (Lenin 1973, 419).

METHODOLOGICAL CONSIDERATIONS

For this study, a census sampling was carried out with the twelve nonagricultural cooperatives (CNA) existing in the municipality at the time, that took into account their form of constitution (induced and not induced)[2] and their field (construction, agriculture, and food and other services).

Our methodology included interviews and surveys with the presidents of the CNAs. We also organized discussion groups with the members, held interviews with experts and municipal government officials, and engaged in participant observation of the organizational structure and internal operation of the cooperatives. As part of the methodological design, we operationalized variables such as *business strategies* and *insertion in and sustainability of the local socio-production structures*.

In order to develop this research process, we took into account theoretical references of the Social and Solidarity Economy and the international cooperative principles to establish the dimensions and indicators that make it possible to evaluate the organizational, operational, and insertion and sustainability strategies of the CNAs as business organizations.

As part of the process to evaluate the implementation of the international cooperative principles, we made emphasis on democratic member control, member economic participation, autonomy and independence, cooperation among cooperatives, social responsibility, and concern for community. Based on these methodological elements, the details of the process are presented below.

PARTICIPATION OF THE MEMBERS IN
THE DESIGN AND MANAGEMENT OF
SOCIO-PRODUCTION STRATEGIES

In Cuba, the participation of the members in the management and control of cooperative enterprises is enshrined in Decree-Law 305/2012 "On
Nonagricultural Cooperatives" and understood to provide for the membership's collective decision-making power and equal rights, which matches
both the principles of the International Cooperative Alliance (ICA) and
the Cuban standards. Its updated version, Decree-Law 366/2019, includes
a change in the sense that it limits participation to the context of the labor
unions. (MINJUS 2012) (MINJUS 2019)

The presence of labor unions in the CNAs is a highly debated question. According to Article 6 of Decree-Law 305/2012 and Article 12.1 of
Decree-Law 366/2019, the constitution of a cooperative is the result of the
contribution of its voluntary members. This can be under a collective ownership regime or a system that preserves the members' ownership of their
personal assets, or else based on the management of the means of production
of the state patrimony. In all three cases, all members have the same rights.

When comparing the ICA principles and the provisions of Decree-Laws
305/2012 and 366/2019 with the steps to design a development strategy
for cooperatives—if it is only by the board of directors, by engaging all
members, or individually by those members—it is clear that said strategy is
designed by all members in an assembly. However, the author's research has
proven that this condition changes among the studied cooperatives depending
on their field (construction, agriculture, or food and other services) and their
form of constitution (induced or not induced).

Our findings show that all the induced CNAs consider the assembly as the
quintessential space for participation. According to the members that we interviewed, they meet "when they have doubts about some internal or external
process that could affect the cooperative," a view that reveals a favorable attitude toward a participatory and collective decision-making process. Fifteen
of the thirty-six interviewees referred to the General Members' Assembly as
the space for participation by voting and making decisions on the running
of the cooperative, in line with Decree-Laws 305/2012 and 366/2019. In the
same sample group, twelve members from three CNAs of the field of services
consider themselves empowered to manage the cooperative and capable of
controlling the processes without any intervention or mandate, be it regarding
warehouse operations, quality control or customer satisfaction.

The results of this research show that the mechanisms approved in the
statutes of these CNAs aim to democratize internal management. However,

some members are unhappy about the prevalence of forms of participation—as typical of the labor culture in the state enterprise model—characterized by Assemblies that remain silent over the predominant views of the president and the board of the directors. In five of the nine induced CNAs—a farmers' market, two dressmaking workshops, and two beauty salons—we were able to establish that the members have participated in discussions about the design and implementation of organizational and operational strategies that best respond to time-saving, cost-cutting, and profit-making needs.

Another incentive for member participation—in service CNAs—is the implementation of strategies that provide more security (in terms of finances, continuance in the job, better use of the working hours and the labor force, etc.), training in cooperative work, more autonomy, and solutions to the lack of a wholesale market.

One negative element hanging over the participation, control, and decision-making processes in the induced CNAs is the presence of centralized management mechanisms that ignore the multiple and varied dynamics and interests of those involved in the said processes. This is a consequence of the poor knowledge about management and cooperative principles among those involved in the constitution and running of the CNAs, for the most part their presidents and managers. All this is the result of haste, insecurity, and, in many cases, improvisation.

The results of intra-sectorial comparisons reveal that the induced CNAs of the service field have implemented strategies to streamline their forms of organization and operation, motivated mostly by the need to adapt to the country's new economic reality.

With regard to development strategies and member participation, they took steps to strengthen security in the workshops and made internal changes to improve the working conditions. In the case of the beauty salons, they included sauna and gym facilities for the benefit of both the customers and the members.

In the case of the three non-induced CNAs, the comparative analysis of the characteristics of the members' participation in the development strategies shows that all three of them have implemented dynamic and creative mechanisms in accordance with their needs, the circumstances and the current legal framework. In one of them—involved in construction—the members show that participation in and control over every area is a responsibility that they all share equally, based on a strong sense of belonging and proper knowledge of every specialty. While this strategy is a form of organization and operation in the short run—as the president and the members recognize—it promises to become one of the keys to medium- and long-term success in this CNA.

The same analysis of the comparison between induced and non-induced CNAs shows that they are more flexible and dynamic in terms of organization and performance. Our assessment reveals that, in the short and medium term, the non-induced CNAs are economically more successful than the induced ones. Therefore, we can conclude that the non-induced CNAs have managed to be more sustainable than the induced ones. In general, the limitations in the latter could compromise the success of the management model because of the reproduction of a centralized management and the little respect for participation and control on the part of the members.

MATERIALIZATION OF THE PRINCIPLES OF MANAGEMENT AUTONOMY, SOCIAL RESPONSIBILITY, COLLABORATION, AND COOPERATION

In our opinion, the implementation or non-implementation of these principles is what makes it possible to evaluate the social relations, participation dynamics, and the logic behind the organization of socioeconomic and power-sharing actions that take place therein, as well as their impact on the institutional fabric and political system of the nation. Let us address now the implementation of the principles of management autonomy, social responsibility, and joint work and cooperation in the CNAs of Centro Habana municipality.

Management Autonomy

Under the principle of autonomy and independence, according to (ICA 1995), the cooperatives are autonomous organizations controlled by their members, which is highly valuable for their development and sustainability as a social movement. This international principle differs substantially from the provisions of Article 4, item d) of the Cuban Decree-Law 305/2012—with special emphasis on economic-fiscal overseeing mechanisms that specify tax obligations, fund creation and profit sharing at the expense of social aspects underlined by ICA. Hence its important role in the search for collective solutions to concerns and interests of the community and its contribution to the CNA's engagement in local structures and to the provision of a better service for their benefit and positive transformation. A substantial difference related to this principle is noticeable in Article 6, item d) of Decree-Law 366/2019 regarding the recognition of the cooperatives as economically self-sufficient inasmuch as they are free to use their patrimony within the terms set by law.

In this process of transition between Decree-Laws 305/2012 and 366/2019, the CNAs of Centro Habana municipality have met difficulties, mostly related to *intermediation*, purchasing basic consumables. In the case of the induced CNAs, the results show that the state mediates in the access to resources, with a strong participation of former buyers and suppliers of the state entities that brought the cooperatives into being. These processes hinder the CNA's management autonomy as much as their sustainability and development strategies, often undermined by the rise in the price of basic commodities, among other reasons.

As to the induced CNAs, a determining factor is the lack of knowledge among the members about the real scope of their management autonomy. An intra-sectorial analysis of the access to technological resources shows that the three farmers' markets consider their relationship with the Empresa de la Agricultura y de Mercado (Agriculture and Market Enterprise) as "not very reliable" because of its failure to deliver the contracted products.

As can be seen, all these problems are the cause and consequence of the lack of a wholesale market, which reveals paradoxes in the implemented policies that limit the development of the strategies of the CNAs and favor the opportunistic designs of the intermediaries. Obviously, despite the lack of a wholesale market, the non-induced CNAs enjoy greater autonomy because they have more possibilities of gaining access to resources without intermediaries.

As to the non-induced CNA in the food service sector, we found that this is the only one that uses a bank loan—granted by CIMEX Corporation—to buy some of its technological and basic products. What is unusual in this case, according to its members, is that this has no influence on its management autonomy. On its end, one of the non-induced CNAs in the construction sector has implemented a number of purchasing strategies, subject to the availability of the products, without state mediation. However, its offices and construction sites are so spread out throughout the country that they have to implement internal mechanisms for consultation between its provincial branches and the board of directors in Havana—a feature that distinguishes this CNA from other similar ones.

Another studied indicator is the control over the cooperatives: who controls them, what is controlled and how frequently. Our comparative analysis—of the non-induced CNAs in the food service sector and the non-induced one in the construction sector—shows that they have been audited only once in two years by the General Comptroller's Office, not by the municipal government or any of its entities. Such a lack of control is inconsistent with the regulations and revealing of the great confusion that prevails about the CNAs as forms of ownership and management, the reason that they are mistaken for a form of self-employment. This is one of the main reasons that the CNAs are not included in this municipality's local development strategy (AMPP Centro Habana 2015), as evidenced by the analysis of the Business Social Responsibility (BSR).

Business Social Responsibility

BSR is considered as one of the fundamental values of this movement (ICA 1995) as well as an ideology that should be reflected in every step of this kind of enterprise (Castilla y Gallardo 2011). Contradictorily, the provisions of Article 4, item f) of Decree-Law 305/2012 reveal limitations in terms of theory and sustainability because of its marked emphasis on the economic-fiscal dimension. This reduces the social responsibility of the CNAs regarding its contribution to planned economic development and to the well-being of its members and their families and of the environment, to the detriment of a well-balanced systemic vision. Something similar happens with the objectives of the Guidelines on the Economic and Social Policy (PCC 2011). Its goal is to reestablish the role of labor and income in favor of social and community development, the fulfillment of individual and family needs—which guarantees the systematic and sustained improvement of public services, creates sources of income and expands the work of the non-state sector—and the assistance to vulnerable sectors of the community and their basic needs.

As to the ethical positioning of the BSR, all the presidents and members of our study sample claim to be aware of the topic of social responsibility, but it is obvious that they all lack a systemic conception that goes beyond the reductionist vision of the regulatory framework.

Our findings prove that all the presidents, as well as seventeen members of the induced CNAs, believe that their prime goal is profit maximization, as do twenty-one members of the non-induced CNAs. As a significant detail, the entire sample only identifies as solidarity relations those that they have established within their own CNAs and not their links with both the community and other regional institutions (be they state or cooperatives). This has to do perhaps with the misconceptions hanging over this form of management since its inception in Cuba, including an incomplete interpretation of the solidarity cooperative principles. If we bear in mind that Decree-Law 305/2012 does not provide for the qualification of human resources and take into account the limitations in terms of training on cooperative principles, it is significant that 11 members mention education as part of BSR.

On the other hand, we found similar views in the non-induced CNAs. Our findings from the collective interview have it that thirteen members associate BSR with "improved individual and family well-being." Seven members of the same study sample referred to BSR as the regional contribution,[3] five were concerned about the environment, four linked BSR with the qualification of human resources, and only two mentioned the community.

As to the social work of the CNAs, the entire sample tends to favor a philanthropic approach subject to voluntary actions rather than BSR, which assumes the latter as an obligation. This behavior defined as philanthropic could explain the poor performance of the studied CNAs regarding their commitment to the solution of social or environmental problems from a systemic and organized viewpoint.

Based on the ethical positioning on BSR and after comparing the results of the interviews with municipal government officials, we found that the limitations of the municipal government are not only caused by their ignorance of the role and place of the CNAs—including their potential to help local and community development and to protect the environment. This is also because of their inability to deal with society's growing intricacies and needs, as stated in the Guidelines of the Economic and Social Policy (PCC 2011) and the Conceptualization of the Economic and Social Model (PCC 2016).

The analysis of the environmental aspects deserves special attention. A look at the government documents on the Environmental Management Strategy of Centro Habana municipality (2015–2020) would suffice to reveal that none of the production or service NCAs controls these aspects. We can infer from this that such a lack of supervision of the environment-related BSR provisions laid down in Article 4, item f) of Decree-Law 305/2012 reveals not only the lack of control that prevails in regional government management, but also little or no knowledge or awareness of such a sensitive issue. Only the president of the CNA Ornitología Habana maintains that they carry out some actions for the benefit of the environment.

In the case of the non-induced CNAs, our findings show that they participate in neither community nor local development projects. However, 12 percent of their members recognize that they generate employment for the community, and 37 percet hold that they carry out actions for the benefit of the environment. A comparative analysis of these results shows that the non-induced CNAs are not very different from the induced ones.

A particularly interesting case is the induced CNA in the food service sector, in which the president and two members liken their conception of BSR to "lending their premises, chairs and tables and other resources." The three CNAs (farmers' markets) in the agricultural sector claim to have created "produce-off-loading jobs for the benefit of the local residents" and made "donations" to nursing homes for the elderly. One of these CNAs holds that they donate its surplus produce to the local Family Care System at the end of the day. These facts reveal their limited participation in local development projects, which they ascribe to the "poor convening power" of the regional authorities.

A different behavior was noticeable in CNAs in the service sector, which undertake "actions in various institutions of the region," such as homes for the elderly, special schools and a polyclinic, by providing "own resources" such as pajamas, tablecloths and sterilized cloths. In our collective interviews with the non-induced CNAs, we found a coincidence between the CNA in the

food service sector and the CNA in the construction sector: the poor participation of their members in community or local development projects. They
ascribe it to the lack of convening power, saying that they "have never been
convened to do anything in favor of the community." However, three members (12 percent) point out that their cooperatives have created jobs for the
benefit of the community, whereas six others remark that they have engaged
in actions of benefit to the environment.

Particularly significant in the analysis of the contribution to the environment is the fact that five of the nine members of one of the CNAs in the
construction sector that we interviewed narrowed their environmental impact
down to the noise they produce while working, saying that "they try to bother
the neighbors as little as possible." In this connection, we noticed a marked
contrast between the poor condition of the multifamily building where their
workshops are located and the excellent economic results they claim to
achieve, which would be sufficient to undertake a comprehensive restoration
of the building.

Starting by its theoretical ambiguity, the lack of risk perception to assess
the responsible behavior of the various economic entities in the region
becomes evident in the municipal government documents that we consulted.
Consequently, it is not surprising that the members of the CNAs studied see
themselves as neither local development nor social transformation actors.
This issue, mostly ascribed to the lack of knowledge about BSR, has become
worse due to discrepancies among the municipal government officials that we
interviewed and, obviously, made an impact on the design, implementation,
development and control of environmental policies.

Among the possible reasons for both their disagreement and the deviations
witnessed in the CNAs of Centro Habana municipality are not only the flaws
in policy-making—from design to implementation. There is also the existing economistic approach to the CNAs—which speaks of theoretical and
methodological limitations of Decree-Law 305/2012—and the absence of a
systematic and well-structured conception of BSR based on the principles and
values of cooperative culture.

Cooperation Among Cooperatives and with
Other Organizations

A comparative analysis between the ICA principles (1995) and the provisions of Article 4, item g) of Decree-Law 305/2012 about cooperation among
cooperatives and with other organizations shows that these instruments have
at once concurrent and conflicting elements. Both promote cooperation, albeit
the Decree-Law has markedly economic, commercial, and fiscal purposes

that deviate from the principles, values, and actions of solidarity cooperation proposed by ICA.

If we compare Article 4, item g) of Decree-Law 305/2012 with Article 6, item g) of Decree-Law 366/2019—about cooperation among cooperatives—we will find no discrepancy between them. A comparison between the provisions of both Decree-Laws and the relations established by the induced CNAs reveals that 86 percent of their links are with state entities in other municipalities and only 16.6 percent with the Centro Habana municipal government entities. Meanwhile, only five of these CNAs claim to have links with agricultural cooperatives and other CNAs.

These relationships stem from bonds of cooperation, trust, commitment, and mutual assistance. However, because of their characteristics, these ties are not strengths, nor do they entail medium- or long-term sustainability for the regional cooperative movement or socio-production structure or point to social transformation or local development. These characteristics, observed in all the CNAs that we studied—as compared to the international cooperative models—make it possible to confirm that they have elements in common with the workers' self-management experience in Yugoslavia, specifically in the 1950s (Lebowitz 2015). In this case, the relations between cooperatives were very poor and only noticeable when established within or among cooperatives of the same sector, as in the cases of the dressmaking workshops, beauty salons, and three farmers' markets. From this data it is safe to conclude that, in the entire sample, the view of a partnership among the cooperative members is that of a market with which they maintain business relations, a notion revealing of a total absence of a spirit of solidarity and cooperation.

Again, it is possible to establish a similar behavior between the induced and non-induced CNAs. In latter, 79.4 percent of relations are with entities of the business sector in other regions of the capital city and only 33.8 percent with entities within the Centro Habana municipality. Among the most notable examples is that of the two non-induced CNAs in the construction sector as the only ones that maintain relations with the municipal government, whereas the other non-induced CNA in the food service sector is noticeably lacking in any direct links with municipal entities. Similarly, the results obtained show that the municipal government also lacks the capacity to implement strategies to promote relations between the CNAs and other economic and social actors who, together with the state enterprise, would contribute to the strengthening of the local socio-production structures.

From the behaviors observed in 100 percent of the sample, we can conclude that the existing problem is not only what we call lack of public awareness or willingness to demand the municipal government to fulfill its duties as coordinator of the various economic and social actors (Morillas Valdés 2018). Also noticeable is the dissatisfaction on the part of the members regarding the government's performance, almost exclusively aimed at profit maximization to the detriment of social values such as solidarity, cooperation and mutual assistance.

We verified in this respect that, owing to the excessive degree of constraint and dependence that prevails among the municipal government officials, they lack both the willingness and the capacity to follow up effectively on cooperative performance or render accounts to society of the structure of relations established by the NCAs.

CONCLUSIONS

The strategies implemented in the induced CNAs reveal the growing presence of vertical management structures typical of the state-owned enterprise, which hinders member participation, unlike the case of the non-induced NCAs, where the members participate more. In 100 percent of the cases, the implemented strategies are designed to fulfill the cooperative's need to adapt to the new realities and to make to most of the labor potentials in all sectors, even if they are focused on profit maximization.

In the case of the strategies that the induced CNAs have in place, the principle of management autonomy has become conditional on the culture of centralization. These cooperatives have implemented control and mediation policies through state entities that curb their management autonomy. By contrast, the non-induced CNAs are less controlled, but also less attended to, probably because they are perceived as entities based on self-employment in terms of their form of management and ownership.

As to social responsibility, there is no clear definition at the level of the municipal government and, therefore, the CNAs' contribution to society is reduced to the taxes paid by and the voluntary engagement of their members. As to the environmental strategy, the main difficulty is that the municipal government has no noise-reducing or waste-handling strategy for the various local economic actors, so the CNAs have no proper environmental control mechanisms in place. Concerning the social engagement of the cooperatives, what prevails is a philanthropic approach to BSR, which relates to their poor results when it comes to finding joint solutions to any social or environmental problem.

In the strategies implemented by the CNAs, the solidarity relations of joint management shared management have been reduced to the internal links among the members and little concern for the community or other institutions. The municipal government has not been able to implement strategies in favor of relations between the CNAs and other regional economic and social actors. The strategies that they have in place respond to instrumental rather than solidarity purposes largely conditional on the orientation of the policies, the deformations of the regulatory framework and the individual and collective occupational history of their members.

NOTES

1. International Cooperative Principles: voluntary and open membership; democratic member control; member economic participation; autonomy and independence; education, training and information; cooperation among cooperatives; and concern for community.

2. Induced refers to cooperatives created by the State through converting preexisting enterprises or enterprise units into cooperatives with the workers as their members. Non-induced are grassroots cooperatives created by the voluntary association of private workers. N.E.

3. Refers to the Regional Contribution for Local Development (Contribución Territorial para el Desarrollo Local—CTDL in Spanish). N.E.

BIBLIOGRAPHY

AMPP Centro Habana. "Estrategia de Gestión Ambiental del municipio Centro Habana 2015–2020" [Strategy for the Environmental Management of Centro Habana municipality 2015–2020]. La Habana, 2015.

Castilla, F., and D. Gallardo. *Socio-économie des Organisations cooperatives* [Social economy of cooperative organizations]. Paris: CIEM, 2011.

Consejo de Estado. "Decreto Ley 305/2012. De las Cooperativas No Agropecuarias" [Decree-Law 305/2012. On Nonagricultural Cooperatives]. *Gaceta Oficial de la República de Cuba, Edición Extraordinaria, No. 53*, diciembre 11, 2012.

———. "Decreto Ley 366/2019. De las Cooperativas No Agropecuarias" [Decree-Law 366/2019. On Nonagricultural Cooperatives]. *Gaceta Oficial de la República de Cuba, Edición Ordinaria, No. 63*, September 30, 2019c.

Da Ros, G. "La Cooperativa: Herramienta de valorización del potencial humano y de desarrollo de capacidades sociales, organizaciones y empresariales" [The cooperative: Tool for appreciating the human potential and of developing social capacities, organizations and enterprises]. *Revista de la Pontificia Universidad Católica del Ecuador* (75), 2005.

Esteller, O. D. *Manual para Organizar Cooperativas* [Manual for organizing cooperatives]. Caracas: Vadell Hermanos Editores, 2002.

Hesselbach, W. *La importancia de las empresas de interés general en la economía alemana* [The importance of general interest enterprises in the German economy]. México: Siglo XXI editors, 1978.

ICA. *Statement on the Cooperative Identity.* ICA Bulletin, International Cooperative Alliance, 1995. Retrieved from: http://ica.coop.

Laville, J. L. "La Economía Social en Europa" [The social economy in Europe]. *Otra Economía,* Red Latinoamericana de Economía Social y Solidaria (RILESS) 1 (1), 2001. Retrieved from: www.riless.org/otraeconomia.

Lebowitz, M. *La alternativa socialista. El verdadero desarrollo humano* [The socialist alternative: True human development]. La Habana: Editorial Ciencias Sociales, 2015.

Lenin, V. I. "Sobre la cooperación" [On cooperation]. In *Obras Escogidas en tres tomos*, 414–417. Moscú, URSS: Editorial Progreso, 1973. Originally published in 1923.

Monzón, J. L. *Las cooperativas de trabajo asociado en la literatura económica y en los hechos* [Associative Labor Cooperatives in the economic literature and in reality]. Madrid: Ministerio de Trabajo y Seguridad Social España, 1989.

Morillas Valdés, F. D. *Estrategias empresariales de las Cooperativas No Agropecuarias para su inserción y sostenibilidad en el entramado socio-productivo local* [Business strategies of Non-Agricultural Cooperatives for insertion and sustainablity in the local economic-productive matrix]. La Habana: CIPS Grupo de Creatividad para la Transformación Social, 2018.

PCC. *Conceptualización del Modelo Económico y Social Cubano de Desarrollo y Plan Nacional de Desarrollo Económico y Social hasta 2030* [Conceptualization of the Cuban Economic and Social Development Model and National Plan for Economic and Social Development until 2030]. La Habana: VI Congreso del Partido Comunista de Cuba, 2016a.

———. *Lineamientos de la Política Económica y Social del Partido y la Revolución* [Guidelines for the Economic and Social Policy of the Party and the Revolution]. La Habana: VI Congreso del Partido Comunista de Cuba, 2011.

Chapter 13

Committing to Cooperative Solidarity Labor

The Taxi Rutero 2 Experience

Mirell Pérez González

The approval of the establishment of urban cooperatives stemmed from the process of updating the economic and social model in the country proposed in the Sixth Congress of the Communist Party of Cuba (2011) and ratified in its Seventh Congress (2016).

In this regard, the development of actions to incorporate these cooperatives into the economic life of the country was evaluated as positive. The debates on this economic and social model address a range of proposals and critical analyses on the possibilities that this form of production and ownership offers. The reforms currently underway entail resizing the state, decentralizing the economy and dismantling the absolute and vertical state hegemony model in order to make it more flexible, effective, and sustainable. It is in this scenario where the urban and private cooperative sectors are growing.

Chapter II, Article 22 of the Constitution of the Republic submitted to a popular referendum on February 24, 2019, and brought into force on April 10 that year (ANPP 2019) provides for different forms of ownership, including the cooperative. It also establishes that a cooperative is based on the collective work of its owner-members and on the effective application of the cooperative principles. Therefore, the fact that our constitution recognizes this form of ownership is, without a doubt, a sign of state support and a guarantee that the essential conditions for its development are in place.

For this reason, it is appropriate that these urban cooperatives recover the central role of labor and its importance and take into consideration the assessment of its activity by its members. Based on these considerations, this article intends to provide a perspective on an urban cooperative in Havana, given the need to recover the central role of labor and the importance of cooperative and solidarity labor as a reference for assessment of the TR2 cooperative in La Lisa municipality.

To this end, we take into consideration the structure of the cooperative, its management model, an evaluation of the cooperative management, and the importance that TR2 members attach to cooperative and solidarity labor.

Therefore, the main contribution of this research is that it makes it possible to create new values within the labor process and to propose a cultural change in the attitude toward labor taking into account the need to provide the required conditions to expand human social labor. This is a challenge to the practice of socialism, since it is about reestablishing labor as the main measure of distribution, recognition and prosperity.

THE IMPORTANCE OF COOPERATIVE AND SOLIDARITY LABOR: THEORETICAL NOTES.

The need to recover the central role of labor involves portraying it as an activity that promotes creativity, solidarity, cooperation, participation and a participatory democracy that is worthy of the individual, aimed at profit-making as much as at their social recognition for what they do. Consequently, this section summarizes some theoretical notes and values for consideration by the workers in their daily practice.

Labor vis-à-vis the Logic of Capital

Labor is the activity that mediates between nature and man; it expresses the human being's efforts to regulate their relationship with nature in such a way that, by transforming it, they form themselves. This involves the human ability to transform resources into means of livelihood by fostering the development of knowledge about their own capabilities and needs and their self-consciousness as productive subjects capable of utilizing their environment and changing it with a view to their own reproduction as human beings (Carrera 2012, 3).

Marxist literature reevaluates this category, mainly with the publication of Marx's early works titled *Economic and Philosophic Manuscripts*, which he wrote between 1843 and 1844 (Marx 1961). This view reconnects with the critique on political economy, developed for the most part in *Capital* (Marx 1973).

Marx describes it in the context of the capitalist system, stating that the key to understand social alienation lies in the alienation of labor and in the processes of production of material means of life. He refers to labor as an alienated human activity and to the worker as the most wretched of commodities. He holds that the greater the size of the workers' production is, the greater their wretchedness will be, and that they will become all the poorer the more wealth they produce, since the immediate result of competition is the accumulation of capital in a few hands, so that society is always divided into two classes: property owners and destitute workers.

Another argument that he employs refers to the devaluation of the human world and the increasing value of the world of things, as well as to the fact that labor produces not only commodities for competition, it also reproduces itself and the worker as another commodity. Therefore, alienated labor becomes a central category to understand and describe capitalist political economy.

Alienation is understood as the hostile, dominant and independent relationship established with something that places the producer in a position of servitude and estrangement.

In capitalism, productive labor becomes oppressive and leads to suffering, both physical and mental. It is outside the production process where the workers feel fulfilled and can develop their creative power. Thus labor becomes an activity solely intended to live better or to survive. It is not a spontaneous activity and the workers are not self-conscious; instead, they alienate the product of their activity, the sensuous nature around them, and other workers (Marx 1972, Marx 1961).

Later, in *Capital*, Karl Marx presents the phenomenon of the fetishism of commodities to show as well how political economy operates. In this respect, labor gains a characteristic feature based on the analysis of the effect created by the circulation of commodities, which only disguises the social character of labor and discloses the exchange and valuation of commodities as "the fantastic form of a relation between things" (Marx 1973, 103).

This process appears as if things come to life and work regardless of labor and social relations, which consequently portrays these relations as links between things that express values beyond their usefulness and interchange according to market laws whose dynamics is independent from the producers. What happens is that there is no equality of all forms of human labor, but of the objective value of their products. The same applies to the mutual relations of the producers, within which the social character of their labor affirms itself and takes the form of a social relation between the products of their labor.

A significant feature of labor in this context is that it is determined independently and privately and it produces values to meet social needs, because it results in a product directly exchangeable under the market rules. Therefore, the workers are free to decide on their productive activity, but their ultimate goal is to produce according to a law of value and to the demands of the market. This means that they do not participate actively in the social organization of the process or its own reproduction because they have to abide by the rules and logic of capitalism.

From the above we can conclude that labor under capitalism fails to meet basic needs and it is replaced with preferences. In other words, it constantly generates new needs. By this logic, therefore, the use-values are replaced with exchange-values in favor of the constant maximization of profit and the atrocious consumerism that enslaves human beings.

As sociologist Ricardo Antunes explains, labor under contemporary capitalism has gained various dimensions and undergone modifications that make it contradictory. On the one hand, there is a de-proletarianization of industrial manufacturing labor in advanced capitalist countries, which has significant repercussions on third-world countries and entails a reduction of the working class. On the other hand, wage-earning labor has expanded and become significantly heterogeneous as women join the job market and the oldest and youngest workers are pushed aside. There is also under-proletarianization, made worse by the increase of part-time, unstable, temporary, and subcontracted labor (Antunes 1999).

Such unstable and part-time labor falls within the kind of informal economy that we have seen grow since the 1980s and 1990s and give rise to lower salaries, a decline in basic working conditions, a shrinking labor market, and the ubiquitous legal loopholes that deprive the working class of steady labor rights. This is why Antunes (2000) speaks of service societies and distances himself from the thesis of the suppression or elimination of the working class under advanced capitalism, replaced with a wide and growing range of segments that make up the "class that lives off labor" (Antunes 2000, 84).

These transformations in the labor world were so intense that the class that lives off labor suffered the most severe crisis of this century, as highly detrimental to its material and subjective nature as it was to the close relationships in between.

Antunes also considers that it was a decade of great technological leaps and automation in which Fordism and Taylorism combined with neo-Fordism and neo-Taylorism. Another notorious consequence is the replacement of "living labor" for "dead labor," where the tendency is that a worker becomes a supervisor and regulator of the production process. This strong crisis affects the universe of the conscience and subjectivity of the workers and has a negative impact on their creative and cooperative nature.

Coraggio (2013) points to these elements as part of a crisis of the "salaried citizen" model (Coraggio 2013, 9) that has given rise in the last few decades to a universe of popular survival strategies such as self-employment, family assistance, mutual assistance ties, and microenterprises (individual, family-run, associations). Likewise, bartering networks, revolving funds, local or neighborhood fairs, and community orchards, soup kitchens, and closets, as well as recovered enterprises, unemployed workers' organizations, mutual cooperatives, and forms of relief services, clientelism, or crime-oriented activities.

All these strategies are part of a so-called social solidarity economy and pave the way for the possible emergence of a broad spectrum of initiatives that organize, through self-management, labor-centered, and solidarity forms of production to supply public goods.

The multiple domination system makes no room for alternatives and proposals of change that go against the homogenization and power that sustain capitalism, as power itself is a social relation of dominance, exploitation, and conflict over the control of each sphere of human social life.

References to Assess Cooperative and Solidary Labor

The neoclassical model praises rationality and scientific knowledge as the way to gain knowledge at the same time as it undervalues the meaning of facts and things and turns efficiency, productivity, rationalization and competitiveness—among others—into supreme values. This is why it is necessary to give reality some meaning and people some references for assessment.

In his book *For an Economy Oriented towards Life* (2014), the philosopher Franz Hinkelammert refers to the irrationality of what has been rationalized, calling it the inefficiency of efficiency because the process of growing rationalization that comes with today's whole squandering leads to increasing irrationality and outlives progress to the extent that its consequences are regressive, which makes it meaningless. (Hinkelammert and Mora 2014)

On its end, the social and solidarity economy suggests placing labor as part of life, not as a means to the end of living, as living is an end that conditions all ends. Hence the importance that it be appraised, that individuals recognize themselves in it and that it foster effective relations for development. Labor is seen then as a useful task and, in this connection, steps can be taken to de-alienate the process, precisely because the starting point to understand the labor process lies not in ownership or management, but on the workers themselves.

It is appropriate to assign labor other meanings associated with cooperation and solidarity and create an awareness that differs from the capitalist and predatory view of the relations of production. This is the mission of cooperative and solidarity work, because every civilization is defined by the role that labor plays in it and by the workers' appreciation of their activity.

In this connection, labor should be an activity that promotes creativity and a worthy participatory democracy in which people earn social recognition for what they do. Attention should turn not to ownership as the driving force of the process, but to the production process itself and the person who does the work. People should encourage cooperation, mutual assistance, and creativity as the proper references for the assessment of labor, in addition to social and environmental justice, protection, equality of rights, and respect for diversity. Labor is a vital necessity, but it should not be seen as a job in the strict economic sense of the word.

Labor should take place in conditions that allow people to grow, develop, and enjoy a decent standard of living, definable in relation with the results of their labor, with other people, with themselves, and with nature. It should also allow them to recognize their capacity to look beyond their immediate needs toward future life projects by transforming reality through social action based on collective knowledge, experience and memory.

So "labor" in these conditions means:

- Creation of use-values: referred to human creativeness; it is labor with a sense of usefulness that needs human creativeness; related to the creation of objects, instruments, processes and ideas to transform human and natural life.
- Means of livelihood: referred to labor as a way of meeting basic individual and collective needs (personal and common).
- Conscious vital need: recognizes the contribution to society based on the workers' awareness of the importance of their work for living; includes the ability to come up with ideas and plans, learn more and get organized.
- Social recognition: broadens the meaning of labor and gives workers real power as owners of their output as they share responsibilities and social commitments; enhances personal and collective self-esteem; it is enjoyed collectively and it gives recognition within society.

Cuba is committed to a prosperous and sustainable model; however, given the meaning of labor, said prosperity should not be associated with the accumulation of wealth but with the possibility of creating conditions and human capacities to produce it. Sustainability should not only be about the capacity to last, but to the possibility that human and natural life continue.

Labor and the Cuban Context

Up to this point, we have described the international context and the great metamorphosis of the labor world during the last few decades. The 1990s in particular witnessed a spate of neoliberal hegemonies and became a momentous milestone regarding the ideal of lifelong job and employment security. This pressing context has placed labor on a spot considered from the perspective of employment and of the need to maintain job security, not just from the notion of low-cost production.

Our country is no stranger to this context, as the updating of the social and economic model and the debates on a socialist model of sustainable development have aroused great interest in analyzing the topics related to the world of labor. Guideline No. 142 refers to the need to rescue the role of labor in order to create quality products with a view to meeting the basic needs of the workers and their families (PCC 2011). Likewise, this idea also appears in the Constitution (2019) to recognize the diversity of forms of production and ownership in Cuba (cooperative, mixed, associative, and private) and social-ist ownership by all the people as the fundamental form of property over the means of production (ANPP 2019).

Cuba boasts a great deal of studies on labor developed by different fields of the social and economic sciences.[1] After the triumph of the Revolution, these studies became institutionalized as scientific fields to respond to the specific demands of the construction of a new kind of society. Therefore, social research has been linked to decision-making, which to some extent determines the topics of the studies. According to other authors, the topic of the present study has maintained its theoretical development closely linked to the changes in the economic model by broadening or limiting the scope of the research or its impact on social practice as a function of the changes in the economic model.

The research carried out in Cuba during the past ten years shows that the main labor-related problems are: working conditions, labor discipline, labor fluctuation, participation of the workers, salary, and the payment of incentives. There is also on-the-job political-ideological work, the performance of young people in the workplace, the reproduction of the workforce and the socio-classist structure of the workers' collective.

The approval of the Guidelines in the 6th Congress of the Party (2011) produces and consolidates new changes in the world of labor, marked by a socioeconomic coordination between the state—with its modified role in the country strategy and in society—and local governments, community, family, the new economic actors with various competencies and levels of perfor-mance in the labor world, and the necessary coordination among the different forms of production and ownership in the country.

The process of reorganization has facilitated the existence of greater auton-omy and redesigned the model of absolute state hegemony with a view to achieving greater effectiveness and sustainability. The rise in production- and ownership-related initiatives in Cuba has fostered decentralization in certain sectors of the economy; therefore, as a result of this process, society shares in judgments, proposals, and critique.

This resizing of the state provides the legal framework for cooperation between state and non-state forms of management (cooperatives and private sector), which has resulted in a number of challenges based on the socialization of the production and reproduction of life. It has also paved the way for full cooperative management, participatory budgeting, community self-management and the commitment to the community and the region. This is just to mention a few not yet fully deployed or considered in their entirety because of the mercantile and centralized character of the economy.

This changing environment led to the establishment of non-agricultural or urban cooperatives (both induced and by individuals). The induced cooperatives are former state enterprises, either economically inefficient or of limited production, that the government helps convert into cooperatives in order to decentralize their activity. These cooperatives reproduce the old-style state logic that permeated them and the dirigisme that detracts from the self-management system of a cooperative movement, precisely because their creation lacked the objective and subjective mediations that a truly cooperative management requires.

On their end, the cooperatives established by individuals are the result of the initiative of a group of people who decide to join forces and engage in a given activity in order to solve a common problem, based on their collective willingness to associate, common property over the means of production, and equal rights and duties.

This context is still pervaded with legal uncertainty and faced with a broad spectrum of difficulties and challenges as they try to socialize production and reproduce life. The subjective approaches to and interpretations of reality lay out a diversity of solutions and alternatives inherent in the structure of Cuban society. Therefore, this study presents the work undertaken since 2013 by the Latin America Group: Social Philosophy and Axiology (GALFISA) in a former state enterprise in Havana turned urban cooperative.

TAXI RUTERO 2 AND THE IMPORTANCE OF COOPERATIVE AND SOLIDARITY LABOR

The urban transportation cooperative Taxi Rutero 2, established on June 26, 2013 by Resolution No. 1 of the General Members' Meeting, is located in Avenida 27-A No. 26431 e/ 264 y 270, Ampliación de Arroyo Arenas, La Lisa municipality of Havana. TR2 is based on the voluntary association and contribution of its members, whose work relies on their collective control to meet social needs as well as their own.

According to its statutes, TR2 is an organization with economic and social purposes, legal status, and its own assets that uses, enjoys, and decides on its property, covers its expenses with its revenues, and meets its obligations with its patrimony. Its social object is to provide transportation services to passengers along a regular scheduled route and to take care of the maintenance, repair and parking of its vehicles.

TR2 was an unprofitable state enterprise, turned into a cooperative through a vertical designation process. Its main means of production—namely facilities and vehicles—remain state property, leased out to TR2, which entails no transfer of ownership. All this is laid down in Article 6, item c) of Decree-Law 305/2012.

In addition, TR2 enjoys preferential prices for electricity and fuel for its fleet of minibuses and cars, made up of vehicles that TRANSTUR (the enterprise in charge of transportation services for tourism) eventually discontinued and sold to Cubataxi, which leases them in turn to TR2.

Havana's Provincial Transport Administration establishes the transportation routes as per Resolution 216/2015, albeit the cooperative may choose new ones if it fulfills the approved Trip Schedule. If the cooperative wishes to expand its services, it must submit the relevant proposal to the Passenger Transportation Directorate and to the Transportation Planning Directorate, which analyze whether the request is feasible or not.

This resolution contains a number of quality requirements that both the drivers and their vehicles must meet in order to provide a service that meets specific user needs and expectations. Among others, these requirements have to do with the vehicle's hygiene, cleanliness, aesthetics, neatness, and good technical condition, as well as to the driver's conduct, courtesy, and manners during the service.

The president of the cooperative, his substitute, and the secretary were elected by a secret and direct vote of the founding members of the cooperative upon its constitution. Although this took place by means of an election, it is worth mentioning that the members of the board of directors are the former managers of the original state enterprise. The remaining members of the cooperative were designated at a later date by a show of hands of the founding members.

At its inception, the cooperative had 40 founding members; then the number of members rose to 116, of whom 99 are men and 17 are women (see Chart 1). Five are hired workers and 37 are founding members. Of all the members, 8 percent are over 60, whereas 36 percent and 56 percent are in the 20-to-35 and 40-to-59 age-groups, respectively.

As to their main jobs and tasks, membership is made up of eighty-four drivers (of whom only two are women) as well as six mechanics, two electricians, one person in charge of logistics, two shift managers, one person in charge of general activities, one janitor, eight night watchmen, and the president of the cooperative.

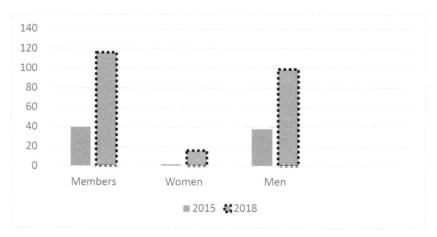

Figure 13.1.   Structure of the Cooperative Taxi Rutero 2.
Source: Author.

TR2's Management Model

TR2 plays a major role in the city of Havana's social life as one of the first two official cooperatives whose mission is the daily transportation of people in vehicles that stand out from the regular public buses for their speediness, safety and comfort.

Following its constitution in June 2013, TR2 worked with twelve vehicles, but this figure has gradually increased. By 2016, it had fifty-eight minibuses in operation, and the number grew to sixty-five in 2018 as part of a strategy to extend its services.[2]

TR2 holds its general assembly once a month to approve its profit and expense budgets, analyze the financial statement and distribution of profits, and evaluate the amount of the advance payments, and it is where the members are apprised of any disciplinary action taken against a worker in cases of breach of duty. It is important to point out that TR2 has not modified its statutes since it was established.

The board of directors is the organ in charge of management and responds directly to the general members' assembly. The board is the one entitled to operate TR2's bank account and, therefore, responsible for submitting to the general assembly the financial statement, the annual balance, and all the documents governing the cooperative's work.

The board of directors also renders a proposal for the distribution of profits and amounts for advance payments. It is in charge of drafting labor, safety, and health standards and defining procedures for the labor process in the cooperative. The board is made up of the president, the treasurer, an administrator, a secretary, and the shop stewards elected in the general assembly.

TR2's assets consist of the contribution made by the members when the cooperative was established—a monetary contribution entirely in Cuban pesos—and any other subsequent contribution provided by them. They also include fixed tangible assets, implements, and tools purchased by the board. However, any other major purchase, for instance, computer equipment, is contingent on approval by the general assembly.

As regards the cooperative accounting system, it is necessary to point out that its operations should conform to tax purposes, using the Cuban standards on financial information and complying with the generally used and accepted accounting principles, as is the case with internal control. In addition, the system should guarantee the fulfillment of the State requirements, as is the case for the control and payment of tax obligations in order to endorse their reliability.

For the purposes of this study, we selected fifty-eight (50 percent) of all the cooperative members engaged in TR2's main activity and included the whole board of directors, based on their responsible and honest attitude. Of all the members involved in the study, forty-eight (83 percent) were men and ten (17 percent) women. Obviously, men are in the majority, a tradition in this sector. It is very difficult for a woman to be hired as a driver, since this is considered a man's profession and a highly lucrative job.

During our study, the board of directors showed interest in being part of the process. In the beginning, the board instructed the drivers to participate, and our research produced direct results for the benefit of the cooperative and its profits, they were more willing to get involved.

It is also necessary to mention that the drivers are not in the premises all the time because they each do their job independently, which is the reason that the number of drivers that we took as a sample for our study was intentional so that we could facilitate a better interaction and communication among them.

Evaluation of Cooperative Management

Based on GALFISA's diagnosis in 2015 (Galfisa 2017) we defined the indicators to evaluate cooperative management from the perspective of the centrality of cooperative and solidary labor. Those designed to measure the labor process based on the objectives of our study correlate the negative tendencies found by the study of the Cooperative and solidarity work network[3] and the results reported by the members of TR2. These indicators were evaluated on a scale of 1 (lowest) to 5 (highest) and organized in four categories: organization, participation, cooperation, and ethics.

Ever since it came into being, TR2 has made significant progress in terms of organization of the labor process and implementation of the cooperative principles. The members admit that they enjoy more autonomy and take

Table 13.1 Indicators to Evaluate the Management of the Cooperative Taxi Rutero 2 (Scale of 1 [negative] to 5 [positive])

INDICATORS	2015	2017
ORGANIZATION		
Improve production and service efficiency	3	4
Increasing profits and income	2	3
Expansion of the market	1	3
Stability of resources	1	3
Exchange with good production experiences in Cuba	1	2
Coordination of relations with other forms of ownership and economic-productive management	1	3
PARTICIPATION		
Strengthening the workers' collective with labor as the unifying factor	2	4
Greater participation of women in the production processes	1	2
Inclusion of more women in decision-making positions	1	2
Inclusion of the cooperative principles in the work strategy	2	3
Strengthening the production process by giving workers more decision-making power	1	3
Increasing the participation of young workers in the production process	1	3
COOPERATION		
Establishing links with government decision-makers	2	3
Establishing links with neighboring communities	1	3
Establishing links with specialists on the subject	2	3
Establishing links with academic institutions engaged in labor studies	1	3
Insertion into spaces of national and international coordination	1	2
ETHICS		
Respect for those who work harder	2	4
Acceptance of the cooperation and solidarity principles in the labor process	2	3
Honesty of the workers' efforts to develop the enterprise	2	3
Shared collective values	2	3

Source: Developed by the author

advantage of some experiences from back when they were a state enterprise. While mostly focused on the renovation of the internal labor process, the cooperative considers the need to establish links with other cooperatives as a challenge. Since it is an offshoot of a state enterprise (Cubataxi), the culture and ethics typical of a state entity still pervades TR2, which limits the consistent deployment of the cooperative principles.

The members of the board acknowledge TR2's greater productive efficiency based on its profits. They fail to consider participation and cooperation as relevant in terms of labor organization with a view to profit maximization. As a rule, it is the workers—most of them young—who refer to these topics.

It is worth stressing that, in some cases, the state enterprise logic proves unsuitable for a cooperative form of management, so the process needs to aim at a different way of thinking and doing things. The cooperatives create new jobs that give capable and qualified young people the opportunity to excel themselves in the performance of their duties, as long as they feel motivated in and identified with them and the labor process falls within their expectations.

There is still a latent need to strengthen solidarity among the cooperative members and with other cooperatives. Even if TR2 has obviously established more relations with other forms of management, the results are still insufficient. Therefore, the cooperative needs to take steps to increase those links.

Something similar happens in TR2 regarding its relationship with the community. The cooperative has managed to prepare a proposal to provide free services to hemodialysis patients and others with serious diseases in the polyclinic of San Agustin, in La Lisa municipality. This proposal is a step forward in the process to raise awareness on the links with the community, except that it has not been systematically implemented. TR2 should not disregard the need for a commitment to the community where it is located, which would contribute to improve the quality of life of the local residents and honor the principle of social responsibility.

The cooperative members acknowledge that most of the female employees hold administrative and decision-making positions and are not involved in the kind of work linked to the production process that the drivers, mechanics and electricians perform. For this reason, TR2 should design a strategy that facilitates the inclusion of women in the processes that contribute to the social objective of the cooperative.

Havana's urban transportation system has been the object of continual changes since August 2018, which has been a new challenge for the cooperative, as this new stage makes its mission even more complicated. GALFISA is still engaged in this experience, mindful of their joint commitment to the strengthening of cooperative and solidarity management.

The Importance of Cooperative and Solidarity Labor for TR2 Members

Any change of attitude toward the cooperative members' labor process must be of necessity the result of their conscious self-assertion as productive subjects, which becomes manifest in four significant and mutually complementing dimensions. Furthermore, it is essential to understand that the starting point for change is not in what the workers appropriate or manage, but in themselves.

It is important to bear in mind the important aspects of labor (creation of use-values, means of life, conscious vital necessity, and social recognition) as they lead the entire process of productive and reproductive labor. Recovering the central role of labor based on these meanings and their critical and creative potential is crucial for a consistent and systemic implementation of the Cuban economic and social model. Chart 2 shows data on the importance of labor as assessed by the workers in 2015 and in 2017.

There is consensus about the need to reestablish the value of labor as the main basis for distribution, recognition, and social differentiation. To that end, a change of attitude toward labor becomes necessary that is neither spontaneous nor casual, as the proper conditions that favor change must be in place. This change leads in turn to major transformations in all spheres of life, not in a fragmented manner, but as a harmonic and consistent whole. Making the forms of production and reproduction more consistent, pursuant to the real conditions for economic development, is a challenge for the Cuban model of economic and social development, as this entails considering not only the specific material and spiritual needs of the workers' everyday life, but also their references for assessment.

Committing to cooperative and solidarity labor involves a lengthy process that requires the workers' dedication to the development of a different way of working based on various approaches and practices that will make the success of these daily practices visible. Cuba has amassed a strong culture of labor marked by qualities such as cooperation, solidarity and honesty. Therefore, the country is in good condition to make the effective implementation of the economic and social model possible. This way of working is also part of political life and certainly an exercise of popular participation.

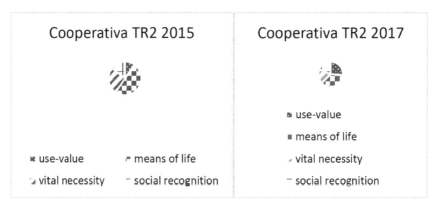

Figure 13.2. The Importance of Labor According to the Workers.
Source: Author.

CONCLUSIONS

For sixty years, Cuba has lived in a system that places cooperation, solidarity and humanistic complementarity at the center of its raison d'être as a society in Revolution. Using this historical experience to conceive and coordinate the various forms of cooperative production and ownership forms on the basis of productive efficiency and effectiveness is a challenge to our society.

Therefore, broadening the political, ethical, economic, and cultural meaning of labor, based on diverse forms of participation, management, and the sustainability of life, is a pressing need.

Cuba has real capacity and competency, especially if we consider the experience gained from the urban cooperative system and the appropriation of a culture of solidarity and cooperative labor.

As research has found, moving labor, the production process, and the workers center stage favors people's creativity and ennobles their lives.

Labor should not be seen as just a job; as it is both a process that should help fulfill our needs and a creative act that facilitates the development of our capacity to transform human and natural life. Likewise, it is a conscious process of construction of new meanings, which entails social recognition of the outcome.

Based on the commitment to cooperative and solidarity labor, this research work reveals that it is possible to have a different kind of labor process, one that involves the daily effort of the workers. How they organize their creative production process and daily practices will define this new way of doing, which will contribute to the effective implementation of the updating of the economic and social model in Cuba.

The findings of this research work do not prove that the TR2 experience takes into account every aspect of cooperative and solidarity labor, but they do reveal that it is actually possible to integrate them into the internal organization of the cooperative's production process and daily practices.

NOTES

1. As found by studies conducted by Centro de Investigaciones Psicológicas y Sociológicas [Center for Psychological and Sociological Research] (CIPS), Centro de Estudios Demográficos [Center for Demographic Studies] (CEDEM), Centro de Estudios de la Economía Cubana [Center for Studies on the Cuban Economy] (CEEC), the School of Philosophy of the University of Havana and the School of Social Sciences of Universidad Central "Marta Abreu," among others.

2. In the second half of 2018, TR2 launched a new service with light vehicles, at first with thirty of them. In line with this strategy, designed to improve the quality and

number of urban transport vehicles in Havana, TR2 increased to sixty the number of hired employees, who would work on a trial basis for three months and then decide whether they wished to become members of the cooperative. This process is still under way, so we did not use it as a sample in our research.

3. The Red de Trabajo Cooperado y Solidario [Cooperative and solidary labor network] (state enterprises, urban and rural cooperatives, private sector and inclusive social, cultural and community development projects) was established by GALFISA in 2014 as an initiative to design and coordinate experiences based on the diversity of the forms of production, ownership and participation in Cuba. It is useful to study and foster economic initiatives based on regional solidarity and cooperation, as well as to improve the synergy between the experiences that decided to join the network and organize training workshops and annual meetings.

BIBLIOGRAPHY

ANPP. *Constitución de la República de Cuba* [Constitution of the Republic of Cuba]. La Habana: Asamblea Nacional del Poder Popular, Febrero de 2019. Retrieved from: http://www.granma.cu/file/pdf/gaceta/Nueva%20Constituci%C3%B3n%20240%20KB-1.pdf.

Antunes, R. "Ensayo sobre la metamorfosis y el rol central del mundo del trabajo"[Essay on the metamorphosis and central role of the world of labor]. In *¿Adiós al trabajo?* Buenos Aires: Editorial Antídoto, 1999.

―――. "La centralidad del trabajo hoy" [The centrality of labor today]. *Papeles de Población* 6(25), México: Universidad Autónoma del Estado de México, julio–septiembre 2000.

Betancourt, Rafael. "La economía social y solidaria y la actualizacion del modelo económico cubano" [Social and Solidarity Economics and the updating of the Cuban economic model]. La Habana: *Blog Catalejo de la Revista Temas,* 2015. Retrieved from: http://temas.cult.cu/blog/?p=2071#more-2071.

Carrera, I. "El fetichismo de la mercancía bajo su forma de teoría de la crisis del trabajo abstracto" [The fetishism of commodities according to the theory of the crisis of labor|. *Marxismo Critico.* http://marxismocritico.com/2012/09/07/el-fetichismo-de-la-mercancía-bajo-suforma-de-teoría-de-la-crisis-del-trabajo-abstracto.

Coraggio, J. L. "Cómo construir otra economía" [How to build another economy]. In *Desafíos para cambiar la vida Economía Popular y solidaria. Cuadernos de solidaridad no 6*, by C. López. La Habana: Editorial Caminos, 2013.

Echeverría, D. "Procesos de reajuste en Cuba y su impacto en el empleo femenino: entre dos siglos y repetidas desigualdades" [Readjustment processes in Cuba and their impact on female employment: between two centuries and repeated inequalities]. In *Miradas a la economía cubana IV*. La Habana: Editorial Caminos, 2013.

Echeverría, D., and J. L. Martín Romero. *Cuba: trabajo en el siglo XXI. Propuestas y desafíos* [Cuba: work in the XXI century. Proposals and challenges]. La Habana: Editorial Instituto Cubano de Investigación Cultural Juan Marinello, 2017.

Galfisa. *Desafios del cooperativismo en Cuba* [Challenges of cooperativism in Cuba]. La Habana: Coleccion Hipotesis. Instituto de Filosofia. www.filosofia.cu/site/institucion.php 14/06/2018 2017.

Hinkelammert, F., and H. Mora. *Hacia una economía para la vida* [Toward an economy for life]. La Habana: Editorial Caminos, 2014.

Izquierdo, O., and H-J. Burchardt. *Trabajo decente y sociedad. Cuba bajo la óptica de los estudios sociolaborales* [Decent wok and society. Cuba under the optic of socio-labor studies]. La Habana: Editorial UH, 2017.

Marx, K. *El Capital* [Das Kapital]. La Habana: Editorial Ciencias Sociales, 1973. Originally published in 1867.

———. *Manifiesto Comunista* [Communist Manifesto]. La Habana: Editorial Pueblo y Educación, 1972.

———. "Manuscritos económico-filosóficos de 1844" [Economic-philosophical Manuscripts]. In *Escritos económicos varios*, by C. Marx, edited by Traduccion y recopilacion W. Roces, 25–125. Editorial Grijalbo. 1961. Originally published in 1844.

PCC. *Lineamientos de la Política Económica y Social del Partido y la Revolución* [Guidelines for the Economic and Social Policy of the Party and the Revolution]. La Habana: VI Congreso del Partido Comunista de Cuba. 2011.

Piñeiro, C. *Cooperativas y Socialismo: una mirada desde Cuba* [Cooperatives and Socialism: A view from Cuba]. La Habana: Editorial Caminos, 2011.

Chapter 14

Cooperative Social Balance

A Useful Tool to Establish a Social and Solidarity Economy

Oscar Llanes Guerra, Mercedes Zenea Montejo, Annia Martínez Massip, and Lienny García Pedraza

In a globalized economy in which corporations rule financial fates and direct technology and the markets by setting the standards of the distribution policies—without taking into account the needs for food security—infinite problems dominate, operating under economic models that are not very useful to solve them. It is therefore important to improve the way to operate cooperative enterprises and to apply practices of cooperative social responsibility (RSC in Spanish). According to Jiménez, "The cooperatives have the ability to produce wellbeing and increase the standard of living of its members and other people who live nearby, through its alternative productions and services" (Jiménez 2008, 7).

For more than twenty years, steps have been taken in Latin America in the design of different models of social balance, with the objective to evaluate the compliance of its management within the framework of RSC. In the Cuban context, the majority of the cooperatives carry out activities that are of benefit to the communities and the environment, but still rare are cases of these productive forms that consider social policies in their strategic plans and form organized lines of work. The Cuban economic model and its governing document—the Lineamientos de la Política Económica y Social del Partido y la Revolución [Guidelines of the Economic and Social Policies of the Party and the Revolution] (PCC 2011)—indicate in these productive forms ways to arrive at sustainable development, highlighting their principles as benchmarks of the standards and rights of the members.

In this context, the ICAFLACSO-PC Modelo de Balance Social Cooperativo [Cooperative Social Balance Model] (Mena 2014) was designed, within the framework of the Joint Program of Support for the New Initiatives of Decentralization and Production Stimulation in Cuba, as shown in Figure 1. It was carried out with financing from the European Union and UNDP and the participation of several national organizations, and implemented in the territories of five municipalities of the country, with the inclusion of cooperative agricultural organizations. Contextualized for Cuban cooperative organizations, among its novelties it includes the intervention area of equity relations, which analyzes inequalities related to territory, age, gender, class, and occupation; it enables the evaluation of behavior and the modification of attitudes in the identification and elimination of equity gaps, to the benefit of the cooperative and the community.

The methodology establishes a guide for the steps to be taken for its implementation by evaluating the indicators defined for each variable and for each area of intervention independently. In addition, its flexible design makes possible the adaptation of the model to the context in which it is applied, and allows its incorporation to evaluate social responsibility in cooperative agricultural and nonagricultural organizations.

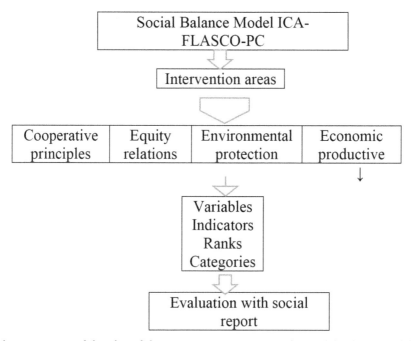

Figure 14.1. Modular Plan of the ICA-FLACSO-PC Cooperative Social Balance Model.
Source: Authors.

It was implemented for the first time in the Basic Unit of Cooperative Production (UPBC) Las Cadenas, of La Palma municipality, in the province of Pinar del Río. The results achieved in this experiment supported its inclusion in the international cooperation project Vía Láctea [Milky Way]—carried out in Cuba by the Italian NGO COSPE and the National Association of Small Farmers (ANAP), in order to evaluate, with similar objectives, the social and environmental contribution of five Credit and Services Cooperatives (CCS). As a result, with its flexible and contextual design, it was also adjusted and implemented in the Nonagricultural Cooperative (CNA) of Waste Recycling in San José de las Lajas municipality, Mayabeque province.

METHODOLOGY

The conception and the design of the ICA-FLACSO-PC Cooperative Social Balance Model originated in the context of the UBPC Las Cadenas, La Palma municipality, Pinar del Río, funded by the European Union and UNDP. It was a concerted effort with the IV Edition of the Masters in Management and Development of Cooperatives of the Latin American Faculty of Social Sciences (FLACSO) of the University of Havana.

It was observed that the supply of equipment and technology, and the training carried out based on the prior diagnostic, were not sufficient to solve the socio-environmental problems that coexisted in the cooperative and affected its community. The participatory observations in this context made it possible to determine that in that cooperative there was no conscious implementation of social responsibility. In addition, different socioeconomic and environmental gaps were found which subsequently shaped the areas of intervention, variables, and indicators of the ICA-FLACSO-PC Model of Cooperative Social Balance.

The literature review that was carried out (Alfonso 2008; Cruz and Cárdenas 2018; Instituto Ethos 2003; Zabala Salazar 2008; Mirabal, Marín and Alfonso 2015; Nova González, Prego Regalado and Robaina Echevarría 2018) provided the state of the art in the international context, with emphasis on Latin America, supported by the studies carried out on the subject in Cuba, begun at Universidad de Pinar del Río, on the topic of social responsibility and the tools to evaluate it.

All this work allowed the definition of the different areas of intervention of the Model, its variables and indicators, which were properly validated in a consultation with experts: twenty specialists of different areas of knowledge, belonging to universities and research institutions, with more than ten years of experience on the topic of cooperatives; as well as agricultural cooperativists and directors with expertise based on daily practices—all with a university-level education: nine PhDs and five Masters of Science.

The implementation of the ICA-FLACSO-PC model in the cooperatives that were the subject of the study was conceived based on the methodological combination of the participatory and the conventional approaches of social research (Hernández 2003; González, et al. 2005; Alejandro, Romero and Vidal 2008; Guzón, et al. 2011). This proposal allowed us to make the most of their merits and reduce the weaknesses of each of the approaches based on the careful and coherent combination of their theoretical foundations, techniques, and stages of practical implementation. For one thing, the implementation methodology of the model is based on the participatory and transformative approach of popular education, which allows the beneficiaries to understand, study and profoundly analyze the specific conditions of their reality, in order to project new actions of change in a more active, conscious and committed manner. Also adopted were components of the triple analysis to direct reflection and debate. With a self-critical view, the implementation of the model is meant to start from the members, added to the participatory view, and in that way, decision-making is guaranteed to be through the assembly of members.

RESULTS OF THE IMPLEMENTATION OF THE MODEL IN THE UBPC LAS CADENAS

The ICA-FLACSO-PC Cooperative Social Balance Model was implemented for the first time in the UBPC Las Cadenas of Pinar del Río. In the results, the following gaps were observed:

- The relations among cooperatives is not sufficiently developed; although some actions are carried out, they are not supported by any program.
- The attention to the community is not supported by programs, nor are there budgets assigned to this objective. Actions that are sometimes relevant are carried out, but they are not quantified.
- Equity relations show little development at the cooperative level. Only eight of the seventy-five members are women; only one woman is in a management position; only one woman is an agricultural producer; and only one woman has a university-level education.
- The average salary of the women members of the cooperative is only 60.9 percent of what men earn.
- Women members of the cooperative claim that they make decisions on the use of their income and about the expenses of the household, but the women of the community depend entirely on their husband's earnings.

- The rate of female unemployment in the community is high, and the cooperative is the main source of employment.
- It is the women—both cooperative members and housewives of the community—who carry out the domestic tasks, without the cooperation of the men.
- The women members do have some environmental education, but the women of the community do not; they are burdened by household tasks and do not have access to additional training.
- There are no policies at the cooperative level related to the protection of environment, although the national policies are being respected.
- Groundwater is being used, but there is no control of the water being used for crops and livestock.
- There are no wooded areas, nor are there plans for forestation.
- The national plans and actions to protect the soil are known, but are not extensively practiced; also, no records are kept on the indiscriminate use of the land.
- There is no organized system to cultivate values related to biodiversity; there are no groups of interest, nor any areas identified with agroecological farming, although in the cooperative these principles are being practiced.

Based on socialization and the analysis developed by the board of directors and the members on the results of the application of the model, the implementation of recommended solutions to the problems found, and the development of the potentials of the cooperative enterprise, the following effects were achieved:

- More autonomy and independence for the management of the cooperative.
- More participation in decision-making at the level of the general assembly.
- Greater fluidity of the information exchanged between the board of directors and the members of the cooperative.
- Increase in the commitment of the cooperative toward the community.
- Important results in the application and use of economic-productive indicators based on the productive management of the cooperative.
- More willingness and sensitivity in the board of directors and the members toward the achievement of affirmative action and a reduction in gender gaps.
- Increase in the sensitivity of the board of the directors and the members on topics of environmental protection.

Four years after the implementation of the ICA-FLASO-PC Model of Cooperative Social Balance, a look at the UBPC Las Cadenas shows the following:

- The collaboration with other cooperatives and state enterprises has been organized.
- A greater inclination toward support of the community has been observed, fundamentally related to the repair and construction of homes (90 percent of the members live in the community).
- Equity gaps have been reduced; two more women have been hired for agricultural jobs.
- The system of linking salaries to productive results was applied to the women, which meant an increase in their salaries to 85 percent of that of the men.
- Agroecological farming in the agricultural production of the cooperative has been sustained, although the recuperation from a marabú[1] infestation of some areas, and the unavailability of other technologies has necessitated the use of herbicides.
- A student interest group on livestock production was established in coordination with the agricultural polytechnic school of the area.
- Relations are maintained with the cooperative related to external decisions that limit its autonomy, finances, and access to the technical and technological resources necessary for the compliance of its production and services plans that it offers the community.

RESULTS OF THE IMPLEMENTATION OF THE MODEL IN FIVE AGRICULTURAL COOPERATIVES

The implementation of the cooperative social balance process—with the application of the ICA-FLACSO-PC Social Balance Model—was carried out from 2016 to 2018 in the context of the Vía Láctea project. It was set up in five de Credit and Services Cooperatives (CCS): the CCS Frank País of Camajuaní, and the Jesús Menéndez CCS in Placetas—both in the central province of Villa Clara; the Juan Manuel Márquez and the Conrado Benítez CCSs—both in the municipality of Aguada de Pasajeros in the central province of Cienfuegos; and the Sabino Pupo CCS in the municipality of Colón in the western province of Matanzas. In these five cooperatives a total of thirty-two interviews were carried out with the directors of the cooperatives, eighty-six with members, and forty-nine with other stakeholders, for a total of 167 interviews; in addition, twenty-one workshops were carried out up to the planning stage.

The quality of the participation and commitment shown in each working group is revealed by the results that were obtained. Although there are differences among the different cooperatives, in general they all respond to a common tendency, and there is a high coincidence in the results that were analyzed in the previous experiment. The following aspects are identified:

- The cooperative principles are only partially fulfilled, because of the presence of external factors that affect the self-management of the cooperative, related to the production plan established from above and the buying and selling relations. The impact on self-management does not constitute a cause clearly or explicitly identified by the CCSs, rather it comes from the collective debate in the participatory workshops that were organized. This means that in general, neither the CCSs nor the boards of directors acknowledge impacts on their management autonomy when decisions are made by external subjects. This is not because they do not exist, but because of the concern that any acknowledgement of interference and its confrontation might provoke other effects on the cooperative, since there are contractual and logistical relations maintained with the state enterprise to which the decision-making power is linked, and because of the decision-making powers of other related organizations in the region.
- Actions of education and training are being carried out, but plans prepared based on the priorities of the cooperative and of the nearby communities are still lacking.
- In general, the cooperatives carry out activities that show a social commitment with the community—spontaneously or induced—but in many cases there is no economic quantification of these contributions to the development of the community.
- In general, the economic and productive indicators are favorable. Profits are generated, and there is economic capacity for actions of support toward the community, but the accounting and financial information is not always complete. The main reason that the interviewed CCS representatives offer is that these activities are managed and processed by the agricultural state enterprise to which they are linked.
- Women members are a minority in the cooperatives. The productive contribution of the women is not always promoted or acknowledged. An important portion of the female jobs are generally associated with service or reproductive tasks.
- There is an acknowledgment of the masculinization and aging of the productive jobs in the fields.
- A greater awareness of environmental issues was observed, as basic knowledge of the absolute need to protect and conserve the environment,

although agroecological practices do not take precedence, nor do awareness activities or organized presentations in the members' assemblies.
- The reduction of chemical agricultural inputs is more due to the fact
  that these products are often not available than to the awareness of the
  damage these products can cause. The use of these toxic products is also
  supported by the lack of availability of biological products to control
  plagues and diseases in the region, and of other necessary resources.
- The majority of the cooperative social management measures are not
  implemented based on the development plan of these enterprises. There
  are no strategic action plans in any of the four regions of intervention
  defined in the model.
- The implementation of this model culminates in a final statement and a
  plan of action, prepared in a participatory way by the members of the
  cooperative, and which is approved in the general assembly. This plan
  of action is focused on overcoming the gaps that were revealed in the
  implementation stage.
- Coordinating actions to the benefit of the community and local development are expressed between the principal community agents, and which
  involve the local decision-making units and the state and cooperative
  management forms, in which the cooperatives generally have leadership.
  This allows for the confirmation of the existence of primary forms of
  social and solidarity economy in the communities.

RESULTS OF THE IMPLEMENTATION OF THE
MODEL IN THE WASTE RECYCLING CNA

The ICA-FLACSO-PC Cooperative Social Balance Model was conceived
with a view to the possibility of its adaptation and implementation in other
cooperative management forms, beyond the agricultural sector in which it
originated. Therefore, within the framework of the project, agricultural, nonagricultural, and second-level cooperatives—which the University of Havana
implements—the adaptation and implementation of the model was carried
out in the Nonagricultural Cooperative (CNA) of Waste Recycling in San
José de las Lajas municipality, Mayabeque province. Its main result was the
accessibility of a social balance model that is appropriate for similar cooperative organizations in the country; to date there are fifteen waste recycling
cooperatives.

The main conclusions described in the social report that resulted from the
application of the model are the following:

- The economic and productive indicators are favorable; profits are generated and there is economic capacity for actions in support of the community. In spite of this, no actions of social benefit to the community, or of increasing the recycling practices are planned.
- There is general interest in growth and in searching for tools that improve the management process, but no training activities are planned; these occur spontaneously and are limited to the board of directors.
- There is a high sense of belonging and commitment on the part of the members, which transforms them into an integrated and efficient collective as related to the use of the labor force and the organization of its labor.
- External regulations affect autonomy and slow down management, fundamentally due to the lack of knowledge of the normative framework on the part of the liaison organizations. The judicial personality of the cooperatives is not always acknowledged, which provokes confusion in the results.
- There is gender equity. Of the fourteen members, six are women. The board of directors consists of three members, all women. The monthly pay is equal for all members of the cooperative, but only one woman participates directly in the productive process.

CONCLUSIONS

The implementation of the ICA-FLACSO-PC Cooperative Social Balance Model in seven cooperatives—six agricultural (one UBPC an five CCS) and one nonagricultural (CNA)—in the current Cuban context shows the usefulness of this tool in identifying and minimizing the gaps found in the areas of intervention described in the model. Moreover, it allowed for the preparation of a plan of action and, with its implementation, for the improvement of the management to the benefit of the cooperative itself and its community, as well as identifying the primary social and solidarity forms in these communities.

The methodology of the implementation of the de Cooperative Social Balance Model—based on the participatory and transformative perspective of popular education—allowed the cooperatives that were analyzed, as well as all the stakeholders involved, to profoundly understand, study and analyze the specific conditions of their reality. This allowed them to design new transformative actions in a more active, conscious and committed way.

The implementation of the ICA-FLACSO-PC Cooperative Social Balance Model has been useful in strengthening the integration of the community members linked to the cooperatives that were analyzed, as well as in demonstrating the energizing role that the universities and research centers—in conjunction with the local governments—have in a new way of managing social and solidarity economy for local development.

NOTE

1. Marabú is a thorny bush with a strong root system, inedible for livestock.

BIBLIOGRAPHY

Alejandro, M., M. I. Romero, and J. R. Vidal. *¿Qué es la Educación Popular?* [What is popular education?]. La Habana: Editorial Caminos, 2008.

Alfonso, J. L. Modelo de Gestión de la Responsabilidad Social Cooperativa Directa. Estudio de caso: Cooperativa de Producción Agropecuaria Camilo Cienfuegos, Pinar del Río [Model for managing Direct Cooperative Social Responsibility. Case study: Agricultural Production Cooperative Camilo Cienfuegos, Pinar del Río]. Tesis en opción al grado de doctor en Ciencias Económicas, Pinar del Rio: Universidad de Pinar del Rio, 2008.

Cruz, J., and F. Cárdenas. "Mercado y principios cooperativos en conflict" [Markets an cooperative principles in conflict]. *Estudios del Desarrollo Social: Cuba y América Latina* 6 (3): 53–65, 2018.

González, N., Z., Alfaro, M. Pérez, and A. R. Padrón. *Técnicas participativas y juegos didácticos de educadores populares* (t. IV) [Participatory techniques and didactic games for popular educators]. La Habana: Asociación de Pedagogos de Cuba, 2005.

Guzón, A., A. Alberto, R. Berriz, and V. Pérez. *Cataurito de Desarrollo Local* [Local Development Basket]. La Habana: Editorial Caminos, 2011.

Hernández, R. *Metodología de la investigación* [Research Methodology]. La Habana: Editorial Félix Varela, 2003.

Instituto Ethos. Guía de elaboración del balance social [Guide to creating a social balance]. Brasil, 2003. Retrieved from: https://www.academia.edu/4228606/GUIA _ELABORACION_BALANCE_SOCIAL_ETHOS_2003.

Jiménez, R. "Cooperativas agrícolas en Cuba y su relación con el desarrollo local" [Agricultural cooperatives in Cuba and their relation to local development]. *Universitas Forum* 1 (1), 2008.

———. Diagnóstico del estado actual de la educación cooperativa en el sector de las Unidades Básicas de Producción Cooperativa. [Diagnosis of the current state of cooperative education in the sector of Basic Units of Agricultural Production]. La Habana: FLACSO-UH, 2002.

Mena, C. Modelo de Balance Social Cooperativo, implementado en la UBPC Las Cadenas, municipio La Palma, Pinar del Río [Cooperative Social Balance Model, implementes at UBPC Las Cadenas, La Palma municipality, Pinar del Rio]. Tesis en opción al grado de máster en Gestión y Desarrollo de Cooperativas, La Habana: Universidad de La Habana, FLACSO Cuba, 2014.

Mirabal, Y., I. Marín, and J. L. Alfonso. "Educación Cooperativa y Modelo de Gestión de la Responsabilidad Social Cooperativa" [Cooperative education and the Cooperative Social Responsibility Management Model] *Avances* 16 (1): 9–17, 2015. http://www.ciget.pinar.cu/ojs/index.php/publicaciones/article/view/62.

Nova González, A., J. C. Prego Regalado, and L. Robaina Echevarría. "La Intercooperación entre Cooperativas Agrícolas en la actualización del Modelo Económico Cubano" [Intercooperation between agricultural cooperatives in the Cuban economic model]. *Estudios del Desarrollo Social: Cuba y América Latina* 6 (3): 167–78, 2018.

PCC. "Documentos del 7mo Congreso del Partido aprobados por el III Pleno del Comité Central del PCC (18 de mayo de 2017) y respaldados por la Asamblea Nacional del Poder Popular" [Documents of the VII Party Congress approved by the II Plenum of the PCC Central Committee (May 18, 2017) and sustained by the National Assembly of Popular Power (June 1st, 2017]. La Habana: PCC, 2017.

———. Lineamientos de la Política Económica y Social del Partido y la Revolución [Guidelines for the Economic and Social Policy of the Party and the Revolution]. La Habana: VI Congreso del Partido Comunista de Cuba. 2011

Zabala Salazar, H. *Construcción de un Modelo de Balance Social para el Cooperativismo de una Región Latinoamericana: El caso de Antioquia* [Construction of a Model of Social Balance for Cooperatives of a Latin American Region: The case of Antioquia]. Medellín, Colombia: Fundación Universitaria Luis Amigó, 2008.

Chapter 15

Gender Perspective Viewed from the Model of Social Balance in Agricultural Cooperatives in Villa Clara

*Annia Martínez Massip, Lienny García Pedraza,
Oscar Llanes Guerra, Mercedes Zenea Montejo,
Lázaro Julio Leiva Hoyo, Anelys Pérez Rodríguez,
and Elianys de la Caridad Zorio González*

Cooperative social responsibility constitutes a pressing challenge which appears implicitly in the cooperative principles (Alianza Cooperativa Internacional 1996) and in the Law of Agricultural Production Cooperatives and of Credits and Services in Cuba (Consejo de Estado 2022). However, the implementation of the Cooperative Social Balance Model in two cooperatives in Villa Clara (from 2016 to 2018) shows dissatisfactions, contradictions, and possible potentials that could be used toward the organization of the cooperative social responsibility.

The implementation of this model was carried out in two Credit and Services [agricultural] Cooperatives (CCS in Spanish) of the province, which take part in Project Vía Láctea: a proposal for actions to strengthen the chain of milk production in four Cuban provinces.[1] They are the Jesús Menéndez CCS of the Placetas municipality—which has 151 associates, of whom 28 are women and 27 are young people of less than 35 years of age—and the Frank País CCS of Camajuaní—which has 230 associates, of whom 21 are women and 38 are members less than 35 years of age—according to the information available at the end of 2018.

The CCS are simple integrated forms of cooperatives. They consist of landowning farmers, farmers that cultivate lands owned and allocated by the State (in usufruct, or rent-free) and families of both, who partner together in order to receive credits and services. As common assets they can rely on certain funds and some means of production (Valdés Paz 2009; Nova González 2011). In Cuba, for several decades

> the most successful form [of cooperative organization] has been the CCS. However, there has been a tendency [by the Ministry of Agriculture] to increase excessively the control over the CCS, by creating an administrative group with resources, machinery, transport, land, etc., which administers the marketing, supplies, etc. of the cooperative. This makes the management of the cooperative difficult. (Nova González 2011, 331)

Since 2008, research on the cooperative social balance has been carried out in Cuba by the Cooperative Study Center on Cooperative and Community Development (CEDECOM in Spanish) at the University of Pinar del Rio, and the Institute of Animal Sciences (ICA in Spanish) in Mayabeque Province. However, the lack of knowledge and specific demands on the part of Cuban agricultural cooperativism reveal that the national scientific production is still insufficient, in spite of the fact that, for the last twenty years, Latin America presents social balance as the instrument for evaluation of social cooperative responsibility.

The first manifestations of the social responsibility movement in the Americas came in the 1970s, with the emergence of the Association of Christian Regulators of Brazilian Companies (1964), but it is not until the 1980s that it achieved prominence. In general, Latin American practice is characterized by a philanthropic design, which disconnects the organization from the environmental and social dimensions, although examples of good experiences are known in Brazil, Argentina, Uruguay, and Ecuador, among others (Mena Lazo 2014).

This article aims to evaluate the most important results achieved during the implementation of the Cooperative Social Balance Model in Project Vía Láctea of Villa Clara from the perspective of gender, so as to reflect on the record and challenges of the social responsibilities of the relevant CCS. The application of the model included participatory workshops based on the methodological guidelines of the "Transform to Educate" project of the Asociación de Pedagogos of Cuba (Isla Guerra 2013), inspired in popular education.[2] Eight participatory workshops were organized—convened by the CCS themselves and by the provincial and municipal ANAP chapters. The following methods were also used: documentary analysis techniques and structured interviews with producers, directors, and community agents.

Six interviews were held with directors of both cooperatives, seventy-nine interviews with associates of both sexes—of which thirty-six (45.57 percent) were with women—as well as twenty-six interviews with directors of political and mass organizations of the communities in which the CCS are situated. The premeditated sample was selected based on the criteria of a connection to Project Vía Láctea.

The implementation of the model is based on the methodological convergence that combines the participatory and transformative perspective of popular education with the traditional concept of social research. Conflicting methodological limitations are synthesized in the epistemological gap between the participatory character of the process and the conventional objective of the model, marked by the particularities of the rural context. The fundamental risk resides in the lack of appropriation of the model as a participatory instrument to evaluate and transform the social responsibility of the cooperative, starting from the associates themselves. Communication and dialogue regulate the methodology with characteristics of fluidity and horizontality, based on respect for the different conceptions of the social agents. This methodological proposal aims to contribute to strengthening the chain of milk production and the social responsibility of the cooperatives based on an inclusive, efficient, and sustainable process.

The link between the model and the chain of milk production through Project Vía Láctea in Villa Clara aims to consolidate social equity, participation, and the sustainability of its practices. The general intention of the project consists of taking part in an integral way in the chain of milk production so as to reduce the losses and increase the quantity and quality of production. This proposal addresses a context of multiple adversities in the agricultural, environmental, economic, and social spheres in Cuba: low productivity and seasonality of milk production, the effects of climate change (prolonged droughts, hurricanes, high temperatures); limited access to supplies, technology and services; deficient genetic improvement and lack of technical knowledge on the part of the small producers; problems in the hygiene, manipulation, and conservation of the milk; insufficient coordination among the agents of the production chain; and the low participation of women.

The current proposal conceives cooperative social responsibility as a process that is constructed from the beginning of the decision-making, that values the impact of economic efficiency in the reduction of gender inequalities and in the protection/conservation of the environment in a participatory way, so as to incorporate such interests into the operation and production results of the organization. Therefore, cooperative social balance is understood as a participatory and systematic process that evaluates, plans, reorganizes, and controls cooperative social balance through organizational, economic, environmental, and social indicators of the management of the unit during a specific period.

NOTES ON THE GENDER PERSPECTIVE DURING THE IMPLEMENTATION OF THE COOPERATIVE SOCIAL BALANCE MODEL IN TWO COOPERATIVES OF VILLA CLARA

Conceived as a self-evaluative working instrument, the model is comprised of four areas of procedures: 1) Cooperative principles, 2) Productive economic area, 3) Gender relations, and 4) Environment.[3] Each one includes a set of dimensions, indicators, levels, and categories that should be validated in real-life experiences in order to find the particular value that pertains to it. Although the categories are flexible in the quantitative category, the plan to support all data with qualitative information is emphasized. The qualitative-quantitative combination of the analysis of the situation establishes the best-known expression of methodological convergence, which is still lacking in Cuban social studies.

The sphere of gender relations proposes the analysis of the quantitative and qualitative state of women's empowerment and emancipation in the cooperative, in the farm and the family. It only has one variable, equitable gender relations, which considers the following: the gender-based distribution of the male and female associates of the cooperative, women's contributions and power in the community, the cooperative, and the family; as well as other data of interest, such as the level of the women's qualification; the use of their free time; men's participation in domestic reproductive roles; and policies toward equity. The intent is to evaluate the level of gender equity achieved in order to determine the balance of opportunities and the level of participation of male and female associates according to their jobs, resources, and the making of decisions. In this way the gaps in gender equality in the rural environment of both CCS is reduced.

The results that were obtained differ slightly between the cooperatives, but in general they respond to tendencies of the common needs. In the area of gender the following issues—known and incorporated in later studies such as (Martínez Massip 2018)—are stressed: female presence in the assemblies is in the minority; the productive contribution of women is not always promoted or recognized; an important proportion of the jobs of women are associated with service or reproductive tasks; the tendency toward masculinization of productive and rural labor is marked.

In addition, it is very interesting to note certain tendencies in the paths taken by women—of the associates themselves or, denounced by them based on their experiences—which reveals even more the gender gap in rural areas, specifically in the agricultural cooperatives.

The patriarchal agrarian culture, framed by socioeconomic needs, has an influence on women when they make decisions. It legitimizes their reproductive role in the productive sector (food preservation, production of ornamental plants and flowers, poultry breeding, cooking and office work at the cooperative) or they tend to stay in their private space as a solution to personal dissatisfaction. There is a tendency in young rural women under thirty-five years of age to be satisfied with domestic *comfort* as a life project or as a way out of the crisis, if the patriarch has a stable source of high income in the cooperative.

When they are on this road to *comfort*, women's preferences remain distanced from the labor options of the rural environment. They do not identify with the successful women agricultural producers of the rural area. One concern is that the widening gap in equality between female identity and regional identity, in terms of emancipation and empowerment. A complex challenge of current Cuban socialist feminism is precisely to confront the patriarchal conception of complacency in women. "For various reasons, there occurs a return of the Cuban woman to the home and a re-adjustment of the gender relations towards patriarchal practices" (Valdés Gutiérrez, et al. 2018, 48).

On the other hand, women agricultural directors and producers (proprietors and usufruct farmers) in both cooperatives represent a minority archetype that deserves more encouragement and social recognition. According to current determinants, these women follow a path of *transgressing* the key patriarchal features of the cooperative labor and rural cultures that reproduce the sexual division of labor. The old discussion on the relation between reproductive and productive jobs constitutes a pending issue on the feminist agenda, which is more acute in the rural context. These women challenge the outdated view of the triplicate role through participatory forms—more improvised than innovative, but effective—and they also have the support of access and control of material resources (supplies, land, financial capital). In general, they have minimal social capital which allows for exchange and cooperation; at the minority tend toward knowledge management and capacity training.

Counterproductively, these *transgressing* women do not succeed in becoming visible in the basic statistics of the cooperatives mentioned. When cooperative directors are asked how many women agricultural producers there are in their cooperative, the replies given followed this order: the total number of women associates, the number of women proprietors or usufruct farmers, and the quantity of women that work in the offices of the cooperatives. When it was explained that the women agricultural producers are those who contribute to the agricultural production of the CCS—because of their direct link to agriculture or animal farming, because of their recognized knowledge of the daily practices and because of their economic contributions to the cooperative—the directors stopped to think, and even to consult others on who could be these women members, mostly landowners or usufruct farmers. The *transgressing* women need to go beyond their personal context; they need to transgress institutional practices and discourse.

Years of training and interactive learning through participatory gender equity workshops, and media and organizational campaigns in favor of rural female empowerment on the part of Cuban institutions, incite in a large proportion of the men, and in some women, what is called the *complacency* discourse. The appropriation of the technical language of the gender perspective and its main hypotheses—as seen from the common sense of the residents of the rural settlements—constitutes an anti-liberating resistance mechanism. With the *complacency* discourse, the patriarchal agrarian culture has discovered another disguise for gender inequalities to pass unseen or to convince, based on (self-)deceit related to the existence of sexist practices.

The *complacency* discourse treats with irony, distorts and minimizes the importance of promoting social equity, reduces the addition of more women directly linked to the agricultural activities and to management, diminishes the equidistant setting of the reproductive roles between men and women in the family. Male expressions like "I do all kinds of things in my house," "in my house it is my wife who is in charge," "I am not a male chauvinist," "women do more than men," become part of the *complacency* discourse when they partially or totally collide with a contrasting practice. It really is a sad defeat when women are an echo of *complacency*.

The patriarchal agrarian culture does not have a defined gender. The obstacles can be as difficult when they come from men as when they do from women. In this sense, a third path is oriented toward the *entrenched* power of women that favors the social status of women empowered by productive, economic, political, or family ways, but which does not succeed in diffusing, increasing, incorporating, and contributing so other women follow the same path. It is an arduous task to achieve that a majority of rural women in an advantageous position could share, include and cooperate with others who suffer less-propitious circumstances. The causes can be different, like a lack of material or cognitive resources, of communication capacities, of time and support. Communication, participation, and cooperative labor form guidelines of positive action, helping to overcome gaps in social inequality, and not only in gender. The rural context and the patriarchal agrarian culture conspire against the formation of solid networks between women, be it because of economic interests, the management of knowledge, or cooperation. Collective female rural power should make the potentials and the weaknesses more visible.

The *entrenched* female rural power contributes to the patriarchal agrarian culture. Training requires one to be more attractive, more stimulating, in touch with the needs of the beneficiaries, and, above all, with the collectivity and the context. Women leaders should be trained not for themselves, as isolated beings or for individual triumphs, but for the challenge of thinking and acting in networks directed at the rest of the women and society. The innovative organizational and institutional practice includes new goals in that sense; it is not an exclusive mission of the Federation of Cuban Women and ANAP, and much less of women only. It is a key objective for a country that aims to perfect its Economic and Social Model of Socialist Development.

In this sense, the issue of gender—or more specifically in this case of the rural women and producers—also requires special attention. Not only for equity and social development arguments, but also because women "in decision-making positions increase the profitability of the cooperative" (Hernández Nicolás, Martín Ugedo and Minguez Vera 2016, 155), which represents an economic interest. The promotion of feminine leadership and its feasibility should be emphasized more in the evaluation process, as part of the cooperative social balance, as well as its link with the optimization of cooperative social responsibility. Because rural Cuba is predominantly agrarian, the CCS constitute fundamental sources of female employment. However, for the majority of nonproducing women cooperative members, this does not represent an attractive option, even having the need or the possibility to work, while for the cooperative producers, their work is an opportunity linked to a strong vocation for agricultural work.

The rural transcends the agrarian. "Thus, the most important re-evaluation should be cultural: the view of the rural as a new, acceptable and better life alternative" (Pérez Correa 2002, 27), which requires changes in the economic and political sphere. It requires being part of transgressing old power structures and patriarchal domination, centralized and authoritarian, through innovative proposals such as the new rurality,[4] the rural or local development that is not divested of its rural component. Such initiatives are considered to be a pending national task.

Today it is a pressing need to further strengthen cooperative management based on strategic planning, in dialog with the academic sector, the enterprises and the government, which should include cooperative social responsibility, and not only the productive and economic aspects. The strengthening of the milk production chain based on an efficient process represents an essential ingredient for fomenting cooperative social responsibility, but the components of participation, inclusion, equity, training and sustainability should go shoulder to shoulder with any cooperative economic development. This means that it is imperative that the implementation of the model needs to be known and recognized not only by the cooperatives, but also by all social agents that interact with them and have an influence on their social objective.

CONCLUSIONS

A fundamental benchmark for the agricultural cooperativism that was studied is rooted in the presence of a patriarchal culture that rests on a masculinized cooperativism. Therefore, full compliance with cooperative social responsibility is of great urgency—a compliance that does not tend toward the economic to solve only formal and basic problems, but one which goes deeper, using cooperative social balance in a planned strategy and directed toward reducing or solving the gender inequalities identified in three streams: *comfortism*, invisible *transgression*, and *entrenched* female power. Thus, in one sense the challenge resides in the application of a participatory methodology of the Model of Cooperative Social Balance and, in another, in the promotion of agricultural and rural policies for the benefit of the health of the cooperatives, their associates, and their lifestyle.

NOTES

1. The Vía Láctea project (2015–2018) also includes other cooperatives in the central province of Cienfuegos and in the western provinces of Matanzas and Mayabeque. The project is coordinated by the Cuban National Association of Small Farmers (ANAP in Spanish) as its national counterpart, and by the international nongovernmental organization Cooperazione per lo Sviluppo dei Paesi Emergenti (COSPE) [Cooperation for the Development of Emerging Countries] as the Italian foreign counterpart. Other national entities of academic, scientific, and civil profiles in the central and western regions of the countries also participate.

2. Popular education has been promoted in Latin America since the end of the 1950s and the 1960s. The noted personality in Cuban popular education, Nydia González Rodríguez, refers to it as an "integrating conception of multiple dimensions that has as its objective to stimulate the transformation of the subjects and their practices based on a participatory process of committed self-reflection, based on their concrete historical reality" (Isla Guerra 2013, 18).

3. This has as its predecessor the model of Mena Lazo (2014), which is characterized as being more flexible in the processing and evaluation of compound variables than the traditional accounting systems. This proposal emphasises areas 3 and 4, because these are not included in the previous models studied by Mena Lazo.

4. The Latin American view of the new rurality does not accept fragmented and insufficient criteria that limit the rural to the importance of the agricultural activity, to the type of settlement, to the distance from urban centers, to the density, the size

of the population, the traditional behavior, or the culture of its residents—but rather in a balanced compendium of all these factors. This is the rural society composed of its economic, cultural, and political relations (beyond the agricultural), in mutual dependence with the rest of society (Teubal 2001).

BIBLIOGRAPHY

Alianza Cooperativa Internacional. *Los principios cooperativos para el siglo XXI* [The cooperative principles for the XXI century]. Fondo Nacional Universitario, 1996.

Consejo de Estado. "Ley 95/2002 Ley de Cooperativas de Producción Agropecuaria y de Créditos y Servicios" [Law 95/2002. Law of Agricultural Production and Credit and Services Cooperatives]. *Gaceta Oficial de la República de Cuba, Edición Ordinaria, No. 72 de 29 de noviembre de 2002*, 11 27.

Hernández Nicolás, C. M., J. F. Martín Ugedo, and A. Minguez Vera. "La influencia del género en la dirección de las sociedades cooperativas españolas sobre la rentabilidad y el endeudamiento: un análisis empírico" [The influence of gender in the management of Spanish cooperative societies on profitability and indebtedness: an empirical analysis]. *REVESCO Revista de estudios cooperativos* (122): 135–64. http://dx.doi.org/10.5209/rev_REVE.2016.v122.52021, 2016.

Isla Guerra, M. A. *Pistas metodológicas. Proyecto Transformar para educar* [Methodological leads. Project Transform to educate]. La Habana: Asociación de Pedagogos de Cuba, 2013.

Martínez Massip, A. "Innovar redes de difusión de innovación agropecuaria para la productividad agropecuaria del municipio Camajuaní" [Innovating networks of dissemination of agricultural innovation for agricultural productivity in the municipality of Camajuani]. Tesis de doctorado, Universidad de La Habana, La Habana, 2018.

Mena Lazo, C. Modelo de Balance Social Cooperativo, implementado en la UBPC Las Cadenas, municipio La Palma, Pinar del Río [Cooperative Social Balance Model, implementes at UBPC Las Cadenas, La Palma municipality, Pinar del Rio]. Tesis en opción al grado de máster en Gestión y Desarrollo de Cooperativas, La Habana: Universidad de La Habana, FLACSO Cuba, 2014.

Nova González, A. "Las cooperativas agropecuarias en Cuba: 1959–presente" [Agricultural cooperatives in Cuba: 1959–present]. In *Cooperativas y socialismo: Una mirada desde Cuba*, by Camila Piñeiro Harnecker, 321–36. La Habana: Editorial Caminos, 2011.

Pérez Correa, E. "Lo rural y la nueva ruralidad" [Rural and new ruralness]. In *Políticas, instrumentos y experiencias de desarrollo rural en América Latina y Europa*, by E. Pérez Correa and J. M. Sumpsi, 15–32. Madrid: Ministerio de Agricultura, Pesca y Alimentación, 2002.

Teubal, M. "Globalización y la nueva ruralidad en América Latina" [Globalization and new ruralness in Latin America]. In *¿Una nueva ruralidad en América Latina?*, by N. Giarraca, 58–64. Buenos Aires: CLACSO, 2001.

Valdés Gutiérrez, G., G. Alfonso González, Y. León del Río, A. Pérez Lara, M. Febles Domínguez, and M. Pérez González. *¿Feminismo en Cuba?* [Feminism in Cuba?]. La Habana: Editorial Filosofí@.cu, 2018.

Valdés Paz, J. *Los procesos de organización agraria en Cuba 1959–2006* [The processes of agrarian organization in Cuba 1959–2006]. La Habana: Fundación Antonio Núñez Jiménez de la Naturaleza y el Hombre, 2009.

Chapter 16

Business Social Responsibility in Local Development

A Look at the Training of Local Actors in the Province of Mayabeque

*Orquídea Hailyn Abreu González, Yuneidys
González Espinosa, and Joanna Gasmury Roldán*

Cuba is currently going through a number of social and economic changes and transformations designed to achieve greater development in the country. This development is conceived to be generated at the grassroots level, with creativity, participation, business social responsibility (BSR), and communication as the drivers of an inclusive society. To this end, it is necessary to take into account all the economic tiers of society (state and private entities, associations, joint ventures), so that this conglomerate of social actors can contribute to their own well-being.

The question of BSR has become prominent in economic, social, and political debates. It is proposed beyond the academic environment as an option for change, a complement of local development strategies, and a tool for social transformation aimed at social equity and inclusion (Rojas, Gómez, Piedra, Cabello, and Barrera 2016; Rojas Piedrahita et al. 2019).

Today, the municipality becomes the geographic space where the needs and hopes of the citizens converge with the potential of their context, based on the close link that should exist between the government and the population. In addition, it is the basis of the nation-government-territory link expected to favor the collective participation of all actors involved in local development.

The processes of local development are based on the local installed capacities and endogenous resources of each region, and the residents' motivation, together with the creation of networks, are essential to set them in motion. The training of human capital is the catalyst that determines the progress of municipal development (Del Castillo Sánchez et al. 2007).

Major socioeconomic changes facilitated by new opportunities offered by the Conceptualization of the Cuban Economic and Social Model of Socialist Development (PCC 2016) have been made throughout the province of Mayabeque in order to increase the effectiveness of the production of goods and services. The forms of nongovernmental ownership and management,[1] intended to revitalize the local economy and use BSR as a harmonic link with the locality, have noticeably developed.

After participating in government meetings,[2] and meeting with nonagricultural cooperatives[3] and self-employed workers, it became clear that there is little recognition—among both government leaders and even the actors involved in them—of the importance of non-state forms of management for local development. There is also poor knowledge among the latter about the multidisciplinary nature and the contribution of the BSR process. The role of the university[4] in raising awareness and training local actors on BSR for the benefit of provincial development is also insufficient.

The training of local actors on BSR for local development is essential to foster the socioeconomic transformations that the country needs and improve the competence of government leaders, the producers-businessmen, and the academics, among others. Furthermore, it makes it possible to coordinate actions and have an impact on local public policy-making for the benefit of municipal development from the standpoint of fairness and equity.

In this connection, an objective of this article is to identify the role that BSR plays in local development based on the training of stakeholders of the province of Mayabeque. The article has three sections, starting with an approach to BSR based on the review of the various definitions of the term adopted nationally internationally, followed by a theoretical analysis of the relationship between BSR and local development based on the training of local players. Finally, the current context of the province of Mayabeque and the actions to train local actors are discussed.

A REVIEW OF THE CONCEPT OF BUSINESS SOCIAL RESPONSIBILITY IN THE CURRENT CONTEXT

In order to understand the concept of BSR it is necessary to review the works of AVINA (2011), Rojas, Gómez, Piedra, Cabello, and Barrera (2016), and the Ethos Institute (Instituto Ethos 2016). It is a form of business management of a multidimensional nature (ethical, social, economic, legal, environmental, and participatory), which entails a commitment to generate value in line with the development of sustainable, verifiable, and intended practices. It becomes manifest in the interaction of the enterprise with its stakeholders in a specific context that favors equity and social justice (Rojas Piedrahita et al. 2019).

Therefore, BSR is considered a multidimensional management process that advocates for a more equitable world where every social, ethical, environmental, public, and economic action taken responds to the needs of society. The close relationship between the state and non-state sectors and the social actors allows for an equitable and egalitarian balance based on actions and measures required to promote sustainable human development at the local level. The definition also indicates the relationship established between the enterprise and its stakeholders,[5] as they are referred to in international literature.

BSR originated in the 1920s and gained strength in the 1950s and 1960s. It starts from the premise that, if the enterprises use the resources of society, this use of itself creates an ethical duty and, therefore, it should give back to society part of the benefits derived from it. The enterprises create wealth by using productive factors, so they must take responsibility for it beyond the generation of jobs and wealth for the owners of the financial resources. They should also safeguard the well-being of the community where it is located (Olaya Garcerá and Rojas Muñoz 2018).

Another element that contributed to the development of BSR originated objectively from the Global Compact initiative (1999) between the United Nations and the capitalist world.[6] According to the United Nations, the ethical, results-oriented approach of the Global Compact is to promote social dialogue for the constitution of a global corporate citizenry that makes it possible to reconcile business interests with the needs and values of civil society, labor unions, and nongovernmental organizations (NGOs) based on principles that crosscut enterprise activities related to fundamental values such as:

- Human rights
- Labor standards
- The environment
- The fight against corruption

It is safe to say then that, at the international level, BSR is not just devoted to responding to legal (environmental and labor) obligations of the enterprise, but also ensuring the internal and external well-being of society. In other words, BSR goes beyond what the law states to care about the sustainability of the workers, their surrounding environment, the community to which they contribute, and the country in general.

According to the economist Rafael Betancourt, BSR has gone through three major stages at the international level:

1. Corporate philanthropy: donations and contributions by the enterprise to community institutions and groups.
2. Social investment: strategic contributions to community institutions and groups.
3. Social responsibility: contributes a view of a responsible business citizenry integrated into the business strategy beyond legal obligations (Betancourt 2016).

In spite of the benefits and advantages that BSR offers, we should keep in mind that it originated in capitalism with the intention of cleaning up the image of exploitative enterprises which, as part of their marketing strategy, engage in a number of charitable works in the community and use said image as a tool to achieve a better positioning in the market (Reyes 2018). This is beneficial to their relationship with the surrounding environment inasmuch as they seem to be socially responsible enterprises, which has brought discredit and disrepute to the image of BSR.

On the other hand, the role of BSR in the present Cuban context aims at a management process that builds capacity and engages the government, the social actors, and the private sector in the fulfillment of development strategies, seizing the regional potential and the role of innovation in the management of public policies and the design of programs and projects.

BSR plays an essential role at the business level, extending its scope to not only environmental but also social variables and, for that purpose, internalizing ethical values through local innovation and social entrepreneurship processes (Mora Mayoral and Martínez Martínez 2018).

This author agrees with the conceptualization provided by Rojas Piedrahita et al. (2016, 2019) since it identifies with the multidimensional character of BSR. The link between the enterprise and the locality benefits from a conscious, participatory, and sustainable process that responds to the needs of the population through the best use of the existing potential and brings benefits and opportunities that favor local development.

The concepts associated with BSR, in terms of values such as honesty, solidarity, and transparency, have been part of the very nature of the public Cuban business system. Its structure builds on the same values that sustain the socialist economy and on the requirements enshrined in the rules for public enterprises, which are expected to guarantee the participation of the workers in organizational management—as owners of the means of production—and to improve their working conditions, evaluate their satisfaction and upgrade their technical and cultural knowledge. In general terms, "promote the human growth of their workers through the development of professional and human competencies" (ISO 2010).

Strictly speaking, Cuba has no legislation or corporate law that mentions BSR. Nor do we have a ministry or governmental structure in charge of its promotion, control, or certification. We do have a number of cross-sectional standards, laws, decrees, and regulations at macro, mezzo, and micro level that contribute jointly to BSR management. Compliance with these norms allows for the existence of a first BSR level. Transcending this level and contributing more than what is required would make it possible to speak of higher BSR levels (Gómez Arencibia and Rojas Piedrahita 2019).

An analysis of Decree 281/2007, "Rules for the implementation and con-solidation of the system of the State Business Management System," reveals a generic approach to the enterprise's responsibility toward society, whereas its role in environmental management is only specified in Chapter VIII. The topic remained as is, without any change or modification, in the recent revi-sion of the document in Decree 281/2018. (Consejo de Estado 2013; Consejo de Estado 2018)

In this respect, the Guidelines for the Economic and Social Policy of the Party and the Revolution for 2016–2021 (PCC 2017a) recognize ownership by the state and joint ventures, as well as private ownership by Cuban or foreign individuals or entities and by political, mass, social, and other orga-nizations of civil society, as forms of production in the national economy. Guideline 99 lays down the need to keep developing a legal and regulatory framework that facilitates the systematic and accelerated use of the results of science, innovation, and technology in the production and service pro-cesses, taking into account the current standards on social and environmental responsibility.

Given that the Cuban state acknowledges a legal vacuum in certain concepts that markedly influences the country's current economic context, actions are under way to change this situation. One example is the announce-ment made by the president of the republic and the minister of economy and planning on new forthcoming economic measures. Cuba's intention is to fos-ter the use of production linkages as an option for local coordination, favor the relations between state and non-state forms of management, and extend self-employment as a driver of local economy. The overall aim is to boost national socioeconomic development (Cubadebate 2020).

The above envisages the legal recognition of the coexistence of various forms of property and management in the Cuban economy that can be the starting point for BSR-related action. However, the regulatory framework that could encourage their development is insufficient, as it leaves this kind of action to voluntariness and to the fulfillment of legal standards (health, tax, and other regulations).

By its very nature and because of its social object (legal status) and its pro-jection as protector of the workers, the state enterprise is socially responsible.

In addition, it contributes to the education of the people, establishes mechanisms of participation, and supports the link of the enterprise with its stakeholders (community, environment). However, the BSR approach is associated with a biased conception of the term (environmental management, in some cases) without specifying its scope. There is an intention to meet people's demand, but stated in such a way that it leans more toward the old culture of assistance rather than encourage participation and feedback between the enterprise and the region in the interests of empowering the population to solve their needs.

BSR is intended to facilitate the development, recreation, growth, and well-being of all residents of the community and contribute to the creation of jobs and production linkages with other enterprises and to make a positive environmental impact. Its implementation relies on objective and subjective factors that determine its contribution to society in the most just and equitable manner. This is why it needs knowledge (the role of universities and research centers), creativity (innovations by businesspeople and decision-makers), participation (being and taking part), sustainability (balance among social, environmental, and economic), awareness (internally and externally favorable), dissemination (promotion of the measures to be taken), a holistic vision (cover everything that benefits or contributes to sustainability), commitment, and voluntariness (feeling like a participant who is free to take action and relies on a regulatory framework).

The implementation of this and other concepts in different contexts is largely contingent on the levels of awareness and knowledge about the topic among the decision-makers. In this regard, the training of actors plays a key role based on the existing university-government-enterprise-territory linkages, as a function of recognizing training needs and facilitating their satisfaction.

BSR AND LOCAL DEVELOPMENT: CONTRIBUTION OF TRAINING

In the case of Cuba, "Local development is recognized as an essentially endogenous, participatory and innovative process that coordinates the interests of actors, regions and levels (municipal, provincial and sectorial/national). It relies on the leadership of the municipal and provincial governments to manage their development strategies, from knowledge and innovation management to the promotion of projects leading up to economic-productive, sociocultural, environmental and institutional transformations in order to improve people's quality of life" (Ministerio de Economía y Planificación 2020).

The municipality is considered as the springboard of local development in Cuba, according to its definition in Article 168 of the Constitution of the Republic, which states that the municipality is the local legally established society that constitutes the primary and fundamental political-administrative entity of national organization. It has autonomy and legal capacity for all legal purposes, and its territorial extension is determined by necessary neighborly, economic and social relations of its population and by the national interests, with the aim of meeting local needs (ANPP 2019, 12).

We should see and understand local development as a holistic process that brings together institutional, environmental, economic-productive, sociocultural, political, and social aspects that define the municipality's situation and encourage the development of an all-inclusive approach to local problems based on the integral conception of its endogenous conditions and capacities.

The Regional Development Policy launched by the Ministry of Economy and Planning (Ministerio de Economía y Planificación 2020) based on the coordinated effort of different academic and government bodies and institutions provides legal guidelines for the definition of concepts, principles and tools to organize development at municipal and provincial level. This document presents the classification of local projects[7] and the figures recognized as their owners, which contributes to local and sustainable development management.

From the theoretical point of view, this concept gained strength in the last decades of the twentieth century, given the failure of large-scale development strategies to generate equitable and sustainable development. These new proposals place emphasis on the transition toward gender, generational, and regional equity based on endogenous development. To this end, social transformations that take advantage of the strengths and potential of the smaller areas are encouraged. These favorable elements build on every region's potential resource base: different forms of social organization, availability of a given natural resource, traditions and identity and sociocultural characteristics. By this logic, small and medium state and private enterprises are municipal assets, as they foster socioeconomic progress, create jobs, are profitable, and engage in exports and, therefore, can contribute to regional development and to the emergence of other entities. In light of these facts, the BSR concept can contribute to the preparation of a flexible business management model that would facilitate the implementation of strategies shared by both the enterprise and the community (Gómez Arencibia and Rojas Piedrahita 2019).

Any change at the local level depends to a large extent on the capacity and willingness of the local actors. The enterprises play a key role in the endogenous and integral development of regions because of their capacity to boost business ventures and thus foster the growth and development of their surrounding environment.

Strengthening the capacity of local actors to manage—in a decentralized manner—the strategies, public policies, programs, and projects that underpin local development becomes essential in this process.

We have remarked in previous pages the importance of the role that universities play or should play in BSR and local development processes, since training is pivotal to their management. Speaking of training necessarily entails identifying specific needs of preparation (topics), as well as who will be trained and where (Mirabal Patterson 2006).

As to the training of local actors, it should respond to the needs identified in the strategic design of the community to develop a system of knowledge that feedbacks constantly on local needs and practical experiences, promotes teamwork and a multidisciplinary approach to problem-solving and encourages the exchange of updated information and permanent training (Del Castillo Sánchez et al. 2007).

This activity should include from the beginning the engagement of various actors from academia, government and production to conciliate together the needs of knowledge and the existing potential, based on theoretical and practical principles.

The BSR process promotes self-management capacity and relies on collective efforts in which not only the population makes demands and the structures find solutions, but spaces for and forms of participation emerge as a result of the tools that it provides (Mirabal Patterson 2006).

The municipal development strategy (MDS) is an instrument of integration that helps municipal governments in managing the priorities defined according to national and regional interests (Guzón 2020). It is an essential working tool to organize the training of local actors, develop a cross-sectional approach to knowledge management throughout the municipal lines of work, and define training priorities according to the potential and needs of enterprises, institutions and the population in general. It also facilitates the coordination of the actions of local leaders and improves the processes of knowledge management and technology transfer that strengthens both the links between the structures and the population and the engagement of various regional actors (Mirabal Patterson 2006).

BSR takes a fresh look at the local context that is in keeping with the objectives of the country. Therefore, it is necessary to find the tools required to motivate and deploy a local movement that develops practical experience. The training of local actors needs to engage the Municipal University Centers (SUN, in Spanish), higher education institutions and research centers, government leaders, and productive actors who can work together on the creation of knowledge networks that make municipal transformation possible.

BSR AWARENESS AND TRAINING OF KEY
ACTORS IN THE PROVINCE OF MAYABEQUE

Mayabeque is one of the provinces in the western part of the country, established as such on August 1, 2010, following an amendment to Act 1304/1976 on Political and Administrative Division of the National Assembly of People's Power. It has eleven municipalities, and the provincial capital is San José de las Lajas.

One characteristic of the creation of the new province was the approval to undertake a far-reaching experiment, setting limits to state and government functions in Mayabeque as per Decree-Law 301/2012 and the new Rules and Regulations for the Municipal Assembly (2013). Consequently, a new institutional design was developed that is today considered a first approximation, highly relevant to the development of a new system of public administration for the country, following the Guidelines for the Economic and Social Policy (Proenza 2016).

Given its geographical location—bordering the provinces of La Habana and Matanzas—a particular feature of the province of Mayabeque is that it is home to a large number of enterprises with a national scope. On one hand, while these enterprises are sources of employment and contribute to regional taxation, they use local resources and market their production elsewhere, which means that the strengths of these entities and the opportunities that they represent are not fully taken advantage of.

These facts, together with the integration of the Centro de Estudios para la Gestión del Desarrollo [Center for Development Management Studies] (CEGED) of Universidad Agraria de La Habana (UNAH) and the Red de Economía Social y Solidaria y Responsabilidad Social Empresarial [Network of Social and Solidarity Economy and Business Social Responsibility] (ESORSE), led to the introduction of the topics of BSR and Social and Solidarity Economy, pursuant to the approach to local development in CEGED's plans and scope.

According to its mission, CEGED[8] is a university institution engaged in research, education, training, and extension to develop human competencies with a view to business management and public administration, based on a cross-sectional multidisciplinary and innovative approach to local development in the province of Mayabeque. For this reason, its functions include building capacity at the level of municipal and provincial governments for the implementation of development strategies and projects, consulting for and coordinating local development management with the SUMs, and strengthening social innovation of knowledge to create innovative local systems.

The institutional recognition of CEGED as a department of UNAH that coordinates these issues in the province has made it possible to develop a joint working system that helps to raise awareness and train government, academic and production actors, as well as to take steps toward the organization of BSR-oriented projects.

One of the first activities undertaken in the province was the National Workshop Aportes de la Economía Social y Solidaria al Desarrollo Local [Contributions of the Social and Solidarity Economy to Local Development] (2019), organized by ESORSE and attended by CEGED's directors, the head of the Provincial Administrative Council, and the head of its Development Division. This workshop allowed for the participation of these actors in working groups organized as part of the program to study and discuss the tools for the institutionalization of the strategic management of local development. It also helped them learn about BSR and ESS and about the province's potential to put them into practice.

With a view toward their greater preparation to deal with this topic, the first step was to include CEGED directors (June 2019) and then the head of the provincial Development Division (October 2019) in the Diploma Program in Management of Cooperatives and Social and Solidarity Economy Organizations, organized by the Escuela Andaluza de Economía Social [School of Social Economy of Andalusia] in Osuna, Sevilla, Spain. This has made it possible to delve deeper into the theory and basic principles of SSE and to learn about different success stories of its use at national and international level. Likewise, sharing views with actors from other provinces has facilitated a dialogue about ongoing experiences.

The dissemination of the topic has encouraged participation in other events, such as the symposiums organized by the Psychological and Sociological Research Center (CIPS) in 2018 and 2019, attended by professors and students who do research on these subjects. This adds to the investigation under way in the province on the role of self-employment in local development from the BSR standpoint, such as of the student Yohana Jasmury's thesis work about the link between self-employed workers and local development in the provincial municipality of San José de las Lajas from the perspective of social responsibility.

In January 2020, UNAH organized an international postgraduate course, coordinated and attended by the ESORSE Network, CIPS, the Provincial Administrative Board and CEGED and cosponsored by Andalusian School of Social Economy, the Center for Management, Local Development, Tourism and Cooperative Studies of the University of Pinar del Río (CE-GESTA) and the Cuban Psychology Society. The course was about the management of local development based on social and solidarity economy and was delivered to thirty-five provincial development official and actors, including SUM directors, municipal local development managers, and provincial government officials from the Ministry of Science, Technology and the Environment (CITMA), as well as industry representatives, the provincial development division, and presidents of agricultural cooperatives. Among the topics covered were SSE and BSR as drivers of local development through different forms of management, strategic local development and environmental management of local development and environmental management, and the various forms of funding local projects. Moreover, as a practical exercise, the trainees visited two cooperatives: the agricultural credit and service cooperative (CSC) "Orlando Cuellar" and the nonagricultural raw material recycling cooperative (CNA) of San José de las Lajas.

The trainees learned to design SSE- and BSR-related actions to implement at the local level as a function of a working system coordinated by the government, the university, the enterprises and the community, and to understand SSE and BSR as drivers of local development.

CEGED's role includes consultancy for and assistance to local actors with a view to development management. This is one of its main lines of work, that is, development models and programs as the basis of the link between local development and BSR, education for development—which covers the training of actors on BSR and SSE as part of its educational program—and management for development. As part of the latter, state and non-state actors involved in food chains are working on a production linkage project. CEGED is also assisting the abovementioned raw material recycling cooperative with the management of projects that promote a culture of recycling in the beneficiary community, as well as private businesses, cooperatives and enterprises with the design and management of BSR-related projects. Besides, its communication and dissemination strategy includes the publication of related articles in the journal *Revista de Gestión del Conocimiento y el Desarrollo Local* coordinated by CEGED.

Adopting the BSR approach allows CEGED to focus attention on the community, in line with its own research on university social responsibility, as well as to direct its efforts toward the coordination of related research in the province based on the recognition of the input of local researchers and professors and the plans to design cross-sectional working strategies. Moreover, it paves the way for new research projects and outcomes of regional benefit through the coordination of various actors involved in local development management and for the training of a greater number of local actors by promoting new local projects based on existing opportunities. All this springs from local policies established by governments who know about the topic through an improved university-government-enterprise-community coordination.

CONCLUSIONS

The Cuban state has promoted a process of changes and transformations for the benefit of national development, engaging various economic actors, guaranteeing productivity and efficiency, and recognizing the role of the non-state forms of management in boosting the economy by making the most of new opportunities and responding to local needs.

The current circumstances call for non-state actors committed to their society and aware that applying BSR to management entails broadening their perspective to include not only the environmental but also the social variable, based on the recognition of ethical values and the generation of innovation and social business in favor of local development.

Since Mayabeque is a young province where BSR is still a new concept, it is necessary to train local actors on the topic. CEGED's work in this connection as part of the ESORSE Network allows raising awareness among government leaders, producers, and other local specialists with a view to making transformations that favor social well-being and strengthen the university-government-enterprise-community link.

NOTES

1. Of the 245,642 people of working age in the province of Mayabeque in 2019, 18,155 (7.4 percent) are self-employed (ONEI, 2020).

2. Municipal and provincial meetings of the Administrative Council and the Municipal Development Committees.

3. Cooperativa No Agropecuaria de Reciclaje de Materias Primas [Nonagricultural Raw Material Recycling Cooperative] San José de Las Lajas.

4. Universidad Agraria de La Habana UNAH is not conducting any BSR research projects in the province of Mayabeque, and very few theses have produced research findings about this topic.

5. In this article, stakeholders are understood to be groups and organizations that interact directly or indirectly with the enterprise—business owners, suppliers/providers, workers, consumers, clients, community, region, government, political, and mass organizations (Communist Party of Cuba, labor unions, Young Communist League, labor unions)—that work for social change (Rojas, Gómez, Piedra, Cabello, and Barrera 2016).

6. Announced by then UN Secretary-General Kofi Annan at the World Economic Forum held in Davos, Switzerland, on January 31, 1999. See www.unglobalcompact .org/about.

7. According to their nature, they can be classified as economic-productive, sociocultural, environmental, institutional, and research, development, and innovation projects.

8. Resolution 42/2017 of the minister of Higher Education, dated April 6, 2017, approved the resizing of CEDAR (Center for Agrarian and Rural Studies) and established CEGED.

BIBLIOGRAPHY

ANPP. *Constitución de la República de Cuba* [Constitutiom of the Republic of Cuba]. La Habana: Asamblea Nacional del Poder Popular, 2019. Retrieved from: http://www.granma.cu/file/pdf/gaceta/Nueva%20Constituci%C3%B3n%20240%20KB-1.pdf.

AVINA. *En busca de la sostenibilidad. El camino de la Responsabilidad Social Empresarial en América Latina y la contribución de la Fundación AVINA* [In search of sustainability. The path to Business Social Responsibility in Latin America and the contribution of the AVINA Foundation]. Buenos Aires: Fundación AVINA, 2011.

Betancourt, R. "La Responsabilidad Social Empresarial en Cuba" [Business Social Responsibility in Cuba]. *Estudios de Desarrollo Social: América Latina y Cuba* (FLACSO UH) 4 (2): 34–43. Mayo–Agosto 2016. Retrieved from: www.revflacso.uh.cu.

Consejo de Estado. Decreto 281/2007. *Gaceta Oficial de la República de Cuba, Edición Ordinaria, No. 007.* 18 febrero de 2013.

———. Decreto 281/2018. *Gaceta Oficial de la República de Cuba, Edición Extraordinaria, No. 31.* 28 junio de 2018.

Cubadebate. Gobierno cubano informa sobre nuevas medidas económicas [Cuban government announces new economic measures]. Cubadebate 16 julio 2020. Retrieved from: http://www.cubadebate.cu/noticias/2020/07/16/gobierno-cubano-informa-nuevas-medidas-economicas-video/.

Del Castillo Sánchez, L., et al., "El papel de la universidad en la capacitación y la investigación acción para el desarrollo económico local. Experiencia del municipio Yaguajay" [The role of the university in training and active research for local economic development]. *Economía y Desarrollo*, 142(2), julio–diciembre 2007.

Gómez Arencibia, J., and M. Rojas Piedrahita. "Responsabilidad Social Empresarial en Cuba: controversias inconclusas" [Business Social Responsibility in Cuba: inconclusive controversy]. In J. L. (Coordinadores), *Hablemos de trabajo en Cuba. El debate necesario y el futuro a construir,* 2019.

Guzón, A. Guía metodológica para la elaboración de la estrategia de desarrollo municipal [Methodological Guide to developing the municipal development strategy]. In A. G. (Coordinadora), *Cataurito de Herramientas para el desarrollo local 2.* La Habana, 2020.

Instituto Ethos. *Conceptos Básicos e Indicadores de Responsabilidad Social Empresarial* [Basic Concepts and Indicators of Business Social Responsibility]. São Paolo, 2016.

ISO. *INTERNATIONAL STANDARD ISO 26000. Guidance on social responsibility.* Switzerland: International Organization for Standardization, 2010.

Ministerio de Economía y Planificación. *Política para impulsar el desarrollo territorial* [Policy for promoting regional development]. La Habana, 2020. Retrieved from https://www.mep.gob.cu/sites/default/files/Documentos/POLITICA-PARA-IMPULSAR-EL-DESARROLLO-TERRITORIAL.pdf.

Ministerio de Trabajo y Seguridad Social. Resolución 33/2011 Reglamento del ejercicio del trabajo por cuenta propia [Guidelines for the exercise of self-employment]. *Gaceta Oficial No. 29 Extraordinaria de 7 de septiembre de 2011.*

Mirabal Patterson, A. "La capacitación de actores locales y el desarrollo local" [Training local actors and local development]. In A.G. (Compiladora), *Desarrollo Local en Cuba: Retos y Perspectivas.* La Habana: Editorial Academia, 2006.

Mora Mayoral, M., and F. Martínez Martínez. "Desarrollo local sostenible, responsabilidad social corporativa y emprendimiento social" [Sustainable local development, corporate social responsibility and social businesses]. *Equidad y Desarrollo*, (31), 27–46, 2018. Retrieved from http://dx.doi.org/10.19052/ed.4375.

Olaya Garcerá, J., and A. Rojas Muñoz. *Responsabilidad Social Empresarial: Su origen, evolución y desarrollo en Colombia* [Business Social Responsibility: Its origin, evolution and development in Colombia]. Alicante: Escuela Superior de Marketing y Management, 2018.

ONEI. *Anuario Estadístico de Cuba, 2019* [Statistical Annual of Cuba, 2019]. La Habana: Oficina Nacional de Estadística e Información de Cuba, 2020.

PCC. *Conceptualización del Modelo Económico y Social Cubano de Desarrollo y Plan Nacional de Desarrollo Económico y Social hasta 2030* [Conceptualization of the Cuban Economic and Social Development Model and National Plan for Economic and Social Development until 2030]. La Habana: VI Congreso del Partido Comunista de Cuba, 2016.

———. Lineamientos de la Política Económica y Social del Partido y la Revolución [Guidelines for the Economic and Social Policy of the Party and the Revolution]. La Habana: VII Congreso del Partido Comunista de Cuba, 2017.

Proenza, D. "La gestión descentralizada como componente esencial de la actualización del modelo en Cuba: el caso de Güines, provincia Mayabeque" [Decentralized management as an essential component of updating the Cuban model: the case of Güines, Mayabeque province]. *Estudios del Desarrollo Social: Cuba y América Latina*, 4(2): 1–19, 2016.

Reyes, A. *Reflexiones sobre la Responsabilidad Social Empresarial ante contradicciones del cuentapropismo y la empresa estatal en Cuba* [Reflections on Business Social Responsibility and the contradictions between self-employment and the state enterprise in Cuba]. La Habana: Fondos biliográficos del CIPS, 2018.

Rojas Piedrahita, M., J. Gómez, Y. González, A. Reyes, J. C. Campos, and I. Caballero. *La Responsabilidad Social Empesarial en el Centro de Inmunología Molecular* [Business Social Responsibility in the Center for Molecular Immunology]. La Habana: Fondo bibliográfico del CIPS, 2019.

Rojas, M., J. Gómez, H. Piedra, L. Cabello, and B. S. Cabello. *La Responsabilidad Social Empresarial desde espacios estatales cubanos. Aproximación a una propuesta de modelo de gestión* [Business Social Responsibility from state-owned spaces in Cuba. Approximation to a proposal for a management model]. La Habana: Fondo bibliográfico del CIPS, 2016.

Chapter 17

"Go for it: You can do it!"

The Solidarity Experience of Female Entrepreneurs

Jusmary Gómez Arencibia

As a concept and proposal for social transformation, the social and solidarity economy (ESS in Spanish) has gradually found a place in contemporary scientific thought. It is addressed from the perspective of different fields such as economics, sociology, law, and studies on social development. The epistemological starting point assumed by their authors prefigures the accepted meanings: popular and solidarity economy, social economy, economic solidarity, and solidarity economy, just to mention a few.

This proposal is based on organizations and enterprises that have a double objective: economic and social—and often also environmental—which produce goods and services according to principles and practices of cooperation, association, solidarity, and the satisfaction of basic needs. These include not only traditional forms of cooperative organizations or mutual societies (such as health services, for example), but also associations of independent workers, organizations and networks of fair trade and ethical consumers, self-help women's groups, social enterprises, community initiatives related to forestry, and nongovernmental organizations (NGOs), that are beginning to generate income through economic activities and community- financed initiatives (Arriagada 1990; Fonteneau et al. 2011).

Within the ESS trends there exists the inclination to associate it to the targeting of the poorest and most vulnerable groups.[1] The precariousness of employment is female, because the largest numbers of the precarious jobs, part-time and with minimal pay, are labored by women (CEPAL 2019). It is possible to distinguish a significant number of experiences of this type which are practiced by women, or meant for them, and in which they occupy an important space as workers, integrators, participants, and users (Nobre 2015).

ESS cannot be a palliative or a focalized group of actions for healthcare, but a process in which the capacities of all citizens are stimulated. It should encourage the development of social links connected to satisfying a wide range of material and social needs, and to the recuperation of the rights of everyone. It is necessary to make it visible in the strategies of local development and in the national regulatory structures.[2]

The term used to characterize this model in Cuba is socialist economy, not social and solidarity economy, in spite of their resemblances. This model was created by the state through the socioeconomic and political system, the central planning, and the state enterprises. These enterprises have implicit solidarity objectives, but they are rarely explicit or drawn up by their directors and workers. Up to now, they also do not have any financial autonomy that would allow them to assign part of their income to social or environmental activities not explicitly so designated in the National Economic Plan (Betancourt 2015, 2).

Currently, Cuba finds itself in a process of modernizing its economic and social model. Based on the programmatic documents that govern these actions[3] we can identify a workable institutional structure for ESS and local development. These reforms display a political will to encourage the processes of developmental self-management at the municipal level, based on their strategies, so that they can become empowered as a fundamental institution with the necessary autonomy; they have an impact in the vertical productive links, which requires their reconfiguration, opens new spaces and challenges for the planning and development of the Cuban regions; they imply the active participation of the population in the governing processes; and they reflect the need to integrate economic actors and types of property and management.

Among the changes that this great modernization process has brought, the strength that local development has today is evident, as well as the deployment of a popular, cooperative and solidary economy in the regions, which include cooperative, associative and community sectors. Even so, there are still many popular experiences and initiatives that should be encouraged to become spaces of hegemonic reconfiguration practices of popular power. Some of these experiences have happened against the current, and they still have much to offer as an anti-capitalist sustainability model. (Galfisa 2017, 2).

The reform that is being carried out has a different impact on women than on men. The measures adopted are not discriminatory or based on gender, but neither do they necessarily constitute opportunities for women (Echevarría and Lara 2012). National statistics reveal that by the end of 2018 the non-state sector employed 31.6 percent of the working population and, in that group, only 5.8 percent were women (ONEI 2019). In the nonagricultural cooperatives that existed in Cuba in 2016, only 19.6 percent of the total members were women (Piñeiro 2018). In addition, there is a difference in the access to productive activities like land, houses and capital, to the disadvantage of Cuban women (Echevarría and Lara 2012)

The jobs permitted in the private undertakings include basic and traditional activities like repair shops, blacksmiths, passenger transportation, repair services, and equipment maintenance—just to mention a few. These have been classified by specialists as being traditionally masculine (Benería and Roldán 1987; Borderías, Carrasco, and Alemany 1994; Wanderley, Sostres, and Farah 2016).

All of this encompasses the fundamental questions of this article: What are the challenges and the opportunities that women have within the ESS in Cuba? What is the role that they should play in this process?

An approach to these questions can be sketched out based on the analysis of the Atelier project *Go for it: You can do it!* organized by women entrepreneurs of the municipality of Marianao in the capital. We take into consideration the form of the organization/management, socially responsible actions, community impact, the different types of stakeholders, and the obstacles and possibilities they have lived through in their career path. The approach to a practical experience—and the presentation of the scope and the limitations of the ESS in Cuba—are the contributions of this article.

ESS in Cuba should transcend philanthropy, and be more than an economy *of the poor and for the poor, of women and for women.* It should be a mobilizer of the local economy, a generator of jobs, of productive links and empowerment of the stakeholders, while promoting and consolidating solidarity activities. Its rationale leads to social protection, equity, fair growth, the progress of foundational democracy, and sustainable development (Guzón 2018).

This chapter is organized in two main sections. The first deals with a theoretical approach to the topic of ESS and the role of women in this process, both in the international and in the national context. The second reflects the process of empowerment that Cuban women experience. In addition, in this section the experience of *Go for it: You can do it!* is presented from the ESS perspective.

SOCIAL AND SOLIDARITY ECONOMY: THEORETICAL NOTES

This section intends to present the theoretical paths that have guided the ESS points of view, both in the international and in the national context. In addition, the role that women have played in these processes is also shown.

The International Approach of the Social and Solidarity Economy

As a practice, ESS goes back to the years 1830 and 1840, in England and France. It was born with the workers' movement, as a reaction to uncontrolled industrial capitalism, the cause of the miserable conditions of the working classes. The first forms of cooperatives appear in Paris and in western France, as credit cooperatives and mutual aid societies. They intended to offer a response to basic solidarity needs, like burying family members and access to basic services (Laville 2006).

Although the concept emerged among the French people several centuries ago, it reached a greater scope in the 1970s, by going through a profound reorientation during the second half of the twentieth century. The high point of the concept in the public sphere came about through the international crisis of the 1970s.[4] During those years it was defined as:

> that form of economics that is integrated by private organizations, mainly coop-eratives, mutual societies and associations whose ethics respond to the follow-ing principles: processes of democratic discussions, the precedence of people and work over capital in the distribution of income, the objective of service to its members or the collective over profit, and autonomy of management. (Borge, 2016, quoted by Betancourt 2017, 12)

According to Mutuberría Lazarini (2008) and Oxoby (2010), we can identify two theoretical traditions in the perspective toward the ESS:

- *The European view:* ESS is seen through a democratization of the economy and the acceptance of a plural economy. The idea of identify-ing it only with poverty, with the informal sector, or the rural population is rejected. It assumes a form of democratization of the economy based on citizens' commitments. Frequently there are initiatives created to respond to contemporary social and environmental problems, to the sys-tems of exchange, local commerce, and sustainable agriculture. These organizations or networks of the solidarity economy are also implanted at the local level and are based on a mechanism of reciprocity (Laville 2006; Lévesque and Mendell 2007).
- *The Latin American View*: this is a heterogeneous movement that emerged from neoliberalism and now includes the defense of the rights of nature (Guerra 2008). It is proposed as a return to ancestral practices, in which the *good life* is emphasized. In the region it has been concep-tualized in different ways: solidarity economy (Razeto 2003), popular solidarity economy (Tiriba 2001; Gaiger 2008), or socioeconomics of solidarity (Arruda 2006; Guerra 2008). The role that the movement

of the recuperated enterprises has played in countries like Argentina, Uruguay, and Brazil should be emphasized (Ruggeri 2019).

The debate on this topic is fed by other opinions: the Third Sector,[5] the non-lucrative sector, a diverse economy (Gibson-Graham 2011). These viewpoints coincide with the ESS in their interest in questioning the dominant paradigms, in producing and retrieving other bodies of knowledge and offer different ways of approaching realities.

The International Labour Organization (ILO) has also pronounced itself on this issue. This international entity considers ESS as macroeconomic systems composed of enterprises and organizations that produce goods, services, and knowledge, that make an effort to achieve economic and social objectives, and tat promote solidarity. They include cooperatives, mutual associations, philanthropies, community volunteers, associations, and nonprofit NGOs. Over the years, the concept has evolved and has included networks of fair trade, self-help groups organized to produce goods and services, purchasing groups of solidarity and of consumers for collective provisions, and associations of workers (OIT 2011).

In times of crisis the ESS has transformed into an alternative to mitigate the negative consequences of neoliberalism for society, particularly at the local level. The Spanish Business Confederation of Social Economy (2008) says that it acts in cases where solutions are needed to local employment problems, meeting the needs of the people, achieving economic development, and integrating excluded collectives; at the same time it encourages the building of a more equitable and cohesive society. This option attempts to set social limits to the capitalist market and, if possible, build markets in which the prices and the relations arise from a social matrix that aims for the integration of all, with an effort and results distributed in a more egalitarian manner (Coraggio 2008).

The ESS can become a strong defense that helps to confront, alleviate, and transform the poverty, exclusion, and marginalization that affect multitudes of human beings, social sectors, and entire peoples in different regions of the world. One of these ways can come from the close connection it has with the processes of local sustainable development.[6]

The social and solidarity economy is recognized as an instrument for the generation of work, employment, and income for a significant number of people, and contributes to local sustainable and inclusive development, taking into account the multidimensionality of its experiences and actions (International Center of Training of the ILO, as cited in Betancourt 2016, 35).

The Social and Solidarity Economy in Cuba

The ESS is integrated into the socialist project insofar as it has the people as its center of development; it aims to satisfy the common needs of the population; it is at the service of society, having as its principal organizational commitment offering services to the members of the community; and it recognizes different forms of social organization for its production, in which the society of people takes precedence over the society of capital (Del Castillo 2017).

> As a socialist country, Cuba is a singular case, and potentially paradigmatic of the ESS. It is impossible to conceive that a capitalist economy—no matter how progressive—can in its essence be social and solidary. Its private corporate sector will continue to respond in its majority to the rationale of the production of capital, and the ESS subsists at the margins of this sector, continuously complementing it or confronting it. (Betancourt 2016, 35)

ESS stands before a planned and centralized economy according to the power of the state. In the relevant statutes, the economic system that prevails continues to be based on the socialist property over the fundamental media of production; and planning—not the market—dominates the distribution of goods and services. In this sense, although currently some experiments are being carried out in the western region of the Island—in the provinces of Artemisa and Mayabeque—and some legal efforts are being made, the majority of the state entities do not have the financial autonomy to designate part of their profits to social or environmental activities.

The construction of an ESS in Cuba should assume social, environmental, and business responsibility consciously, from the macroeconomic model to the behavior of all its stakeholders, going through the public policies that facilitate it. It should complement the regulatory structure established by the government, not relieve the state of its civic duty to serve the public interest. It is a question of forging an *entrepreneurial citizenry* capable of contributing to a *prosperous and sustainable socialism* which we are committed to build.

Invigorating the Cuban economy from an ESS base needs multiple alliances and connections that traverse the macro-, mezzo- and micro- social levels. From the local level, the community acts as a bearer of traditions, culture and identity, and its own social, human and economic strengths. Using the opportunities offered by the surroundings to the greatest extent can contribute to sensitizing local abilities, to the production of sustainable employment and the inclusion of vulnerable groups. This assumes the application of fair and solidary principles of redistribution of material resources and of knowledge; the redefinition of normative structures; the production and provision of public goods of high quality; and a new arrangement of multi-stakeholder alliances.

Within the ESS in Cuban reality, an essential place belongs to cooperativism.[7] There is some experience in agriculture, which has slowly begun to spread to other branches of the economy. It is considered to be an option that speeds up the transition toward ESS structures and goes along the path of social, economic, and environmental well-being for the men and women of this country. The opening up of this economic space means an effort to develop an entrepreneurial alternative that could aim to be more participatory, solidary, just, and therefore, consistent with improvement of the Cuban socialist project (D'Angelo, Pinos, and Velázquez 2016).

ESS, in the Cuban context, has the following opportunities: the political will of the government to offer some managerial autonomy to state-owned business; the gradual legitimation of the non-state forms of management, which in its turn contributes to the generation of jobs; the initial experiences of productive links and multi-stakeholder alliances; the processes of education and training in these topics; the development of solidarity enterprises and of others that exercise actions of business social responsibility;[8] and the very nature of Cubans and of our social system.

Within the frame of this article we accept the definition of ESS as given by the Network of Social and Solidarity Economy and Social Entrepreneurial Responsibility (Red de Economia Social y Solidaria y Responsabilidad Social Empresarial—ESORSE in Spanish):

> ESS is a form of economy centered on social protection and equity, which leads to the creation of quality jobs, fair growth, progress of grassroots democracy, and sustainable development, in which the role of the local governments is fundamental. It is a way of making "another economy," by organizing the production, distribution, circulation and consumption of goods and services in an associated or cooperative manner, and not based on obtaining profits on an individual basis, but instead solving needs; by pursuing quality of life for all who participate in the project, their families and communities, in collaboration with other communities; at the same time that social fraternal and solidary links are established in self-managing and democratic ways in the participation in decision-making, assuming the management of the natural resources with responsibility and the respect toward future generations, without exploitation of other people's work. (Betancourt and Gómez Arencibia 2019, 3)

Women in the Social and Solidarity Economy

The gender-based division of labor means the unequal distribution of social spaces and the activities carried out by the genders, as well as the feminization and masculinization of activities and areas of interaction. From this, a structure of gender relations is derived, sustained in the hierarchization of roles and rules, which places women at a disadvantage in family and public life—including, in the beginning, total exclusion from public life and the prescribed confinement to the home (Fleitas Ruíz 2006).

> During the twentieth century, women thinkers made visible the irreversible trend of the public participation of women and of family, social and economic transformations. An early group of studies showed women leaving the private sphere of the homes, and their growing incorporation into the world of labor and the public world more generally (Benería and Roldán 1987; Arriagada 1990; Borderías, Carrasco and Alemany 1994). Their studies showed the occupational segregation, the income gaps between men and women and the discriminatory practices in the labor market. They argued that the segregation of women into certain activities and occupations (horizontal segregation), their greater presence at the lower levels of each profession (vertical segregation), and the resulting larger income gaps, are not only the result of productivity differences between masculine and feminine professions in a competitive market model (free and self-regulated). (Farah and Wanderley 2016, 10)

ESS has demonstrated that it is one of the forms in which women and families can find new and wide-ranging possibilities for participation, development, and empowerment of their searches based on gender identity. In a general sense, it is a space that includes an important feminine participation component (Fournier and St-Germain 2011; Nobre 2015). In spite of being the carrier of values like sustainability and social justice, in this sector women continue to have less access than men to jobs of greater responsibility, and occupy many of the part-time jobs. We are in the presence of an alternative that is likely to reproduce the hegemonic gender patterns, which puts us on the alert when these enterprises are being established.

ESS is an opportunity for society in general, through which women can find a space for personal and professional realization. However, the other face of this coin can present a woman regressing, because rather than a space toward independence and empowerment, she finds an oasis to combine the labors of the home and care with those of the working world. A study carried out by Nobre (2015) warns that a considerable portion of the women who participate in ESS groups value the possibility to organize their time and value the understanding of other participants when, at some point, they have to decrease their participation in order to care for a family member who is ill. At the same time, they tell of how other members of the family end up transferring all their responsibility for this care to the working women, because they have the possibility of combining it with their paid jobs.

It is necessary to question the opportunities and spaces for reflection, promotion, and strengthening that women in ESS have. Another issue that needs an answer relates to the question of whether social and solidarity enterprises take into account the obstacles and deterrents that women encounter in general, in order to insert themselves in the working world, to obtain access to credit and training.

FEMALE AND SOLIDARITY ENTERPRISES IN CUBA: "GO FOR IT: YOU CAN DO IT!"

The following pages show the progressive empowerment that Cuban women have experienced. We now present the experience of women entrepreneurs from the perspective of the ESS: "Go for it: You can do it!"

The Starting Point for Cuban Women

Beginning with the impact of the changes that happened in January 1959, Cuban women have been the protagonists of a progressive process of empowerment. They have raised their level of education, and as a result, since several decades they constitute the greater part of university graduates; they have invaded the workforce; they are the sponsors of important victories such as the Maternity Law (1974),[9] and that of pay equal to men for equal work; they have occupied important positions in the social, economic, cultural, and political life of the country; they can vote and be elected; they have reproductive, sexual, and family planning rights. In a general sense, measures have been taken to improve the condition and position of women.

These achievements have also had their darker side. It is possible to see the salary gaps between women and men associated with the occupational segregation that is being maintained in the sexual division of labor; as well as the cultural distribution of jobs, activities, and hierarchies in paid employment typically associated with women and with men (Díaz and Echevarría León 2020). Women have a smaller presence among workers; during the past decade their numbers have been around 37 percent. The rate of female economic activity shows that of the total number of women of employment age and able to work, only 49.5 percent have a formal job or are looking for one (Díaz and Echevarría León 2020).

In the non-state forms of property (self-employed, SMSE, cooperatives) Cuban women are not a majority. However, it is possible to identify the development of enterprises and cooperatives that are led by women who in turn promote ESS logics.[10] Systematizing these types of experiences, their good practices, their obstacles and successes, is a pending exercise that can bring light to this process in Cuba, and can especially be enriched by a gender perspective. This would afford a view of the extent to which the stereotypes still in force from patriarchy are being removed or reproduced.

Atelier: "¡Atrévete, eres más!" ["Go for it: You can do it!"]

The Project Cooperative management among Women, an experiment result-ing from the Talleres de Transformación Integral del Barrio—TTIB [Integral Neighborhood Transformation Workshops] in 2015, began with the objec-tive of strengthening the abilities and values of the Popular and Solidarity Economy (EPS in Spanish) in women.[11] This project is led by the Marianao TTIB and emphasizes the importance of women needing to learn to ana-lyze the unequal power relations between genders with a marked prejudice towards women and the effect this has on the development of their com-munities (González Achón, Caballero León, and Sarda Noriega 2018). The creation of the atelier "Go for it: You can do it!" is among the results of these actions.[12] The analysis of this experience is presented here based on the fol-lowing indicators: the form of the organization or management, the actions of social responsibility, the community impact, multi-actor alliances, and the obstacles and possibilities they have lived through during their trajectory. The information that was obtained comes from the analysis of documents that bring together parts of the activities of the atelier, from interviews with its members, and from the presentations that its leaders have given on the issue in different places.

The aim of this initiative was to convert it into a nonagricultural coop-erative, a process that has been at a standstill since 2014. "This restated the original idea of this group of women, who found a creative way to produce and decide together: a cooperative process among self-employed women" (González Achón, Caballero León, and Sarda Noriega 2018, 9). They have a collaborative view both for decision-making and for the distribution of profits. Their economic and financial management is transparent, and the payment of their taxes is done on time.

> Each entrepreneur obtains her working license on her own, but they join their enterprises and put into practice the values of EPS, through which they collec-tively decide how to produce, where and how to market, how to distribute their profits, what will be the aim of their social responsibility. They agree based on formal-legal principles and on their feelings of being more sisterly. (González Achón, Caballero León and Sarda Noriega 2018, 9)

They organize themselves based on a system of values that has become their philosophy of life: mutual aid, solidarity, the pursuit of the common good above the personal, cooperative labor, sisterhood, reasonable and defined prices, equitable distribution of the surplus, and inclusion of and response to the need of the community or the surroundings.

It is an economic enterprise led by and totally comprised of women. It has as its social objective to organize, transform, and produce pieces of clothing. The activities that are performed can be included in the range of those considered to be feminine which, according to the dominant structures, are those who have the worst working conditions and the lowest salaries (Mies and Shiva 2014). In spite of this trend, they have built a secure, innovative space, with working conditions that respond to the requirements of the activity they carry out; they have aimed for professional and personal improvement; the income they have received guarantees their economic independence by throwing off the dependence that in this sense they were experiencing.

In the words of one of the entrepreneurs of the atelier, "economic empowerment leads to economic solvency and that means a feeling of having an important role because you generate economy." The participation of the women in the solidarity economy, while it makes possible the generation of income, also involves an organizational process in which they are political subjects. It thus contributes to their personal and political autonomy (Dantas 2015).

These are women who have lived through violence and discrimination and who have found a space in which to fulfill themselves as persons, and which allows them to break these cycles. As one of them said, from this reality another objective is born: "to empower women psychologically so they can identify situations of violence they are experiencing, the aggressions, the types of violence." The foregoing finds resonance in what Nobre stated, that women evaluate their participation not only from the point of view of the economic remuneration, but they also value the learning, the conviviality, the possibility to deal with topics like violence against women or reproductive health (Nobre 2015). In general, the women who participate feel stronger, more valued, with better self-esteem because of their knowledge and their capacity for innovation.

They develop several activities with direct impact in their community:

- They train women to become involved in economic enterprises, through an initiative called Mariposas Emprendedoras [Enterprising Butterflies].
- They work with boys and girls with Down syndrome, with those who are deaf and autistic.
- They carry out activities with young people, with the aim of contributing to their involvement in society; among them: making rugs, handkerchiefs and other articles that are sold in the fairs that are held; in this way, they generate income for themselves and for their families.
- They differentiate prices for women who live alone and are older.
- They devote themselves to repairing uniforms, at different prices, during the time before the beginning of the school year.

During recent times, they have developed their main alliances with other enterprises—by holding commercial fairs—and NGOs[13]—for whom they make sweaters and handbags, both for events and for campaigns. Contacts with the municipal government are rare, and the women don't feel included within the local development strategies of the municipality, in spite of several exchanges.[14]

They recycle and reuse the leftovers from their sewing, because they start from the premise of care and protection of the environment.[15] They have a Facebook page where they share what they do and they receive feedback from their clients or from people who are interested. They have some difficulties with the supply of raw materials, although they do receive significant donations—from the community—of remnants and pieces of clothing they can reuse. This enterprise does not have growth potential that would create new local jobs, but its activities and practices inspire other women and enterprises. They receive training on the topics of sewing, delving into questions of gender, equity and EPS.

They consider that the main impacts they have had are the personal growth of the women involved; the multiplication of other economic initiatives with the same viewpoint; and the recognition on the part of the community. For these women, EPS does not mean thinking of oneself, it is to see and feel the needs of others; it is something that is done from the heart, it is the growth of all, and how we can collectively help ourselves. They have a thought that marks their daily routine: "Together we learn, together we produce, and together we receive."

CONCLUSIONS

- From the Cuban perspective, ESS implies a collective knowledge and a sharing of its scope, objectives, and development of actions based on the needs of the people of the country, which must be founded on the principles of responsibility with society (families, workers, clients, and other stakeholders in the enterprise and the community), with the natural environment, and with the existing culture.
- Within the frame of ESS women can find support for their difficulties, but they, in turn, should convert that into a battlefront in order to validate their rights and the legitimate practices that empower and support an inclusive and participative social development.
- There exist experiences in the ESS developed by women which should be studied, systematized, and socialized with a view to extend these types of good practices.

- The experience that has been presented shows how ESS can be an option for the empowerment and personal fulfillment of a group of women.

NOTES

1. Within these groups are the unemployed, workers in the informal economy, young people, women, black people, and different ethnic groups.

2. Three countries have placed the ESS into their Constitution: Ecuador, Venezuela, and Bolivia. These initiatives contribute to the legitimation of this way of working, and allow for it to progress toward its inclusion in the constitutional documents. This is combined with a new way to conceive democracy and develop a politics that is participative.

3. Conceptualización del Modelo Económico y Social Cubano de Desarrollo Socialista [Conceptualization of the Cuban Economic and Social Model of Socialist Development]; Plan Nacional de Desarrollo Económico y Social hasta 2030 (PCC 2016) [National Economic and Social Development Plan to 2030]: Propuesta de Visión de la Nación, Ejes y Sectores Estratégicos (1–6) (PCC 2016b) [Proposal for a National Vision, Strategic Lines and Sectors]; Lineamientos de la Política Económica y Social [Economic and Social Policy Guidelines] (12, 13, 17, 49, 91, 107, 119, 163, 173, 174 191, 196, 233, 243, 262, 263, 265, 269, 272) (PCC 2011); Constitución de la República (168) (ANPP 2019).

4. The variations of the development models have characterized the role of ESS based on the needs that are not covered by the economic model that is valid at the time.

5. The Third Sector includes all those organizations which, due to the type of activity they carry out, are considered different from the government entities and the private enterprises.

6. "Sustainable local development" refers to the process in which local advantages are put to good use, their strengths to minimize problems, to achieve socioeconomic growth and to positively transform the levels of equity and well-being of a particular area. This progress is nuanced by economic and environmental sustainability and the decentralization of the decision-making process. It encourages social participation by strengthening the institutions and local stakeholders. At the same time, it also takes place in smaller regions, such as, in this case, the communities (Gómez Arencibia 2009).

7. As stated in the Declaration of the International Cooperative Alliance on cooperative identity (ACI 2013), a cooperative is an autonomous association of people who have joined voluntarily to satisfy together their needs, their economic, social and cultural desires by means of a business that is joint property and has a democratic administration.

8. Experiences of this type have been recognized all over the country. In Pinar del Río there are recognized businesses that develop the concept of ecotourism, others "from farm to table," and barbershops and hairdressers that offer free services to children and seniors. In Havana there is the Jíbaro restaurant with an interesting

sociocultural project for boys and girls, in addition to the Akokán, in the Callejón de los Peluqueros [Barbers' Lane], among others. In Holguín, the Plaza de la Marqueta.

9. It gives paid leave to women workers for childcare and encourages the formation of nurseries once that period concludes. In 2003, this law was modified; among the changes was the permission for fathers to also receive paid paternity leave. Recently other modifications have been made which extend the beneficiaries of this law to include grandmothers and grandfathers who are employed. In 2017, Decrees 339 and 340 were approved, which continue to broaden the rights of the working woman-mother.

10. The Recycling Cooperative (Mayabeque), the Bar-Restaurant Beisbolerito 360 (Mayabeque), the Muñeca Negra [Black Doll] project (Havana), the Jíbaro restaurant (Havana), the CTEX Comercial cooperative (Matanzas), among others.

11. In this article we have used the definition of Economía Social y Solidaria (ESS). The term Economía Popular y Solidaria (EPS) is used in Cuba by the Centro Memorial Martin Luther King, and has been discussed by Dr. Luis del Castillo of the Faculty of Economics of the University of Havana (UH) (Del Castillo 2017).

12. This belongs to the Red de Mujeres por la Equidad Social desde la Economía Popular Solidaria [the Network of Women for Social Equity in the Popular Solidarity Economy]. It receives support of the Centro de Reflexión y Diálogo Oscar Arnulfo Romero, the Faculty of Social Communications (UH), the Network of the Popular Educators (Centro Memorial Martin Luther King), the Latin American Social Sciences Faculty (UH), the Network of Cooperative and Solidary Employment (GAL-FISA, Instituto de Filosofía), the Red Feminista Bertha Cáceres and the Network of Women for Local Development.

13. Among these are: The Centro Memorial Martin Luther King, the OXFAM program in Cuba, the Centro de Reflexión y Diálogo Oscar Arnulfo Romero.

14. For some time they have been requesting a place to rent and make it into a store, so as to have more visibility.

15. The residues that cannot be reused are donated to the Muñeca Negra project, where they are used as filling for the dolls.

BIBLIOGRAPHY

ACI. *Declaración sobre la Identidad Cooperativa* [Declaration on Corporate Identity]. Alianza Cooperativa Internacional, 2013.

ANPP. *Constitución de la República de Cuba* [Constitution of the Republic of Cuba]. La Habana: Asamblea Nacional del Poder Popular, 2019. Retrieved from: http://www.granma.cu/file/pdf/gaceta/Nueva%20Constituci%C3%B3n%20240%20KB-1.pdf.

Arriagada, I. *Participación desigual de la mujer en el mundo del trabajo* [Participation of women in the world of labor]. Santiago de Chile: CEPAL, 1990.

Arruda, M. *Tornar Real o Possível: Economia Solidária, Desenvolvimento e o Futuro do Trabalho* [Make Real or Possible: Solidarity Economy, Employment and the Future of Work]. Petrópolis, Brasil: Editora Vozes, 2006.

Benería, L., y M. Roldán. *Las encrucijadas de clase y género. Trabajo a domicilio, subcontratación y dinámica de la unidad doméstica en la Ciudad de México* [The crossroads of class and gender. Homebased work, outsourcing and the dynamic of the domestic unit in Mexico City]. México: El Colegio de México y FCE, 1987.

Betancourt, R., ed. *Construyendo socialismo desde abajo: la contribución de la economía popular y solidaria* [Building socialism from the bottom up: the contribution of popular and solidarity economics]. La Habana: Editorial Caminos, 2017.

Betancourt, R. "Grupo de Trabajo sobre Economía social y solidaria para el Desarrollo Local" [Work group on Social and Solidarity Economics for Local Development]. In *Sector cooperativo y desarrollo local. Visión desde las redes cubanas de investigación*, J. García, D. Figueras and E. González (editors). Santa Clara, Cuba: Editorial Feijóo, 2016.

———. "La economía social y solidaria y la actualizacion del modelo económico cubano" [Social and solidarity economics and the updating of the Cuban economic model]. La Habana: *Blog Catalejo de la Revista Temas*, 2015. Retrieved from: http://temas.cult.cu/blog/?p=2071#more-2071.

Betancourt, R., & Gómez Arencibia, J. *Sinopsis de la Red Cubana de Economía Social y Solidaria y Responsabilidad Social ESORSE* [Synopsis of the Cuban Network of Social and Solidarity Economics ESORSE]. La Habana: Centro de Investigaciones Psicológicas y Sociológicas CIPS, 2019.

Borderías, C., C. Carrasco, and C. Alemany. "Las mujeres y el trabajo: Rupturas conceptuales" [Women and work: Conceptual breaks]. *Revista de Sociología*, (47) (Icaria/FUHEM) 175–76, 1994.

CEPAL. *Panorama social de América Latina, 2018* [Social panorama of Latin America, 2018]. Santiago de Chile: Publicación de las Naciones Unidas, 2019.

Coraggio, J. L. *Necesidad y Posibilidades de Otra Economía. América Latina en Movimiento. Economía Social y Solidaria* [Need for and Possibilities of Another Economy. Latin America in Movement. Social and Solidarity Economy]. Publicación Internacional de la Agencia Latinoamericana de Información, 2008.

D'Angelo, O., P. Pinos, and S. Velázquez. *Participación en la gestión de cooperativas no agropecuarias (CNA) y su interpretación desde la Autonomía Integradora. Estudio de caso Centro Habana* [Participation in the management of nonagricultural cooperatives and its interpretation from Integrative Autonomy. Case study in Centro Habana]. Informe de Investigación, La Habana: GCTS, CIPS, 2016.

Dantas, C. "Autonomía económica de las mujeres rurales en los Territorios de la Ciudadanía" [Financial autonomy of rural women in the Territories of Citizenship]. In *Las mujeres en la construcción de la economía solidaria y la agroecología. Textos para la acción feminista*, N. Faria, R. Moren, and M. Nobre (editors). Brasil: Publicación de SOF Sempreviva Organização Feminista, 2015.

Del Castillo, L. "La concepción de la Economía Popular para la renovación del modelo económico cubano" [The concept of Popular Economy for the renovation of the Cuban economic model]. In *Construyendo socialismo desde abajo. Contribución de la Economía Social y Solidaria*, R. Betancourt (editor). La Habana: Editorial Caminos, 2017.

Díaz, I., y D. Echevarría León. "Ingresos en Cuba, brechas entre mujeres y hombres en el sector no estatal" [Earnings in Cuba, gaps between women and men in the non-state sector]. In *Miradas a la Economía Cubana*. La Habana: Editorial Caminos, 2020.

Echevarría, D., and T. Lara. "Cambios recientes: ¿oportunidad para las mujeres?" [Recent changes: opportunity for women?]. In *Miradas a la economía cubana*, edited por O.E. Perez y R. Torres. La Habana: Editorial Caminos, 2012.

Farah, I., and F. Wanderley. "El feminismo y la otra economía. Una mirada desde América Latina" [Feminism and the other economy. View from Latin America]. In *Economía social y solidaria en movimiento*, by J. L. Coraggio (editor). Buenos Aires: Ediciones UNGS Universidad Nacional de General Sarmiento, 2016.

Fleitas Ruíz, R. "La identidad femenina: las encrucijadas de la igualdad y la diferencia" [Female identity: the crossroads of equality and difference]. In *Selección de Lecturas de Sociología y Política Social de Género*, C. Proveyer Cervantes (editor). La Habana: Editorial Félix Varela, 2006.

Fonteneau, B., et al. *Social and Solidarity Economy: Our Common Road towards Decent Work International.* Montreal: Training Centre of the International Labour Organization, 2011.

Fournier, D., y L. St-Germain. *Las Mujeres, Corazón de la Economía Social y Solidaria* [Women Are the Heart of the Social and Solidarity Economy]. Montreal: Documento redactado para el comité organizador de FIESS, 2011.

Gaiger, L. I. "A dimensão empreendedora da economia solidária: notas para um debate Necessário" [The entrepreneurship dimension of the solidarity economy: notes for a necessary debate]. *Revista Otra Economía*, (3), no. 2 (2008). Retrieved from: www.riless.org/otraeconomia.

Galfisa. *Desafíos del cooperativismo en Cuba* [Challenges of cooperativism in Cuba]. La Habana: Coleccion Hipotesis. Instituto de Filosofia, 2017. Retrieved from: www.filosofia.cu/site/institucion.php 14/06/2018.

Gibson-Graham, J. K. *Una política poscapitalista* [A postcapitalist polity]. Bogotá: Siglo del Hombre Editores, coedición con la Editorial Pontificia Universidad Javeriana, 2011.

Gómez Arencibia, J. *El desarrollo local: una alternativa frente a la pobreza. Un estudio de caso en Bejucal.* [Local development: an alternative to poverty. Case study in Bejucal]. Tesis de maestría, La Habana: FLACSO -UH, 2009.

González Achón, L., I. Caballero León, and T. Sarda Noriega. "Gestión cooperada entre mujeres. Un reto desde los Talleres de Transformación Integral del Barrio" [Cooperative management among women: A challenge for the Neighborhood Integral Transformation Workshops]. La Habana: Editorial Caminos, 2018.

Guerra, P. "La economía solidaria y el cambio socioeconómico" [Solidarity economics and socioeconomic change]. *Kolping Cartilla No. 2*, 2008. Retrieved from: http://www.kolping.org.uy/sites/default/files/contenidos/publicaciones/archivos/cartilla2.pdf.

Guzón, A. "Ingresos en Cuba brechas entre mujeres y hombres en el sector no estatal" [Earnings in Cuba gaps between men and women in the non-state sector]. *Rebelion*,

2018. Retrieved from: https://rebelion.org/ingresos-en-cuba-brechas-entre-mujeres -y-hombres-en-el-sector-no-estatal/.

Laville, J. L. *Economía Solidaria, Economía Social, Tercer Sector: las apuestas europeas* [Solidarity Economy, Social Economy, Third Sector: European wagers]. Biblioteca Virtual TOP sobre Gestión Pública, 2006. Retrieved from: www.top.org .ar/publicac.html.

Lévesque, B., and M. Mendell. *La création d'entreprises par les chômeurs et les sansemploi: le rôle de la microfinance* [The creation of enterprises for the unemployed: the role of microfinance]. Research report submitted to the International Labour Office (ILO), International Labour Organization (ILO), Montréal: PROFONDS-CRISES, 2007.

Mies, M., and V. Shiva. *Ecofeminism: Theory, Critique and Perspectives*. London: ZedBooks, 2014.

Mutuberría Lazarini, V. "El debate en torno a la economía social: discusiones fundamentales desde la perspectiva de los países de la periferia" [The debate about social economics: main discussions from the perspective of peripheral countries]. *Revista Idelcoop,* 35(183), 2008. Retrieved from: http://www.socioeco.org/bdf _fiche-document-3908_es.html.

Nobre, M. "Economía solidaria y economía feminista: elementos para una agenda" [Solidarity economics and feminist economics: Elements for an agenda]. In *Las mujeres en la construcción de la economía solidaria y la agroecología. Textos para la acción feminista*, M. Nobre, N. Faria, and R. Moren (editors). Brasil: Publicación de SOF Sempreviva Organização Feminista, 2015.

OIT. *Panorama Laboral 2011. América Latina y el Caribe* [Émployment Panorama 2011]. Organización Internacional del Trabajo, 2011.

ONEI. *Anuario Estadístico de Cuba, 2018* [Statistical Annual of Cuba, 2018]. La Habana: Oficina Nacional de Estadística e Información de Cuba, 2019. Retrieved from: http://www.onei.gob.cu/sites/default/files/07_empleo_y_salarios_2019.pdf.

Oxoby, P. "Una aproximación a las divergencias e implicaciones de los distintos abordajes a la Economía Social: países centrales europeos y América Latina" [An approximation to the divergences and implications of the different approaches to Social Economy]. *Unisinos* 4(6). 2010. Retrieved from: http://revistas.unisinos.br/ index.php/otraeconomia/article/view/1286.

PCC. *Conceptualización del Modelo Económico y Social Cubano de Desarrollo y Plan Nacional de Desarrollo Económico y Social hasta 2030* [Conceptualization of the Cuban Economic and Social Development Model and National Plan for Economic and Social Development until 2030]. La Habana: VI Congreso del Partido Comunista de Cuba, 2016.

———. *Lineamientos de la Política Económica y Social del Partido y la Revolución* [Guidelines for the Economic and Social Policy of the Party and the Revolution]. La Habana: VI Congreso del Partido Comunista de Cuba, 2011.

———. *Propuesta de Visión de la Nación, Ejes y Sectores Estratégicos* [Proposed Vision of the Nation, Strategic Lines and Sectors]. La Habana: VI Congreso del Partido Comunista de Cuba, 2016.

Piñeiro, C. "Desempeño socioeconómico de las cooperativas no agropecuarias: contribución de sus principales determinantes. Estudio de casos" [Socioeconomic performance of nonagricultural cooperatives: contribution of its principal determinants. Case studies]. *Oibescoop,* 2018. Retrieved from: https://www.oibescoop.org/noticias/nuevas-investigaciones-sobre-el-cooperativismo-cubano/.

Razeto, L. *Economía de la solidaridad y mercado democrático* [Economy of solidarity and democrtaic markets]. Santiago de Chile, 2003.

Ruggeri, A. *¿Qué son las empresas recuperadas?* [What are the recuperated enterprises?]. 2019. Retrieved from: https://www.casadellibro.com/libro-que-son-las-empresas-recuperadas/9789507544576/2365942.

Tiriba, L. *Economia popular e cultura do trabalho: pedagogia da produção associada* [Popular Economics and culture of work: pedagogy of associated production]. 2001. Retrieved from: http://www.socioeco.org/bdf_auteur-4186_es.html.

Torres Páez, C. "La Economía Social y Solidaria en Cuba: su impacto en el desarrollo local. Experiencias desde la provincia Pinar del Río" [Social and Solidarity Economics in Cuba: its impact on local development]. *Ponencia presentada al Taller Internacional de Economía Social y Solidaria.* Pinar del Río, 2015.

Wanderley, F., F. Sostres, and I. Farah. "La economía solidaria en la economía plural: Discursos, prácticas y resultados en Bolivia" [Solidarity economics in the plural economy: Speeches, practices and results in Bolivia]. *Revista de Economía Mundial* (Sociedad de Economía Mundial España), 2016.

Chapter 18

Business Social Responsibility Does Not Go Unnoticed in Cuban Private Enterprises

William Bello Sánchez

In 2020 we were witness to many Cuban businesspeople responding to the challenge of avoiding the spread of the coronavirus by placing their enterprise in tune with the measures that the situation demanded. This attitude was surprising, because for several years businesspeople have demonstrated the social values with which they have built their enterprises. They had shown this previously, with their involvement in the recovery after the disasters caused by hurricane Irma, the tornado that ravaged Havana in January 2019, and when they adopted the measures relating to the cholera outbreak that affected Cuba a few years ago.

The norms of business social responsibility (RSE in Spanish) are applied and developed in several private enterprises—either empirically or consciously. This is a business practice that in the *Libro Verde [Green Book]* (Comisión Europea 2001) is defined as a voluntary action on the part of enterprises to integrate social and environmental concerns into their commercial processes and in their relations with the people in their surroundings.

Self-employed workers in Cuba have learned to administer their enterprises in a brief period of time, as a result of the general training that our society has been able to provide. However, in order to achieve better economic, social, and environmental results, undertaking a business would require more knowledge, especially for businesspeople, in addition to economic resources and the promotion of a legislative framework that favors this setting. The training of businesspeople is not incorporated into the traditional teaching systems of the country, and this works against the success of business initiatives; it becomes a hindrance to the development of a responsible involvement of enterprises with society and the environment.

The Oasis Program of business social responsibility of the CubaEmprende Project[1] has been able to complement and stimulate the incorporation of social and environmental activities—internal and external—into the management of private enterprises and self-employment. This chapter—based on the context and the responsibilities of businesses in Cuba—follows this same path, so as to offer an approach to the methodology and some of the results obtained by the program, for the development of socially responsibly management of Cuban enterprises.

The Cuban businesspersons and those who have been linked to the Oasis Program have shown that they are willing to learn more, and to also perform in the context of a new business law, pending legislation. In addition, they have understood the importance of managing with a social commitment, a topic which the most advanced countries in the world continue to raise awareness. In Cuba it has taken us only seven years to arrive at a working concept on social responsibility in private enterprises, despite the growth limitations this sector has experienced.

The process of incorporating private business into our national life has been marked by periods of development and decline, under restrictive legislation and administrative obstacles. Now, based on recent official discourse, a more conciliatory and stimulating setting can be foreseen (Alonso et al. 2020).[2] In this context of a possible aperture, it is important to analyze some of the impacts that self-employed workers (TCP in Spanish) have had on the progress of recent Cuban society.

The coordination between the state sector, the TCPs, and the nonagricultural cooperatives in 2020 shows that a productive chain and its alliances can bring greater benefits for the economy, society, and the environment in our country. This is an issue which undoubtedly contributes positively to the sustainable development of the country (Bello 2020).

AN INSIDE VIEW OF RSE, A PREMISE FOR ITS APPLICATION IN CUBAN BUSINESSES

Charity, solidarity, volunteerism, and altruism have been aspects of Cuba in its development as a nation. These are the values that are expected of a society that intends to have an economic organization that is tied to social and environmental commitment. Social responsibility is part of the idiosyncrasy of Cubans, though that does not imply that they are unencumbered by challenges to be overcome at the social, legislative, political, and economic levels.

A business in Cuba is different from those in other economic models in the world. In the current legislation there is as yet no way to speak effectively of private enterprise. This form of economic organization fundamentally operates through decrees that regulate the TCPs, without a legal personality, and being closer to self-employment from the legal standpoint, though a part of the private enterprises function as MIPYMES [Spanish acronym for Micro, Small and Medium-sized Enterprises, or MSMEs]. State-owned enterprises continue to dominate the business context in Cuba, and the model of national development rests on them.

In the meantime, the development of RSE has been limited by the centrality that for many years has governed the state business system in Cuba. The restricted framework for decision-making and the limitations under which they operate limit the development of RSE in the state sector, although in their very conception all Cuban institutions have a social mission. (Betancourt Mayo-Agosto 2016) For their part, the TCPs are not directly anchored in central mechanisms, although they face the same lack of resources as the state enterprises, and during the greater part of their development they cope with limited access to raw materials, equipment, supplies, and wholesale markets. However, they do have greater flexibility in the organization of their priorities and in the management of their social or environmental commitment.

In the search for an inside view of RSE, it is worthwhile to evaluate alternatives for the promotion of responsible practices in the Cuban business context, particularly relating to the TCPs. Looking at a group of models of RSE is an indispensable step in the search for aspects that contribute to the conceptual and methodological construction of a proposal on RSE for Cuban enterprises. These include:

- Regulation ISO 26 000 on Social Responsibility (ISO 2010)
- The Green Book of the European Commission (Comisión Europea 2001)
- The Social Doctrine of the Catholic Church (Camacho 1995)
- Guide for the Preparation of Sustainability Records of the Global Reporting Initiative (GRI 2020)
- Ethos Indicators for Sustainable and Responsible Enterprises (Instituto Ethos 2016)
- The Cuban socioeconomic context

The result has made possible a holistic view of a business organization that is connected to its time and space—a view in which several criteria coexist and which leaves antagonism aside; they understand and complement each other.

Being practical allows for obtaining results, but for this to happen it is also necessary to understand good practices and the group of terms that orbits around the enterprises that aim for a management with positive impacts in its various surroundings (internal and external) and dimensions (economic, social, and environmental). The fundamental debate on the social and environmental commitment of enterprises is going in the direction of whether there should be talk of sustainable enterprises, according to the Institute for Global Prosperity (IGP), or of RSE, according to the Dutch Institute of BSR (MVO Netherlands).[3]

RSE is also related to other concepts: social and solidarity economy, economy of communion, or popular economy, which are connected to different realities and circumstances; they coexist with each other and not necessarily in detriment to each other.

As has been mentioned, in the case of Cuba, RSE is an issue of idiosyncrasies, this desire that characterizes us: to help one another. Even when for many the fundamental purpose of developing RSE in enterprises could be to eliminate weaknesses, a survey carried out with more than fifty entrepreneurs shows a higher probability that it increases the risks.[4] However—as per the author's research[5]—it is the values that end up defining the decisions of many businesspersons on whether to apply social responsibility in Cuba.

Since current legislation limits the possibilities for association, RSE as a concept has been closer to Cuban enterprises, and thus looking for social forms of businesses from the point of view of self-employment is not possible, nor legal at the moment. Until now in 2020, the closest things to a collective organization based on the private sector would be the community projects or those of local development, to which the authorities—who are responsible for their approval—should offer a speedier process.

RSE depends on the businessperson; in his or her hands rests the decision on how to carry out the business, and it is she or he who can decide on a more responsible organization. Because of the education that our society has provided, Cuban entrepreneurs have learned how to run their business in a brief time period, which allows for ideas and concepts to be assimilated quickly. So it is not too audacious to move toward an RSE concept that is vanguard, even when the regulatory framework for MIPYMES is still not in view,[6] and even when RSE or a social and environmental commitment of the enterprises needs a better legislative framework of regulation and promotion, in agreement with the outline of a socialist, prosperous, and sustainable development model.

Based on what has been presented, business social responsibility is defined as follows: a voluntary strategy that aligns the economic growth of an enterprise with a positive impact on its internal and external settings in the economic, social, and environmental surroundings, beyond what is established by law (CubaEmprende 2017).

THE TRAINING OF BUSINESSPERSONS FOR AN RSE APPROACH: THE EXPERIENCE OF THE OASIS PROGRAM

Finding a space to talk and work on RSE in the business community has been a seven-year-long comprehensive effort. As part of the objective of supporting sustainable business through CubaEmprende, there has been gradual work on RSE in private enterprises. With this effort there is an intent for private enterprises to have a positive impact—in the long and medium term—on the environment and on society in general, without denying the production of economic benefits.

Through all its actions, the project has been able to preserve the meaning of community and solidarity for Cuban society, by taking a stance as a socially responsible and innovative entity. Its Oasis Program is the result of this, and it has as its mission to promote social responsibility in the enterprises based on the CubaEmprende Project, as a culture to raise well-being and promote active participation of the enterprise in sustainable development through training, coaching, a connection between businesspersons, and the visualization of a socially responsible business environment in Cuba.

Bottom right: Social Networks. Spaces in the social networks to discuss RSE] *Source:* CubaEmprende. Programa OASIS de Responsabilidad Social

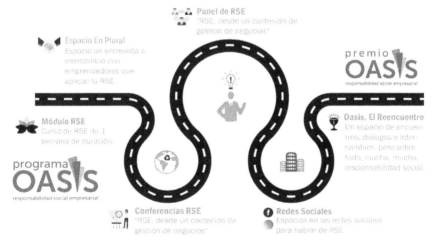

Figure 18.1. Spaces of the Program [Business Social Responsibility]. [Top center: RSE Panel. *RSE, based on a business management perspective* Middle left: Spaces, plural. Space for interviews and exchange with businessmen who apply RSE. Bottom left: RSE Conferences: *RSE, based on a business management perspective* Middle right: Oasis, the Reunion. A space for meetings, dialogue and exchanges, but especially much, much social responsibility.

Empresarial [OASIS Program of Business Social Responsibility]. La Habana: CubaEmprende, 2017.

As can be seen in Figure 1, the CubaEmprende Project offers conferences and training modules on RSE. In both areas there is an effort, with different intensity, to bring knowledge to the business community about the fundamental elements of RSE, its principles and benefits, as well as how the enterprises can work with RSE and elaborate strategies to organize the enterprise based on that perspective. The two-hour conferences—which have a strong motivational component—synthesize the fundamental topics of RSE, while the module—which is conceived as a twenty-hour workshop over five days—broadens and deepens the perspective. As part of the activities of the project, there have so far been fifteen conferences and thirteen workshops on RSE, the latter composed of 211 participants.

The conferences do not always originate in RSE; rather, RSE links to various issues of business management. The aim is to insert the topic of RSE indirectly into the conferences associated to the theme of the month, with the objective of creating a new option. The idea is to use topics that will be attractive to the businesspersons and through them introduce the role of RSE in them. This is to create greater awareness on the topic on the part of the entrepreneurs, and at the same time continue to offer them valuable information on elements that could be overwhelming for them.

The module is established based on a structure that decreases traditional in-person teaching and promotes direct interaction between the businesspersons through a series of dynamics that encourage the collective building of knowledge and the development of the group. And with that, the functions of the workshop are improved, in addition to other teaching methods in which vertical teaching dominate. The intent is for the businesspersons to find knowledge through mechanisms outside the course, with the objective of bringing the acquired knowledge from the classroom into the enterprise.

Through infographics, fundamental issues of RSE are reviewed by taking all important information to the social networks. With respect to social responsibility, the networks offer a space in which every fifteen days publications are shared relating to the substance of RSE which contribute to the understanding of how to work a socially responsible business. The contents should contribute to the knowledge and the tools that businesspersons need to start implementing responsible management of their enterprise.

Achieving an approach to RSE on the part of the community of entrepreneurs—and of all those who are interested in the topic—requires different spaces for knowledge and relations—an idea that is materialized in the panels with business persons and academics, as well as in the spaces, El plural and Oasis, el rencuentro [the reunion].

El plural is a space for encouraging the training and relations between businesspersons by presenting the experiences of enterprises that have a socially responsible management. For this, and before an audience, several stakeholders of a business (owners, workers, clients, suppliers, members of the community, authorities, etc.) are interviewed, and where they explain how this socially responsible management is carried out. This dialogue lasts for an hour and a half, prioritizing the questions asked by the moderator, but also always leaving space for the participation of the audience. The questions can be directed to any of the invitees.

Oasis, el rencuentro proposes an exchange with winners of the Premios Oasis [Oasis Prize] and Reconocimiento Oasis [Oasis Recognition]. The objective of this space is to prepare a better version of the Oasis prizes, by including the criteria of those who participated in previous meetings, making them the leading agents of the development of the new versions. At the meeting the intent is to have dialogues relating to the good and bad choices of previous editions of the program. Also presented are other enterprises who work with RSE, or projects of enterprises that have planned to participate in a new edition of the Premios Oasis in order to motivate the spontaneous appearance of counseling, coaching, and tutelage. The expected result of that space would be a business that is more committed to RSE, and a greater number of enterprises that foresee their participation in the Premios.

Top right: Recognition: to all businesses that have done significant work related to RSE.

Premio OASIS
Dedicado al mejor negocio que aplique la RSE

Premio Plan de Negocio
Al Plan de Negocio con la mejor estrategia de RSE

Reconocimientos
A todos los negocios que hayan tenido un trabajo significativo en materia de RSE

Premio Honorífico
A la persona que haya tenido una trayectoria y trabajo sostenido en materia de RSE

Premio Novato RSE
Al novato del año que se presenta por primera vez al concurso y tiene resultados relevantes

Figure 18.2. Premios [Prizes]. [Top left: Oasis Prize. Offered to the best business to apply RSE. Top middle: Business Plan Prize: Offered to the Business Plan with the best RSE strategy.

Bottom left: Honorary Prize: Offered to the person who has taken a sustained course of action related to RSE Bottom right: Novice RSE Prize: Offered to the novice of the year in which they participate for the first time in the competition and have relevant results.] *Source:* CubaEmprende. Programa OASIS de Responsabilidad Social Empresarial [OASIS Program of Business Social Responsibility]. La Habana: CubaEmprende, 2017.

The Oasis Prizes (Figure 18,2 above) intend to promote the practice of RSE in the sector of Cuban business. The prizes are offered biannually, with a three-month convocation period, which allows the entrepreneur to prepare for their selection, and which intends to encourage responsible practice in a positive manner. In order to be eligible for the prize, the entrepreneurs have to present a brief outline of up to two pages on the elements and actions they undertake, together with basic required documentation, which should include the information that shows the legal status of the enterprise, its description, owners, and name.

With the objective of facilitating the process, a guide of statements and questions is provided to assist in responding to the five variables presented below with their corresponding indicators that confirm them:

1. Communication: This deals with every mechanism of participation that the enterprise uses to obtain or transmit information from and toward the interested parties, internal or external. There should be a compilation, consultation, or transmission of the effects of their management, as well as setting up and discussing with all the partners integrated in a management system.
2. Quality control: This goes from taking responsibility for bad service to being sure to work with suppliers who take responsibility for the quality of their products. Mechanisms should be established to find the origin of the products, form alliances, or maintain a trustworthy network of suppliers, which facilitates such aims and guarantees a positive result.
3. Community development: The enterprise clearly establishes in its community who can have a relation with the business, or who has established a group of actions with them. Jobs in the local community must be encouraged, as well as social or environmental actions with positive results, and integrate the community into their business decisions.
4. Environmental protection: This deals with the reduction, reuse, and efficient management of energy, water, waste, and residuals. All elements or actions that the business undertakes in relation to these issues must be included.
5. Human development: This deals with actions for personal training; work that encourages a sense of belonging in the business; the establishment of mechanisms of financial support; scheduling of adequate

free time; transparency in the access channels for workers re: higher level jobs in the enterprise, etc. There must be a favorable response to these elements.

The recommendations and procedures—the result of the validation process—are followed by an evaluation. In this process there is a jury, which is composed of three members with a proven knowledge of RSE, and who do not form part of the business being evaluated. Among its functions is the corroboration of the veracity of the information supplied by the entrepreneurs on the applications.

Up to now, there have been two editions of the Premios Oasis, in which twenty-two private enterprises have participated. However, the awarding of the prizes has had to be adapted to the circumstances, as the frequency was changed from being annual to every two years. The extension of the awards makes it possible for the entrepreneurs to have a longer time to work, and move forward in their social and environmental commitment.

In the four years of the Premios Oasis, the working environment of the enterprises has become difficult for long periods: TCP licenses were held up, tourism decreased because of the measures taken by the administration of Donald Trump in the United States; the country is suffering one of its worst periods of shortages, and because of these, the pressure on business has increased. The Oasis Program has therefore postponed its certification and has looked for recognition and alternatives of support appropriate to the times that the business community is living through.

In 2020, given the restrictions imposed by COVID-19, the contest was postponed. Given the measures of social distancing and the closing of several enterprises, it was not possible to comply with the methodology and the procedures. In addition, to continue with the competition in the midst of this situation would not have been a responsible act by the program.

However, the circumstances did not prevent Cuban businesspersons from responding to the challenge to avoid the spread of the new coronavirus, placing their enterprises in tune with the measures that the situation demanded. During the two phases of strong propagation of SARS-CoV-2, Cuban businesspersons developed a group of actions to contribute to the efforts to reduce the effects and transmission of the illness. These initiatives were noted by the Oasis Program and collected in the pamphlets titled "Emprendedores responsables, un jaque a la COVID-19" [Responsible entrepreneurs, checkmate to COVID-19] (Bello et al., 2020).

This situation drove the Oasis Program to create a new recognition as part of its awards: the "Recognition of social and environmental commitment." In its first edition, the prize was given to enterprises that developed actions of social work in the midst of COVID-19. This prize will support Cuban enterprises in the future, when other adverse phenomena could force them to put their business at the services of reducing negative effects for the environment and our society.

Achieving a better commitment to social responsibility on the part of the entrepreneurs is not only connected to motivation or knowledge of what a business can do for the environment and society, but it also evidences that they need resources and experience on how to encourage responsible activities in the Cuban context. The development of RSE should be an initiative of the enterprise itself and, with support, we can find the experience, motivation and resources for the social and environmental commitments to become truly sustainable.

With this objective in mind, the Club Oasis was started; it aims to establish a platform that guarantees the development of RSE in a sustainable manner with the leadership of the business sector. This way, the connection between entrepreneurs and their participation in social impact actions is strengthened. Entrepreneurs with experience in RSE would become mentors of others who are looking to develop RSE in their business. The members could present RSE projects to the club in their search ways to overcome factors that hinder the implementation of individual socially and environmentally responsible actions.

The Business Community and RSE Actions

The spaces developed by the Oasis Program have in certain ways contributed to place social responsibility on the working agenda of many businesspersons—although charity, solidarity, and commitment have always been part of the values of many Cubans. During the past few years we have attended many activities that different entrepreneurs have developed to solve or lessen a social or environmental problem. Activism has been present in difficult moments that the country has lived through.

In September 2017, Hurricane Irma caused loss of belongings and homes for many people. The country encouraged support for those affected, and private enterprises responded, raising funds for different articles and food that were be needed, in addition to contributing to the involvement of the business community.

In January 2018, Havana was devastated by a category EF4 tornado, on a scale of 5. The damage caused was catastrophic, especially because many of the areas in its wake are among the most disadvantaged in the city. In those difficult circumstances and with a great uncertainty about the scope of what had happened, the business community mobilized spontaneously in record time. The assistance was varied and of all kinds, but during the first moments the actions taken by the restaurants and private cafeterias were significant.

These establishments, which had to negotiate the lack of supplies, were able to provide more than fifty meals daily for those affected, over several days.

The negative results caused to the environment by human activities have also been the subject of responses offered by the entrepreneurs. In this sense, the actions carried out by the Junky's Pan restaurant at the mouth of the Quibú River west of Havana are notable. There, through announcements in its social networks, and on two occasions, they gathered together more than three hundred people—clients, neighbors, authorities, students, and members of other enterprises and institutions—with the objective of cleaning the beach of all kinds of waste along one of the shores of the river.

Recently, COVID-19 has put the social commitment of the business community to the test. Amid the difficulties there are examples of good strategies, initiatives, and actions that show the Cuban spark, and our tradition of standing up and being counted when faced with problems. During the consequences of the pandemic, entrepreneurs collaborated, from designing and producing security tools for the health personnel who were in the front lines of COVID-19 response and, for those quarantined at home, sending a variety of products: soaps, vegetables, cold cuts, and all kinds of prepared food, etc. Examples of these actions and the enterprises that carried them out are mentioned in (Bello et al. 2020).

The illustrations of actions of social responsibility by private businesses are not limited to those that have impact in the media. The competition for the Premios Oasis shows how to be socially responsible through quality control, human development, and communication, both internal and external.

Quality control has led several enterprises—especially in the gastronomic area—to be closer to the producers, encourage them to adopt ecological farming practices, provide financial support, and in some cases become agricultural producers themselves. With that, they succeed in guaranteeing fresh products, without artificial ripening agents, and with traceability.

There are enterprises that dedicate resources to the training of their personnel; they pay salaries that are higher than the cost of living; they reconcile the work schedule with the families' responsibilities, and they see the relationship with their workers as being a big family. The goal is to be include them in decision-making and strategizing discussions, because it is a question of being a team, in which everyone has something to contribute. Internal communication is also directed toward this idea. In several enterprises there are mechanisms for things to flow in two directions: top to bottom and bottom to top, so that a strong feedback loop is incorporated into the business strategies. In the area of external communications, several entrepreneurs understand that clients come to get a product, but that they come back because of the connections they make, and they logically look for these connections to accompany them through the social networks.

Final Considerations

Incorporating socially responsible management in private enterprises has been a challenge in the Cuban context, because the stigmas associated with private enterprise have not yet been erased, with a prevalence among some of an exploiter-exploited relationship, or those who only follow the rules of the market. To think only of this would be to underestimate the development of humanity, ignore the idiosyncrasy of our country and the solidarity values promoted during the last sixty years. Many of the members of the business community are professionals; for example, doctors, who until recently—or until now—received salaries very close the cost of living, but who extended their schedules on a voluntary basis in order to care for their patients. These same people form part of the business community, with the same values—which are not exclusive to a job or an institution. This is why in 2020, only ten years after resuming the promotion of self-employment in Cuba, there are so many examples of business social responsibility.

The Oasis Program of the CubaEmprende Project considers the idiosyncrasy and the values of the entrepreneurs to be an important catalyst toward the development of RSE in Cuba. Training, coaching, and awards have encouraged an important platform for learning, knowing, and acknowledging the social, economic, and environmental commitment that businesspersons can have in our society. Greater support for RSE at the national level will depend on a greater legal recognition of private enterprises, which would make them part of a regulatory legal framework that, in a reactive or proactive—though still limited—way, could encourage social responsibility in state enterprises and cooperatives.

The country is living a time of transformation; at their own risk, several entrepreneurs, as private enterprises or as self-employed workers, have decided to also transform their role in a responsible manner. Responsible enterprises could increase in number and contribute to the sustainable development of the country, because we have seen that for many of them, RSE does not pass by unnoticed.

NOTES

1. Proyecto Social del Arzobispado de La Habana [Social Project of the Archbishopry of Havana], which took place in 2012. From its beginnings, the project aimed to broaden the possibilities of success for the private sector. Workshops, conferences, counscling, and events were placed at the disposal of those who wanted to start or improve their business.

2. N.E. In August 2021, the Cuban government adopted legislation which allows the creation of micro, small, and medium-sized enterprises (MIPYMES, in Spanish), both private and public, and expanded the attributes of self-employment (Consejo de Estado 2021a, 2021b).

3. The result of the 2019 exchange of members of the Oasis Program team with specialists of the Institute for Global Prosperity (IGP), University College London, and of MVO Netherlands (Dutch Institute of BSR).

4. They explain these criteria through the fact that actions of social responsibility are seen by part of some authorities as having secondary intentions, questioning their legitimacy—following which they can investigate the enterprise in question.

5. A survey carried out in 2015 by those in RSE responsible for the Proyecto CubaEmprende, as part of the investigation to validate the variables and indicators of the Premios Oasis (results not published).

6. See Note 1.

BIBLIOGRAPHY

Alonso, R., et al. "Gobierno cubano informa sobre nuevas medidas económicas" [Cuban government announces new economic measures]. *Cubadebate*, 16 de julio, 2020. Retrieved from: http://www.cubadebate.cu/noticias/2020/07/16/gobierno -cubano-informa-nuevas-medidas-economicas-video/.

Bello, W. *Emprendimiento responsable en Cuba. Historias de creatividad y audacia* [Responsible business in Cuba: Stories of creativity and audacity]. La Habana: Programa Oasis, 2020a. Retrieved from: https://drive.google.com/file/d /1uvUzPJuqWY3q2-VsiofRR1sF5PSesUWR/view.

Bello, W., et al. *Emprendedores responsables, un jaque a la COVID-19. Iniciativas de apoyo social. Folletos I y II* [Responsible entrepreneurs check COVID-19. Initiatives of social support. Booklets I and II]. La Habana, 2020b. https: //bit.ly/emprendedorescovidv2. Retrieved from: https://drive.google.com/file/d /1zPQOBTOvpJw_Lg5NpCpJO7eYNw5faBWZ/view.

Betancourt, R. "La Responsabilidad Social Empresarial en Cuba" [Business Social Responsibility in Cuba]. *Estudios de Desarrollo Social: América Latina y Cuba* 4(2): 34–43. Mayo–Agosto 2016. Retrieved from www.revflacso.uh.cu.

Betancourt, R., and J. Gómez Arencibia. *Sinopsis de la Red Cubana de Economía Social y Solidaria y Responsabilidad Social ESORSE* [Synopsis of the Cuban Network of Social and Solidarity Economics ESORSE]. La Habana: Centro de Investigaciones Psicológicas y Sociológicas CIPS, 2019.

Bruni, L., and C. Calvo. *El precio de la gratuidad: Nuevos horizontes en la práctica económica* [The price of gratuity: New horizons in the economic practice]. Buenos Aires: Editorial Ciudad Nueva, 2008.

Bruni, L., and S. Zamagni. *Persona y comunión* [Person and communion]. Buenos Aires: Editorial Ciudad Nueva, 2009.

Camacho, I. *Creyentes en la vida pública. Iniciación a la Doctrina Social de la Iglesia* [Believers in public life. Initiation to the Social Doctrine of the Church]. Madrid: San Pablo, 1995.

Cecchini, S., and A. Madariaga. "Programas de transferencias condicionadas: balance de la experiencia reciente en América Latina y el Caribe" [Programs of conditional transferences: balance of recent experience in Latin AMerica and the Caribbean]. *Cuadernos de la CEPAL* (Comision Economica para America Latina) (95), 2011.

Comisión Europea. *Libro Verde. Fomentar un marco europeo para la Responsabilidad Social de las Empresas* [Green Book. Promoting a European framework for Business Social Responsibility]. Bruselas: Oficina de Publicaciones Oficiales de las Comunidades Europeas, 2001.

Consejo de Estado. "Decreto-Ley 44/2021 Sobre el ejercicio del Trabajo por Cuenta" [Law-Decree 44/2021. On the practice of self-employment]. *Gaceta Oficial No. 94 Ordinaria de 19 de agosto de 2021*, 19 agosto 2021 (a).

———. "Decreto-Ley 46/2021 Sobre las micro, pequeñas y medianas empresas" [Law-Decree 46/2021. On micro, small and medium-sized enterprises] (GOC-2021–777-O94)." *Gaceta Oficial*, 19 agosto 2021 (b).

Coraggio, J. L. *Economía social y solidaria. El trabajo antes que el capital* [Social and Solidary Economics. Work before capital]. Quito, Ecuador: Ediciones Abya-Yala, 2011. Retrieved from: https://www.coraggioeconomia.org/jlc/archivos %20para%20descargar/economiasocial.pdf.

———. "Desarrollo humano, economía popular y educación" [Human development, popular economics, and education] *Papeles del CEAAL No. 5 a ser publicado en: Economía y Trabajo, Programa de Economía y Trabajo*, 1993.

CubaEmprende. *Programa OASIS de Responsabilidad Social Empresarial* [OASIS Program of Business Social Responsibility]. La Habana: CubaEmprende, 2017.

Friedman, M. "The Social Responsibility of Business Is to Increase Its Profits." *New York Times Magazine*, September 13, 1970: 122–26.

GRI. "Guía para la elaboración de memorias de sostenibilidad" [Guide to creating chronicles of sustainability] Version 3.1. Global Reporting Initiative, 2020. Retrieved from: https://www.globalreporting.org/how-to-use-the-gri-standards/gri -standards-spanish-translations/.

Guthrie, J., and F. Farneti. "GRI sustainability reporting by Australian public sector organizations." *Public Money and Management* (28), 2008.

Instituto Ethos. *Conceptos Básicos e Indicadores de Responsabilidad Social Empresarial* [Basic Concepts and Indicators of Business Social Responsibility]. São Paolo, 2016.

ISO. *INTERNATIONAL STANDARD ISO 26000. Guidance on social responsibility.* Switzerland: International Organization for Standardization. 2010a.

———. *Norma ISO 26000 Responsabilidad Social* [Norm ISO 26000 Social Responsibility]. Suiza: International Organization for Standardization, 2010.

Lubich, C. *Economía de comunión: Historia y profecía* [Economy of communion: History and prophesy]. Buenos Aires: Editorial Ciudad Nueva, 2007.

OIT. *El desafío de la promoción de empresas sostenibles en América Latina y el Caribe: un análisis regional comparativo* [The challenge of promoting sustainable enterprises in Latin America]. Lima: OIT/ACTEMP, Oficina Regional para América Latina y el Caribe, 2012.

Chapter 19

Institutional Social Responsibility and Subjectivity

Consuelo Martín Fernández and Jany Bárcenas Alfonso

When we think of social responsibility, economists resonate with an expression from their area of knowledge, especially as related to the ideas of social and solidarity economy and business social responsibility (RSE in Spanish); and they also refer to social environmental responsibility, cooperative social responsibility (Betancourt 2015), and corporate social responsibility (Fernández 2004). The same holds for pedagogy in higher education (Valverde, et al. 2011), which approaches university social responsibility. From the viewpoint of politics or ideology, we have heard that in Cuba social responsibility is assumed by the socialist system that already includes it. In this way we could give free rein to the creation of these and many other related hypotheses. However, it is not often—if ever—associated with psychology as a science, when in reality human subjectivity is at the core of all the processes that are related to social responsibility, since its protagonists are people, social actors in groups, businesses, universities—that is, in the institutions that, at different levels, are focused on the daily life of a particular society, and in every concrete cultural context or historical period. And it is precisely in the areas of daily knowledge where the scientific contribution of the psychosocial perspective is found.

Etymologically, responsibility refers to the ability to respond to situations from an evaluative reflection of the possible responses. Focused on the social, it is related to the ways to measure citizen responsibility and institutional transparency, which has been evaluated from the perspective of business organizations. Today, social responsibility has been studied as a way to recover the commitment of the business sector with the social and environmental surroundings; becoming aware of the impacts that they can cause in the territory is emphasized, as well as their engaged participation in the solutions of problems that affect society.

RSE has been much studied in the literature, even when there has not been a common concept accepted by the majority of the authors (Betancourt 2016). In general, almost everyone agrees that the concept goes beyond the simple generosity toward society, and the aim is that it be converted into a key process in the strategy of the enterprise that practices it, seeing it as a guide that orients procedures which will be of benefit to all.

Social responsibility thus has to do with the ways of thinking, feeling, and acting of people in their different environments of daily life, family, work, and free time. And, above all, from the subjective point of view, their expression in the dynamics of the institutions to which they belong, personally and collectively, is very important. This is how we understand institutional social responsibility (RSI in Spanish).

It is important to specify that the reference to institutional includes any organizational area of society, which we can demand to be socially responsible. All forms of social organization, public or private, with a set of norms, roles, and functions, is an institution, and reaches from the family to the state.

The etymology of the word "institution" refers to the action and the effect of situating and being inside, that is, to encourage a sense of belonging in order to inspire the capacity to organize projects from within and act as a result of them, and whose effect is aimed at the personal, collective, and social. The emphasis in this case is the subjective realization of the institution as the highest level of every organization, while upholding the exercise of authority of the members in their different roles. As understood in its root, "authority" is a word that refers to being author, creator, to the creative quality of being and moving forward; someone who makes something grow and prosper.

Thus, the realization and putting into practice of RSI necessarily includes the subjective dimension of each of the assembled institutional processes with the characteristics and the regional potentials that are involved. This analysis is contextualized in daily life, defined as the direct expression in a concrete time, space, and rhythm of the social activities and relations that, mediated by their subjectivity, regulate the life of the person in a concrete historical cultural context (Martín 2000). In this way the day-to-day subjectivity refers to the way joint relations[1] and habitual events are experienced, which condition and are conditioned by needs, motivations, perceptions, representations, stereotypes, prejudices, and attitudes that stimulate the exercise of the roles through individual, group, and social behaviors.

Day-to-day subjectivity is the form of expression of social subjectivity in daily life. It is necessary to reflect on the relation between the social and the individual. First, we need to emphasize that it is not a linear nor a homogeneous relation, because the social is not added to the individual; it is not a sum total, rather the social is built from the heterogeneity that the subject constitutes. Second, there is a contradictory and complex relation between individual and collective needs, in which the personal sense is what allows its social expression. And third, social subjectivity is constituted by the subjective senses that are configured at the institutional, group, or social level (González 1997). That is to say that the personal implication is determined by, and is expressed in the group and institutional spaces of day-to-day life.

THE SUBJECTIVE DIMENSION IN RSI

From a psychosocial perspective, in order to follow the reasoning expressed on day-to-day subjectivity it is relevant to reflect on how to incorporate the subjective dimension into RSI. Specifically, we will here present essential aspects that integrate subjective indicators of RSI, as related to: motivations and satisfaction of needs; the carrying out and transformation of institutional roles; social participation; processes of social inclusion and exclusion; representational perceptions and contents (and in this latter category, examples of the results of applied research, carried out in Havana in 2015 and 2018, are included).

RSI: Motivations and Satisfaction of Needs

Where do I see my needs satisfied? This is a question we only occasionally ask ourselves in order to reflect and discern, but nevertheless it is present in daily life. The topic of the satisfaction of personal and collective needs is one of the fundamental mobilizers of human behavior for how they constitute the source of motivations. The needs can be felt from an absence, as well as from a desire; both mobilize the search for satisfaction (Calviño 2004). So, conceiving RSI implies that it be built on the basis of motivations, that is, it should be accompanied by the satisfaction of the needs that the subjects and the institutions indicate. It is fundamental to start from a diagnostic of personal, institutional, and community needs, and it should be the first step in this dynamic process. From that diagnostic, it is important to work on the collective construction of the object of satisfaction, starting from the common needs, and then move on to the particular ones. Encouraging social responsibility from good intentions can be successful if the needs are considered, which is key to the development of the desired motivations and behaviors, starting from the conscious activities of the institutions.

RSI: INSTITUTIONAL ROLES AND
INSTITUTIONAL TRANSFORMATION

RSI requires a dynamic process to assign and assume socially responsible roles, that is, conceive of human resources committed to institutional values meant to promote the well-being of the people and the social environment. The interaction between the individual and the collective favors the development of the sense of group belonging, which articulates the capacity to become involved in the institutional processes.

Becoming sensitized to the needs and problems of colleagues—subordinates or not—should be a set standard and, even more, a daily practice in all roles exercised in institutions. It could be assumed that this has to do only with the working environment; however, the affective component is really fundamental for a task that aims to be fulfilled responsibly. Everything that could be beneficial to that end will be of benefit to RSI, because it is precisely the task—more so than interpersonal relations—which guides institutional activity, that is, the one that ultimately brings together all processes. It is a question of mainly establishing a commitment with the task and, in this sense, interpersonal relations should not be an impediment. In this way, being more responsible implies facilitating the task based on performing the roles and accomplishing the specific transformative actions as identified directly by the people.

Exercising leadership is possible in every one of the institutional roles. Being a good leader starts with knowing how to be a good follower, and a good follower can be a good leader. This question is based in the exercise of authority in every role. The difference between authority and power is fundamental for understanding this matter. Working from the desire to form part of the collective group and institutional construction has to do with the authority of the role. On the other hand, to assume the role from a position of hierarchical power—beyond the one assigned to the levels of each function—is a vertical, unilateral exercise, without interdependencies. RSI implies the exercise of authority in the carrying out and the transformation of roles through the capacity and the will to build together, which should be expressed through the proper specific daily practices and, again, this collective gain will give institutions solidity and trustworthiness. Authority in the performance of the roles for institutional transformation (Gutmann 2003, 2005) is a process that is learned by experience (Barcenas 2018), and whose training should be explicitly included in the institutional development strategy and in its social plans.

RSI: Participation, or the Passion to Form a Part

The objective of social participation points to the accomplishments of projects with other actors, so that links are made for mutual learning and social development. In that way, RSI envisages intra- and interinstitutional cooperation based on dialogue, negotiations satisfactory to all participants, conflict mediation strategies, and the strengthening of consensus; it includes the formation and improvement of workers based on their interests and those of the institution, and in which personal and collective capacities and competences are stimulated, rather than a rivalry which affects common well-being. As a subjective indicator, social participation is real when the passion of forming a part of the institution is felt, and this is achieved through actions that are implicated in the process of decision-making, with clarity in the personal and collective processes, rights, and duties. The experience of being a protagonist in collective projects generates feelings of personal and institutional commitment. Sharing experiences with other people of the community can project the creativity of the institution, based on other collective strengths. Assertive communication is a psychological resource that favors participatory institutional dynamics and their projection toward the social environment.

RSI: Social Inclusion vs. Exclusion

The importance of a psychological viewpoint toward questions of social inclusion and exclusion is rooted in the interdependence that has been confirmed between social responsibility and social and group subjectivity which intercedes in the effectiveness of what has been established (Batista 2018). Stereotypes, prejudices and attitudes are historically conditioned and are transmitted through daily practices that culture has made invisible, reinforced by self-evident truisms, and crystallized in day-to-day knowledge (Martín 2006).

RSI should be seen in subjective and naturalized terms as a practice in any context. An intentional practice—not at all ingenuous—which responds to the social transformations that are necessary in every area. In this sense, RSI should deal with the transformation of the spread of social exclusion—a theoretical category that emerged in order to make visible those sectors that are disadvantaged, and to recognize the inability of the system to uphold social guarantees for everyone—and support social inclusion. For this, it is necessary to face the challenges of the growing social heterogeneity and its economic, political, as well as psychological intersections; this includes macro-structural elements, in which the mechanisms of differentiation have been legitimized by politics and institutions (Batista 2018). It is essential to identify the presence of stereotypes and prejudices related to gender, race, ethnicity, religion, age, profession, elitism, regionalism and any attitude that threatens social inclusion. When identified clearly, they are associated to specific roles, and their existence is recognized so that they can be transformed in institutional practices by specific actions. It is a question of having diversity as a principle, this being an institutional strength for its own development, which enables the conscious transformation of that which causes disadvantages for certain social sectors. Thus, RSI projects should be conceived to counteract any type of social discrimination and marginalization; it should be based on social inclusion and directed toward the diversification of options to raise well-being and the quality of life.

RSI: Representational Perceptions and Contents in Daily Life

Daily life expresses the relations that people have with their environment, which are influenced by their needs in each of the areas in which they take place. The day-to-day thinking integrates the cognitive referents with those that the person uses, and is habitually based on their referential behavioral pattern; that is, the perceptions of everyday objects and processes determine the links that energize behavior. So the approach to the topic of RSI should start with the exploration of the representational contents that constitute it—whether shared or not by the institutions involved. What people associate with social responsibility indicates their knowledge and affective link with the topic, in such a manner that all information that is offered to them passes through this perceptual lens by which their behavior is conditioned. Incorporating this subjective indicator to the institutional diagnostic allows for the transformation of the representational contents toward a better comprehension and practice of RSI.

What does social responsibility mean to you? This question, which we seldom ask ourselves, would be the first to be raised in any institution bent on embracing RSI. The results of a study done at community level[2] using the free association technique to explore the underlying unconscious material as a referential pattern at cognitive level reveals a configuration of representational contents in dimensions associated with the respondent's environment and regular practices.

In the daily lives studied, the subjects used their own words to describe social responsibility in various ways, and one of them had to do with social input: "contributing to a better coexistence and helping those who need it," "collective consciousness and good behavior," "observing social discipline." The topic of care and hygiene also came out in actions such as "protecting the environment," "taking care of what belongs to everyone," "taking care of what little we have," "respecting our surroundings." In addition, they raised

Table 19.1—Representational Contents of Social Responsibility

WHAT IS SOCIAL RESPONSIBILITY?

Neighborhood unity	Protecting the environment	Respect
Having collective consciousness	Taking care of what belongs to everyone	Being an active part of the community
Good behavior	Cleaning up the sidewalk	Cultural and sporting events
Observing discipline	Contributing to a better coexistence in the neighborhood and helping those who need it	Attending the meetings of the Committees for the Defense of the Revolution (CDR) and do volunteer work

Every person's awareness of the environment where they live, be it the people with whom they interact or their place of residence.

Source: Authors' elaboration

the topic of participation: "attending the CDR[3] meetings and doing volunteer work," "being an active part of the community," "participating in cultural and sporting events," "taking part in whatever is being done." They also mentioned other important elements such as "respect," "setting an example," "not bothering the neighbors," "being polite," "getting along with everyone," and helping the elderly." In general, the study highlights the relational aspect of responsibility and recognizes the active role that those who have that conception play as transforming agents of their reality. They also associate RSI with "every person's awareness of the environment where they live, be it the people with whom they interact or their place of residence."

The value of this information is precisely that it is the starting point to work on RSI, since it provides referents of the daily subjectivity that people usually deploy that serve to gain new knowledge from the information about their behavior.

Let us now look at the results of another applied research project, in this case on the symbolic representation of social and environmental responsibility, conducted in an institution[4] to explore representational contents from a symbolical perspective. This important indicator reveals perceptions of opposing contents in the notions of daily life regarding social and environmental responsibility.

Using the technique of drawing, the symbolic projection of processes and objects of daily life appears as a graphic representation of subjectivity that reveals the unconscious component underlying every kind of conscious evaluative inquiry. Asked to make a free drawing about social and environmental responsibility, the subjects matched it mostly with nature, as most of them drew rural landscapes. The drawing of one of the respondents, whom he titled *Ciudad limpia* (clean city), a representation of a rural landscape (Figure 19.1), provided conclusive evidence of this. In addition, symbols such as the sun, clouds, birds, mountains, trees, flowers, and rural houses are accompanied by rivers, with the specific characteristic that they stressed the need to protect them in order to have clean water.

Another two basic notions related to institutional issues emerged among some of the interviewees. One involves security in terms of the need to use name tags to authorize and control access to the institutions, the management of solid waste in garbage containers, and measures to prevent the dumping of contaminated water. The other has to do with the education of children and young people in the schools, respect, the care of children and senior citizens, and the contribution to the development of the country. Emphasis is placed on the links between people, which is interesting because such issues are absent from the notions about nature (only five of the rural drawings showed a person, and alone at that).

These representational designs reveal a contradiction in the image that the interviewed workers in an urban institution have of social and environmental responsibility. At a conscious level, it is paradoxical that they mostly depict rural areas; however, such is the reference that appears at an unconscious level and with which they usually function, except that it shows up only during projective explorations. It is important to keep this symbolic material in mind with a view to institutional management based on social and environmental responsibility, since it reveals the need for a comprehensive environmental concept that facilitates the identification of the individual role within the RSI.

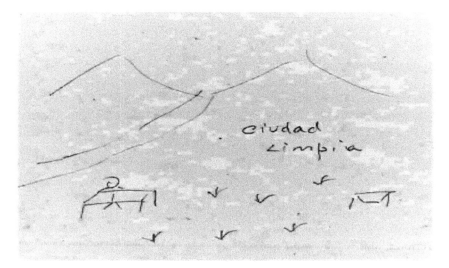

Figure 19.1. Symbolic Representation of Social and Environmental Responsibility.
Source: Author.

METHODOLOGIES FOR IMPLEMENTING RSI

The social sciences provide a broad range of methods and techniques according to each of the disciplines that they cover, which interact to develop integrative scientific approaches to objects and phenomena that intersect some of them, as is the case of RSI. We need a combination of methodologies, both quantitative and qualitative, to organize the proposed objectives in a recursive relation with a view to RSI management. In other words, to design planning, diagnostic, implementation and assessment actions as in an RSI spiral in the making, which means that they must be implemented every time that the process is implemented.

So, how to implement RSI? In the planning processes—be it strategic planning, a cooperative social assessment, a triple business bottom line (economic, social, and environmental) or another form described in the literature on the topic in the case of enterprises—the most important thing to emphasize is the moment of working out the RSI indicators. These are designed according to the relevant sector of the economy, services, labor unions, education, etc. and to the different forms of property. There must be general indicators for every sector, but specific ones for the different institutions, addressed to their internal public (workers and their families) and to the external one (clients, partners, all those engaged in the value chains of the institutions in question, and the community in general).

Preparing the indicators is a conscious process—including its subjective dimension—coordinated by both the professional staff of the institution and external consultants specialized in RSI management. Although Cuba has no institution dedicated to offering this type of consultancy, there are professionals in different fields of the social sciences who are qualified to provide this service with an integrative approach. One methodological strategy to incorporate the subjective dimension into RSI begins with the preparation of its indicators.

There are various methodologies to study and evaluate social responsibility in its different environments, for example, the indicators of the Instituto Ethos of Brazil (Martín, Abín, and Barcenas 2015), which constitute a model for the study of social responsibility, at the business and the environmental level, in addition to the thematic axes of the university social responsibility (Vallaeys 2009). In both cases the person is included, but without specifying the subjective dimension and its practical applicability. Therefore, in what follows we propose some techniques and analytical methods that can be incorporated into the interdisciplinary strategies to implement RSI.

- The semi-structured interview: It permits an individual approach that encourages communication with the investigator in order to facilitate the procurement of information. Because of the characteristics of the investigation and the method that is employed, its use has a flexible character, because of which it is the fundamental technique of the investigation. It allows the researchers a joint construction of meaning related to the object of the study, and for the participants to openly express their opinion. This technique guides the entire process of applying the tools, because during a unifying interview other, more specific techniques, can be applied, together with those previously prepared.
- Free word association: This was initially developed from the psychoanalytic perspective in order to access the complex unconscious mechanisms of the patients. Subsequently, it went beyond the limits of psychoanalysis and has enjoyed a broad use both in psychological research and in clinical practice, as in the study of social representations produced by S. Moscovici, D. Jodelet and others (Martín 2000). The leading words in this case could be: social responsibility, institutional social responsibility, environmental social responsibility, and social and solidarity economy.
- Drawing: As a psychographic element, it indicates the capacity to represent the concepts, ideas, experiences, beliefs, perceptions, feelings, attitudes about the object being studied on a surface, from the psychical reflection of the person doing the drawing (Cancio-Bello 2014). The graphic representation should be accompanied by feedback on the part of the interviewee, which would allow for an understanding of the meanings that the forms being represented have for the subject. The feedback exercise is extremely valuable for collecting both information and evaluations relating to the object of the representation (Ortega 2010). In this case it offers rich information on how people conceive social responsibility.
- Oral graphic representation: This is a variant of the drawing technique, in which it is possible to obtain graphic images or representations of the object under study by oral means. The use of this technique is relevant for the studies on social representations, in contexts in which the use of drawing may be unwise or impossible to do because of the deficiency of its premises. The graphic representation variant provides for the formation of constitutive symbols of the representation by oral means.
- Facial technique: This is essentially projective; it allows grasping the affective-emotional component that emerges in each selection that the interviewees make about how they feel with respect to the aspect being evaluated, and it complements the information obtained in a direct way by the reason for their choice. In this way, the subjectivation of the

concrete situations in the daily lives of the interviewees is expressed; that is to say, the facts are expressed mediated by their personal experiences, which supposes that similar circumstances can produce different perceptions, attitudes, evaluations, behaviors—among other subjective productions, and vice versa. The facial expression of the caricature that is offered is graded on a type of scale that has seven option ranges, from the number 7 (feeling well, happiness, and satisfaction) to the number 1 (feeling badly, sadness, and dissatisfaction). This technique allows for the expression of individual differences relating to an attitude that ranges between the extremes of pleasure-displeasure, acceptance-rejection, satisfaction-dissatisfaction. To the degree that the attitude of the person is more favorable, there will be a choice of a face near the number 7 and, on the contrary, feeling worse would bring the choice to the number 1 face. The information is processed from the answers indicated by the interviewees, and the general qualification is taken from the average considered for each of the categories studied, which allows for a comparison between them (CESBH-UH 2012).

- The technique of the ten wishes: Created in Belgium by J. Nuttin and retaken in Cuba by Diego González Serra (1972) as part of the methodology he proposes for the motivational study called Register of the activity and direct and indirect method (Registro de la actividad y método directo e indirecto. RAMDI in Spanish). Its objective is to explore what areas of people's lives their main needs and motives are directed toward, in addition to discovering which is the hierarchical place in which these are located (Cancio-Bello 2014).

- Focal group: This is characterized as a planned conversation, with investigative objectives, and coordinated by an expert moderator or team. The topic to be broached is presented for the participants' considerations, and they can express their evaluations and commentaries in a friendly, flexible and non-managerial environment. "It offers the possibility to enter into subjectivation and defining processes" (Montaño 2004, 6). As it is a planned debate, it is based on an established design which has a flexible character. "It includes forms of interaction, as well as role playing; there is a regulation on the forms of interaction which to some extent are different and, in some ways, more flexible or open than those in the surroundings" (Montaño 2004, 8). Generally, the groups are made up of an approximate number of between seven and twelve participants who present some common characteristic relevant to the investigation's objectives.

- Observation: This accompanies the entire research process; it allows for a global study of the phenomenon, as it occurs in reality. This technique

favors especially the knowledge of the affective-emotional dimensions
in the communication.

- Experimental workshops: These are based on learning through experience, with objects, processes, and social phenomena that encourage
the identification of roles assumed in the source institutions and their
representational expressions for the institutional transformation with
RSI. They are conceived as a temporary institutional apprenticeship created for one or several days of group work with two types of sessions
(of reflection and of *the here and now*). They deal with the structure of
interpersonal relations that is established from the articulation between
the large system, subsystems and small groups. During the sessions the
opportunity is offered to study how myths, beliefs, stereotypes, prejudices, and fantasies arise and that structure the life of the organization.
In addition, they encourage the awareness of repetition in the noncritical
exercise of the institutional functions. Multiple types of languages are
used (rational, emotional, corporal, artistic) in order to problematize and
identify actions of transformation in the roles and behaviors to perform
in the respective institutions. In this way, the aim is to find the rupture of the noncritical familiarity[5] as a way of democratically building
knowledge with RSI, focused on discovering and putting into practice
the personal and collective resources to confront the various problems
of institutional life. In addition, the participants can become producers
of the lived experience (Barcenas 2018).

- Content analysis: For some authors this consists of a technique, for
others it is a method or a set of procedures applied to the analysis of
the information that was obtained. It allows for the investigation of the
nature of the communication by offering the possibility to find consis-
tencies and common points among the results of the direct, indirect and
projective techniques, as well as between each of the case studies. It
consists of the identification and explanation of the cognitive elabora-
tions which give meaning to all communicative procedures. Six types
are defined: exploratory analysis of content; analysis of content verifi-
cation; analysis of quantitative content; analysis of qualitative content;
analysis of direct content; analysis of indirect content. For our particular
case, the last two modalities can be used together. The analysis of direct
content, which is focused on taking the literal meaning of the material
studied, does not intend to reveal an eventual latent meaning in the communications; it remains at the level of the patent meaning. The analysis
of indirect content aims to extract the latent content that is hidden behind
the patent content, and for that purpose it resorts to the interpretation of
the meaning of the components, their frequency, their place in relation
to the rest, and their associations (Perera 2005).

A NEW GLOBAL CONTEXT

We are living in a difficult year; in a worldwide crisis, which has managed to transform the turbulent rhythm of daily life but has also offered us the opportunity to reflect, to value what is really important, to question our traditional ways of thinking, feeling and acting. In the context of the COVID-19 pandemic, social responsibility takes on a special meaning and interest. It is taking on new meanings and now appears as associated to concepts such as responsible self-care, the need to care for ourselves so we can care for others, flexibility, adaptation, and resilience, among others. So for RSI it is indispensable to incorporate the subjective dimension, and reach out to the articulation of personal, family and social projects. When personal projects find meaning within collective projects, we will be able to really advance toward a more just and healthy society, a daily life with physical, material and spiritual well-being. From the perspective of the social sciences it is possible to contribute to this effort, with inter-, multi-, and transdisciplinary viewpoints, through which psychology complements its professional performance in favor of the human essence, here located in the axes of subjectivity and institutional social responsibility.

CONCLUSIONS

1. Institutional social responsibility is a far-reaching concept that is applied to any of the components identified as socially responsible, especially to businesses, be they state, collective, or privately owned.
2. When the subjective dimension is included in any organization, there is an opportunity to transform it into an institution that belongs to and acts according to the social responsibility it aims for.
3. The knowledge of institutional information is necessary, but not sufficient, to motivate behaviors; recognition and affective commitment is required to mobilize the passion to become a part of it, from the perspective of day-to-day subjectivity.
4. In the interdisciplinary strategies to implement RSI the conscious incorporation of the subjective dimension is necessary to achieve an integrative vision and action, inclusive and participative, in which the human resources can be salvaged as the essential and indispensable factor for its successful implementation.

RECOMMENDATIONS

1. Identify personal and collective needs in the institutions so as to put the human being in the central axis of the good RSI practices in social and solidarity economy of all sectors and levels of society.
2. Incorporate the subjective dimension in the management of RSI, with psychosocial, generational and gender perspectives, which communicate with the necessary interdisciplinary practices that are required in the social and solidarity economy.
3. Carry out pilot projects for the implementation of the development strategies of an integrative RSI, starting from the application of techniques set in the subjective dimension so as to revitalize behaviors, participation, perceptions, commitments and feelings of belonging desired in the institutional management of a specific area, where its pertinence and its capacity to respond will be demonstrated, and generalize the results.
4. Given that in Cuba there is no institution dedicated to RSI-related consultancy, we propose to create one, staffed with professionals from different social sciences who are qualified to offer this service with an integrative and coaching approach, which is feasible, given the government-university alliances established as regional strengths for local development.

NOTES

1. Life experience is considered as being the smallest unit of the cognitive and the affective component (Vigotsky 1993), and the link of the elemental relational unit of the subjects with him/herself, with others and with reality (Pichón Rivière 1985).

2. Transforming daily life in the Las Cañas Popular Council, Cerro Municipality (Martín, Abín, and Barcenas 2015a). This study was part of the Parallel Pilot Project—Patrimony and local identity, developed by the University of Havana and the Technological University Jose Antonio Echeverria (CUJAE) in the context of the Alfa ADU2020 Network. Transformando . . . was an interdisciplinary project conducted with twenty-three students of architecture (CUJAE) and three students of psychology (UH). The purpose of this research was to make a critical analysis of daily situations involving social misbehavior and suggest specific feasible actions based on social responsibility to contribute to transforming daily life in that Havana Popular Council. A mixed methodology including 158 questionnaires and the free association technique was used with the local residents.

3. Committees for the Defense of the Revolution—neighborhood groups.

4. Case study on social and environmental responsibility, carried out in 2017 and 2018 in a closed loop center (research, production, and marketing) at the University of Havana, to explore people's perceptions of social and environmental responsibility

and their consistency with the work of this center. Twenty-three workers (53 percent of the labor force) were interviewed as the internal public in the case in question. (Martín and Abín 2019).

5. This refers to the psychological phenomenon of habituation and naturalization of customs, routines, and roles which crystallize in daily self-evident truths which, because they are well-known, close-by, or familiar, are repeated without thought and are not questioned (Martín 2006).

BIBLIOGRAPHY

Barcenas, J. 2018. "Transformar ESTUDIA en ES-TU-DÍA desde el aprendizaje experiencial y la crítica de la vida cotidiana." Tesis de Maestría en Psicología Educativa. La Habana: Facultad de Psicología, Universidad de La Habana.

Batista, P. 2018. "El grupo escolar y el proceso de inclusión-exclusión: estudios en instituciones docentes de la capital." Tesis de Maestría en Psicología Educativa. La Habana: Facultad de Psicología, Universidad de La Habana.

Betancourt, Rafael. 2015. "La economía social y solidaria y la actualizacion del modelo económico cubano." *Blog Catalejo de la Revista Temas.* http://temas.cult.cu/blog/?p=2071#more-2071.

———. 2016. "La Responsabilidad Social Empresarial en Cuba." *Revista Estudios del Desarrollo Social: Cuba y América Latina* (FLACSO Universidad de La Habana) 4 (2): 34–43. http://www.revflacso.uh.cu/index.php/flacso/issue/view/17.

Calviño, M. 2004. *Análisis dinámico del comportamiento.* La Habana: Editorial Félix Varela.

Cancio-Bello, C. 2014. "Identidad de género y proyectos futuros: su relación desde la perspectiva de género en mujeres jóvenes que ejercen la prostitución." La Habana: Facultad de Psicología, Universidad de La Habana.

CESBH-UH. 2012. *La cohesión social como valor en el Municipio Centro Habana.* Informe final de Investigación del PTCH-CITMA "Los procesos de socialización para el desarrollo de valores en La Habana," La Habana: Editorial Félix Varela.

Fernández, D. 2004. "La responsabilidad social corporativa en materia ambiental. Estado de la cuestión." *España: Boletín económico* (Universidad de Salamanca).

González, F. 1997. *Epistemología cualitativa y subjetividad.* La Habana: Editorial Pueblo y Educación.

Gutmann, D. 2005. *La Transformación: Deseo y liderazgo en la vida y en las instituciones.* Barcelona: Icaria Editorial, S.A.

———. 2003. *Psychoanalysis and Management: The Transformation.* UK: The Studio Publishing Services Ltd.

Martín, C. 2000. *Cuba: Vida cotidiana, familia y emigración.* Tesis de doctorado en Ciencias Psicológicas, La Habana: Centro de Estudios de Alternativas Políticas, Ciudad de La Habana.

———. 2006. *Psicología social y vida cotidiana.* La Habana: Editorial Félix Varela.

Martín, C., O. Abín, and J. Barcenas. 2015. "Acciones prácticas de Responsabilidad Social y Medioambiental: dos experiencias desde la Universidad de La Habana.

Cuba." Martín, C., Abín, O., Barcenas, J. (2015). *Acciones prácticas de Responsabilidad Social y Medioambiental: doPrimer Seminario Internacional de Economía Social y Solidaria, MARDELTUR.* Pinar del Rio, Cuba: Universidad de Pinar del Río.

———. 2015a. "Transformando la vida cotidiana del Consejo Popular Las Cañas, Municipio Cerro." Informe de investigación del Proyecto Piloto Paralelo (PPP) "Patrimonio e Identidad local" UH-CUJAE, La Habana.

Martín, C., and O. Abín. 2019. "Un estudio de caso sobre responsabilidad social y medioambiental." "Debates contemporáneos sobre Economía Social y Solidaria y Responsabilidad Social Empresarial en el contexto latinoamericano y caribeño." La Habana: Simposio Internacional CIPS 2019.

Montaño, R. 2004. "El dispositivo grupal como instrumento de intervención e investigación en el campo de la Psicología Social." *Liberaddictus.* https://www.liberaddictus.org.

Ortega, D. 2010. "Delegado/a del Poder Popular: un estudio sobre su representación social en el Consejo Popular Jesús María." Tesis de Maestría en Psicología Social y Comunitaria. La Habana: Facultad de Psicología, Universidad de La Habana.

Perera, M. 2005. "Sistematización crítica de la teoría de las representaciones sociales." Tesis de doctorado en Ciencias Psicológicas. La Habana: Centro de Investigaciones Psicológicas y Sociológicas.

Pichón Rivière, E. 1985. *El proceso grupal. Del Psicoanálisis a la Psicología Social.* Buenos Aires: Editorial Nueva Visión.

Vallaeys, F. 2009. *Responsabilidad Social Universitaria. Manual de primeros pasos.* México: McGraw-Hill Interamericana.

Valverde, J., W. Beita, J. C. Bermúdez, G. Pino, and G. Rodríguez. 2011. *Gestión de la Responsabilidad Social Universitaria: Dimensiones y estudios de caso.* San José: Universidad Nacional de Costa Rica.

Vigotsky, L. 1993. *Pensamiento y lenguaje.* Buenos Aires: Editorial Fausto.

Index

Note: Italicised page numbers refer to figures and bold refer to tables. Page numbers followed by "n" refer to notes.

VI Congress of the Communist Party of Cuba, 2, 6n1, 168, 197, 203; Conceptualization of the Economic and Social Cuban Model of Socialist Development, 7, 18, 31, 168, 169; National Plan of Economic and Social Development to 2030, 7; Proposal of the Vision of a Nation, Axes and Strategic Sectors, 7

VIII Congress of the Communist Party of Cuba, 2–3, 168, 197

2011 Guidelines of the Economic and Social Policies of the Party and the Revolution, 12, 13, 31, 105–6, 141, 143, 168, 169, 171, 190, 191

2017 Guidelines of the Economic and Social Policies of the Party and the Revolution, 105

2018 Peoples' Summit (Confederación Latinoamericana y del Caribe de Trabajadores Estatales 2018), 112

2030 Agenda of the United Nations, 102

ACI/ICA. *See* International Cooperative Alliance [Alianza Cooperativa Internacional (ACI/ICA)]

Act 1304/1976 on Political and Administrative Division of the National Assembly of People's Power, 245

Administrative Municipal Council/ Municipal Administration Council, 57, 58

Agencia Nacional de Vigilancia Sanitaria (ANVISA), 135n13

AGROCADENAS Project, 84, 94n5

Alianza Bolivariana para las Américas [Bolivarian Alliance for the peoples of America], 129

Alianza de Mujeres Cooperativistas de Centroamérica [Alliance of Women Cooperative Members in Central America], 76

altruism, 272

AMPP. *See* Asamblea Municipal del Popular Power [Municipal Assembly of Popular Power (AMPP)]

ANAP. *See* National Association of Small Agriculturalists [Asociación Nacional de Agricultores Pequeños (ANAP)]

Andalusian School of Social
Economy, 246
anti-capitalist sustainability model, 254
Antunes, R., 200
ANVISA. *See* Agencia Nacional de
Vigilancia Sanitaria (ANVISA)
Argentina, 228
Asamblea Municipal del Popular Power
[Municipal Assembly of Popular
Power (AMPP)], 56, 58, 61
Asia, social and solidarity
economy of, 21
Asociación de Pedagogos of Cuba:
"Transform to Educate" project, 228
Association of Christian Regulators of
Brazilian Companies, 228
Auge Consultancy, 15
autonomy, 43, 46, 56, 58, 74, 112,
129, 166, 169, 184, 185, 187, 203,
207, 219, 220, 223, 243; of the
cooperatives, 140, 146–50, 152,
154; entrepreneurial, 4, 18, 32, 152;
financial, 254, 258; integrative,
33; management, 28, 178, 188–89,
194, 221, 256; managerial, 33, 259;
municipal, 53, 58; operational, 51;
personal, 263; political, 263
AVINA, 238

Bases of the National Economic and
Social Development Plan for 2030,
99, 168, 170
Betancourt, R., 121, 164, 239–40
BEU. *See* Forestry Base Enterprise
Unit (BEU)
BioCubaFarma, 120, 126
Bonilla-Molina, L., 54–55
Brazil, 228; participatory budgeting, 54
BSR/RSE. *See* business social
responsibility (BSR/RSE)
bureaucratic socialism, 49
business social responsibility
(BSR/RSE), xiv, 8, 18–20, 22,
119–36, 259, 287; applications
of, 272–74; approach, 124–26;

awareness and training of actors
in Mayabeque, 245–47; business
community and RSE actions,
280–81; businesspersons, training
of, *275*, 275–82, *277*; in Centro
Habana municipality, 190–92;
in Cuban private enterprises,
271–83; dimensions of, 125–26;
international context, 120–24; in
local development, 237–49; training,
contribution of, 242–44
business sustainability, 121

Cabello, B. S., 238
Cabello, L., 238
Callejón de los Peluqueros
[Hairdressers Alley], 109
capital: cultural, 74; foreign, 108; labor
vis-à-vis the logic of, 198–201;
social, 74; symbolic, 74
capitalism, 5, 39n2, 47, 199–201, 240;
industrial, 256
care for the environment, 28
Casa Productora de Audiovisuales
Palomas, 79n5
Castro, Raúl, 13
Catedral Popular Council, 109
CCS. *See* Cooperativas de Créditos
y Servicios [Credit and Service
Cooperatives (CCS)]
CCSNA. *See* Cooperatives of
Non-Agricultural Credits and
Services (CCSNA)
CCS "Orlando Cuellar," [Orlando
Cuellar Credit and Service
Cooperative] 247
CECMED. *See* Centro Estatal
para el Control de los
Medicamentos (CECMED)
CEDECOM. *See* Cooperative
Study Center on
Cooperative and Community
Development (CEDECOM)
CEDEL. *See* Centro de Estudios del
Desarrollo Local y Comunitario

[Center of Local and Community Development Studies (CEDEL)]

CEDEM. *See* Centro de Estudios Demográficos de la Universidad de La Habana (CEDEM)

CEEC. *See* Center of Study on the Cuban Economy, University of Havana (CEEC)

CEGED. *See* Centro de Estudios para la Gestión del Desarrollo [Center for Development Management Studies] (CEGED)

CE-GESTA. *See* Center for Studies on Management, Local Development and Tourism, University of Pinar del Río (CE-GESTA)

CEMEFI. *See* Centro Mexicano para la Filantropía (CEMEFI)

Center for Molecular Immunology [Centro de Inmunología Molecular (CIM)]: business social responsibility of, 119–36; *Manual of Communications Management*, 127; mission of, 127; Security, Health, and Environmental Policy, 131; as socially responsible enterprise, 128–33; social objective of, 127; Training Plan for Good Productive Practices, 130; Union of Young Communists, 131; vision of, 127–28

Center for Studies on Management, Local Development and Tourism, University of Pinar del Río (CE-GESTA), xviiin2, 246

Center of Research on the International Economy, University of Havana (CIEI), xviiin1

Center of Study on the Cuban Economy, University of Havana (CEEC), xviiin1, 112, 211n1

Central America, feminism in, 76

Central State Management Entities (Organismos de la Administración Central del Estado—OACE), 143, 145, 178

Centro de Estudios del Desarrollo Local y Comunitario [Center of Local and Community Development Studies (CEDEL)], xviiin1, 60

Centro de Estudios Demográficos de la Universidad de La Habana (CEDEM), 84, 94n5, 211n1

Centro de Estudios para la Gestión del Desarrollo [Center for Development Management Studies] (CEGED), 245–48

Centro de Intercambio y Referencia de Iniciativa Comunitaria [Center for Exchange and Guidance of Community Initiatives (CIERIC)], 60, 79n4

Centro Estatal para el Control de los Medicamentos (CECMED), 135n13

Centro Félix Varela, xv, 100, 112

Centro Habana municipality: cooperative principles, role and implementation of, 183–85; nonagricultural cooperatives, participation in strategies and social management of, 183–95 (business social responsibility, 190–92; cooperation among cooperatives, 192–94 cooperation with other organizations, 192–94; management autonomy, 188–89; member participation in design and management of socio-production strategies, 186–88; methodological considerations, 185)

Centro Mexicano para la Filantropía (CEMEFI), 135n6

CEPAL (Economic Commission for Latin America and the Caribbean), 102

CERES. *See* Consorcio Ecuatoriano de Responsabilidad Social (CERES)

CETED. *See* Facultad de Economía y Centro de Estudios de Técnicas de Dirección (CETED), Universidad de La Habana

charity, 272
China: Communist Party of China, 103; public-private partnerships, 103
CIEI. *See* Center of Research on the International Economy, University of Havana (CIEI)
CIERIC. *See* Centro de Intercambio y Referencia de Iniciativa Comunitaria [Center for Exchange and Guidance of Community Initiatives (CIERIC)]
CIM. *See* Center for Molecular Immunology [Centro de Inmunología Molecular (CIM)]
CIMEX Corporation, 189
CIPS. *See* Scientific Committee of the Center for Psychological and Sociological Research (CIPS)
CITMA. *See* Ministry of Science, Technology and the Environment (CITMA)
Club Oasis, 280
CMLK. *See* Martin Luther King Memorial Center (CMLK)
CNAs. *See* Cooperativas no Agropecuarias [nonagricultural cooperatives (CNAs)]
CODESPA Foundation, 89
Colombia: Gender Equity and Equality Policy for Associated and Working Women and a Gender Committee, 76
comfortism, 231
Comité Nacional de Mujeres Cooperativistas [National Committee of Women Cooperative Members (CONAMUJER)], 76
Commission on the Implementation of the Guidelines of the Party and the Revolution, 171
Committees for the Defense of the Revolution, 300n3
complacency, in women, 231, 232
CONACOOP. *See* Consejo Nacional de Cooperativas de República Dominicana (CONACOOP)

CONAMUJER. *See* Comité Nacional de Mujeres Cooperativistas [National Committee of Women Cooperative Members (CONAMUJER)]
Consejo Estatal de RSE [RSE State Council], 123
Consejo Nacional de Cooperativas de República Dominicana (CONACOOP), 79n4
Consejo Popular Catedral [Popular Council of the Cathedral]; "Por tu Barrio" [For your Neighborhood] project, 58–62, 64
Consorcio Ecuatoriano de Responsabilidad Social (CERES), 122, 135n6
Constitution of the Republic of Cuba, 31, 63, 203; Article 1, *167*; Article 3, 55; Article 4, item d, 188; Article 4, item f, 190, 191; Article 4, item g, 192, 193; Article 10, 56; Article 13, *167*; Article 18, *168*; Article 22, 165, 197; Article 53, 56; Article 80, sub d, 56; Article 101, sub d, 56; Article 101, sub h, 56; Article 168, 53, 57; Article 200, 53; Article 305, 57; Chapter II, 197
Contribución Territorial para el Desarrollo Local [Regional Contribution for Local Development (CTDL)], 57, 58, 64, 195n3
cooperation, 28, 73, 100, 113, 185
Cooperativas de Créditos y Servicios [Credit and Service Cooperatives (CCS)], 29, 33, 39n4, 159n7, 171, 217, 227–29, 247
Cooperativas de Producción Agropecuaria [Agricultural Production Cooperatives (CPA)], 29, 33, 39n4, 159n7, 171
Cooperativas no Agropecuarias [nonagricultural cooperatives (CNAs)], 12–14, 27, 29, 33, 39n4, 39n5, 106, 109, 142, 171, 217, 238, 247; in Centro Habana municipality,

participation in strategies and
social management of, 183–95;
waste recycling, implementation of
CA-FLACSO-PC Cooperative Social
Balance Model in, 222–2
cooperative as energizing agent
in, 171–79
cooperatives, 33, 261; autonomy,
140, 146–50, 152, 154; as
energizing agent of SSE model,
163–80; higher-tier, creation of,
150–54; management, proposals for
improvement of, 172, *173–77*; multi-
stakeholder, creation of, 150–54;
non-statement management forms,
33; in restarted reforms, 139–60;
socioeconomic agents *vs.*, 165–66
cooperative social balance, 215–24;
methodology, 217–18
cooperative social responsibility, 178,
180n4, 227
cooperatives of industrial labor and
service workers (CTIS), 12–15, *13*
Cooperatives of Non-Agricultural
Credits and Services (CCSNA), 17
cooperative solidarity labor: committing
to, 197–212; labor vis-à-vis the logic
of capital, 198–201; references to
assess, 201–2
Cooperative Study Center on
Cooperative and Community
Development (CEDECOM), 228
cooperativism, 33, 74; movement,
28; new, 29; transformative
potential of, 30
Cooperazione per lo Sviluppo dei Paesi
Emergenti [Cooperation for the
Development of Emerging Countries
(COSPE)], 217, 234n1
Coraggio, J. L., 29, 30, 49, 200
corporate social responsibility
(RSC), 88, 215
corruption, 3, 4, 45, 54, 239
COSPE. *See* Cooperazione per lo
Sviluppo dei Paesi Emergenti

[Cooperation for the Development of
Emerging Countries (COSPE)]
Costa Rica, 76
COSUDE. *See* Swiss Agency
for Development and
Cooperation (COSUDE)
Council of Ministers, 12;
Decree 309, 171
Council of Ministries, 145
Council of State: Law Decree 305, 171;
Law Decree 306, 171
COVID-19 pandemic, 7, 8; Plan for the
Prevention and Control of COVID-
19, 16–17; social impact of, 15–16
CPA. *See* Cooperativas de Producción
Agropecuaria [Agricultural
Production Cooperatives (CPA)]
CTDL. *See* Contribución Territorial
para el Desarrollo Local
[Regional Contribution for Local
Development (CTDL)]
CTIS. *See* cooperatives of industrial
labor and service workers (CTIS)
Cuba and its Economic and
Social Challenges. Summary
of the Economic and Social
Strategy, 99–100
Cubadebate, 180n5
CubaEmprende Project, 275, 276,
283n5; Oasis Program of business
social responsibility, 272
Cuban Communist Party, 159n4
Cuban Economic and Social Model of
Socialist Development, xiv, 43, 99,
125, 141, 163, 233, 238
Cuban Psychology Society, 246
CUJAE. *See* Technological University
Jose Antonio Echeverria (CUJAE)
cultural capital, 74

dead labor, 200
Decree 281/2007, 241
Decree 281/2018, 241
Decree-Law 301/2012, 245

Decree-Law 305/2012, 188, 192, 193;
Article 6, 186
Decree-Law 366/2019, 188, 193;
Article 12.1, 186
*Democratización de las Diferentes
Instancias de Decision del
Movimiento Cooperativo*
[Democratization of the Different
Decision-Making Entities of the
Cooperative Movement], 80n6
Díaz-Canel Bermúdez, Miguel, 8
DL. *See* sustainable development (DL)
Dutch Institute of BSR (MVO
Netherlands), 274

EAES. *See* Escuela Andaluza de
Economía Social [School of Social
Economy of Andalusia (EAES)]
EAP. *See* economically active
population (EAP)
ECLAC. *See* UN Economic
Commission on Latin America and
the Caribbean (ECLAC)
economically active population
(EAP), 85–86
economic inefficiency, 1
Economic Plan for 2020 and 2021, 8
Ecuador, 89, 228
egalitarianism, 8–15
El Negocio [The Business], 80n5
El oficio de crecer [The profession of
growing], 79n5
El Troudi, H., 54–55
EMEA. *See* European Medicines
Agency (EMEA)
Empresa de la Agricultura y de
Mercado (Agriculture and Market
Enterprise), 189
Engels, F., 29, 154
entrenched power of women, 232–33
entrepreneurial autonomy, 4, 18, 32, 152
entrepreneurial social responsibility, 34
EPS. *See* popular and solidarity
economy (EPS)

equality, 76, 112; of opportunity, 17–18.
See also inequality
equity, xvi, 2, 4, 5, 28, 34, 38, 48, 70,
71, 93, 124–26, 152, 164, 166, 179,
233, 238, 239, 255, 259, 264, 265;
gaps, 216, 220; gender, 76, 89, 223,
230, 232, 243; generational, 74, 243;
regional, 243; relations, 218; social,
35–36, 73, 90, 114, 229, 232, 237
Escuela Andaluza de Economía
Social [School of Social
Economy of Andalusia (EAES)],
79n4; Diploma Program in
Management of Cooperatives and
Social and Solidarity Economy
Organizations, 246
ESORSE. *See* Red Cubana de Economía
Social y Solidaria y Responsabilidad
Social Empresarial [Cuban
Network of Social and Solidarity
Economy and Social Business
Responsibility (ESORSE)]
EU. *See* European Union (EU)
Europe, social and solidarity
economy in, 21
European Medicines Agency
(EMEA), 135n13
European Union (EU), 94n3

Facultad de Economía y Centro de
Estudios de Técnicas de Dirección
(CETED), Universidad de La
Habana, 135n7
FDA. *See* Food and Drug
Administration (FDA)
Federation of Cuban Women, 233
Felix Varela Center: "Strengthening
environmental transformation for
adaptability to climate change in
Cuban communities," 110
female entrepreneurs, solidarity
experience of, 253–66
feminism, 76; socialist, 231
financial autonomy, 254, 258
FLACSO-Cuba, 79n4

Fondo Cubano de Bienes Culturales (Cuban Stock of Cultural Assets), 111
Food and Drug Administration (FDA), 135n13
Fordism, 200
Forestry Base Enterprise Unit (BEU), 111
Forja (blacksmiths), 109
Fundación Avina, Argentina, 122

GALFISA. *See* Group on Latin America, Social Philosophy and Axiology (GALFISA)
García Linera, A., 48
GDIC. *See* Grupo para el Desarrollo Integral de la Capital (GDIC)
gender, 77; equity, 76, 89, 223, 230, 232, 243; gender-based division of labor, 259; perspective, in cooperative social balance model (Villa Clara), 227–35
General Comptroller's Office, 189
generational equity, 74, 243
GEPAC. *See* Gestión participativa local de la rehabilitación del Centro Histórico de la Habana [Local participatory management of the rehabilitation of the Historical Center of Old Havana (GEPAC)]
Gereffi, G., 87
German codetermination experience, 160n10
GEST. *See* Social Labor Studies Group [Grupo de Estudios Sociales del Trabajo (GEST)]
Gestión participativa local de la rehabilitación del Centro Histórico de la Habana [Local participatory management of the rehabilitation of the Historical Center of Old Havana (GEPAC)], 59
Gibbon, P., 87
Gil, Alejandro, 16
Go for it: You can do it!, 255, 262–64

Goldfrank, B., 55
Gómez, J., 238
Gómez Arencibia, J., 164
González Rodríguez, Nydia, 234n2
Governmental Accountability Office of the Republic of Cuba, 135n11
Great Depression, 149
Group on Latin America, Social Philosophy and Axiology (GALFISA), xvi, 204, 207, 212n3
Grupo para el Desarrollo Integral de la Capital (GDIC), 79n4

Harnecker, M., 54–55
Health Products and Food Branch (HPFB), 135n13
hegemonic culture, 4
Hesselbach, W., 30, 184
higher-tier cooperative, creation of, 150–54
Hinkelammert, F.: *For an Economy Oriented towards Life*, 201
Historical Center of Havana: comprehensive management for development, 109; participatory budgeting in, 58–63
HPFB. *See* Health Products and Food Branch (HPFB)
Humphrey, J., 87

IARSE. *See* Instituto Argentino de Responsabilidad Social Empresarial (IARSE)
ICA-FLACSO-PC Modelo de Balance Social Cooperativo [Cooperative Social Balance Model], *216*, 216–24; in agricultural conservatives, implementation of, 220–22; in UBPC Las Cadenas of Pinar del Río, implementation of, 218–20; in waste recycling CNA, implementation of, 222–23
IDB. *See* Interamerican Development Bank (IDB)

IGP. *See* Institute for Global
Prosperity (IGP)
ILO/OIT. *See* International Labor
Organization (ILO/OIT)
INCA. *See* Instituto Nacional de
Ciencias Agrícolas (INCA)
independence, 1, 74, 179, 184
individualism, 79
inequality, 9, 69, 72–73, 77; class-based,
74; race-based, 74; socio-economic,
48; structure, 72. *See also* equality
Institute for Global Prosperity (IGP),
274, 283n3
institutional social responsibility (RSI),
xvii, 287–301; implementation
methodologies, 295–98; motivations,
289; new global context, 299;
participation, 291; recommendations
for, 300; representational perceptions
and contents, in daily life, 292–94,
293, 294; roles and transformation
of, 290–94; satisfaction of needs,
289; social inclusion *vs.* exclusion,
291–92; subjective dimension of, 289
Instituto Argentino de Responsabilidad
Social Empresarial (IARSE), 135n6
Instituto de Cooperativismo o
Cooperativas, 144
Instituto Ethos, Brazil, 122, 135n6
Instituto Nacional de Ciencias Agrícolas
(INCA), 79n4
Instituto Panameño Cooperativo
(IPACOOP), 79n4
Interamerican Development Bank
(IDB), 122
Interinstitutional Committee (Comité
Interinstitucional), 145
International Conference on
Harmonization of Technical
Requirements for Registration of
Pharmaceuticals for Human Use, 129
International Conference on Population
and Development, Cairo (1994), 83
International Cooperative Alliance
[Alianza Cooperativa Internacional

(ACI/ICA)], 28, 30, 183, 184, 186,
188, 192, 193, 228, 265n7
International Labor Organization (ILO/
OIT), 122, 123, 163, 257; on social
and solidarity economy, 163–64
IPACOOP. *See* Instituto Panameño
Cooperativo (IPACOOP)
ITTIB. *See* Talleres de Transformación
Integral del Barrio [Integral
Neighborhood Transformation
Workshops (TTIB)]

Jiménez, R., 215
job insecurity, 88
Jodelet, D., 296
Joint Program of Support for the New
Initiatives of Decentralization and
Production Stimulation in Cuba, 216

labor alienation, 35–36
labor institutions, condition of, 4
Las Cañas Popular Council, Cerro
Municipality, 300n2
Latin America: new rurality, view of,
234–35n4; popular and solidarity
economy, 50; popular education in,
234n2; public–private partnerships,
101; social and solidarity economy,
21; social and solidarity economy
proposal, 88–92; social cooperative
responsibility, 228
Law of Agricultural Production
Cooperatives, 227
Law of Commercial Enterprises and
Societies, 32
Law of Cooperatives [Ley de
Cooperativas], 139–60; autonomy
of the cooperatives, 146–50;
higher-tier cooperative, creation of,
150–54; institutional ecosystem,
establishment of, 142–45; multi-
stakeholder cooperatives, creation of,
150–54; proposal for, 141–42; time
management, 155–58
Law of Credits and Services, 227

Lenin, V. I., 44, 45, 47, 154, 185; "On Cooperation," 29–30
Libro Verde [Green Book], 271
Lineamientos de la Política Económica y Social del Partido y la Revolución para el periodo 2016–2021 (Guidelines of the Economic and Social Policies of the Party and the Revolution for 2016–2021), 57, 99, 215, 241
living labor, 200
local self-management, 36
Los poderes vitales del éxito [The vital powers of success], 79n5

Malthus, T. R., 94n2
management autonomy, 28, 178, 188–89, 194, 221, 256
managerial autonomy, 33, 259
Manzano, A., 115n5
marginalization, 72
Mariposas Emprendedoras [Enterprising Butterflies], 263
Martin Luther King Memorial Center (CMLK), 60, 79n4, 266n11
"Mártires del Corynthia" primary school, 131
Marx, K., 29, 31, 47, 151, 198–99; *Capital*, 198, 199; *Economic and Philosophic Manuscripts*, 198
Master Plan of the Office of the Historian of the City of Havana, xviiin1
Maternity Law (1974), 261
Mayabeque, BSR awareness and training of actors in, 245–47
MDS. *See* municipal development strategy (MDS)
Meidner Plan, 157
Mena Lazo, C., 234n2
Mesa Redonda, 107
micro, small and medium enterprises (MSMEs), 10, 12, 14, 17, 18, 22–23n1, 44, 51n1, 157, 158, 273

MINAG. *See* Ministry of Agriculture (MINAG)
Ministry of Agriculture (MINAG), 84
Ministry of Economy and Planning (Ministerio de Economía y Planificación): Regional Development Policy, 243; Resolution 427, 171; Resolution 570, 171
Ministry of Finances and Prices, 171
Ministry of Labor and Social Security (MTSS), 11; Consejo Técnico Asesor [Technical Advisory Council], 73
Ministry of Science, Technology and the Environment (CITMA), 247
MINJUS 2012, Art. 305–315, 57
MIPYMES, 273, 274
Monreal, Pedro, 16
Moscovici, S., 296
MSMEs. *See* micro, small and medium enterprises (MSMEs)
MTSS. *See* Ministry of Labor and Social Security (MTSS)
Mujeres tejedoras del Guano Cano (Women Weavers of Guano Cano), 113
multi-stakeholder cooperatives, creation of, 150–54
municipal autonomy, 53, 58
municipal development strategy (MDS), 244
Municipal University Centers (SUN), 21, 244
mutual aid, 22, 28, 256, 262
Mutuberría Lazarini, V., 256

National Association of Small Agriculturalists [Asociación Nacional de Agricultores Pequeños (ANAP)], 33, 159n7, 217, 228, 233, 234n1
National Economic Plan, 254
National Workshop Aportes de la Economía Social y Solidaria al Desarrollo Local [Contributions of

the Social and Solidarity Economy to Local Development], 246
neo-Fordism, 200
neo-Taylorism, 200
New Public Management, 100
Nobre, M., 260, 263
non-statement management forms, 31–34; cooperatives, 33; difficulties of, 32; self-employed workers, 33–34; socialist state enterprise, 32–33
North America: social and solidarity economy, 21
Nuttin, J., 297

OACE. *See* Central State Management Entities (Organismos de la Administración Central del Estado—OACE)
OECD. *See* Organization for Economic Cooperation and Development (OECD)
Oficina del Historiador de la Ciudad de la Habana [Office of the Historian of the City of Havana (OHCH)], 59; Master Plan (Plan Maestro), xviiin1, 59; participatory budgeting, 53–64; School Workshop, 109
OHCH. *See* Oficina del Historiador de la Ciudad de la Habana [Office of the Historian of the City of Havana (OHCH)]
Organización Superior de Desarrollo Empresarial (OSDE), 120, 126, 134n3, 135n8, 135n9
Organization for Economic Cooperation and Development (OECD), 122
OSDE. *See* Organización Superior de Desarrollo Empresarial (OSDE)
Oxoby, P., 256

participatory budgeting (PB), 53–64; democratization of, at municipal level, 55; in Historical Center of Old

Havana, 58–63; legal foundations for promoting, 55–58
participatory responsibility, 28
PB. *See* participatory budgeting (PB)
personal autonomy, 263
PIAL. *See* Programa de Innovación Agrícola Local (PIAL)
Piedra, H., 238
Piketty, T., 157
political autonomy, 263
Polytechnic School of Industrial Chemistry: "Mártires de Girón," 135n14
popular and solidarity economy (EPS), xv, 43–51, 75, 262, 266n11
Popular Councils, 57
popular economy, 28; social (solidarity) economy *vs.*, 29
population: as object and subject of development, 85–86; population-development relation, 88–92; studies, 83
Porter, M., 87; *America's Green Strategy*, 95n8; *Competitive Advantage*, 88; *Competitive Advantage of Corporate Philanthropy, The*, 95n8; *Creating Shared Value: Redefining Capitalism and the Role of the Corporation in Society*, 95n8; *Strategy and Society: The Link between Competitive Advantage and Corporate Social Responsibility*, 95n8
"Por tu Barrio" [For your Neighborhood] project, 58–62, 64
poverty, 75; conditions of, 38
Premios Oasis [Oasis Prize], *277*, 277–79, 283n4
price-gouging regulations, 148
private sector, evolution of (2010–2020), 9–12, *10*
privatization, 100
Programa de Innovación Agrícola Local (PIAL), 79n4

Programa OASIS de Responsabilidad Social Empresarial [OASIS Program of Business Social Responsibility], 275–76, 278, 279, 282

PROhumana, Chile, 122

Project *ArteCorte* [Art of haircutting], 109

Provincial Administrative Board, 246

Provincial Enterprise of Local Industries, 110, 112

Proyecto Social del Arzobispado de La Habana [Social Project of the Archbishopry of Havana], 282n1

public–private partnerships/alliances, 19, 20, 99–115; expectations of, 102–3; as management techniques, 100; promotion of, 110–13; types of, *104–5*

RAMDI. *See* Register of the activity and direct and indirect method [Registro de la actividad y método directo e indirecto. (RAMDI)]

"Ration Card" ["Libreta"], 159n8

Razones [Reasons], 79n5

reciprocity, 28, 91, 164, 256

Reconocimiento Oasis [Oasis Recognition], 277

Red Cubana de Economía Social y Solidaria y Responsabilidad Social Empresarial [Cuban Network of Social and Solidarity Economy and Social Business Responsibility (ESORSE)], xiii–xiv, xviiin1, 5, 135n7, 245, 246, 248, 259; *Construyendo socialismo desde abajo: la contribución de la economía popular y solidaria* [Building socialism from the bottom up: the contribution of the popular and solidarity economy], xiii

Red de Trabajo Cooperado y Solidario [Cooperative and solidary labor network], 212n3

Regional Contribution for Local Development, 5

Regional Development Policy, 243

regional equity, 243

Register of the activity and direct and indirect method [Registro de la actividad y método directo e indirecto. (RAMDI)], 297

República Bolivariana de Venezuela 1999, Art. 70, 54

Resolution 216/2015, 205

Revista de Gestión del Conocimiento y el Desarrollo Local, 247

Rochdale Society of Equitable Pioneers, 39n1

Rojas Piedrahita, M., 238, 240

RS. *See* social responsibility (RS)

RSC. *See* corporate social responsibility (RSC)

RSI. *See* institutional social responsibility (RSI)

"salaried citizen" model, 200

Sanders, B., 157

SARS-CoV-2, 7, 279

Schmitz, H., 87

School of Philosophy of the University of Havana, 211n1

School of Social Sciences of Universidad Central "Marta Abreu," 211n1

Scientific Committee of the Center for Psychological and Sociological Research (CIPS), xviiin1, 5, 119, 135n7, 211n1, 246

self-employed workers (*trabajadores por cuenta pro pia*, TCPs), 9–12, *10*, 16, 17, 33–34, 38, 75, 114n4, 271, 273, 279

self-employment, 2, 79, 106, 115n4, 261, 274

self-management, 50, 165; local, 36; social, 36–37

Serra, D. G., 297

shared value, 88

Singer, P., 30

small and medium enterprises (SMEs), 106, 107; nonrecognition of, 75

small and medium-sized enterprises (SMSEs), 34, 35, 38, 39–40n6, 261

SMEs. *See* small and medium enterprises (SMEs)

SMSEs. *See* small and medium-sized enterprises (SMSEs)

social and solidarity economy (SSE/ESS), xiii, xiv, 75, 84, 88, 185, 201, 247, 255–61, 266n11, 274; C Factor, 28; cooperative, as energizing agent, 163–80; cooperative social balance, 215–24; and Cuban social system, common aspects between, 166–71, *167–68*; European view of, 256; ILO on, 163–64; international approach of, 256–57; Latin American view of, 256–57; in new normal, 20–21; non-statement management forms, 31–34; principles of, 164; relevance of, 17–20; in socialism, 7–23, 29–31, 37–39; versions of, 28–29; women in, 259–61

social capital, 74

social class, 77

social complexity, 8–15

social economy, 29

social equity, 35–36, 73, 90, 114, 229, 232, 237; levels of enrichment *vs.*, 35–36

social inclusion *vs.* exclusion, 291–92

socialism, 1–6, 156; bureaucratic, 49; construction of, 19–20; development of, 37–39; distributive ethics of, 17; real, 46, 49; social and solidarity economy in, 7–23, 29–31

socialist state enterprise, 2, 32–33, 44, 106, 129, 132

social justice, 1, 5

social labor relations, 34–35

Social Labor Studies Group [Grupo de Estudios Sociales del Trabajo (GEST)], 119

social responsibility (RS), xiii, xiv, 4; business, xiv, 8, 18–20, 22, 119–36, 237–49, 259, 271–83; institutional, xvii

social security, 32

social self-management, 36–37

social stakeholders, empowerment of, 38–39

socioeconomic agents: cooperatives *vs.*, 165–66; integration of, *178*

socioeconomic coherence, 39

socioeconomic solidarity, formation-diffusion of, 38

socio-labor structure, diversification of, 75

solidarity, 4, 28, 73, 262, 272; group, 79. *See also* social and solidarity economy (SSE/ESS)

Son del Barrio, 80n5

Soto, L., 106

sovereignty, 1, 48, 55

Spanish Business Confederation of Social Economy, 257

Special Tabloid Cuba and its Economic and Social Challenges. Summary of the Economic and Social Strategy, 107

SSE/ESS. *See* social and solidarity economy (SSE/ESS)

"state commitments" [encargos estatales], 160n8

State Entrepreneurial Units, 171–72

SUN. *See* Municipal University Centers (SUN)

Superintendence (Superintendencia), 143

sustainable development (DL), xiii, xiv, 102

sustainable local development, 265n6

Swiss Agency for Development and Cooperation (COSUDE), 59, 94n3

symbolic capital, 74

Talleres de Transformación Integral del Barrio [Integral Neighborhood

Transformation Workshops (TTIB)], 77, 79n4, 262

Taxi Rutero 2 (TR2): cooperative management, evaluation of, 207–9, *208*; cooperative solidarity labor, 197–212, *206*, *210*; management model, 206–7

Taylorism, 200

TCPs. *See* self-employed workers (*trabajadores por cuenta pro pia*, TCPs)

Technological University Jose Antonio Echeverria (CUJAE), 300n2

Texier, J., 36

Third Sector, 29

Torres, R., 11

"Transform to Educate" project, 228

transgression, 231–32

TRANSTUR, 205

Triana, J., 108

Trotsky, L., 47–48

Trump, D., 7, 279

UBPC. *See* Unidades Básicas de Producción Cooperativas [Basic Units of Cooperative Production (UBPC)]

UN. *See* United Nations (UN)

UNAH. *See* Universidad Agraria de La Habana (UNAH)

UNDAF. *See* United Nations Development Assistance Framework (UNDAF)

UNDP. *See* United Nations Development Programme (UNDP)

UN Economic Commission on Latin America and the Caribbean (ECLAC), 122

UNFPA. *See* United Nations Population Fund (UNFPA)

Unidades Básicas de Producción Cooperativas [Basic Units of Cooperative Production (UBPC)], 33, 39n4, 159n7, 171, 217; agricultural

cooperative, 110; ICA-FLACSO-PC Cooperative Social Balance Model, implementation of, 218–20

United Nations (UN), 19, 159n6; 2030 Agenda, 102; Global Compact, 123, 134–35n5, 239; on population dynamics, 85

United Nations Development Assistance Framework (UNDAF), 84

United Nations Development Programme (UNDP), 84, 102

United Nations Population Fund (UNFPA), 94n5; Country Programme (2014–2018), 84

Universidad Agraria de La Habana (UNAH), 245, 246

Uruguay, 228

value chains, 84–92

value creation, 86–88

Varcacel, Amelia, 78

Vía Láctea Project [Milky Way], 217, 227–29, 234n1

Villa Clara, model of social balance in agricultural cooperatives in: gender perspective of, 227–35

Vitria (glaziers), 109

volunteerism, 272

vulnerable groups as subjects of development, inclusion of, 69–80, **70**, *70*; development opportunities and inequalities, 72–73; social work and engagement, 73–77; social work challenges, 77–79

WHO. *See* World Health Organization (WHO)

Williamson, O., 101

World Bank, 102

World Health Organization (WHO), 129

Yarual Workshop, 110–13; design stage, 112; monitoring and evaluation stage, 113; organization stage, 112–13

About the Editors and Contributors

EDITORS

Rafael J. Betancourt

PhD (ABD) in economy (University of Florida), master's in regional organization and urbanism (ISPJAE, Cuba), bachelor of arts in economy (University of Florida). Coordinator of the book *Construyendo socialismo desde abajo: La contribución de la Economía Popular y Solidaria* [Building socialism from the bottom up: the Contribution of the Popular and Solidarity Economy] (Ed. Caminos, La Habana, 2017). Founder and cocoordinator of the Red Cubana de Economía Social y Solidaria (ESORSE) [Cuban Network of Social and Solidarity Economy], Collaborator of the Centro de Investigaciones Psicológicas y Sociológicas (CIPS) [Center for Psychological and Sociological Research] and of the Centro de Estudios Demográficos (CEDEM) at the Universidad de La Habana. Member of the Equipo Editorial [Editorial Team] of *Temas* magazine. rbetancourt3114@gmail.com.

Jusmary Gómez Arencibia

Bachelor's in sociology from the Universidad de La Habana (2005), master's in desarrollo social (FLACSO-Cuba, 2009). She is assistant researcher of the Grupo de Estudios Sociales del Trabajo at the Centro de Investigaciones Psicológicas y Sociológicas of the Ministerio de Ciencia, Tecnología y Medio Ambiente, and secretary of the Consejo Científico [scientific council] of that institution. She is co-coordinator of the Red de Economía Social y Solidaria y Responsabilidad Social Empresarial (ESORSE), Associate Professor of the Departamento de Sociología of the Universidad de La Habana, and collaborator of the Cuban NGO Centro Félix Varela. She has completed several research projects and published scientific articles on Responsabilidad Social Empresarial, the Economía Social y Solidaria and other topics related to labor. jusmarycips@ceniai.inf.cu.

CONTRIBUTORS

Orquídea Hailyn Abreu González

Bachelor's in Estudios Socioculturales from the Universidad de Pinar del Río (2007). Master's in Desarrollo Social [Social Development] (2013). She has participated in research projects with international financing, directed toward local development based on community labor, local innovations, and training of local stakeholders. She has published articles on these topics in national and international journals. She is currently employed as the Director of the Centro de Estudios para la Gestión del Desarrollo (CEGED) [Center for Studies of Development Management] of the Universidad Agraria de La Habana. orquidia@unha.edu.cu

Jany Bárcenas Alfonso

Bachelor's in psychology (2014), master's in educational psychology (2018), and doctoral student in psychological sciences at the Universidad de La Habana (UH). Teaching professor in the Department of Psicología Social, Laboral y de las Organizaciones [Social, Labor and Organizational Psychology] at the Facultad de Psicología of UH. Member of the board of directors of the Sección InterCreAcción of the Sociedad Cubana de Psicología (SCP) and also of the Sociedad Interamericana de Psicología (SIP). jbarcenas@psico.uh.cu

William Bello Sánchez

Bachelor's in Geografía and master's in Medioambiente y Ordenamiento Territorial [Environment and Regional Organization] from the Universidad de La Habana. MBA from the UCAM in Murcia, Spain. For five years he was a professor at the Facultad de Geografía at the Universidad de La Habana. He is now professor of the CubaEmprende project and coordinator of the OASIS program of Social Business Responsibility. williambs82@gmail.com

Luis del Castillo Sánchez

PhD in Economic Sciences, MBA, bachelor's in political economy; full professor in the department of Ciencias Empresariales [Business Sciences] at the Facultad de Economía of the Universidad de La Habana. He develops research linked to the topics of the Sistema de Dirección y Gestión Empresarial [Business Management and Organization System], Gestión Empresarial en Apoyo al Desarrollo Local [Business Management in Support of Local Development], and on the foundations and application of the Economía Popular y Solidaria. luiqui@fec.uh.cu

Ovidio D'Angelo Hernández

PhD in Ciencias Psicológicas from the Universidad de La Habana (1994). Bachelor in Psychology and in Sociology. Postgraduate studies in Economy and in Philosophy. Full researcher at the Centro de Investigaciones Psicológicas y Sociológicas (CIPS) and Director of the Grupo Creatividad para la Transformación Social [Creativity Group for Social Transformation]. President of the Section Psicología y Sociedad of the Sociedad Cubana de Psicología. Member of the Sociedad Económica de Amigos del País [Economic Society of the Friends of the Country]. odangelocips@ceniai.inf.cu

Orestes J. Díaz Legón

PhD in Ciencias Jurídicas, Universidad de La Habana. PhD in Derecho Público [Public Law], from the Université Paris-Nanterre, France. Assistant Professor in the Facultad de Derecho at the Universidad de La Hana. In this faculty, he is the head of the teaching department of international consultation. He develops research on topics of local development, municipal property, and taxation and on economic topics in Cuba. orestes@lex.uh.cu

Geydis Fundora Nevot

PhD in Ciencias Psicológicas and full Professor at FLACSO-Cuba and the Universidad de La Habana. She teaches undergraduate and graduate courses and carries out research on topics of development, social policies, intersectionality, and social economy. She has published six books and some twenty articles in important journals. geidys@flacso.uh.cu

Lienny García Pedraza

Bachelor's in sociology from the Universidad Central "Marta Abreu" de Las Villas (UCLV). She is associate professor at the Departamento de Sociología at the Facultad de Ciencias Sociales (UCLV), and is currently vice dean of continuing education, communication and computer Science of this same faculty. She is a member of the Grupo de Estudios de Desarrollo Rural y Cooperativisimo [Study Group on Rural Development and Cooperativity] and of the Grupo de Estudios del Trabajo [Study Group on Labor] of UCLV. She is a student in the doctoral program on Desarrollo Local Comunitario [Local Community Development] of the Centro de Estudios Comunitarios of the UCLV. She carries out research on local development and cooperativity. liennygp@uclv.cu

Joanna Gasmury Roldán

Third-year student in the program Gestión Sociocultural para el Desarrollo at the Universidad Agraria de La Habana (UNAH). She has carried out research on the sociocultural impact of the local agricultural directive on the organization of science and innovation based on Higher Education, and currently carries out research on the non-state forms of organization and their relation to local development. jgasmuri@nauta.cu

Enrique Gómez-Cabezas

PhD in sociology, University of Camagüey, Cuba (2015). Master's in community social development from the "Marta Abreu" Central University of Villa Clara, Cuba. BS in Engineering from the "José Antonio Echevarría" Technical University of Havana. Currently he is associate professor and vice director for science of the Cuban Center for Psychological and Sociological Studies (Centro de Estudios Psicológicos y Sociológicos). His research interests include public policies, social work, citizenship, problems of development, and socio-structural dynamics in contemporary Cuba. ejgcabezas@gmail.com

Yuneidys González Espinosa

Bachelor's in Estudios Socioculturales, matster's in Trabajo Sociocultural Universitario. Researcher in the Department of Manejo de Agroecosistemas Sostenibles [Management of Sustainable Agro-ecosystems] in the Instituto Nacional de Ciencias Agrícolas (INCA). Her main lines of research have been directed toward local agricultural innovation, agroecological training, and continuing education. She has published in scientific journals such as *Agrotécnica de Cuba* and *Congreso Universidad*, as well as in national and international books such as *Hélices y anclas para el desarrollo local* [Propellors and anchors for local development]. She has participated in prestigious international scientific congresses such as AGRODESARROLLO, INTERJOVEN of the Congreso Cubano de Desarrollo Local, among others. yuneidys@inca.edu.cu

Dianné Griñan Bergara

Bachelor's in sociología (2012) and master's in estudios de población [population studies] (2018). Professor at the Centro de Estudios Demográficos of the Universidad de La Habana (2012–present). She has published several articles in scientific journals and books and has participated in national and international scientific events related to labor resources, social studies on labor, and value chains. She has coordinated research on international cooperation projects on value chains. dianne@cedem.uh.cu

Maidolys Iglesias Pérez

Sociologist, with a master's in Desarrollo Social from the Facultad Latinoamericana de Ciencias Sociales [Latin American Faculty of Social Sciences] [FLACSO]. Principal specialist at the Plan Maestro de la Oficina del Historiador. Professor at the Colegio San Gerónimo of the Universidad de La Habana. She carries out research on the topics of social participation, social and solidarity economy, urban sociology, and integral management of local development. maidolys@planmaestro.ohc.cu

Reynaldo Miguel Jiménez Guethón

PhD in Ciencias de la Educación, full professor and academic coordinator of the Facultad de Ciencias Sociales—FLACSO-Cuba—of the Universidad de La Habana. He has published articles in national and international journals and has given conferences in universities and study centers in Argentina, Belgium, Bolivia, Brazil, Canada, Chile, Costa Rica, Finland, Ecuador, Spain, the United States, South Africa, Sweden, and Turkey. rejigue@flacso.uh.cu

Lázaro Julio Leiva Hoyo

Bachelor's in Filosofía (2003) and master's in Sociología (2008) from the Universidad de La Habana. Associate professor and director of the Department of Sociology at the Universidad Central "Marta Abreu" de Las Villas. He collaborated in the VIA LACTEA project on the application of the Modelo de Balance Social Cooperativo. He is a doctorate student in Sociological Sciences at the Universidad de La Habana on the topic of gender. In this field, he also participates in the Programa de Innovación Agropecuaria Local in Villa Clara. lazaro@uclv.edu.cu

Oscar Llanes Guerra

PhD in Ciencias Técnicas (2001) from the Universidad Agraria de La Habana (UNAH); master's in Gestión y Desarrollo de Cooperativas [Organization and Development of Cooperatives] in the FLACSO-Cuba program of the Universidad de La Habana; full professor and associate researcher. He has a diploma from the Escuela Andaluza de Economía Social. Since 2013 he has been associated with local development projects and cooperative organizations based on local development. oscarllanesguerra@gmail.com

Iriadna Marín de León

PhD in Ciencias Económicas; professor. Master's in Administración de Empresas Agropecuarias. Associate of the Centro de Estudios de Dirección, Desarrollo Local, Turismo y Cooperativismo (CE-GESTA) of the Universidad de Pinar del Río. Director of the Sociedad Científica Cubana de Cooperativismo (ANEC). Member of the Comité Académico de la Maestría en Administración de Empresas Agropecuarias [Academic Committee for the Master in Agricultural Enterprises Administration]. Director of the journal *Cooperativismo y Desarrollo* (COODES). iriadi@upr.edu.cu

Consuelo Martín Fernández

PhD in Ciencias Psicológicas (2000); full professor and researcher at the Universidad de La Habana (UH). She coordinates the master's in Migraciones Internacionales y Emigración Cubana, and the Grupo de Migraciones Internacionales of the Centro de Estudios Demográficos (CEDEM-UH). She is professor of Psicología Social y Vida Cotidiana [Social Psychology and Daily Life] in the Faculty of Psicología-UH. In that institution, she is vice president of the PhD jury panel, and member of the doctorate in Demografía. She is associate director of the TransformAction 2017 and 2018 and of the Seminario Internacional del Foro Internacional para la Innovación Social of Paris. She won the Premio Nacional de Psicología in 2018 for her scientific research. cmartin@rect.uh.cu

Annia Martínez Massip

PhD in Ciencias Sociológicas from the Universidad de La Habana (2018). From 2010 to 2014 she was the director of the Departamento de Sociología de la Universidad Central "Marta Abreu" de Las Villas. She collaborated in the VIA LACTEA Project. She is currently full professor in the same department and teaches courses at the undergraduate, master's, and doctorate levels on rural sociology and the sociology of gender. She coordinates the field of gender studies in the Programa de Innovación Agropecuaria Local in Villa Clara. massip@uclv.edu.cu

Yamira Mirabal González

PhD in Ciencias Contables y Financieras [Accounting and Financial Sciences]. Master's in Administración de Empresas Agropecuarias. Subdirector of the Centro de Estudios de Dirección, Desarrollo Local, Turismo y Cooperativismo (CE-GESTA) of the Universidad de Pinar del Río. National President of the Sociedad Científica Cubana de Cooperativismo (ANEC). Coordinator of the master's in Administración de Empresas Agropecuarias. Member of the Comité Académico del Doctorado en Ciencias Económicas. Member of the Comité Editorial de la Revista Cooperativismo y Desarrollo (COODES). National Accounting prize "Abel Santamaría Cuadrado" (2011). yamira@upr.edu.cu

Francisco Damián Morillas Valdés

Bachelor, master's, and doctorate studies in sociology at the Universidad de La Habana. Researcher at the Centro de Investigaciones Psicológicas y Sociológicas (CIPS). He studies the topics of Economía Social y Solidaria, el Trabajo por Cuenta Propia [Self-Employment], and the Cooperativas no Agropecuarias and their potential to positively transform society. fmorillas-valdes@gmail.com

Mirell Pérez González

Researcher at the Instituto de Filosofía de Cuba and member of the Grupo América Latina, Filosofía Social y Axiología (Galfisa). Bachelor's in Filosofía from the Universidad de La Habana and master's in Gestión de Desarrollo de Cooperativas from FLACSO-Cuba. She specializes in topics of urban cooperativity and labor studies. mirell91perez@gmail.com

Anelys Pérez Rodríguez

Bachelor's in Sociología (2018) from the Universidad Central "Marta Abreu de Las Villas." Teaching professor in the Departamento de Marxismo, Dirección Marxismo Leninismo e Historia at that same University. Master's student in Intervención Psicosocial. She has collaborated in the VIA LACTEA project on the application of the Modelo de Balance Social Cooperativo. She works with the Programa de Innovación Agropecuaria Local Villa Clara on the subject of the organization of knowledge. anelys@uclv.cu

Camila Piñeiro Harnecker

PhD in Ciencias Económicas and master's in Procesos Gerenciales from the Universidad de La Habana. Master's in Desarrollo Sostenible from the University of California, Berkeley. Professor of the master's in Gestión y Desarrollo de Cooperativas of the Facultad de Ciencias Sociales (FLACSO) at the Universidad de La Habana. For more than fifteen years she has been a researcher, professor, and consultant on social and solidarity economy, specializing in cooperativity and public policies in that sector. She is the author of three books and more than fifty chapters and articles on these topics. camila.ph@gmail.com

Mirlena Rojas Piedrahita

Associate researcher of the Centro de Investigaciones Psicológicas y Sociológicas [CIPS]. Master's in Ciencias Sociológicas from the Universidad de La Habana, specializing in Relaciones Laborales. She does research on topics related to employment, the labor market, social equity, and labor policies. She coordinates the Red Cubana de Estudios Sociales del Trabajo and the Grupo de Estudios Sociales del Trabajo in CIPS. She has published several articles in books and national and international journals. mirlenacips@ceniai.inf.cu

Mercedes Zenea Montejo

Bachelor's in Economía Agropecuaria (1985), master's in Consultoría y Desarrollo Organizacional and PhD in Ciencias Económicas. She is full professor at the Centro de Estudios de Técnicas de Dirección at the Universidad de La Habana, with more than thirty-five years of experience in the training of specialists. She is a member of the Comisión de Grado Científico de Economía of the UH and of the academic curriculum committee of the doctorate in that field. mercle@ceted.uh.cu

Elianys de la Caridad Zorio González

Bachelor's in Sociología from the Universidad Central "MartaAbreu" de las Villas (2018), she is currently a teaching profesor in the Dirección de Marxismo Leninismo e Historia de Cuba, and teaches the Teoría Marxista I course at UCLV. She participates in the area of knowledge management in the Programa de Innovación Agropecuaria Local in Villa Clara. She collaborated in the VIA LACTEA program on the application of the Modelo de Balance Social Cooperativo. ezorio@uclv.cu

TRANSLATOR

Catharina Vanderplaats Vallejo

MA McGill University (Montreal), PhD Université de Montréal (1991). Professor of Spanish at Concordia University (Montreal) until 2016 (currently retired). Courses taught on Spanish American culture, literature, translation. Many research grants received at the university, provincial, and national level. Many conference publications in English and Spanish; articles and books published, mainly on women's writing in nineteenth-century Spanish Caribbean. For example: *The Women in the Men's Club*: *Women Modernista Poets in Cuba, 1880–1910* (2017) (translated into Spanish by C. Vallejo as *La rosa azul. Mujeres poetas modernistas en Cuba 1880–1910)* (2018). *Ecce Felicia: Virginia Felicia Auber, 1821–1897, prolífica novelista y periodista en la Habana* (in press).

Milton Keynes UK
Ingram Content Group UK Ltd.
UKHW011600010224
437106UK00005B/57